Praise for *Plan of Attack*

"An astonishing book. . . . Here, in abundant detail, is a convincing portrait of a president. . . . Remarkably revealing."

—Robert Scheer, *Los Angeles Times Book Review*

"A virtuoso piece of storytelling."

—*Financial Times* (London)

"[President Bush] fairly leaps off the page."

—Joe Klein, *Time*

"Riveting . . . Full of gems."

—Al Hunt, *The Wall Street Journal*

"The best and I judge the most accurate picture yet of how the United States got into war with Iraq . . . Woodward has established himself as the best reporter of our time. He may be the best reporter of all time."

—Bob Schieffer, CBS News *Face the Nation*

"How good is this book? Well, if discomfort caused is the measure of greatness achieved, forget the Pulitzer—Mr. Woodward deserves a Nobel. . . . This is the craft of a journalist without peer."

—Robert Sam Anson, *New York Observer*

"Washington's premier investigative reporter . . . has not lost his knack for opening up otherwise secretive government officials."

—Evan Thomas, *Newsweek*

"Woodward is a masterful recorder of the fascinating doings of our republican court . . . the most accomplished political reporter of his generation."

—Walter Russell Mead, *The Washington Post Book World*

"Digs deep . . . projects a reassuring neutrality. . . . Woodward is manifestly a great reporter—an unparalleled getter of facts."

—Hendrik Hertzberg, *The New Yorker*

"The prose is irresistible. . . . The conversations between the players grip the reader with their verisimilitude. Worst of all for would-be novelists, this is journalism. . . . Woodward is sui generis."

—Andrew Sullivan, *The Sunday Times* (London)

"*Plan of Attack* is flesh-and-blood history."

—Fritz Lanham, *Houston Chronicle*

"A gripping read."

—*The Economist*

"Woodward captures the frenzy and emotion of the final prewar diplomacy, strategizing and speechmaking."

—Thomas Frank, *Newsday*

"What is stunning is the detail. . . . [A] penetrating account of the way Mr. Bush operates his presidency."
—Ivo Daalder, *Financial Times* (London)

"A compelling, instructively nuanced tale."
—Peter Preston, *The Observer* (London)

"Delivers on all counts. . . . Puts readers inside meetings in the White House, the Pentagon, U.S. Central Command in Florida, and the secret base the CIA set up."
—Robert Schlesinger, *Pittsburgh Post-Gazette*

"A book everyone should read."
—Jeff Guinn, *Fort Worth Star-Telegram*

"Woodward is tireless and industrious . . . the best at what he does."
—Andrew Ferguson, *The Weekly Standard*

"There's plenty of ammunition here for the most fervent fans of Bush as well as his foes."
—Frank Davies, *The Miami Herald*

"Incomparable."
—Jim Rowen, *Milwaukee Journal Sentinel*

"In Bob Woodward's new book, *Plan of Attack*, readers get a privileged insider's look at the preparations for the war in Iraq. The veteran Washington journalist demonstrates once again that truth is indeed stranger than fiction."
—Susan Larson, *The Times-Picayune* (New Orleans)

"Woodward's real contribution is the meticulous documentation of how long, carefully, and secretly the war was planned."

—Michael D. Langan, *The Boston Globe*

"Add[s] significant new documentation to the story of the rush to war in Iraq."

—Sidney Blumenthal, *The Guardian* (London)

"His most compelling book about a living U.S. president since *All the President's Men* and *The Final Days*."

—Steve Weinberg, *The Plain Dealer* (Cleveland)

"Packed with the kind of high-grade information that traditionally stays hidden until the publication of memoirs years after the event. Here is the inside track on a crisis that is still unfolding."

—Jonathan Freedland, *The Guardian* (Manchester, U.K.)

ALSO BY BOB WOODWARD

Bush at War

Maestro: Greenspan's Fed and the American Boom

Shadow: Five Presidents and the Legacy of Watergate

The Choice

The Agenda: Inside the Clinton White House

The Commanders

Veil: The Secret Wars of the CIA 1981–1987

Wired: The Short Life and Fast Times of John Belushi

The Brethren
(with Scott Armstrong)

The Final Days
(with Carl Bernstein)

All the President's Men
(with Carl Bernstein)

PLAN

SIMON & SCHUSTER PAPERBACKS

OF ATTACK

Bob Woodward

NEW YORK · LONDON · TORONTO · SYDNEY

To Elsa

SIMON & SCHUSTER PAPERBACKS
Rockefeller Center
1230 Avenue of the Americas
New York, NY 10020

SIMON & SCHUSTER PAPERBACKS and colophon are
registered trademarks of Simon & Schuster, Inc.

First Simon & Schuster trade paperback edition 2004

Map by Laris Karklis

CREDITS FOR INSERT PHOTOGRAPHS: Shawn Thew (Agence France-Presse): 1; Rich
Lipski *(The Washington Post):* 2, 17, 20, 25; Associated Press: 3; Ray Lustig *(The Washington
Post):* 4, 7, 12, 13, 14; Eric Draper (The White House): 5, 9, 10, 23, 24, 26, 28, 30, 31;
Dayna Smith *(The Washington Post):* 6; Jeff Mitchell (Reuters): 8; Mark Humphrey
(Associated Press): 11; James A. Parcells *(The Washington Post):* 15; Kevin Lamarque
(Reuters): 16; Frank Johnston *(The Washington Post):* 18; Remy de la Mauviniere
(Associated Press): 19; Mike Segar (Reuters): 21; Richard Drew (Associated Press): 22;
Todd Cross *(The Washington Post):* 27; Tina Hager (The White House): 29.

For information regarding special discounts for bulk purchases,
please contact Simon & Schuster Special Sales at
1-800-456-6798 or business@simonandschuster.com.

Manufactured in the United States of America

10   9   8   7   6   5   4   3   2   1

The Library of Congress has catalogued the hardcover as follows:

Woodward, Bob.
    Plan of attack / Bob Woodward.
      p. cm.
    Includes index.
    1. Iraq War, 2003—Causes. 2. Bush, George W. (George Walker), 1946— 3. United
States—Foreign relations.

DS79.76.W66 2004b
                                                        56.7044'31—dc22
                                                        200113591133

ISBN 0-7432-5547-X
    0-7432-5548-8 (Pbk)

AUTHOR'S NOTE

Mark Malseed, a 1997 architecture graduate of Lehigh University who was my assistant on *Bush at War,* stayed on for this book, the next volume in the Bush saga. I have been blessed to have him assist me full-time in the reporting, writing, research and conception of the book. Mark blossomed in every way, particularly as an editor who knows how to compress, clarify meaning and find the proper words and rhythm for a story. He is incredibly well-informed on everything from literature to geography and current events. He is a computer and Internet whiz, one of the younger generation whose technical skills are a sixth sense. Though he retains a natural tough-mindedness, his hallmarks are a deep sense of fairness and an insistence that we reflect with precision what people said, meant and did. Ours is a friendship that has grown and one I continue to treasure. Last time he was a collaborator. This time he was a partner.

A NOTE TO READERS

The aim of this book is to provide the first detailed, behind-the-scenes account of how and why President George W. Bush, his war council and allies decided to launch a preemptive war in Iraq to topple Saddam Hussein.

Information in the book comes from more than 75 key people directly involved in the events, including war cabinet members, the White House staff and officials serving at various levels of the State and Defense Departments and the Central Intelligence Agency. These interviews were conducted on background, meaning I could use the information but not identify the sources of it in the book. The main sources were interviewed a number of times, often with long intervals between interviews so they could address new information I had obtained. In addition, I interviewed President Bush on the record for more than three and a half hours over two days, December 10 and 11, 2003. I also interviewed Secretary of Defense Donald Rumsfeld on the record for more than three hours in the fall of 2003.

Many of the direct quotations of dialogue, dates, times and other details of this history come from documents, including personal notes, calendars, chronologies, official and unofficial records, phone transcripts and memos.

Where thoughts, judgments or feelings are attributed to participants, I have obtained these from the person directly, a colleague with firsthand knowledge or the written record.

I spent more than a year researching and interviewing to obtain this material. The reporting started at the bottom of the information chain with many sources who are not mentioned in the book but were willing to share some of the secret history.

The decision making leading to the Iraq War—concentrated in 16 months from November 2001 to March 2003—is probably the best window into understanding who George W. Bush is, how he operates and what he cares about.

I have attempted, as best I can, to find out what really happened and to provide some interpretations and occasional analysis. I wanted to take a reader as close as possible to the decision making that led to war.

My purpose is to recount the strategies, meetings, phone calls, planning sessions, motivations, dilemmas, conflicts, doubts and raw emotions. The most elusive parts of any history are often the critical moments in the debates and the key turning or decision points that remain secret for years and are not revealed publicly until presidents and others leave office. This history presents many of those moments, but I am aware I have not found all of them.

Bob Woodward
March 1, 2004
Washington, D.C.

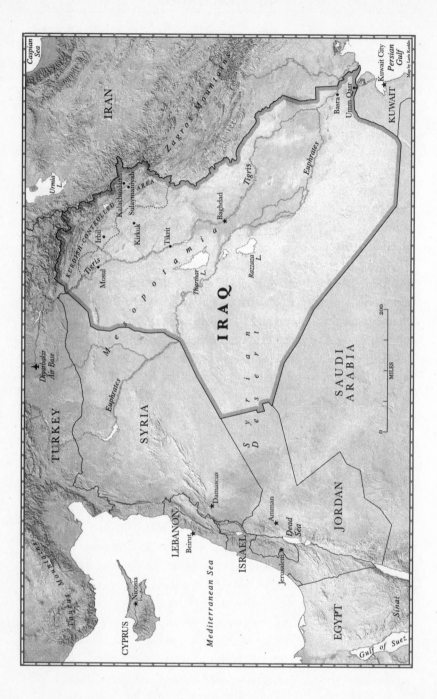

Caspian Sea

IRAN

Zagros Mountains

Kuwait City
Persian Gulf
KUWAIT
Map by Lars Katlin

Urmia L.

Basra
Umm Qasr

Euphrates

KURDISH-CONTROLLED AREA

Kalachualan
Sulaymaniyah
Kirkuk
Irbil

Tigris

Baghdad

Tikrit

Tharthar L.
Razzaza L.

Mosul

Tigris

M e s o p o t a m i a

IRAQ

S y r i a n
D e s e r t

200

SAUDI
ARABIA

MILES

0

Diyabakir
Air Base

Euphrates

TURKEY

SYRIA

Damascus

Amman

JORDAN

LEBANON

Beirut

Dead
Sea

ISRAEL

Jerusalem

Tautus Mountains

Nicosia

CYPRUS

Mediterranean Sea

EGYPT

Sinai

Gulf of Suez

PROLOGUE

P RESIDENT GEORGE W. BUSH clamped his arm on his secretary of defense, Donald H. Rumsfeld, as a National Security Council meeting in the White House Situation Room was just finishing on Wednesday, November 21, 2001. It was the day before Thanksgiving, just 72 days after the 9/11 terrorist attacks and the beginning of the eleventh month of Bush's presidency.

"I need to see you," the president said to Rumsfeld. The affectionate gesture sent a message that important presidential business needed to be discussed in the utmost privacy. Bush knew it was dramatic for him to call the secretary of defense aside. The two men went into one of the small cubbyhole offices adjacent to the Situation Room, closed the door and sat down.

"I want you . . ." the president began, and as is often the case he restarted his sentence. "What kind of a war plan do you have for Iraq? How do you feel about the war plan for Iraq?"

Rumsfeld said he didn't think the Iraq war plan was current. It didn't represent the thinking of General Tommy Franks, the combatant commander for the region, and it certainly didn't represent his own thinking. The plan was basically Desert Storm II Plus, he explained, meaning it was a slightly enhanced version of the massive invasion force employed by Bush's father in the 1991 Gulf War. "I am concerned about all of our war plans," the secretary added. He poured out some of his accumulated frustrations and consternation.

He was reviewing all 68 of the department's secret war and other contingency plans worldwide and had been for months.

Bush and Rumsfeld are a contrasting pair. Large and physical with a deep stare from small brown eyes, Bush, 55, has a quick, joshing manner which at times borders on the impulsive. Focused, direct, practical but not naturally articulate, he had been elected to his first political office as governor of Texas only nine years earlier, a novice thrust into the presidency. Rumsfeld, 69, had been elected to his first political office, congressman from the 13th District of Illinois in the Chicago suburbs, 39 years earlier. Small, almost boyishly dashing, with thinning combed-back hair, Rumsfeld was intense and also focused as he squinted through his trifocals. He is capable of a large, infectious smile that can overwhelm his face or alternatively convey impatience, even condescension, though he is deferential and respectful to the president.

In his semi-professorial voice Rumsfeld explained to Bush that the process of drafting war plans was so complex that it took years. The present war plans tended to hold assumptions that were stale, he told the president, and they failed miserably to account for the fact that a new administration with different goals had taken over. The war planning process was woefully broken and maddening. He was working to fix it.

"Let's get started on this," Bush recalled saying. "And get Tommy Franks looking at what it would take to protect America by removing Saddam Hussein if we have to." He also asked, Could this be done on a basis that would not be terribly noticeable?

"Sure, because I'm doing all of them," Rumsfeld replied. His worldwide review would provide perfect cover. "There isn't a combatant commander that doesn't know how I feel and that I'm getting them refreshed." He had spoken with all the main regional commanders, the four-star generals and admirals for the Pacific, Europe, Latin America, as well as Franks's Central Command (CENTCOM), which encompassed the Middle East, South-Central Asia and the Horn of Africa.

The president had another request. Don't talk about what you are doing with others.

Yes, sir, Rumsfeld said. But it would be helpful to be able to know to whom he could talk when the president had brought others into his thinking. "It's particularly important that I talk to George Tenet," the secretary said. CIA Director Tenet would be critical to intelligence gathering and any coordinated covert efforts in Iraq.

"Fine," the president said, indicating that at a later date Tenet and others could become involved. But not now.

Two years later in interviews, Bush said he did not want others in on the secret because a leak would trigger "enormous international angst and domestic speculation. I knew what would happen if people thought we were developing a potential or a war plan for Iraq."

The Bush-Rumsfeld-Franks work remained secret for months and when partial disclosures made their way into the media the next year, the president, Rumsfeld and others in the administration, attempting to defuse any sense of immediacy, spoke of contingency planning and insisted that war plans were not on the president's desk.

Knowledge of this work would have ignited a firestorm, the president knew. "It was such a high-stakes moment and when people had this sense of war followed on the heels of the Afghan decision," Bush's order for a military operation into Afghanistan in response to 9/11, "it would look like that I was anxious to go to war. And I'm not anxious to go to war." He insisted, "War is my absolute last option."

At the same time, Bush said, he realized that the simple act of setting Rumsfeld in motion on Iraq war plans might be the first step in taking the nation to a war with Saddam Hussein. "Absolutely," Bush recalled.

What he perhaps had not realized was that war plans and the process of war planning become policy by their own momentum, especially with the intimate involvement of both the secretary of defense and the president.

The story of Bush's decisions leading up to the Iraq War is a chronicle of continual dilemmas, since the president was pursuing two simultaneous policies. He was planning for war, and he was conducting diplomacy aiming to avoid war. At times, the war planning aided the diplomacy; at many other points it contradicted it.

FROM THE CONVERSATION in the cubbyhole off the Situation Room that day, Rumsfeld realized how focused Bush was about Iraq. "He should have," the president recalled. "Because he knew how serious I was."

Rumsfeld was left with the impression that Bush had not spoken to anyone else. That was not so. That same morning the president had told Condoleezza Rice, his national security adviser, that he was planning to get Rumsfeld to work on Iraq. For Rice, 9/11 had put Iraq on the back burner. The president did not explain to her why he was returning to it now, or what triggered his orders to Rumsfeld.

In the interviews the president said he could not recall if he had talked to Vice President Dick Cheney before he took Rumsfeld aside. But he was certainly aware of Cheney's own position. "The vice president, after 9/11, clearly saw Saddam Hussein as a threat to peace," he said. "And was unwavering in his view that Saddam was a real danger. And again—I see Dick all the time and my relationship—remember since he is not campaigning for office or his own future, he is around. And so I see him quite a bit. And we meet all the time as a matter of fact. And so I can't remember the timing of a particular meeting with him or not."

On the long walk-up to war in Iraq, Dick Cheney was a powerful, steamrolling force. Since the terrorist attacks, he had developed an intense focus on the threats posed by Saddam and by Osama bin Laden's al Qaeda network, the group responsible for 9/11. It was seen as a "fever" by some of his colleagues, even a disquieting obsession. For Cheney, taking care of Saddam was high necessity.

• • •

THE NATION WAS ON EDGE in November 2001, still in shock from the 9/11 attacks, and continually bombarded with dire-sounding national alerts warning of future terror attacks. Poisonous anthrax in mailings to Florida, New York and Washington had killed five people. But the joint military and CIA paramilitary attack on Afghanistan's ruling Taliban regime and al Qaeda terrorists was meeting with extraordinary and somewhat unexpected success. Already, U.S.-supported forces controlled half of Afghanistan, and the capital of Kabul had been abandoned as thousands of Taliban and al Qaeda fled south to the Pakistan border. In an effective display of American technology, the CIA with millions of dollars and years of covert contacts among Afghan tribes, plus U.S. military Special Forces commando teams directing precision bombing, seemed to have turned the tide of war in a matter of weeks. It was a time of both danger and intoxication for Bush, his war cabinet, his generals and the country.

When he was back at the Pentagon, two miles from the White House across the Potomac River in Virginia, Rumsfeld immediately had the Joint Staff begin drafting a Top Secret message to General Franks requesting a "commander's estimate," a new take on the status of the Iraq war plan and what Franks thought could be done to improve it. The general would have about a week to make a formal presentation to Rumsfeld.

FRANKS, 56, HAD SERVED in the Army since he was 20—a Vietnam and 1991 Gulf War veteran. At 6-foot-3 with a gentle Texas drawl, he could get hot real fast and had a reputation as an officer who would scream at his subordinates. At the same time, he was a bit of a maverick reformer who at times deplored the leaden, unimaginative ways of the military.

It had been a brutal 72 days since 9/11 for Franks. There had been not even a barebones war plan for Afghanistan, and the president had wanted quick military action. Rumsfeld had been the strongest proponent of "boots on the ground," a commitment of U.S. military ground forces. But the first boots on the ground had been a

CIA paramilitary team on September 27—just 16 days after the terrorist attacks. This had driven Rumsfeld to the brink. It took another 22 days before the first U.S. Special Forces commando team arrived in Afghanistan. For Rumsfeld, each day had been like a month, even a year. The excuses were broken helicopters, fouled-up communications and weather delays. He had pounded on Franks very hard with increasing fury.

I don't understand, Rumsfeld had said. Why can't we do this? Soon the secretary was trickling down into lower-level operational decisions, demanding details and explanations.

According to Franks's contemporaneous account to others, he had told Rumsfeld, "Mr. Secretary, stop. This ain't going to work. You can fire me. I'm either the commander or I'm not, and you've got to trust me or you don't. And if you don't, I need to go somewhere else. So tell me what it is, Mr. Secretary."

Rumsfeld's version: "There's no doubt but that at the beginning we had to find our way."

The two had a very emotional discussion and it became a turning point in their relationship. They both pulled back from confrontation. Rumsfeld, the former college wrestler, appreciated someone confident enough to push back and lay it on the line from a subordinate position, maybe even take him down, throw him on the mat for a moment. They agreed to try to work as a team. Rumsfeld also needed Franks, even if he contemplated a replacement. Firing the general in charge at the onset of a war on terrorism of unknown duration and complexity, in the middle of the hopeful but still uncertain campaign in Afghanistan, and at the beginning of who-knows-what in Iraq would, in any practical sense, be difficult.

After the CIA and military campaign in Afghanistan looked successful, Rumsfeld declared that Franks was his man. Military men have always known they have to adapt to their superiors, adaptability having much in common with both subservience and survival. Franks would learn to adapt again. Rumsfeld could be tough, unpleasant, unrelenting, but Franks decided not to take it personally. There was much to be admired in Rumsfeld. The military needed to modernize and Rumsfeld's talk about "transformation," bringing the military into the 21st century, made sense to Franks. Yes, Rumsfeld was bullheaded. And it probably had been ten years since the senior generals and admirals—those like Franks himself—had had anyone chew their asses or even argue with them. So when Rumsfeld said, I don't agree with that! Why do you do that? Let's fix it!, the fellows felt challenged and went into hyperventilation. Not Franks. He was going to go along. It might not be the way he would run things, but it was intellectually absorbing, and he decided to take Rumsfeld's prodding and questions and treat them as a needed stimulus. The tasks before them were large and fit with Franks's sense of national necessity. To reports of lingering tensions, Franks said much later, "Bullshit. He was pushing, and it satisfied me greatly."

THE SAME PRE-THANKSGIVING Wednesday that Bush sent Rumsfeld on the mission about the Iraq war plan, Air Force Major General Victor E. "Gene" Renuart Jr., the director of operations for General Franks at Central Command, headquartered in Tampa, Florida, was in the thick of organizing and monitoring military movements and attacks in the Afghanistan war, 5,000 miles and nine and a half time zones away. Renuart, 51, a balding, brainy fighter pilot with a master's degree in psychology, was the man who knitted it all together for Franks. He had not had a day off since 9/11, and the thick, bound volumes in which he took down notes from endless meetings and extensive lists of tasks to be performed were multiplying. Renuart's executive assistant called each latest volume "The Black Book of Death" because the mounting number of tasks had become a killer.

Renuart picked up a call on a secure line from the Pentagon coming in from his counterpart there, Marine Lieutenant General Gregory S. Newbold, the director of operations or J-3 for the Joint Chiefs of Staff. Newbold was the senior operations officer in the Pentagon, the liaison with the combatants and a reliable pipeline for what was stirring.

"Hey," Newbold said in his best take-notice voice, "I've got a real tough problem for you. The secretary's going to ask you to start looking at your Iraq planning in great detail—and give him a new commander's estimate."

"You got to be shitting me," Renuart said. "We're only kind of busy on some other things right now. Are you sure?"

"Well, yeah. It's coming. So stand by."

The current Iraq war plan, Op Plan 1003, was some 200 pages with 20-plus annexes numbering another 600 pages on logistics, intelligence, air, land and sea operations. According to this plan, it would take the United States roughly seven months to move a force of 500,000 to the Middle East before launching military operations. Renuart went to see General Franks, who had received only a vague indication there had been discussion in Washington about the Iraq war plan. Renuart now had more detail.

"Hey, boss," Renuart said, reporting that a formal request of a commander's estimate was coming. "So we'd better get on it."

Franks was incredulous. They were in the midst of one war, Afghanistan, and now they wanted detailed planning for another, Iraq? "Goddamn," Franks said, "what the fuck are they talking about?"

1

IN EARLY JANUARY 2001, before George W. Bush was inaugurated, Vice President–elect Dick Cheney passed a message to the outgoing secretary of defense, William S. Cohen, a moderate Republican who served in the Democratic Clinton administration.

"We really need to get the president-elect briefed up on some things," Cheney said, adding that he wanted a serious "discussion about Iraq and different options." The president-elect should not be given the routine, canned, round-the-world tour normally given incoming presidents. Topic A should be Iraq. Cheney had been secretary of defense during George H. W. Bush's presidency, which included the 1991 Gulf War, and he harbored a deep sense of unfinished business about Iraq. In addition, Iraq was the only country the United States regularly, if intermittently, bombed these days.

The U.S. military had been engaged in a frustrating low-grade, undeclared war with Iraq since the Gulf War when Bush's father and a United Nations–backed coalition had ousted Saddam Hussein and his army from Kuwait after they had invaded that country. The United States enforced two designated no-fly zones, meaning the Iraqis could fly neither planes nor helicopters in these areas, which comprised about 60 percent of the country. Cheney wanted to make sure Bush understood the military and other issues in this potential tinderbox.

Another element was the standing policy inherited from the Clinton administration. Though not widely understood, the baseline policy was clearly "regime change." A 1998 law passed by Congress and signed by President Bill Clinton authorized up to $97 million in military assistance to Iraqi opposition forces "to remove the regime headed by Saddam Hussein" and "promote the emergence of a democratic government."

On Wednesday morning, January 10, ten days before the inauguration, Bush, Cheney, Rumsfeld, Rice and the designated secretary of state, Colin L. Powell, went to the Pentagon to meet with Cohen. Afterward, Bush and his team went downstairs to the Tank, the secure domain and meeting room for the Joint Chiefs of Staff.

Bush sauntered in like Cool Hand Luke, flapping his arms slightly, cocky but seeming also ill at ease.

Two generals briefed them on the state of the no-fly zone enforcement. Operation Northern Watch enforced the no-fly zone in the northernmost 10 percent of Iraq to protect the minority Kurds. Some 50 U.S. and United Kingdom aircraft had patrolled the restricted airspace on 164 days of the previous year. In nearly every mission they had been fired on or threatened by the Iraqi air defense system, including surface-to-air missiles (SAMs). U.S. aircraft had fired back or dropped hundreds of missiles and bombs on the Iraqis, mostly at antiaircraft artillery.

In Operation Southern Watch, the larger of the two, the U.S. patrolled almost the entire southern half of Iraq up to the outskirts of the Baghdad suburbs. Pilots overflying the region had entered Iraqi airspace an incredible 150,000 times in the last decade, nearly 10,000 in the last year. In hundreds of attacks not a single U.S. pilot had been lost.

The Pentagon had five graduated response options when Iraqis fired on a U.S. aircraft. Air strike counterattacks were automatic; the most serious ones, involving multiple strikes against more important targets or sites outside the no-fly zones, required notification or direct approval of the president. No-fly zone enforcement was dangerous and expensive. Multimillion-dollar jets were put at risk bombing 57-millimeter antiaircraft guns. Saddam had warehouses of them. As a matter of policy, was the Bush administration going to keep poking Saddam in the chest? Was there a national strategy behind this or was it just a static tit-for-tat?

An operation plan called Desert Badger was the response if a U.S. pilot were to be shot down. It was designed to disrupt the Iraqis' ability to capture the pilot by attacking Saddam's command and control in downtown Baghdad. It included an escalating attack if a U.S. pilot were captured. Another operation plan called Desert Thunder was the response if the Iraqis attacked the Kurds in the north.

Lots of acronyms and program names were thrown around—most of them familiar to Cheney, Rumsfeld and Powell, who had spent 35 years in the Army and been chairman of the Joint Chiefs of Staff from 1989 to 1993.

President-elect Bush asked some practical questions about how things worked, but he did not offer nor hint at his desires.

The JCS staff had placed a peppermint at each place. Bush unwrapped his and popped it into his mouth. Later he eyed Cohen's mint and flashed a pantomime query, Do you want that? Cohen signaled no, so Bush reached over and took it. Near the end of the hour-and-a-quarter briefing, the chairman of the Joint Chiefs, Army General Henry "Hugh" Shelton, noticed Bush eyeing his mint, so he passed it over.

Cheney listened but he was tired and closed his eyes, conspicuously nodding off several times. Rumsfeld, who was sitting at a far end of the table, paid close attention though he kept asking the briefers to please speak up, or please speak louder.

"We're off to a great start," one of the chiefs commented privately to a colleague after the session. "The vice president fell asleep and the secretary of defense can't hear."

Cohen, who was leaving the Defense Department in 10 days, believed that the new administration would soon see the reality about Iraq. They would not find much, if any, support among other countries in the region or the world for strong action against Saddam, which would mean going it alone in any large-scale attack.

What could they accomplish with air strikes? Not much, he thought. Iraq was treacherous. When everything was weighed, Cohen predicted the new team would soon back off and find "reconciliation" with Saddam, who he felt was effectively contained and isolated.

In interviews nearly three years later, Bush said of the pre-9/11 situation, "I was not happy with our policy." It wasn't having much impact on changing Saddam's behavior or toppling him. "Prior to September 11, however, a president could see a threat and contain it or deal with it in a variety of ways without fear of that threat materializing on our own soil." Saddam was not yet a top priority.

BUSH RECEIVED A SECOND critical national security briefing a few days later. CIA Director George Tenet and his deputy for operations, James L. Pavitt, gave Bush, Cheney and Rice the so-called secrets briefing. For two and one-half hours, the two ran through the good, bad and ugly about covert operations, the latest technical surveillance and eavesdropping, the "who" and "how" of the secret payroll.

When all the intelligence was sorted, weighed and analyzed, Tenet and Pavitt agreed there were three major threats to American national security. One was Osama bin Laden and his al Qaeda terrorist network, which operated out of a sanctuary in Afghanistan. Bin Laden terrorism was a "tremendous threat" which had to be considered "immediate," they said. There was no doubt that bin Laden was going to strike at United States interests in some form. It was not clear when, where, by what means. President Clinton had authorized the CIA in five separate intelligence orders to try to disrupt and destroy al Qaeda.

A second major threat was the increasing proliferation of weapons of mass destruction, WMD—chemical, biological and nuclear. This was of immense concern, they said. Third was the rise of China, especially its military, but that problem was 5 to 15 or more years away.

Iraq was barely mentioned. Tenet did not have an agenda for Iraq as he did for bin Laden and al Qaeda.

On the 17th day of the Bush presidency, Monday, February 5, Rice chaired a principals committee meeting that included Cheney, Powell and Rumsfeld. Deputy CIA Director John E. McLaughlin substituted for Tenet. The purpose was to review Iraq policy, the status of diplomatic, military and covert options. Among the first taskings were for each principal and his department or agency to examine and consider how intelligence collection could be increased on Iraq's suspected weapons of mass destruction.

At least on paper, the United Nations had an economic sanctions policy directed at Saddam's regime. The principals conceded that Saddam had basically won the public relations argument by convincing the international community that the sanctions were impoverishing his people, and that they were not stopping him from spending money to keep himself in power.

Powell very quickly said they needed to attempt to get the U.N. to revise the sanctions to tighten them on material that might advance Saddam's military and WMD programs. Sanctions could then be eased on civilian goods.

Another issue was the weapons inspections inside Iraq that the U.N. had authorized after the Gulf War to establish that Saddam no longer possessed weapons of mass destruction. The inspectors had helped to dismantle Iraq's chemical, biological and surprisingly advanced nuclear programs, but suspicious accounting of destroyed munitions and elaborate concealment mechanisms left many unanswered questions. In 1998 Saddam had forced the inspectors out, and the question was what might be done to get them back in. No one had a good answer.

What should be the approach to Iraqi opposition groups both outside and inside Iraq? When should weapons and other lethal assistance be provided? Who should provide it—the CIA or Defense? Again no one had a complete answer.

Rice asked for a review of the no-fly zones. What was their purpose? What were the costs and risks? The benefits?

Bush himself worried about the no-fly zone enforcement. The odds of Iraq getting lucky and downing a pilot were bound to catch up with them. He later recalled, "I instructed the secretary of defense to go back and develop a more robust option in case we really needed to put some serious weapons on Iraq in order to free a pilot."

The eventual result was a plan to fly fewer sorties and fly them less predictably to enhance the safety of the pilots. If a plane was shot at, the response would be more strategic, hitting Iraqi military installations important to Saddam.

ON FRIDAY, February 16, two dozen U.S. and British bombers struck some 20 radar and command centers inside Iraq, some only miles from the outer areas of Baghdad. A general from the Joint Staff had briefed Rice beforehand and she in turn had informed the president, saying that Saddam was on the verge of linking some key command and control sites with hard-to-hit underground fiber optic cables. They would be destroyed before they were completed. The attacks would be part of the routine enforcement of the no-fly zones. It was the largest strike in two years.

Somehow no one at the Pentagon or the White House had thought to make sure that Rumsfeld was fully in the loop. In the first month, his front office was not yet organized—"complete and total disarray" in the words of one White House official. His deputy and other top Defense civilian posts had not been filled or confirmed. Within the Pentagon there also had not been adequate appreciation of the location of one of the sites near Baghdad. Saddam or his security apparatus had panicked, thinking the United States had launched a larger attack. Air raid sirens went off in Baghdad, briefly putting Saddam on CNN, and reminding the White House and the Pentagon that Saddam had a vote in these shoot-outs: He could respond or escalate.

Rumsfeld, furious, declared that the chain of command had been subverted. By law, military command ran from the president to him as secretary of defense to General Franks at CENTCOM. The Joint Chiefs' role, again by law, was advice, communications and oversight. He should be the one to deal with the White House and the president on operational matters. Period. "I'm the secretary of defense," he reminded one officer. "I'm in the chain of command."

ON MARCH 1, the principals met again and Powell was given the task of devising a plan and strategy to refocus the U.N. economic sanctions on weapons control. Powell knew that the French and Russians, who had substantial business interests in Iraq, were doing everything possible to pull the sanctions apart, get Iraq declared in compliance, and have the sanctions lifted. On the opposite side, the Pentagon did not want anything changed or eased. Rumsfeld and others from Defense repeatedly voiced concern about dual-use items—equipment that might seem innocent but could be used or converted to assist Iraq's weapons programs.

Look what they are buying, Rumsfeld complained to Powell at one point. They are buying these dumptrucks. They can take off the hydraulic cylinder that pushes the truck bed up and they can use it for a launcher for a rocket. You want to sell them the means to erect rockets to shoot at us or Israel?

For Christ's sake, Powell said, if somebody wants a cylinder to erect a rocket, they don't have to buy a $200,000 dumptruck to get one!

Another issue for Rumsfeld was the so-called HET—Heavy Equipment Transporters—that the Iraqis were buying. These are trailers heavy enough to carry a tank. Intelligence had some overhead photography showing the Iraqis were reinforcing some of the transporters, leading to the conclusion that revised sanctions would allow clandestine development of a fleet of tank transporters. To Powell, it seemed that Rumsfeld was suggesting that the Middle East might be overrun by Iraqi tanks.

"Come on!" Powell said. He had become increasingly skeptical. There was a heated fight that led to some of the most bizarre debates he had within the administration.

Rumsfeld also complained about the no-fly zones. Iraqis were shooting at our planes routinely. Where else in our history have we ever let people shoot at us like that? he wanted to know.

What's the alternative? Powell asked. What did he want? No one ever came up with a viable alternative. Rumsfeld continued to express his discontent, finally saying that the administration was playing "patty-cake."

Okay, what do you want to play? Powell asked. The discussions moved on to the president's request for a better military plan in the event that a pilot was shot down. Was there a "big bang" that would deter Iraq from shooting at our pilots? Was there a way to have strategic impact which might both weaken the regime and send a message of seriousness to Saddam?

A formal alternative was not forthcoming.

IT WAS UNPRECEDENTED for someone who had served as secretary of defense—or for that matter any top cabinet post—to come back 25 years later to the same job. It was a chance to play the hand again. Rumsfeld was determined to play it better.

For a whole series of reasons—some that went back decades, some only months—Rumsfeld was going to push hard. Perhaps pushing was an understatement. Rumsfeld not only preferred clarity and order, he insisted on them. That meant personally managing process, knowing all the details, asking the questions, shaping the presidential briefings and the ultimate results. The questions always before him were: What did the president need to know and what could the president expect his secretary of defense to know? In other words, Rumsfeld wanted near-total control.

In part, this desire stemmed from his experience and deep frustrations from 1975–76 when he had been President Gerald Ford's defense secretary. Rumsfeld was secretary for only 14 months because Ford did not win election in his own right in 1976. Only 44 at the time, he had found the Pentagon difficult and almost unmanageable.

In 1989, some 12 years after leaving the Pentagon, Rumsfeld reflected on the frequent impossibilities of the job during a dinner he and I had at my house. I was writing a book on the Pentagon, and was interviewing all the former secretaries of defense and other top military leaders. The Princeton wrestler had not mellowed. It was just ten days before the presidential inauguration of his longtime GOP rival, George H. W. Bush. In the 1960s and 1970s, Rumsfeld had been a Republican star and a good number in the party, including Rumsfeld, thought he might be president one day. Rumsfeld thought Bush senior was weak, lacking in substance, that he had defined his political persona as someone who was around and available. That night as the two of us ate in my kitchen, he showed no bitterness, perhaps only a sense of lost opportunity. The business was the Pentagon and he stuck to it.

The job of secretary of defense was "ambiguous," Rumsfeld said, because there was only "a thin layer of civilian control." He said it was "like having an electric appliance in one hand and the plug in the other and you are running around trying to find a place to put it in." He added, "You can't make a deal that sticks. No one can deliver anything more than their temporary viewpoint." Even the secretary.

There was never enough time to understand the big problems, he said, adding that the Pentagon was set up to handle peacetime issues, such as the political decision about moving an aircraft carrier. In a real war these would be military questions, and he went so far as to say that in case of war the country would almost need a different organization than the Pentagon.

Rumsfeld recalled how the top senior civilian and military officials, some 15, had come into his Pentagon office about 6:30 one night. They needed a decision on which tank the Army should buy. The choices were the one with the Chrysler engine or the one with the General Motors engine. You've got to decide, they told him, we can't. A press release with the announcement was all ready to go with blanks to be filled in with his decision. By his own description, Rumsfeld began flying around his office, telling them they all ought to be "hung by their thumbs and balls." His voice rising, he had shouted, "You idiots, jerks!" They were not thinking—they would wind up getting neither tank from Congress because "THE BUILDING IS DIVIDED!" Congress would inevitably learn of the divisions. So he refused to decide and the press release was abandoned. It took another three months, but he forced them to reach a decision "unanimously."

"If someone does not know how to wrestle he will get hurt. If you don't know how to move, you will get a black eye. Same in Defense," he said.

RUMSFELD HAD WORKED HARD behind the scenes on the Bush campaign in 2000 on substantive matters, and was at first interested in becoming CIA director in a new administration, having concluded that intelligence was what needed fixing. He had spoken with his one-time aide and friend Ken Adelman, who had been head of arms control in the Reagan administration. Adelman told Rumsfeld bluntly that the CIA would be the wrong job. "It's a mean place and they eat their own," he said. "Secondly, I think it is just totally unrealistic. Let me paint you a picture. You're in the Situation Room and you are going to sit there and say well, here our intelligence shows this and shows that but I'm not going to tell you any policy recommendation." The CIA director is supposed to stay out of policy. "You are just so out the ass. You can fool other people but that's not you, it'll never happen." Rumsfeld would feel compelled to make his recommendation. "I don't think you should go into a job playing a role you can't play."

When the top candidates for Defense flubbed their interviews or turned the job down, Bush and Cheney, who had been Rumsfeld's deputy when Rumsfeld served as White House chief of staff for President Ford, turned to him as the surprise choice.

As an illustration of the way Washington works, when Rumsfeld was being considered for Defense by Bush junior, Vice President–elect Cheney—who headed the transition team—sought a confidential opinion from Brent Scowcroft, who had served as national security adviser to both Ford (1974–77) and Bush senior (1989–93).

As Cheney knew, Scowcroft said, Rumsfeld was secretive. Scowcroft said he did not find it necessarily pernicious, but that it made it difficult if not impossible to read him. He doesn't signal. He asks questions and throws out doubts and rarely says, "I think we ought to do this."

Of course, the description also fit Cheney, who wanted his old boss at Defense.

Before Rumsfeld became George W. Bush's secretary of defense, he had a talk with the president-elect. It was a sort of test. During the eight years of Clinton's presidency, the country's natural pattern when challenged or attacked had been what Rumsfeld called "reflexive pullback." He said he believed that, in contrast, the new Bush administration should be "forward-leaning," and Bush had agreed.

Two months into the job, Rumsfeld drafted a three-page memo called "Guidelines When Considering Committing U.S. Forces." He took the fourth revision to the president and went over it in detail. It was a series of questions to be addressed: "Is a proposed action truly necessary?" "Is the proposed action achievable?" "Is it worth it?"

Rumsfeld argued for being clear-eyed. One passage foreshadowed problems to come: "In fashioning a clear statement of the underpinning for the action, avoid arguments of convenience. They can be useful at the outset to gain support, but they will be deadly later." He also had written, "U.S. leadership must be brutally honest with itself, the Congress, the public and coalition partners." And he added, "It is a great deal easier to get into something than it is to get out of it!"

Rumsfeld found the president responsive, but during the first months of his second Pentagon tour, he discovered that the place was more broken than he had anticipated.

AS DISCUSSIONS on Iraq policy continued at the cabinet level and at the second tier, the so-called deputies committee, attention turned to the support of the opposition groups—both those outside the country, such as the Iraqi National Congress (INC) headed by the controversial Ahmed Chalabi, and groups inside Iraq. Chalabi, an American-educated mathematician who left Baghdad in 1958 as a boy, had become the darling of senior Defense officials who saw him and his London-based exile organization as a potential armed insurgent force. The State Department and CIA viewed Chalabi with skepticism—too slick, they felt, too divisive, out of touch with the horrors of life under Saddam—and he was wanted in Jordan for bank fraud.

Within the deputies committee, which included defense deputy Paul D. Wolfowitz and the No. 2 at State, Richard L. Armitage, the debate was passionate about how far and how fast to go with the opposition. At what point would the U.S. provide weapons? At what point would they support lethal operations inside Iraq if the opposition wanted to go inside and conduct operations there? Would training of the opposition be done by Defense or the CIA? Though Armitage had promoted the idea of rearming opposition forces in Afghanistan, he wasn't enthusiastic about Chalabi.

Armitage, 56, is Powell's best friend, adviser and most outspoken advocate. He graduated from the Naval Academy in 1967 and served four tours in Vietnam, ending his naval career in 1973 after teaching counterinsurgency. In the 1980s, Powell and he both served under Secretary of Defense Caspar Weinberger, Armitage as assistant secretary of defense for international security affairs—the Pentagon's mini–State Department—and Powell as Weinberger's senior military assistant. The two talk on the phone so many times each day that aides think of them as teenagers joined at the hip, committed to sharing absolutely everything.

The common goal among the deputies was to increase pressure on Saddam, to try to create fissures and disagreements within the regime. But then the question was how and to what extent they would be exploited if they could be created? The deputies could not reach anything close to agreement. On June 1, the principals asked the full National Security Council to address a policy that would help the Iraqis help themselves. "Stirring the pot and seeing what happens" is how one participant described it.

But that half-policy carried the danger that Saddam might react. He might attack into the Kurdish areas in the north, or go after the

Shiite population again in the south. He might attack a neighbor—
Israel, Kuwait again. Or he might fire Scud missiles at Israel, Saudi
Arabia or Kuwait. There were no easy answers.

BETWEEN MAY 31 and July 26, 2001, Deputy National Security Adviser Stephen J. Hadley convened the deputies four times to work the
Iraq policy. Hadley, 54, was a smart attorney who had worked for
Cheney in Defense and was known for his workaholic tendencies. As
Rice's deputy, he chaired the deputies committee. On August 1, the
group presented a Top Secret paper to the principals entitled, "A Liberation Strategy." It proposed a phased strategy of pressuring Saddam and developing the tools and opportunities for enhancing that
pressure, and how to take advantage of the opportunities. It relied
heavily on the Iraqi opposition.

The paper had classified attachments that went into detail
about what might be done diplomatically—economic sanctions and
U.N. weapons inspectors; militarily with the no-fly zones and the
contingencies if a pilot were shot down; and what the CIA or others
might do to support, strengthen and empower the Iraqi opposition.

The interagency process had yielded up lots of meetings and
paper but no plan and no action toward regime change. This led to
discussions among the principals and deputies about the circumstances under which the U.S. military might be used directly. Powell
called this the "Suppose-we-ever-have-to-do-this" attack on Iraq to
overthrow Saddam. Though there was a lot going on over in the Pentagon that was never shown to the principals, Powell heard enough
officially and unofficially from his old military contacts—the generals' grapevine.

The intellectual godfather and fiercest advocate for toppling
Saddam was Paul Wolfowitz, the deputy secretary of defense. A 58-
year-old Ph.D. in political science, with long, thick, graying hair and
a soft, almost rabbinical manner, Wolfowitz had edgy, hawkish
views. The reasons for getting rid of Saddam were: It was necessary
and it would be relatively easy.

Wolfowitz believed it was possible to send in the military to overrun and seize Iraq's southern oil fields—1,000 wells, which had about two-thirds of Iraq's oil production—and establish a foothold. All the wells were within some 60 miles of the Kuwait border. "There's nothing to stop you from seizing it," he declared. The proposal was dubbed the "enclave strategy." From the enclave, support would be given to the anti-Saddam opposition, which would rally the rest of the country and overthrow the dictator.

Powell thought that Wolfowitz was talking as if 25 million Iraqis would rush to the side of a U.S.-supported opposition. In his opinion, it was one of the most absurd, strategically unsound proposals he had ever heard.

But Wolfowitz was like a drum that would not stop. He and his group of neoconservatives were rubbing their hands over the ideas, which were being presented as "draft plans."

And Powell, shaking his head, kept saying, "This is lunacy." It was not clear where the off switch was or whether there was an off switch. So the secretary of state sought opportunities to speak directly to the president.

"Don't let yourself get pushed into anything until you are ready for it," Powell advised Bush, "or until you think there is a real reason for it. This is not as easy as it is being presented, and take your time on this one. Don't let anybody push you into it."

"Don't worry about it," the president replied. "It's good contingency planning and I know what they are doing and I'm in no hurry to go look for trouble."

Still alarmed that such a scheme might get traction, Powell again raised the matter of a quick strike or incursion into Iraq to the president. He said, "You don't have to be bullied into this." He urged Bush to take it slowly.

"I've got it," the president replied. "I know it."

Bush never saw a formal plan for a quick strike, he recalled. "The idea may have floated around as an interesting nugget to chew on," he said. Whatever it was, the concept and the loose thinking behind it was a source of continuing and mounting consternation for Powell.

On August 10, U.S. and British jets bombed three air defense sites in Iraq, the largest strikes since February. It wasn't even front page news. *The Washington Post* story the next day on page A18 characterized the attack as one of "relatively limited scope" and business-as-usual. "Yesterday's strikes appeared to continue the Clinton-era pattern of hitting Iraqi air defenses every six months or so."

Most work on Iraq stopped for the rest of August as Bush and his top advisers left for vacation. A policy recommendation on Iraq was never forwarded to the president.

The deep divisions and tensions in the war cabinet with Powell the moderate negotiator and Rumsfeld the hard-line activist meant no real policy would be made until either the president stepped in or events forced his hand.

No one realized that better than Rice. At 46, she had a Ph.D. in political science and had taught at Stanford where she had risen to be provost. A Russian expert, she had been on the NSC staff in the presidency of Bush senior. Graceful and tall with an outgoing smile, she had forged her relationship with George W. Bush during the 2000 campaign when she served as his chief foreign policy adviser. She is not married and has no immediate family; it seemed she was on call for the president 24 hours a day in her West Wing office, with him on trips abroad, at Camp David on weekends or at his Texas ranch. She was the connective tissue with the principals. Tending to the president and his priorities was her primary goal.

2

THE SEPTEMBER 11, 2001, terrorist attacks in New York and Washington that killed nearly 3,000 altered and defined the Bush presidency. It was not an exaggeration when Bush dictated to his daily diary that night that, "The Pearl Harbor of the 21st century took place today." In some respects the attacks were more devastating. Instead of 1941 Hawaii, which was not then a state, the targets were the power centers of the homeland. Instead of Japan, the attacks were conducted by a shadowy enemy that had no country or visible army. Worse for Bush, CIA Director Tenet had explicitly warned him about the immediacy and seriousness of the bin Laden threat. Focusing on domestic issues and a giant tax cut, Bush had largely ignored the terrorism problem. "I didn't feel that sense of urgency," the president acknowledged later in an interview. "My blood was not nearly as boiling."

THE TERRORISTS who struck the Pentagon flew their plane into the building on the opposite side of Rumsfeld's office, tearing a gaping hole and killing 184 people. At 2:40 P.M. that day, with dust and smoke filling the operations center as he was trying to figure out what had happened, Rumsfeld raised with his staff the possibility of going after Iraq as a response to the terrorist attacks, according to an aide's notes. Saddam Hussein is S.H. in these notes, and UBL is Usama bin Laden. The notes show that Rumsfeld had mused about whether to "hit S.H. @ same time—not only UBL" and asked the Pentagon lawyer to talk to Paul Wolfowitz about the Iraq "connection with UBL." The next day in the inner circle of Bush's war cabinet, Rumsfeld asked if the terrorist attacks did not present an "opportunity" to launch against Iraq.

Four days later in an exhaustive debate at Camp David, none of the president's top advisers recommended attacking Iraq as a first step in the terrorism war—not even Vice President Cheney, who probably read where Bush was headed and said, "If we go after Saddam Hussein, we lose our rightful place as good guy." Cheney, however, voiced deep concerns about Saddam and said he would not rule out going after him at some point. Colin Powell was adamantly opposed to attacking Iraq as a response to September 11. He saw no real linkage between Saddam and 9/11. Members of a rapidly forming international coalition of other nations would jump off the bandwagon, Powell said. "They'll view it as bait and switch—it's not what they signed up to do," the secretary of state said bluntly. He was pumping the brakes.

White House Chief of Staff Andrew H. Card said Iraq should not be a principal, initial target. Tenet also recommended that the initial terrorist target for the military should be Afghanistan, not Iraq.

A tally would show that it was 4 to 0 against hitting Iraq initially, with Rumsfeld abstaining, making it 4 to 0 to 1. Powell found Rumsfeld's abstention most interesting. What did it mean? he wondered. Rumsfeld had this way of asking questions—questions, questions, questions!—and not revealing his own position.

As a former chairman of the Joint Chiefs of Staff, Powell was direct with one of his successors, Army General Hugh Shelton, in a private discussion after an NSC meeting. Powell had rolled his eyes at Shelton after Rumsfeld had raised Iraq as an "opportunity."

"What the hell! What are these guys thinking about?" Powell had asked Shelton. "Can't you get these guys back in the box?"

Shelton promised he was trying. The only strong advocate for attacking Iraq at that point was Wolfowitz, who thought war in Afghanistan would be dicey and uncertain. Wolfowitz worried about 100,000 American troops bogged down in the notoriously treacherous mountains six months from then. In contrast, Iraq was a brittle, oppressive regime that might break easily with an opposition yearning to topple Saddam. He estimated that there was a 10 to 50 percent chance Saddam was involved in the 9/11 attacks—an odd conclusion that reflected deep suspicion but no real evidence.

The next afternoon, Sunday, September 16, Bush told Rice that the first target of the war on terrorism was going to be Afghanistan. "We won't do Iraq now," the president said, "we're putting Iraq off. But eventually we'll have to return to that question."

On September 17, the president signed the Top Secret/Pearl order for new CIA and military operations against terrorists worldwide. Afghanistan was the first priority. Rumsfeld was directed to continue working on Iraq war plans but it was not to be a top priority.

In an interview nearly one year later, President Bush said that in the immediate aftermath of September 11, "There were some who discussed Iraq. That's out of the question at this point. I mean, I didn't need any briefings." He added, "Don, wisely—and I agreed with this—was looking for other places where we could show that the war on terror was global." Rumsfeld also wanted ground forces in Afghanistan, not just cruise missiles and bombers launched from afar. "He was the man who was insistent upon boots on the ground to change the psychology of how Americans viewed war," the president said.

Bush believed Clinton had been risk-averse. He had used cruise missiles to attack bin Laden in Afghanistan in 1998 after al Qaeda had bombed two American embassies in East Africa. During the Kosovo war, he had limited U.S. involvement to an air campaign, still spooked by the disastrous mission in Somalia in 1993 when 18 U.S. soldiers died in a fierce urban firefight.

President Bush said, "And Rumsfeld wanted to make sure that

the military was active in other regions. My point was that the degree of difficulty had to be relatively small in order to make sure that we continued to succeed in the first battle."

TWO YEARS AFTER 9/11, during an interview in his office in the White House residence, President Bush said, "September the 11th obviously changed my thinking a lot about my responsibility as president. Because September the 11th made the security of the American people the priority . . . a sacred duty for the president. It is the most necessary duty for the president, because if the president doesn't take on that duty, who else is going to?"

It changed his attitude toward "Saddam Hussein's capacity to create harm," he said, adding that "all his terrible features became much more threatening. Keeping Saddam in a box looked less and less feasible to me." Saddam was a "madman," the president said. "He had used weapons of mass destruction in the past. He has created incredible instability in the neighborhood." Saddam had invaded Iran in the 1980s and Kuwait in the 1990s.

Bush added, "The options in Iraq were relatively limited when you are playing the containment game."

CHENEY, THE 61-YEAR-OLD conservative hard-liner, had already carved out a special position in the administration and held great sway with the president. He was the résumé vice president: White House chief of staff to President Ford at age 34; then 10 years as the only congressman from Wyoming, his home state; briefly the No. 2 House Republican leader before being selected by Bush's father to be secretary of defense in 1989. Thought by many Republicans to be the best qualified in their party for the presidency, Cheney had considered running in 1996. But he found the fund-raising and media scrutiny distasteful, and he was named CEO of Halliburton, the large Texas-based energy and oil service firm, in 1995. He served until Bush picked him to be his running mate in the summer of 2000 with these words, "If times are good, I'm going to need your advice, but not nearly as much as if times are bad."

It was not clear how such a high-powered figure who had a chief executive's instincts and order-giving habits would fit into the new Bush administration, since as vice president he would have no operational responsibility, no department, no agency. But two roles emerged.

After the close election, in which Bush-Cheney won only after a 36-day recount in Florida and a Supreme Court ruling, the conventional wisdom—what Cheney liked to call "the bottled wisdom of Washington"—held that Bush would have to proceed carefully. He was technically a minority president, since Al Gore had won 500,000 more popular votes. But Bush told Cheney up front that they weren't going to have any trimming of sails, no acting like some kind of minority president. "From the very day we walked in the building," Cheney once said privately, "a notion of sort of a restrained presidency because it was such a close election, that lasted maybe 30 seconds. It was not contemplated for any length of time. We had an agenda, we ran on that agenda, we won the election—full speed ahead." Cheney was delighted at this approach. He did not like going wobbly on matters in which he deeply believed.

The first matter was a massive tax cut. As the vice president, Cheney was president of the Senate and had the power constitutionally to break tie votes. Since the Senate was split 50–50 between Republicans and Democrats, he technically held the balance of power. So Cheney was closely involved in the behind-the-scenes negotiations over Bush's first tax cut. At a closed-door meeting on the morning of April 4, 2001, he grabbed one of the small pale yellow napkins with "Majority Leader" printed on it from Senator Trent Lott's office and wrote three numbers:

1.6
1.425
1.25

Bush's proposal for the entire tax cut package was $1.6 trillion, the number being floated by a group of Senate Democrats was $1.25 trillion. In a blue pen, Cheney drew a big circle around $1.425—a compromise, the first time the administration had moved. Bush eventually got $1.35 trillion.

Cheney had been a key administration figure in prolonged, secret negotiations to win Vermont Republican Senator James Jeffords's vote on the tax cut. Not only did the administration lose Jeffords's vote but he resigned from the Republican Party, became an Independent, and gave the Democrats temporary control of the Senate. Legislative compromise was not Cheney's strength.

Bush and Cheney agreed on still another role for the vice president. Given Cheney's background in national security going back to the Ford years, his time on the House Intelligence Committee, and as secretary of defense, Bush said at the top of his list of things he wanted Cheney to do was intelligence. In the first months of the new administration, Cheney made the rounds of the intelligence agencies—the CIA, the National Security Agency, which intercepted communications, and the Pentagon's Defense Intelligence Agency. He was determined to get up to speed on what had transpired in the eight years since he had left government. Bush also asked Cheney to study the nation's vulnerability to terrorism, primarily from biological and chemical threats. By the summer of 2001, Cheney had hired a retired admiral, Steve Abbott, to oversee a program for taking homeland defense more seriously.

With the president's full knowledge and encouragement, Cheney became the self-appointed examiner of worst-case scenarios. Though it was not formalized, he would look at the darker side, the truly bad and terrifying scenarios. By experience and temperament, it was the ideal assignment for Cheney. He felt they had to be prepared to think about the unthinkable. It was one way to be an effective second in command—carve out a few matters, become the expert in them, and then press the first in command to adopt your solutions.

Cheney thought that the Clinton administration had failed in its response to terrorist acts, going back to the first World Trade Center bombing in 1993, and that there had been a pattern of weak responses: No effective response to the 1996 bombing of Khobar Towers, the U.S. military installation in Saudi Arabia, not enough to the 1998 East Africa embassy bombings, none to the 2000 bombing of the USS *Cole*.

After 9/11 it was clear to Cheney that the threat from terrorism had changed and grown enormously. So two matters would have to change. First, the standard of proof would have to be lowered— smoking gun, irrefutable evidence would not have to be required for the United States to act to defend itself. Second, defense alone wasn't enough. They needed an offense.

The most serious threat now facing the United States was a nuclear weapon or a biological or chemical agent in the hands of a terrorist inside the country's borders. And everything, in his view, had to be done to stop it.

BY THAT NOVEMBER 21, when he took Rumsfeld aside, Bush had decided it was time to turn to Iraq. "I want to know what the options are," Bush recalled. "A president cannot decide and make rational decisions unless I understand the feasibility of that which may have to happen. And so in dealing with Don Rumsfeld on this issue, the point I was making to him was at the time, show me what you have in place in case something were to happen. And we had already been through this exercise once [in Afghanistan]."

Bush said he knew it was a big step and that it entailed preparing the country and the world for war. "I have no idea what it takes to cause the Pentagon to respond to a request since I've never been there. I presume Don Rumsfeld . . . was making sure that the product got done and the process didn't linger." The president knew his man.

3

A FTER FRANKS'S MINI-EXPLOSION on November 21 when he had gotten word that Rumsfeld wanted a commander's estimate on the Iraq war plan, the general soon settled down. "We'll give them our best shot at it," he told his operations chief, Renuart. He knew the staff was under immense pressure, that the workload was staggering and round-the-clock because of the war in Afghanistan. "Don't get too worried. We'll just do what we can." Franks added reassuringly, "Man, I just can't imagine this is something we're going to be doing anytime soon."

But Rumsfeld now had his orders and he was not about to waste any time. The president was focused on the Iraq war plan, and when the president was focused, Rumsfeld was focused. Much of the year he had been casting about, some felt stumbling about, trying to answer the question of how to fight the next war. His new, 71-page defense strategy published that fall hadn't really answered that question. But Rumsfeld's method—the constant questioning, interrogations and never-ending reassessments of reassessments—had already unearthed immense problems. He had hit pay dirt months before when he had begun asking to see the war and contingency plans, the actual details for fighting specific wars.

"Let me see the Korean war plan," Rumsfeld ordered soon after he became secretary. The isolated, brutal and militaristic regime of

North Korea, headed by leader Kim Jong Il, was thought by many to be the next potential hot spot and the most dangerous threat. Kim either had or was dangerously on the verge of building nuclear weapons.

So the planners briefed Rumsfeld on Op Plan 5027, the Top Secret contingency plan for war with North Korea.

"I was stunned," Rumsfeld later recalled in an interview. It was years out of date, and focused on the mechanics of transporting large numbers of troops to the region. The plan also had not taken into account that the United States had a new president, Bush, and a new secretary of defense. They had different ideas and strategies. He was appalled.

Did North Korea have nuclear weapons or not? Rumsfeld wanted to know. It sure as hell would make a giant difference if there was war. Were they assuming nuclear weapons or not? The Pentagon war planners and briefers didn't have an answer. Were they assuming the North Koreans were one year away from having nukes? Two years? Again there were no real answers.

As he recalled, he had more questions. "What's happened to their military capabilities? Have they gone up or down in the intervening period?"

Vice Admiral Edmund P. Giambastiani, a nuclear submariner and Rumsfeld's senior military assistant at the time, recognized that the plan provided no options, no intermediate solutions. The choices, as he put it, were: "Would you like to use rhetoric or would you like to bring in 75 sledgehammers to beat that gnat into the ground?" It was either diplomacy or total war.

"What I would like to do is next Saturday," Rumsfeld directed— he liked to haul people in on Saturday—"I want the war planners, the contingency planners, to come in and brief me on *all* of the major contingency plans' assumptions, not the plans, but I want to see the assumptions."

So on a Saturday in early August 2001, the chairman of the Joint Chiefs of Staff and the director of the operational plans staff and all his section chiefs appeared in Rumsfeld's office.

PLAN OF ATTACK   33

Of the 68 war plans, fewer than 10 were massive, fully developed plans such as those for Korea, Iraq and a few other potential hot spots. The rest were smaller contingency plans for civilian evacuations or for defending key areas such as the Panama Canal. After spending hours going through four or five, Admiral Giambastiani, who was supposed to keep the Pentagon train—i.e. Rumsfeld—running on time, said, "We are going to be here for about a week if we keep up this pace. You need to pick this up."

Rumsfeld did. The basic solution in most of the plans was to move a vast portion of the American military machine, and in some cases a portion of the U.S. transportation infrastructure and logistics capability, to the region, whether it be Asia or the Middle East, over many months for a war.

"Well, I don't agree with that guidance," he snapped at one point when someone tried to justify what had been planned.

Rumsfeld recalled the scene two years later. "And I sat there for, in that room down there"—and he pointed across his vast Pentagon office down to his conference room—"so I sat there and these people couldn't believe it. It took most of the day. And then one colonel would pop up and he'd go through the assumptions and I'd discuss them and talk about them." Others in attendance said it was more a grilling with Rumsfeld pointing out that the colonels and others hadn't really isolated the assumptions and didn't know what the new administration wanted. "And then the next guy would come up and we went through one after another after another.

"They were just briefing what was on the shelf." And it was an old, dusty shelf going back four or five years in some cases. The formal guidance to the war planners often went back to the mid-1990s. "Yet it had never been even discussed here," Rumsfeld recalled with disdain, indicating the secretary's office.

"Furthermore, we had a new defense strategy by then," Rumsfeld said, referring to his concept that called for deterring aggression against U.S. interests by demonstrating a capacity to swiftly defeat attacks. "Of course the old plans were not looked at that way at all in that new context. So we had to fix them all.

"I said, 'Look, we've got to do two things. We owe the country and the president war plans, contingency plans, thinking that is current. And the only way we're going to get that is if we can compress that process dramatically and shorten it from years down to some cycle that it can be refreshed with current assumptions.' "

There was a convergence with Rumsfeld's hurry-up agenda on war planning and the lessons of 9/11 as he saw them. In an interview four months after 9/11, he said, "The key thought about this is that you cannot defend against terrorism." He had learned that when he had spent six months as the Middle East envoy for President Reagan in 1983–84. "You can't defend at every place at every time against every technique. You just can't do it, because they just keep changing techniques, time, and you have to go after them. And you have to take it to them, and that means you have to preempt them."

This was four and one-half months before Bush formally announced his preemption doctrine. Rumsfeld was thinking of a future when the U.S. should be ready to strike first.

RUMSFELD WAS GOING to tune up the war machine everywhere. "What I did was I went to literally all of the area-of-responsibility geographic combatant commanders and said, 'Pull 'em out, let's look at them, let's put a priority order and we're going to compress this cycle so that they get done in a much shorter period.' " That meant starting with the assumptions, "which most people don't," he noted, "and most people start with a plan that's there and then tweak it."

Well, there was going to be no more tweaking, micro-steps of change. "I said we're going to start with assumptions and then we're going to establish priorities and each of the combatant commanders are then going to start working through their plans. And the way they're going to work through them is they're going to come back to me every six or eight weeks." He was going to check their homework.

"That way," Rumsfeld continued, "all of the grunt work that people have to do, which is an enormous amount of work, won't get done until we get the front right." The grunt work was the detailed charts and timetables of moving forces, the logistics and communications of assembling an army thousands of miles away.

"I don't know who it was," Rumsfeld said, "[George] Marshall or somebody that said, if you get the strategy right, a lieutenant can draft the plan. If you know what you're doing, and where you're going." Well, he did, and the implication was that no one else really did.

"You can move a long distance in the right way without jerking people around and wasting their time. And it just breaks my heart to see fine, talented people working so hard on something that when you look at it, you say, well my goodness, we never should have gone that way."

Rumsfeld's way was clear, and he was precise about it. "The only way these things can be done well is *if risk is elevated*, put on the table and discussed, instead of trying to mitigate it down below at a level where you don't have the benefit of trading off with and balancing risk." He was willing to assume risk by planning to use less force, or at least he wanted to identify the trade-offs.

No one at the lower levels, the colonels, would embrace risk. They would add another division to a plan, some 20,000 troops, just to be sure. "So it gets dealt with that way, if it's lower. It gets dealt with in a totally different way if it's at a higher level."

After the Saturday review session was over, Rumsfeld pronounced his verdict: "That is insane, that is crazy." The war plans were improperly designed. "Either it's world peace or it's World War III. Either the switch is off or on." His orders were clear. "We're not going to do it that way."

Though he was trying to fix all the major war and contingency plans, after the president asked about the Iraq plan Rumsfeld shifted into high gear. "It at a certain point became much more intense," he said, "and it had the highest priority."

THE MONDAY MORNING after Thanksgiving, November 26, the president welcomed two humanitarian aid workers in the Rose Garden of

the White House. Heather Mercer and Dayna Curry had been res-
cued by the U.S. military in Afghanistan. During a long question session, reporters asked about Iraq and Saddam.

"In order to prove to the world he's not developing weapons of
mass destruction, he ought to let the inspectors back in," Bush said.

"If he does not do that, what will be the consequences?"

"That's up for—" the president replied, "he'll find out."

"Readmit Inspectors, President Tells Iraq; 'Or Else' Is Un-
stated," said the front page headline in *The New York Times* the
next day.

That morning, six days after the president's request on the Iraq
war plan, Rumsfeld flew to see General Franks at CENTCOM headquarters in Tampa. After greeting everyone, he kicked Franks's staff
as well as his own aides out of the room, even telling his military assistant, Vice Admiral Giambastiani, "Ed, I need you to step outside."

"Pull the Iraq planning out and let's see where we are," Rumsfeld told Franks when they were alone. The existing Iraq war plan, the
mammoth Top Secret document, Op Plan 1003, outlined an attack
and invasion of Iraq designed to overthrow the regime of Saddam
Hussein. "Don't start without letting me look at those assumptions
you made," he directed, "because we need to challenge everything
we've done in that regard." One additional focus was what they knew
about the current status of the Iraqi military. What are they capable of
doing? What of their training levels? What is their willingness to
fight for Saddam?

Rumsfeld said that the president to his knowledge does not
have a desire to go do something right now, but it would be prudent
to begin.

The existing plan was a real hodgepodge. Rumsfeld found it
cumbersome; it provided every evidence of refighting the 1991 Gulf
War. It called for a force of some 500,000, including six Army and
Marine divisions on the ground, and essentially envisioned only one
scenario: an action by Saddam like his 1990 invasion of Kuwait that
would require a massive response but also allow an extended period
of time for a force buildup before the start of offensive military ac-

tion. The intricate timelines confirmed it would take some seven months to transport and build up the force in the region before attacking Iraq. It was, Franks thought, the classic kind of plodding, tank-heavy, big-bomb massing of military might from another era. Just the thing that drove Rumsfeld nuts.

The Op Plan 1003 on the shelf had last been fully approved in 1996 and an update done in 1998 had gone through all the approval wickets in the Pentagon except it had not been signed by then Secretary of Defense William Cohen.

Rumsfeld and Franks spent an hour going through the plan, the planning process, the assumptions and the stale thinking behind them.

"Let's put together a group that can just think outside the box completely," Rumsfeld ordered. "Certainly we have traditional military planning, but let's take away the constraints a little bit and think about what might be a way to solve this problem."

After the meeting, Rumsfeld and Franks appeared before the news media to brief on the ongoing Afghanistan war called Operation Enduring Freedom. Franks, a head taller than Rumsfeld, loomed over him physically. But there was no question who was boss. The war in Afghanistan was essentially won, at least the first phase. Widespread predictions of a Vietnam-style quagmire had been demolished, at least for the time being, and Rumsfeld was in a buoyant mood.

"This is fantastic! I've got a laser pointer!" Rumsfeld said to laughter after being handed the latest in briefing tools. "Holy mackerel!" He had not only the Taliban and al Qaeda on the run but also, to a certain extent, the media, and he was enjoying it thoroughly.

"How much of it frankly is a surprise?" one reporter asked, referring to the quick close in Afghanistan.

"I think that what was taking place in the earlier phases was exactly as planned," Rumsfeld said. "It looked like nothing was happening. Indeed, it looked like we were in a"—and he asked the room to join in—"all together now—QUAGMIRE!"

There was scattered laughter.

Rumsfeld then turned to a favorite theme: appearances are deceptive. "It now looks like things are going along quite well, superficially," he added, "just like in the first phase superficially it looked like things were not going along very well. And I would submit that what we have said from the outset is correct, that this is going to be a very difficult period." The Afghanistan cities were not safe. "It's not over, it's going to take some time." Afghanistan was unstable. Bin Laden and Taliban leader Mullah Omar were still at large. "People are going to die because of the risks and dangers that exist there."

Rumsfeld knew that they really hadn't had a plan for Afghanistan, had made it up under great pressure and uncertainty after September 11. Iraq would be different. He wasn't going to be caught short, unprepared and uninvolved.

Four days later, December 1, a Saturday, Rumsfeld sent through the chairman of the Joint Chiefs of Staff a Top Secret planning order to Franks asking him to come up with the commander's estimate to build the base of a new Iraq war plan. In two pages the order said Rumsfeld wanted to know how Franks would conduct military operations to remove Saddam from power, eliminate the threat of any possible weapons of mass destruction, and choke off his suspected support of terrorism. This was the formal order for thinking outside the box.

The Pentagon was supposed to give Franks 30 days to come up with his estimate—an overview and a concept for something new, a first rough cut. "He had a month and we took 27 days away," recalled Marine General Pete Pace, the vice chairman of the Joint Chiefs of Staff and a Rumsfeld favorite. Franks was to report in person three days later.

OVER AT THE STATE DEPARTMENT, Powell's deputy, Rich Armitage, had heard that *The New York Times* was doing a story for Saturday, December 1. He was told that the *Times* story was going to say that Powell was soft on Iraq and Rumsfeld was hard over. It was likely to be one of those stories that are based on the statements, leaks and inferences attributed to unidentified "senior administration officials."

A news story with that attribution often carries a semiofficial stamp, not quite on the record but not against the perceived interests of the president. But such stories can be maddening because it is not always clear whether someone was speaking from the White House or another department or agency, or even what qualified as "senior."

Armitage decided to insert himself somewhat dramatically into the *Times*'s developing story and protect Powell's flank by speaking on the record. It would add unusual weight, not so much because the senior official would be named but because he was the No. 2 in the department and the best friend of the No. 1. Armitage told the *Times* that President Bush was engaged in a calculated effort to use the momentum—"a roll in Afghanistan"—to try to force Saddam to readmit U.N. weapons inspectors. The inspectors, who operated under the treaty signed after the 1991 Gulf War, had been effectively expelled by Saddam in 1998. Powell's State Department was always suspected of subversive tendencies, at least cutting to the moderate or dovish side of any saber rattling, so Armitage wanted to make it clear that State had gotten the message. "The president said it, so that's that—it's back," Armitage was quoted as saying. "I don't think there is any question that an Iraq with weapons of mass destruction is a threat to its neighbors and ultimately to ourselves, and so we will do what we need to do to obviate that threat."

Armitage's comments, along with some on-the-record comments by Rice, were the lead story in *The New York Times* December 1, under a modest one-column headline: "U.S. to Press Iraq to Let U.N. Search for Banned Arms." As far as Armitage was concerned, it was a great story squelching, at least temporarily, the suggestion that Powell was soft. Armitage, whose bald head and barrel chest make him look like a cross between Daddy Warbucks and a World Wrestling Federation champ, has a knack for significantly more expressive language behind the scenes. The story, he later remarked privately, declared, "Oh, State, they're in the game. They want to get these fuckers." That was basically true, but Powell and Armitage wanted to do it later and in a way that would preserve the anti-Saddam international coalition that had supported the 1991 Gulf War. The State

Department account is diplomacy, making their game negotiations and talk, not war, to solve problems such as Iraq.

AN IMPATIENT RUMSFELD wanted the first formal presentation on the Iraq war plan from Franks three days later on December 4 at the Pentagon. It was to be done in the strictest secrecy. Franks asked who he could bring to their meetings. Rumsfeld said that Major General Gene Renuart, Franks's operations director, could attend and even accompany them to the White House for the NSC meetings with the president. Renuart had commanded a fighter squadron during the Gulf War and flown 34 combat missions himself. Before becoming Franks's J-3, he had spent a year in Saudi Arabia commanding the Southern Watch no-fly zone enforcement, so he had the most immediate on-the-ground knowledge of the region and intelligence on Iraq.

"Look, if Gene is around, you can bring Gene into anything as far as I'm concerned," Rumsfeld told Franks.

So on December 4, Franks and Renuart came to Rumsfeld's Pentagon office. Franks began by saying that in the short period of time all he had been able to do was tinker with Op Plan 1003. He now had it trimmed down to a force level of 400,000 over six months, having cut 100,000 and one month from the base plan.

"This is the state of planning as it exists today," Franks told Rumsfeld and a few aides. Though he had gone over it the previous week with Rumsfeld in Tampa, this was the first presentation to the others. "All of us are going to find a lot of difficulties with this plan."

No one more than Rumsfeld, he might have added.

The reason the plan was important, Franks noted, was because it was all they had. As they knew, it normally took two years or maybe three years to write a war plan. So they could work on Op Plan 1003 at the margins without gutting it because they might have to execute it on short notice. "There is uncertainty with respect to when a jet gets shot down in Operation Southern Watch," he said. "There is uncertainty when we may find a linkage between al Qaeda and the Iraqi intel services and this regime." They could not just throw Op Plan 1003 out, declare it no good. If the president woke up one morning—say the next day—and for whatever reason decided to go to war with Iraq this is what the plan was now. "I don't favor this. That's not the point. The point is this is what's here."

Franks and Rumsfeld looked at each other. They had already agreed that this was not where they were going to end up.

"It seems to me that that's going to take a long time," Rumsfeld said.

"Mr. Secretary, that's right," Franks said. "It's going to take a long time to do this."

"I'm not sure that that much force is needed given what we've learned coming out of Afghanistan," Rumsfeld said, citing what that war showed about their advanced precision weapons with laser guidance, and the improvement in intelligence, surveillance and reconnaissance (ISR). The new Predators, the small, unmanned aerial vehicles or drones that provided real-time video, could stay airborne for 24 hours, and could fire two Hellfire missiles. He looked at the charts. "I'm not sure we're going to have to do that."

"You'll get no argument out of me," Franks replied. "I don't think we have to do it either, but it is what it is," he repeated.

They did not know how much time they would have to build up forces, Rumsfeld reminded them. They could not know what would drive a presidential decision. This plan assumed they would have six months. Rumsfeld wanted some alternatives and options, particularly the out-of-the-box thinking and work he had ordered Franks to undertake. How could they minimize the amount of time between the moment the president might be forced to make a decision on war and when military operations could begin? Suppose there was not enough time to move large forces? What was the shortest period of time to get enough there to achieve the objectives?

Franks didn't have the answers. He had, of course, learned the importance of addressing assumptions. He was in the process of making sure he had nailed them all and he could, in the near future, lay them all out.

The mission in an Iraq war was clear: Change the regime, overthrow Saddam, eliminate the threats associated with him—the weapons of mass destruction, the terrorist ties, the danger he posed to his neighbors, especially Israel. It was a tall order. One reality was the U.S. force level currently in place. That consisted of one battalion of 500 combat troops on the ground in Kuwait. Pre-positioned equipment existed in the region for another 1,000 military personnel. That was all. Some 200 aircraft were normally in the region—about 100 Air Force planes based at Prince Sultan Air Base in Saudi Arabia as part of Operation Southern Watch, and out of Turkey for Northern Watch. Another nearly 100 planes were on the Navy aircraft carrier in the region.

Rumsfeld wanted the latest and best intelligence on the Iraqi military. It had been reduced substantially since the Gulf War. How much of a reduction? What did it mean?

This time Franks was given eight days to come back with more, and on December 12 he and Renuart returned to the Pentagon to give Rumsfeld their update. This was called the second iteration of the commander's estimate, and it was kept as secret as possible, delivering on President Bush's strong desire to prevent any leaks. Franks addressed two key questions: Are there efficiencies in how they might create a more robust force in a shorter period of time? Could they use less force?

Rumsfeld thought yes to both, but he had more questions.

"Will it all be visible?" he asked. What parts of an escalating military deployment to the Middle East region could be invisible? Were there things, movement of equipment and forces, that would be below the line, not seen or known publicly?

Of course, yes, Rumsfeld and Franks both knew.

What could they do to increase the invisible component? Rumsfeld asked. What were the things they could get away with without letting Saddam know?

Franks voiced caution about the big parts. If these things were done, large movements of troops, deploying aircraft carriers, they would be seen and they would be reading about it in the newspapers.

What parts would cost lots of money? Rumsfeld asked. He

was always cost-conscious. Were there parts that wouldn't cost much?

Then he had one more thought. "You need to look at things that you could do even as early as April or May." That was four or five months away.

The suggestion took Renuart's breath away. First Rumsfeld had implied there was no urgency, and then implied it was all urgency. The thought of starting a war against Iraq in the spring was daunting.

"Yes, sir," Franks said, "we'll go back and take a look at it." He left frustrated. He wanted to be able to walk in with a 100 percent solution at every briefing. It was impossible, of course, but he pushed Renuart and the planning staff. He wanted them to be out front of his own thought process—addressing and answering questions before Rumsfeld popped them on him.

Franks is an early riser, getting up as early as 3 or 4 A.M., though he normally didn't come to work until 7 A.M. One morning, he was driving especially hard, and Renuart tried to calm and slow his commander with a joke. "Boss, we come in to work at six and are starting to think, and you've been thinking a couple of hours ahead of us already."

FRANKS GOT ONLY another week before Rumsfeld summoned him back to the Pentagon on December 19 for the third iteration. Once again Rumsfeld indicated he was not satisfied—"not fulfilled," as he occasionally termed his sense of dissatisfaction.

Later Rumsfeld recalled during an interview in his Pentagon office, "I tend to ask a lot of questions of the people I work with and I tend to give very few orders. This place is so big and so complicated and there's so much that I don't know, that I probe and probe and probe and push and ask, Well why wasn't this done or shouldn't this be done, but it's generally with a question mark at the end."

Rumsfeld certainly had to be aware that when the secretary of defense asks, "Why wasn't this done?" or "Shouldn't this be done?" or shows even the slightest discontent, it has the force of an order, even if concluded with a sincere question mark. Rumsfeld's questions are not musings, asked in some kind of abstract context or misty wonderment. It is not likely that he misread his authority in the military; the secretary is the boss, period. Or that he did not understand the force of his Type A personality. He was driving, and as he said, the steering had to be done from the top because at the lower levels planners would solve problems by throwing in more force and time. He was willing to accept increased risk in order to get ready faster, and as secretary, he was ultimately the one who could take responsibility for more risk and justify it to the president. "The president wants you to come to Crawford," Rumsfeld told Franks after this latest briefing. Bush was spending the holidays at his 1,600-acre ranch in Crawford, Texas.

"I won't go unless you go," Franks said, half tongue-in-cheek but knowing that Rumsfeld was fierce about the chain of command.

"Well, I'll see," Rumsfeld replied.

Later Rumsfeld recalled that this all had a purpose. "I've read a lot of history in my life and I decided early on and, I don't know if I got it from history, but I decided that it was enormously important, that if I was going to be an effective link between the president of the United States and the combatant commander, I knew my relationship with the president and the access and his interest and how he feels and his body language on things, and I knew that it was that that had to be communicated down to Tom Franks and through him to his people. And so I started spending a lot of time with Tom Franks, and we'd have dinner and what have you and talk on the phone. We'd talk here and we'd talk down there, and I decided that that was just of fundamental importance if we were going to have people's lives at risk. That that be a true channel from the president to me to him and from him to me to the president. I also took great pains to bring him in contact with the president as often as I could and in some instances when I wasn't there."

Rumsfeld talked to the president and called Franks back with a surprising order, "The president wants you to come out there by yourself."

4

———

IN LATE NOVEMBER, the British Secret Intelligence Service, MI6, passed on to Washington the result of an elaborate intelligence operation it was running under a so-called false flag in Pakistan. For the false flag, part of a covert campaign to prevent the spread of nuclear technology and nuclear weaponry, British agents appeared to be tied to extremists or a radical Islamic country to elicit contacts with proliferators. Pakistan, which had nuclear weapons and a relatively sophisticated program, was the focus of worries about proliferation to other Muslim nations, or perhaps worse, to Osama bin Laden's network.

A Pakistani nuclear weapons designer had offered to sell the crude design of a bomb to the SIS false flag. Using the fictitious cover to make the scientist comfortable, the British were able to smoke out more information. At one point the scientist drew a much more sophisticated design of a nuclear weapon, and, according to the British, the drawing was to scale. It reflected a deep understanding of the intricacies of nuclear weapons technology. Included was information on building a crude radiological weapon or "dirty bomb." A dreaded but comparatively simple weapon, the dirty bomb could be made by taking highly radioactive material such as used reactor fuel rods and wrapping them around conventional explosives. If detonated, the device could spread radioactivity over several city blocks or more and have a calamitous psychological impact.

To top this off, another intelligence report said that bin Laden had been present at a gathering when one of his associates produced a canister alleged to contain radioactive material and waved it in the air menacingly to prove that al Qaeda was serious about obtaining a nuclear device. As CIA paramilitary teams were overrunning Afghanistan, bin Laden's sanctuary, they had found a diagram of a dirty bomb and other documents about nuclear weapons. Though crude and of insufficient detail for a weapon, the documents suggested an intent. Bin Laden himself had told a Pakistani journalist recently that he had chemical and nuclear weapons "as a deterrent."

It was an electric moment when all this came together for the president.

"George," Bush told Tenet, "I want you to go over there and get what you need." Get on your plane and fly to Pakistan immediately. Pull out all the stops.

Within hours Tenet was halfway around the world. A large, hulking man with a charged, raspy, infectious voice, he tends to take over whatever space he is occupying. He went to see the head of the Pakistani intelligence service with the intent of raising holy hell. After the 16-hour flight, Tenet was surging. Naturally disinclined to understatement, he cajoled and threatened.

"I can't say to my president," Tenet told the Pakistani chief, "that there isn't a nuclear weapon in the United States! If there is, and it goes off, it will be your fault!"

Tenet met with Pakistani President General Pervez Musharraf to convey the same message, peeling back the eyeballs of the demure, Westernized, English-speaking general as much as possible. Pakistani authorities had picked up several of their scientists and under questioning had pried out information that at least one had met with al Qaeda members.

Tenet insisted the Pakistanis go 24/7 on the case and explore every angle, turn over every rock and scientist.

On the night of December 1, Tenet was flying back to Washington. Five foreign intelligence services, including the Saudis, were alerted to the possibility that a nuclear device in some form, from a dirty bomb to a full-fledged fission warhead, might be loose. The Saudis took extreme precautions at their borders and increased the use of radioactive detection instruments.

The intelligence had a dramatic impact on Bush. He did not want to underreact. A new national terrorist alert was planned for Monday warning vaguely that the "quantity and level of threats are above the norm" and an attack might come in the "next several weeks." Vice President Cheney went off to a secure location outside Washington and had to conduct meetings with visiting senior foreign officials via secure video conference.

Two reporters at *The Washington Post* had got wind of the possible nuclear or dirty bomb threat and a story was about to be published Sunday, December 2, with some of the details. With Tenet out of the country, a very senior CIA official called me at home hours before the story was to be printed and urged it be delayed.

Of Musharraf, the official said, "We leaned on him heavily" and were "turning the screws." The official said, "We just reached the point where they [the Pakistanis] will work with us. A story would cause them to clam up and they would see it as an attempt to pressure them" through the media. The information was sketchy, he said. "What we have is more suggestive than conclusive."

Len Downie, the executive editor of the *Post,* spoke with the CIA official and decided to hold the story.

Several days later, the *Post* ran the story without any reference to Tenet's trip. It was the lead article, Tuesday, December 4, under a two-column headline, "U.S. Fears Bin Laden Made Nuclear Strides; Concern Over 'Dirty Bomb' Affects Security." Four months later, the senior CIA official said the agency "didn't find what we feared in Afghanistan, but is it somewhere else? I don't think we're to the bottom of this yet." *

The fear never went away, and the president and his NSC had to wrestle with the possibility of an attack that would be on such a scale

---

* This was the beginning of the operation that in 2004 uncovered the clandestine sale of nuclear technology by the head of Pakistan's nuclear program, Abdul Qadeer Khan, who later confessed to aiding Iran, North Korea and Libya.

that 9/11 would be a footnote to the history of the era. In this context, it was difficult to determine what *was* an overreaction. After all, hijacked passenger aircraft flown into buildings as missiles to kill thousands had seemed unreal before 9/11. Tenet said that after the Gulf War, the weapons inspectors discovered that Saddam had eight separate ways to get to a nuclear weapon—primitive and inadequate, but threatening.

IN THE DAYS BEFORE CHRISTMAS, when the pace in Washington normally slows, a small, intense 51-year-old attorney was working long, grueling hours up in Room 276 of the Old Executive Office Building next to the White House. It is a dark, modest room with a mantel and fireplace that had seen much history, once used by Theodore Roosevelt when he was assistant secretary of the navy and then by Franklin Roosevelt when he held the job. The current occupant kept neat files and notes in careful penmanship. He might be considered part of a small category of Washington officials—the Unobtrusive Man, ever-present behind the scenes. He was also one of the most important players in the Bush national security apparatus—I. Lewis Libby Jr. A somewhat formal, dignified man, Libby incongruously had the nickname "Scooter," which everyone used.

Libby had three formal titles. He was chief of staff to Vice President Cheney; he was also national security adviser to the vice president; and he was finally an assistant to President Bush. It was a trifecta of positions probably never before held by a single person. Scooter was a power center unto himself, and accordingly, a force multiplier for Cheney's agenda and views.

Libby was a protégé of Paul Wolfowitz, having worked for him in the 1980s when Wolfowitz was an assistant secretary of state, and again in the 1990s when he was policy undersecretary for Cheney in the Pentagon. At the Pentagon Libby's portfolio had been the chemical and biological weapons of Saddam Hussein.

In his current role, Libby was one of only two people who were not principals to attend the National Security Council meetings with the president and the separate principals meetings chaired by Rice. (The other was Rice's deputy, Stephen Hadley.)

From his unique vantage, Libby watched and participated in the debate and development of the president's national security policy. Since Cheney did not have direct operational responsibility for the military, diplomacy, intelligence—or anything else for that matter— neither the vice president nor Libby had to get caught up in the daily firefights or crises, unless, of course, they chose to insert themselves. They both could try to tend to the largest matters of policy and decision. In the end, Libby knew, Cheney's only product was advice—to the National Security Council, and most importantly and most directly, to the president.

Libby had a good lawyer's understanding of the value of caution, patience—and silence. Both Cheney and Libby were artists at just going quiet, closing down completely during a discussion or interview. The style could rattle their colleagues and throw them off stride. Libby also was an expert at deflecting questions about his own views with questions of his own: What does that mean? How are you using the word "decision"?

He had graduated from Yale in 1972—just four years after Bush, and nine years after Cheney would have graduated from Yale if he had not dropped out. Unlike his bosses, Libby had graduated magna cum laude. He had written a little noticed novel in 1996, *The Apprentice*, an adventure tale with some erotic themes set in early-20th-century Japan that *The New York Times Book Review* praised for "delicate prose and stirring descriptive passages."

Libby liked to immerse himself in details—the makeup and characteristics of various tribes in Iraq or even military tactics. During the Gulf crisis of 1990, Wolfowitz and Libby had proposed putting Special Operations commando teams into the west of Iraq to protect Israel, and keep Israel out of the war. Cheney, the secretary of defense, had liked the idea but the CENTCOM commander, General Norman Schwarzkopf, had not been interested. Libby liked to note that during the war, Schwarzkopf had to use up to a quarter of his airpower to secure the western part of Iraq. If the general had only listened.

In the days after the 9/11 terrorist attacks, *The New York Times* ran a front page story on the debate in the Bush administration over whether to go after Iraq in the first wave of military attacks in the war on terrorism. Headlined "Bush's Advisers Split on Scope of Retaliation," the story reported Powell to be opposed, while Wolfowitz and Libby were listed as pressing the case for Iraq. It was an unusual appearance of his name in the newspaper, and he was excruciatingly uncomfortable. The reporters had not called him for comment, and he felt the leak was "scandalous." He tried to tell others that the story was "untrue." Asked if it was "totally untrue," he responded with a lawyerly parsing of language: "It's not totally untrue, but untrue." He had not spoken about Iraq in the large NSC meeting but as he put it, "there were confabs on the margins."

Libby went to see Armitage. "I'm used to seeing Powell's name in print," Libby said. "I didn't like to see my name next to him, particularly in that context. And I don't have a dog in that fight."

"You want me to tell the secretary this?" Armitage asked.

"Please."

"I'll do it," Armitage said, "I'll do it faithfully, but it's not a personal fight. This is about business. And how we do the nation's business, Scooter."

"It's not about who has affection for Iraq or lack of affection," Libby said. "It has to do with what's workable and what's not."

Libby felt that keeping the focus on Afghanistan initially was wise, and now with Afghanistan going well, he believed if the war on terrorism was properly and broadly defined that Iraq had to be dealt with. It was impossible, in his view, to deal definitively with terrorism, as he put it privately, "without facing up to the issue of Iraq." To that extent, he did have a very big dog in that fight.

As defined by his jobs and his own tendency, he was watching the president carefully, noting the body language and the verbal language ordering war planning for Iraq, the questions, attitudes and tone. Maybe it wasn't a war decision, Libby felt, but the president had decided that the Iraq problem was going to be solved one way or the other. Serious military planning was underway, he knew. It was more his own feeling than Cheney's, but he concluded that the president was well on the road to deposing Saddam Hussein. It was an important turning point.

5

———

THE MORNING OF FRIDAY, December 28, the president rose at 5 A.M. at his Crawford, Texas, ranch and spent some time with his wife, Laura. Their place is a small, very modern, even spare ranch-style house on a man-made lake. Except for the various trappings of the presidency—security and stewards who cook and serve—it might be a well-decorated weekend retreat for a wealthy couple. Bush had just read *Theodore Rex* by Edmund Morris, a glowing portrait of President Teddy Roosevelt and his "big stick" diplomacy of the early 20th century. Even a casual reader of the 555-page text, even one inclined to skim, as Bush might have been, could not miss the message: Teddy Roosevelt dominated and defined his era by exercising presidential power decisively, acting, insisting on results and doing it with a personal style that was optimistic and exuberant, even assured to the point of being overbearing and arrogant. Normally Bush would have gone for a run of three or four miles, but a visitor was coming early.

The president went to a special building on his ranch called a SCIF—Sensitive Compartmented Information Facility—where he could be given sensitive briefings in person or by secure video links. The intelligence briefing that morning between Christmas and New Year's included the Top Secret/codeword Threat Matrix, the latest reports on terrorist threats and activities. Item 8 of 19 in the 14-page document described an intercepted communication from an area in Afghanistan apparently still inhabited by Osama bin Laden's terrorist network, al Qaeda. The unidentified person said "good news will be coming in due time," and implied that plans were in place for new attacks. It was precisely the kind of vague but hair-raising intelligence warning that had been received in the months before the September 11 attacks. Whatever it meant, the report was sobering and helped set the tone for the coming meeting.

General Tommy Franks and Major General Renuart joined the president in the secure video conference room. On screens were Cheney from his Wyoming vacation home, Rumsfeld from his Taos, New Mexico, retreat, and Condi Rice, Powell and Tenet from Washington. The president liked to see the faces of his war cabinet.

Franks, who had just been to Afghanistan, gave a summary of operations there. Since the first phase of the Afghanistan campaign had been won, he was accorded the respect of a victorious general by the members of the war cabinet. Someone, probably a remnant of the bin Laden network or the deposed Taliban regime, had fired a surface-to-air missile at his helicopter but missed.

"Franks," Bush said, "the last thing I need is for you to get yourself killed."

Powell noted wryly that captains and majors and those below them in the officer ranks were supposed to be the ones taking the risk, not four-star generals.

Franks turned to the principal reason for the meeting that day, the Iraq war planning.

"Mr. President," Franks said, "we have a lot to do on this thing, but let me show you where we are with this right now." He handed the president a paper copy of 26 briefing slides. Each was inscribed in stark red with the classification Top Secret/Polo Step—the special compartment of information for military operational plans. Access is limited to those who have absolute need to know. In some respects it was the most sensitive compartment, and the 26 pages represented some of the most important classified work being undertaken in the government. Copies had been sent by classified computer to Cheney, Powell,

Rice and Tenet. As if to further establish the point, the first slide and page said in bold letters: HIGHLY CONFIDENTIAL PLANNING.

The plan reflected the rethinking Rumsfeld had urged on Franks. It was nothing less than a new concept for a war with Iraq, one which might be executed as a preemptive strike. The Desert Storm–type operation was still on the shelf as Op Plan 1003, but it now called for 400,000 U.S. military personnel and close to six months for the buildup. Not much surprise could be maintained.

Franks noted that in the Afghanistan war he had tried to move away from the classic military plan of an air campaign of massive bombing followed by ground operations. Instead, he had developed what he called "lines of operations"—actions that could be carried out independently and often simultaneously. Because there had been no staging bases in or close to Afghanistan, he had been forced to rely heavily on Special Operations Forces, the elite small-team commando units. The Afghanistan battlefield demonstrated that Special Operations Forces could be leveraged, for example, by using laser designators to guide bombs from Air Force or Navy aircraft onto precise targets. It was an integration of air and ground that far exceeded past military operations.

So the notion of an air campaign and a ground campaign was now out. There would only be one campaign.

Moving through the charts, Franks explained that as part of the commander's estimate requested by Secretary Rumsfeld on December 1, he had presented three iterations to the secretary on the 4th, 12th and 19th. The secretary's guideline was to think outside traditional war planning.

The lines of operations would be the key. These were the components of things the military, the CIA and even the diplomats could do to apply pressure on Iraq. They were attempting to create a construct that was not just a military operation but one that drew on all elements of national power. Each line of operation would be separate, but taken together they would create a critical mass that would reduce the amount of conventional combat power that would be needed. They were not all of equal weight by any means, but it was a way of defining the U.S. capability. He explained that the seven lines of operations were:

1. Kinetic operations or "operational fires" that would include the traditional air campaign of bombing, but also the use of Tomahawk cruise missiles fired from ships or aircraft, plus long-range ground-to-ground systems such as the Army's Tactical Missile System (TACMS), which fired a 13-foot semiballistic missile 100 to 180 miles. Overall, it was the delivery of precision weaponry deep into enemy territory.

2. Unconventional warfare utilizing Special Operations Forces who could conduct deep penetrations into Iraq—for example, lethal raids to stop the firing of Scud missiles into Israel or Saudi Arabia. Again Afghanistan had demonstrated ever-expanding possibilities for speed and stealth.

3. Operational maneuvers, the traditional ground operations of conventional forces to be carried out by Army and Marine divisions.

4. Influence operations—the dissemination of information, and a wide range of psychological and deception operations.

5. Support of the opposition groups throughout Iraq, including the Kurds in the north and disaffected Shiite groups in southern Iraq or even within the Iraqi military. This would be in full coordination with the CIA. Support might include everything from arms to developing the opposition groups' capacity to gather intelligence, conduct strategic reconnaissance and sabotage.

6. The political-military aspects of diplomacy, including civil-military operations to work with the populace mostly after the major fighting.

7. Humanitarian assistance to the Iraqi population.

These were the things that could be done, Franks said, making it clear that this was an initial cut and that the lines of operations could be expanded and refined.

But here was what he considered the breakthrough. He planned to array these lines of operations against what he called "slices" of the Iraqi regime's capability or vulnerability. These were the centers of gravity in Saddam's government.

Franks had nine at this point. They were:

1. The leadership, the real inner circle of Saddam and his two sons, Uday and Qusay.
2. Internal security and the regime intelligence, including the close-in ring of bodyguards in the Special Security Organization (SSO); the command, control and communications network.
3. Weapons of mass destruction infrastructure.
4. Missile production, maintenance and delivery capability.
5. The Republican Guard divisions and the Special Republican Guard that protected Baghdad.
6. Land and territory inside Iraq where pressure could be exerted such as the northern Kurdish area that was effectively autonomous.
7. The regular Iraqi army.
8. Iraqi commercial and economic infrastructure; and the diplomatic infrastructure abroad that included Iraqi agents working out of their embassies.
9. The civilian population.

Franks then presented a chart in the form of a matrix with "slices" of regime power listed along the top or horizontal axis and the "lines of operations" along the side or vertical axis. In all there were 63 boxes in the matrix—seven lines of operations times the nine slices of regime power.

Little graphic signs of explosions or starbursts indicated where particular "lines of operations" could be effectively employed against "slices" of regime vulnerability.

For example, kinetic bombing could be especially effective against: 1. leadership, 2. internal security services, 5. Republican

Guard divisions, 7. the regular Iraqi army, but obviously not 9. the civilian population. The influence operations, on the other hand, could be used effectively on the Iraqi commercial, economic and diplomatic infrastructure. They might even be used on the leadership and certainly on the regular army, which was not as loyal to Saddam as the Republican Guard.

If you want to cause the regime to fall, a bombing campaign would only do so much for you, Franks said. You've got to create in the minds of the people an overwhelming urge to get rid of Saddam. The influence and information operations would be critical.

The Special Operations Forces could be used to seize the oil fields in the south with relatively small numbers of troops and to take some relatively undefended territory out in the west of Iraq to prevent Scud missile launches. SOF could also go into the north with the Kurds and, with CIA support to the opposition groups and perhaps to unhappy Iraqi army leaders, set up conditions so the internal Iraqi opposition would help in action against the regime.

Franks said he needed to understand more fully the relationship between those lines of operations and the slices of enemy vulnerability. It was a concept in flux and still in development.

Overall, Franks said this approach could avoid the long, drawn-out buildup of moving massive numbers of force to the region, so an attack could start with less notice and less force. On the other hand, beginning too soon could leave them with too little force.

The president was taken with the concept that force could be applied selectively and carefully across the different slices. He saw that it was possible to create and capitalize on Iraqi vulnerabilities more efficiently if military and other power were combined in the right way.

In an interview two years later, Bush specifically recalled "the little starbursts" on the matrix but not much of the detail.

Franks turned to the Top Secret/Polo Step slide on the basing and staging support from other countries that would be necessary for a war. What could they realistically expect? He presented three options—robust, reduced and unilateral.

The first, robust, would require support from the three countries on Iraq's southern and western borders—Kuwait, Saudi Arabia and Jordan—and to the north Turkey, which shared a 100-mile border with Iraq. Help from four small Gulf states, Bahrain, Qatar, United Arab Emirates and Oman, would be required, and the United Kingdom. It was a tall order, requiring some sensitive diplomacy to win the agreements. But generally speaking, this robust level of foreign support would allow the lines of operations to be executed simultaneously.

With this level of foreign support, Franks said he would need only a U.S. force level of 105,000 to start the war. The flow of forces would continue in this initial concept to a level of about 230,000 over the next 60 to 90 days.

Any less foreign support would mean some slices of vulnerability would have to be attacked sequentially, increasing the risk and time involved. Without Turkey or Saudi Arabia, for example, the impact could be immense.

Franks said that for a bilateral attack with the participation of the United Kingdom, they would need at least four other countries for basing and overflight operations—Kuwait, Bahrain, Qatar and Oman.

In a unilateral operation, without U.K. forces, Franks indicated that they would still have to have Kuwait, Qatar and Oman—all but Bahrain.

"Mr. President, if we want to execute something like this, then what we're going to need to do is we're going to need to start posturing and building forces," Franks said. Rumsfeld and he had agreed over the past month that they needed to "incrementally improve our position," as he delicately put it. The U.S. had thousands of personnel in the Middle East but they were engaged in other missions.

In support of the Southern Watch no-fly zone operation, Franks said he kept a small ground task force in Kuwait of just 500 troops, a battalion. It was there for the protection of Kuwait in case Saddam invaded again and quite frankly it was also a trip wire—ensuring that if Saddam attacked, he would immediately engage U.S. forces. That battalion task force and another 500 U.S. support personnel also trained the Kuwaitis.

Right away or very soon, we ought to have three times as many in Kuwait, in all about 3,000, Franks said. Secretary Rumsfeld had agreed, he said, and they were going to proceed.

Fine, the president said. It wouldn't be seen as provocative or committing the nation. It would be a training rotation.

"We're going to hedge our bets," Franks said. Because the U.S. was engaged in Afghanistan, Saddam might misread and not notice a buildup. In the category of doing something else without committing the nation to war, Franks said he wanted to move some of the Army's pre-positioned equipment that was 300 miles to the south in the small emirate of Qatar up to Kuwait. First, this would make the equipment immediately available; troops could be flown in quickly, but the equipment included a lot of gear that took time to move. Franks said the Marines also had pre-positioned equipment that could be brought closer to Kuwait. It would be out of sight and out of mind. Politically no one would be paying much attention to the movement of boats and trucks, he said.

Second, since they would be moving the equipment out of their facility in Qatar, Franks said, "I'd like to put a couple of hundred million dollars into that facility and turn it into a command and control center that looks a lot like warehouses on the outside but looks a lot different on the inside."

Franks carefully said that nothing had been decided about this because of the hefty price tag, but that he was talking with Rumsfeld about it.

The president seemed receptive.

"Thoughts on Timing" was the next slide.

Mr. President, Franks said, we don't know if or when you'd want to do this, but if and when you decide to do this, some things have to happen first.

Certainly the CIA had to be able to get their folks in place inside Iraq. In Afghanistan, the linkup between CIA paramilitary teams on the ground and the military Special Operations Forces had been critical. In fact, the Afghanistan war had initially required only some 115 CIA and 300 SOF on the ground. For Iraq, Franks said it would take 120 to 180 days for the CIA to become active in the region.

To be effective with the influence operations, we need to start immediately, Franks said, not to say we are going to invade Iraq, but to begin to pick away at the Iraqi regime, its intelligence service, for example, and their people in embassies around the world.

On the diplomatic front, it would take at least 30 days to go to the heads of state in Kuwait and Turkey and all the others and say, "Are you with us or are you against us?" borrowing the president's famous line after 9/11 that had challenged other nations with the choice.

The efforts to increase the force and move the pre-positioned equipment to Kuwait would take 60 days. Getting the headquarters into Qatar would also take 60 days.

Staging and moving the entire 3rd Infantry Division, the unit that was already partially deployed, would take as much as 90 days to get everything into Kuwait and to be combat ready. To move in logistics that would be sustainable for combat would take 60 to 90 days if it were done in a relatively unambiguous fashion so everyone would notice; doing it with little steps at a time would take longer.

A close reading of Franks's list would fix a possible start date for combat operations at four to six months from then, conceivably sometime between April and June 2002.

Mr. President, Franks said, we understand that making a decision to do this should be reserved for the last moment that you have. But, he added, there are decisions that we would come to you and ask you to make that would allow us to set conditions to have the capacity to conduct operations.

Franks had a dozen and he listed them:

1. Build the interagency intelligence capability.
2. Commence influence operations.
3. Gain host nation support.

4. Move the pre-positioned equipment and CENTCOM head-quarters.

5. Move the lead division forward.

6. Create a sustainable supply line.

7. Move the alternate air command and control center into Qatar so they would not have to rely on the primary center at Prince Sultan Air Base in Saudi Arabia.

8. Position the Marine Expeditionary Brigade (MEB), which would be the lead Marine force.

9. Establish the necessary Combat Search and Rescue (CSAR) and the intelligence, surveillance and reconnaissance (ISR) aircraft in the region.

10. Bring in a third Navy aircraft carrier battle group.

11. Position the other Marine equipment to be available to units other than the MEB.

12. Pre-position aircraft around the world so the so-called air bridge would be available to transport forces and equipment.

Individually these were prudent, incremental steps. Together they laid the groundwork for war.

Mr. President, here's what we think our assumptions are, Franks said, fulfilling Rumsfeld's demand that the assumptions be laid down on the table ahead of time. He wanted to try to identify all the things that couldn't be controlled, or that the Pentagon, CIA or State Department should try to control. For Iraq, Franks said, the assumptions were:

1. Host nations in the region would be available in some fashion to permit at least the unilateral operation.

2. Iraq possessed WMD capability, so the U.S. would have to plan to fight against it and in a potentially contaminated battlefield.

3. An Iraq war would be the main effort of the U.S. and would

get priority on resources, including cruise missiles from
other theaters. Other contingencies around the world
could be handled, though if there was a choice they would
be put on hold.

4. Some Iraqi opposition groups would support the U.S. military inside Iraq or at least would provide some cooperation.

5. Iraq could attack Israel so they had to build a capacity to defend against that.

6. The Afghanistan operation called Enduring Freedom and
the global war on terrorism would provide a noise level
under cover of which forces could be moved; those operations wouldn't diminish.

7. CENTCOM would have at least a force level of 105,000 in
the region before starting combat operations.

8. The Department of State would promote creation of a
broad-based, credible provisional government as had been
done in Afghanistan through the Bonn Conference earlier
in the month. State would have to engage the United Nations or other countries to do this. The military did not do
nation building very well, Franks said.

9. Regional states would not interfere.

10. CENTCOM would have sufficient munitions.

11. NATO countries would provide adequate basing and overflight rights, though there was concern that France, Italy,
Germany or Belgium might say no.

12. The civilian reserve fleet could help transport troops and
matériel.

The ingenious list put the president and the others on notice of
exactly what would be required or expected from the region, the
State Department, the CIA, Europe and the president himself. In an
interview nearly two years later, Rumsfeld was shown a list of these
assumptions. He agreed with or recalled most, said he didn't recall a
few, helpfully clarified several, and, of course, argued with the way
several were worded.

"You have to put up assumptions that are things that you either can't control or can't be controlled," he said. "In other words, some of them are external to the department so they have to be there so that other people looking at it know that and then some that just aren't controllable."

Rumsfeld wanted everyone to go into war planning, and if need be war, with as few illusions as possible. The list put the president on notice that the military had certain expectations, that the success of any operation would be contingent on others meeting those stated conditions. At the same time, it could be seen as a list of demands.

Finally on page 26, Franks asked, Where do we go from here?

When you get to the point, Mr. President, of wanting, or believing you might consider doing this, Franks said, treading carefully, you have to allow us to increase the HUMINT (human intelligence) activity in the country. Ticking through the list of prewar actions again in sequential order, he said, We've got to develop and provide substance to the opposition groups within Iraq. We need to begin this influence operation, and we need to start to enhance both our ground force and our air capacity under cover of the Afghanistan operation and the enforcement of the no-fly zones. Finally we want to start now to move the equipment out of pre-position storage in Qatar to create space to allow CENTCOM headquarters to move in.

Don, the president said, we need to get started doing some of these things. To Franks, he said, "This is good work. Keep grinding on it."

Rumsfeld had seemed to want to jump in two or three times during Franks's briefing but the technology made him only one remote figure on a screen filled with the others. "Yes, sir, Mr. President," Rumsfeld said. "Tom and I will talk about these things." Of course, he added, they were not recommending any time to start such operations.

"Tom and I will discuss this further, and I will come back to you with some recommendations," he added. Franks was briefing, but Rumsfeld was the Defense Department's voice.

The president said he could see where they might be able to

make some real progress and not expose that many people to combat operations. There were economies of scale, he said. He also could see, he said, that some things had to start. He was particularly caught up with the CIA piece, having watched the agency's covert relationships with opposition groups and leaders in Afghanistan, particularly the Northern Alliance, speed the course of that war.

Tenet put the brakes on. Iraq was very different, he said. The CIA had had relationships with the various opposition groups in Iraq—the Kurds in the north, the Shiites in the south—over the years in too well told stories. The consequences had been disastrous because the groups and individuals had been abandoned. It had happened so many times, he said, that the people in Iraq were skeptical. Until they saw a commitment on the part of the United States, they would not sign up. So you can build all these thoughts, he said, but it's not going to bear fruit unless they see a tangible commitment. Now that could be in the form of weapons, or training, or a hefty U.S. military presence, but you had to invest in that.

Bush told Powell and Rumsfeld that they would have to work the political part. "We've got to work the nations in the region," the president said. "Develop a strategy for me on how best to do that."

Rice had a question: What would happen if Saddam took his forces and pulled back into Baghdad to make a last stand, creating a fortress that we would have to fight through?

That's something we're going to have to focus more on in our planning to preclude it from happening, Franks said.

Cheney had a major concern. "We're going to have to really look hard at how we protect ourselves against the use of weapons of mass destruction, both in the field as well as in the rear."

Yes, sir, Franks acknowledged. Then addressing the president, he said, "Now we're going to want to come back and talk to you about evolving this big plan, or linking this big plan to what you know, Mr. President, as Desert Badger." Bush had already been briefed on Desert Badger, which would allow him to order a small attack in four hours—either with U.S. aircraft or some 50 Tomahawk cruise missiles from Navy ships in the Persian Gulf. He now had modules he could pick from, including a rather substantial, punishing series of strikes on Iraq targets of military significance, up to and including suspected production sites for Iraqi missiles.

Just before 10 A.M., Bush, in a casual ranch outfit of jeans, shirt and boots, and Franks with his high-top combat boots and beret, stepped out for a press briefing.

"We just got off of a teleconference with the national security team," the president said, "to discuss his trip and to discuss what's taking place in Afghanistan." He did not mention the central focus of the teleconference—Iraq. And no one asked. All the questions were about bin Laden, Afghanistan and the recent collapse of Enron, the Texas-based energy trading company.

Asked about the coming new year, Bush said, "I hope 2002 is a year of peace. But I am also realistic."

Bush and Franks walked over to the Governor's House, the small guesthouse on the ranch, where the president signed a defense appropriations bill and prerecorded his weekly radio address.

"Come on, Tommy," Bush said, "jump in my pickup truck and we'll take a drive around the ranch." Bush then drove Franks on a long tour of his ranch.

Afterward, they stopped at the main house to visit with Laura Bush. Both Franks and Laura are from Midland, Texas, and had gone to the same high school but did not know each other. The president invited Franks and Renuart to stay for lunch.

No, Mr. President, said Franks, I need to get back. He was commander for one war that was winding down in Afghanistan, and another war that seemed to be winding up.

On the flight back to Tampa, Renuart complained that Franks should have agreed to stay for lunch. He was hungry, there was no food on the plane and he would have preferred lunch with the president. "Boss," Renuart said, "you're not feeding us on the way home here."

So they had soft drinks and peanuts while sharing their excitement. They were pleased that the president seemed to understand the complexity and the time problems—that this wasn't going to happen tomorrow.

"I think he got it," Renuart said.

"We have made a start," Franks replied.

"I WANT TO KNOW what my options are as the president," Bush said two years later in an interview, explaining how he had approached this first briefing on Iraq war plans. He knew his secretary of defense well, and Rumsfeld wouldn't have gone ahead if he hadn't been satisfied himself with the progress. "They've got the process to a point where he feels comfortable bringing Franks forward," Bush recalled. So he had been most interested in reading Franks.

"I'm trying to figure out what intelligent questions to ask a commander who has just impressed me in Afghanistan. I'm looking for the logic. I'm watching his body language very carefully," Bush recalled. He emphasized the body language, the eyes, the demeanor. It was more important than some of the substance. It was also why he wanted Franks there in Crawford and not as another face on a wall of screens.

"Is this good enough to win?" he recalled asking Franks, leaning forward in his chair and throwing his hand forward in a slicing motion at my face to illustrate the scene.

Absolutely it was, Franks had answered, but the plan could get better.

"We weren't ready to execute then," the president said. "I mean we're not even close." But he left the briefing with two things on his mind: "Saddam's a threat. This is an option."

6

B Y THE BEGINNING OF 2002, CIA Director George Tenet's stock
with the president was way up. His covert action program for
sending CIA paramilitary teams into Afghanistan had provided the
initial contacts and strategy for driving the Taliban from power. He
had dramatically improved human intelligence and expanded the
training of CIA case officers more than tenfold, making such covert
action possible.

At 48, Tenet was the only high-level Clinton holdover on the
Bush national security team. He had risen in the world of secret intelligence first as a staffer on the Senate Intelligence Committee,
then as the Clinton NSC staffer handling the intelligence account.
Clinton had named him deputy CIA director in 1995 and then director in 1997.

High-strung, focused and an extremely talented briefer, Tenet,
the son of Greek immigrants, knew the importance of forging personal relationships and devoted time to the people important in his
professional and personal life. "Everything is mano-a-mano, everything," he once said. He was familiar with the background and families of the heads of important foreign intelligence services, and
regularly asked about them. Occasionally, Tenet had breakfast with
Karl Rove, the president's senior political adviser, in the White

House mess and joked that he would share secrets with Rove that even Rice was not allowed to know.

Most importantly, he had bonded with President Bush, whom he personally briefed in the Oval Office most days at 8 A.M. "I like him," Bush said, "and I trust him, which is more important." Tenet often said he had two constituencies: "Number one, the president. Number two, the 17,000 who work at the CIA."

Even before 9/11, Tenet had seen Iraq was going to be an important concern for the Bush administration. One of the key, behind-the-scenes posts for the CIA would be Chief, Iraqi Operations Group, the person who would run covert action against Saddam. Tenet made it clear to the chain of command in the agency that he wanted a hard-core, tough son-of-a-bitch.

Saul * was a real star in the CIA's clandestine service, the Directorate of Operations (DO), which ran covert action. At 43, balding with a short, perfectly trimmed beard and a fireplug build, he had worked for years in sensitive undercover posts as a case officer and senior operator in CIA stations around the world. Born in a small town in Cuba, his father had been involved in one of the most spectacular CIA failures—the 1961 Bay of Pigs fiasco in which 1,200 Cuban exiles had been abandoned on the beach by their CIA sponsors. As he told associates, "I am here as the result of a failed CIA covert operation."

In the late 1990s, in the effort to train more CIA case officers and step up the rigors of the introduction to the agency, Tenet had decided to assign fast-track officers to run the CIA's secret training facility in Williamsburg, Virginia, known as the Farm. Saul was appointed course chairman, and also taught himself, giving hands-on training to some 250 officers. Then during 2000–01, he was given the plum assignment as executive assistant to Tenet's deputy, John McLaughlin. There Saul saw all the major secrets and watched CIA politics from the inside.

After the one-year stint in the front office, Saul was looking

---

* A nickname. The full names of CIA undercover officers are not used or disclosed.

around for a job at CIA headquarters in Langley. For family reasons such as kids in high school, he had to stay in the Washington area. Within the CIA's Near East Division, which handled the Middle East, Israel, Afghanistan, Iran and Iraq—some of the hardest, most violent countries—the Chief, Iraqi Operations Group post was opening up. There were not a lot of takers. It was viewed as a career killer. In the division, Iraqi Operations was referred to as "The House of Broken Toys." It was largely populated with new, green DO officers and problem officers, or old boys waiting for retirement.

Saul asked for the job. He thought the Bush administration might get serious about Iraq. He'd heard some rumblings. He started as Chief IOG on August 4, 2001.

The National Security Council had asked the CIA what it could do on Iraq. The request wasn't, Can you overthrow Saddam, or, Can you support a military invasion? It was, How do you see Iraq? What can you do? How would you view covert action inside Iraq?

So Saul set about a full scrub or review of the past. He named as his deputy a fellow senior teacher from the Farm who had worked Iraq issues in the DO since the 1991 Gulf War.

The House of Broken Toys was more than a people problem, Saul quickly learned. Past operations read almost like a handbook for failed and stupid covert action. It was a catalogue of doomed work— too little, too late, too seat-of-the-pants, too little planning, too little realism. The comic mixed with the frightening.

During the Nixon administration, Iraq became a pawn in the Cold War. In 1972, then-strongman but not yet leader Saddam Hussein signed a Friendship Treaty with the Soviet Union. To checkmate this Soviet influence in the Middle East, President Nixon signed an order directing the CIA to provide $5 million covertly to the Kurds, which included some 40 mountain tribes totaling about 25 million people spread out across five countries—Iran, Turkey, Syria, the then Soviet Union, and the northeastern corner of Iraq.

The Iraqi Kurds would get $5 million for supplies and weapons. Israel, Britain and Iran (then ruled by Shah Mohammed Reza Pahlavi, who was friendly with the United States) provided another

$7 million in covert aid. By 1973, Secretary of State Henry Kissinger recommended increasing the covert money because Iraq had become the chief Soviet client in the Middle East and the Baath regime under Saddam, as Kissinger put it in his memoirs, "continued to finance terrorist organizations as far afield as Pakistan" and was a force trying to block an Arab-Israeli peace. The Shah in Iran upped his financial support to $30 million, promising $75 million the next year.

In many respects the CIA support of the Kurds was more a favor to the Shah. The CIA reported that the Kurds, who by one count had fielded a force 100,000 strong, were tying down two-thirds of the Iraqi army—a stunning accomplishment even if only partially true. The key was the heavy artillery supplied by the Shah. But in 1975 the Shah reached an accord with Saddam, pulled the plug on the Kurds and stopped CIA arms shipments. The Kurds' anguished personal appeals to the CIA and Kissinger went unanswered. The covert operation collapsed and Saddam slaughtered many of the Kurds.

After the 1991 Gulf War, President George H. W. Bush signed a presidential finding authorizing the CIA to topple Saddam. The CIA had thrown money at almost any anti-Saddam opposition group, including Iraqi exiles in Europe and even Iraqi prisoners taken during the Gulf War who had refused to go back to Iraq. And the president publicly called on Iraqis to "take matters into their own hands" to remove Saddam. When the Kurds in the north and Shiite Muslims in the south rebelled against Saddam, Bush declined U.S. military support. The result was another slaughter.

During the Clinton administration, the CIA continued to dabble, supporting various anti-Saddam efforts. One absurd broken-toy operation included dropping leaflets in Baghdad to mock Saddam on his birthday. In 1996, Saddam's security service penetrated a group of CIA-supported former Iraqi officers plotting a coup, and some 120 former officers were executed. By 1998 when the CIA proposed a new covert plan, the Congress refused and authorized instead $97 million in overt assistance to the Iraqi opposition groups.

Saul brought together a group of seasoned covert operators and analysts from the Directorate of Intelligence (DI) to review the past.

Some had worked Iraq issues for 12 to 15 years, and others had worked covert programs in the Balkans. The central question: How do we view covert action in Iraq?

The CIA of movies and modern mythology is populated by fanatical, can-do warriors eager for new risks and missions impossible. Saul, however, reached a conclusion that was contrary to agency stereotypes. "Covert action is not going to remove Saddam Hussein," he summarized. The CIA had to face the reality that Saddam, in power since 1979, had erected a nearly perfect security apparatus to protect himself and stop a coup. The Iraq Special Security Organization was in charge of his security; a Presidential Guard accompanied him, and the Special Republican Guard protected the presidential palaces and other government buildings in the capital. Four intelligence services supported their work. In practice, dozens of Iraqi army divisions could stop coup plotters.

The Iraqi government functioned with one purpose—to keep Saddam alive and in power. Internal spying, programmed suspicion, overlapping roles and authorities and segmented responsibility put Saddam at the center of everything.

It was going to take the concentration of the entire U.S. government to remove him, Saul concluded. Looking at the overall U.S. policy, he saw a glaring contradiction. Through the United Nations, the U.S. was working to contain and deter Saddam with economic sanctions and diplomacy; through the CIA it was trying to overthrow him. "Bullshit!" Saul said. The bifurcated policy of trying to contain with one hand and trying to overthrow with the other wasn't going to work. The only way to succeed was for the CIA to support a full military invasion of Iraq. That was the only road to possible success. The agency had been in the lead in Afghanistan. It would have to play a supporting role in Iraq. The mission and the target were too hard. Piercing the wall around Saddam was nearly impossible without military operations and an invasion.

On the morning of September 11, 2001, Saul and some of his team were on their way to the Old Executive Office Building adjacent to the White House to brief senior NSC staffers on some of these conclusions. As they were going over a bridge connecting Virginia and the District of Columbia, they heard reports on the radio of the terrorist attacks and the evacuation of the White House complex. "Oh, shit," Saul said, "let's turn around and go home." They had almost passed Director Tenet, who was speeding back to the CIA from downtown Washington where he had been having breakfast.

In the first months after 9/11, Iraq took a back seat, though Vice President Cheney asked the CIA to brief him on what they could do. On January 3, 2002, Saul, Tenet, the deputy chief of the Near East Division and two covert operators who had worked Iraq programs went to see the vice president and Scooter Libby.

Saul did not soft-pedal his message. He told Cheney that covert action would not remove Saddam. The CIA would not be the solution. The one thing the dictator's regime was organized for was to stop a coup, he told them. Saddam had taken power in a coup. He has put down coups. The son of a bitch knows what a coup is. If you are an Iraqi military unit and you have the bullets to launch a coup, you don't have the gas to move your tanks. If you have gas, you don't have bullets. Nobody stays in power long enough to launch a coup.

If we try to launch a coup, we play into the regime's strengths, he told them. Saddam would take the coup plotters apart—limb by limb if necessary. Only a U.S. military operation and invasion that the CIA could support had a chance of ousting Saddam, Saul said. The agency had done a lessons-learned study of past Iraq covert operations, he said, and frankly the CIA was tainted. "We've got a serious credibility problem." The Kurds, the Shiites, former Iraqi military officers and probably most attuned people in Iraq knew the history of the CIA's cutting and running. To reestablish credibility, potential anti-Saddam forces would have to see a determined seriousness on the part of the United States. Preparations for a massive military invasion might send that signal, nothing else.

Saul laid out for Cheney the problems with standing up at the United Nations, talking negotiations and containment, while secretly telling the Saudis and Jordanians the U.S. was going to remove the regime covertly. They needed a single national policy that everyone supported and explained in the same way.

"You're going to have to expect that we are going to take casualties," Saul explained.

Cheney indicated that he understood that.

In addition, Saul said, they had made mistakes in the past in how they handled agents. The tradecraft—source protection, cutouts, communications, payment—had to be more sophisticated.

Another lesson was that the CIA couldn't sustain a covert action program for a lengthy period of time. The regime would find some of the human sources that they might recruit and roll them up. So they had to move fast.

Cheney was used to briefers coming to his office with ambitious declarations and promises that their department or agency would deliver. The CIA message was the opposite, sobering, highly unusual in its judgment that it really could not do the job.

The CIA officers then gave the same briefing to the president.

"Could we do it by covert means?" the president asked.

The answer was no.

"Darn!" the president recalled thinking. There didn't seem to be a sucker punch.

To the agency's objection to a bifurcated policy of moving toward war while continuing diplomacy through the U.N., Bush said that that was the way it was going to be.

"I know I've put you in a difficult position," the president said. "I know this is hard, but this is the course we're on. And we're going to have to keep doing all of these elements at the same time."

For Condoleezza Rice, this was one of the tough dilemmas— working two tracks and having to act and speak forcefully and convincingly about both. Coercive diplomacy meant living with dissonance and inconsistencies, she realized. The CIA made it clear that in order to recruit sources inside Iraq they would have to say the U.S. was serious and was coming with its military. The president's body language suggested he had received the message, but he didn't make any promises.

• • •

WHEN POWELL was told all of this, he concluded that the CIA just
didn't want another fuck-up. On occasion, Tenet dressed it up a little, declaring that covert action alone had only about a 10 to 20 percent chance of succeeding. He seemed really to mean zero. The CIA
had no real sources inside and there was no way to get to Saddam unless there was a military operation. Powell realized that when someone says they can't do something, but oh, they can support the other
guys, it created another substantial pressure for war.

7

A FTER THE DECEMBER 28 Crawford briefing for the president, Rumsfeld ordered Franks to come back in 10 days with a plan that could be executed. A meeting was set for January 9, but that slipped. Rumsfeld and Franks spoke by secure phone. Franks had put a splitter on his phone that allowed a senior aide, a Navy captain, to listen, take notes and write a memo of conversation. This produced thousands of pages of highly classified top-level discussion. The notes from that day showed that Rumsfeld wanted the following questions answered at the next meeting:

- What would be done if Iraq used weapons of mass destruction?
- Exactly how much had the Iraqi military been degraded since the Gulf War in 1991?
- What was the exact use of neighboring countries that Franks wanted for basing and staging?
- What were the targets really out there right now, both strategic and tactical?
- Take the matrix chart of the lines of operations versus the slices of vulnerability that had been used with the president and show targeting priorities. What were the meaningful tar-

gets? How long would it take to have the effect you want on those targets?

- Would there be a difference in the timelines if the unconventional warfare and human intelligence effort were able to pinpoint targets?

- If dozens of key targets could be destroyed simultaneously, would that put pressure on the regime, cause it to crumble and preclude the need for a long war requiring a large force? If you had the intelligence database, could you pinpoint the most critical targets to accelerate the fall of Saddam?

Franks passed the list to a few senior staffers. "Boss, goddamn it," Renuart said. This was overwhelming, it was impossible.

"Okay, boys," Franks told Renuart and the others, "we need to understand. Here's the deal, so let's not try to fight the wrong fight. The good guys are us, so let's fight in the direction we need to go together." In other words, don't make Rumsfeld the bad guy because he had a stack of questions. Franks made it clear that he was going to have to power through Rumsfeld, and so would they. They were going to have to adapt to and mirror Rumsfeld's style. Each time Franks came back to brief him, the secretary lifted more rocks and found more questions under them. It was bound to continue.

In an interview, I showed Rumsfeld the list of questions he had posed. He chuckled and maintained the list was incomplete. It was "not even close" to half the questions he had at that point, he said.

Since Rumsfeld had what he called an "iterative planning" process, which for practical purposes meant nothing was ever finished, Franks developed his own iterative planning process. At his Tampa headquarters, he had regular huddles with Renuart and about 15 others in the key leadership. He had in addition a group of military planners whom Renuart called "the 50-pound brains," young majors, lieutenant colonels, colonels or Navy commanders and captains who were trained in strategy.

A group of operations experts from J-3 and intelligence specialists from J-2, the intelligence directorate, were called the "targeteers." They examined and set priorities on targets. They were sent off and locked away in a back room, presumably not to be seen or heard from until they could answer Rumsfeld's targeting questions.

At one point, Franks's staff addressed the question of what could be done with half the force in half the time. This question was broadened in an attempt to calculate what capabilities could supplant the reduced time and force. What could be leveraged? Better intelligence, precision weapons, attacking Iraq on multiple fronts, Special Operations Forces and information operations were raised.

What real impact could come from information operations? Could effective propaganda really substitute for troops? No one seemed sure.

How could they leverage the opposition elements, especially the Kurds in the north? What real capability could the Kurds bring to a war plan? And what political impact might it have on Turkey with its large, disaffected Kurdish population, since the Turks would view an emerging Kurd force in Iraq, never mind a Kurdish state, with alarm?

Eventually the planners agreed tentatively that Special Operations Forces could go into northern Iraq, which was practically autonomous from Baghdad, and create a force of about 10,000 Kurdish fighters. That seemed feasible; it was also a low enough number that it should not upset Turkish political sensibilities.

Franks brainstormed with his planners on successive days, limited to several hours each time because after a while their brains would fry. He wanted to make sure that very few people knew about any particular line of operation. One small group was assigned to work the information operations, another the operational fires, and others for the remaining lines. He ordered that the groups not talk to one another. Each was assigned a separate Top Secret compartment with its own codeword. Only Renuart and a few others and he would know all the compartments, have an overall understanding of the state of the plan.

As they proceeded, Franks and Renuart began to see where the lines of operations touched and reinforced each other—for example, the Special Operations Forces and the air portion of the operational fires attacking the same target.

POWELL, THE PROUD former general and now chief diplomat, was troubled by what he was seeing and hearing. He had served two tours in Vietnam as a junior officer where he'd seen failure up close. Generals had not spoken the truth to the political leadership, which in turn had not been sufficiently skeptical of the generals. As chairman of the Joint Chiefs of Staff on the eve of the 1991 Gulf War, he had sat alone in his office at the Pentagon, Room 2E878, remembering the famous remark by Robert E. Lee: "It is well that war is so terrible, or we should grow too fond of it." The Confederate general knew the horror of war. Now in 2001, from Washington and the Pentagon and the White House, and even his own State Department, war seemed antiseptic, and at times like a great game.

Powell knew deeply, intimately, that war is fought by kids, even teenagers who would die because of decisions made in Washington. The top echelon of the Bush administration was noticeably free of those who had seen combat. Bush had served in the Texas Air National Guard but had not been in combat. Cheney had never served in the military himself, though he was defense secretary during the Gulf War. Rumsfeld had been a Navy fighter pilot in the 1950s but not during wartime. Rice and Tenet had not seen military service. Only he had been in combat.

During his time as Joint Chiefs chairman, he had loosely formulated a Powell Doctrine. It was commonly stated that he meant the military should use overwhelming force to guarantee success in any use of force in any operation. He felt it had been caricatured and had cast him as the Reluctant Warrior, unwilling to take any chances, eager to avoid limited military engagements. Actually, his doctrine was a bit more subtle: The military should use decisive force to achieve political objectives. Still, he had pled guilty to being the Reluctant Warrior in his 1995 best-selling memoir, *My American Journey*.

He had found too many who were willing to pull the trigger without making sure it was done with decisive force for a political objective that was necessary, and one that was supported by the Congress and the public.

Powell had another problem to contend with. After nearly a year as secretary of state, he had not achieved a personal relationship with President Bush. They were uncomfortable with each other. A sense of competition hovered in the background of their relationship, a low-voltage pulse nearly always present. Powell had considered running for president in 1996. He had had stratospheric poll ratings as the country's most admired man. For personal reasons and after making a calculation that there were no guarantees in American politics, he had decided not to run. But he had been the man in the wings, the former general and war hero, a moderate voice who would not run in 2000 when George W. Bush did.

As secretary, he found himself often frozen out by the White House—in the "icebox" or the "refrigerator" as Armitage and he often joked. The week before the 9/11 attacks, *Time* magazine had done what appeared to be a White House–sanctioned cover story designed to knock Powell down a notch. The headline was, "Where Have You Gone, Colin Powell?" and the article asserted that Powell was isolated, out of step with administration hard-liners who were setting the direction in foreign policy.

Powell asked Richard N. Haass, a Republican foreign policy moderate who was his director of policy planning at State, what he thought of the *Time* article.

"It sucks," Haass said. "The only thing that would have been worse would have been if it had showed you were in charge. Then you would have been totally fucked."

Powell burst out with a loud laugh.

In fact, the administration's foreign policy was pretty much a muddle before 9/11. The president was focused on domestic and tax issues and there was no clear direction.

Powell also noticed that Bush had listened respectfully to the

Polo Step briefing in Crawford, asked some general factual questions but tended not to be very probing, he thought. Bush was not drilling down.

Troubled by what was being planned and how, Powell reached out to General Franks. He had not known Franks in the Army, being almost a decade his senior, but both belonged to the informal network of former and current generals. So Powell had several one-on-one phone conversations with Franks. Such a back-channel contact outside the chain of command was risky for both of them, especially for Franks, who would have to protect himself and might have to let Rumsfeld know there had been conversations. Powell, who had been chairman of the Joint Chiefs when the original Op Plan 1003 was devised, voiced deep concern to Franks that the military would allow itself to be talked into a smaller force than necessary. Don't allow yourself to become too vulnerable under some new theory, he warned. Change—Rumsfeld's notion of "transformation"—could be good but realism was the strength of any military plan. But talk of having a ground force of only 105,000, one-fifth the size of the old Op Plan 1003, was preposterous, out of the question. To Powell, the guidance to Franks seemed to be: Keep it small, the smallest you can get away with.

Franks made it clear that he was first a military officer and had no intention of losing a war on his watch.

ON JANUARY 17, 2002, Franks and Renuart appeared to present the fourth iteration of their planning to Rumsfeld.

Franks said up front that they and the intelligence people had done an assessment of the strength of the Iraqi military compared with 12 years ago before the Gulf War. Economic sanctions had slowed their equipment maintenance, Franks said, and prevented them from modernizing their force, substantially diluting their offensive capability.

The numbers: Pre–Desert Storm there were seven Republican

Guard divisions, now six—a drop of 15 percent. The regular army had 27 divisions before and presently only 17—a drop of 35 percent. The tactical aircraft had gone from 820 to 310—down 60 percent. Many Iraqi aircraft were sitting hulks because they had run out of spare parts. Surface-to-air missiles had gone from 100 to 60. The Iraqi navy had always been somewhat of a joke with 15 to 20 ships. It was now down to two or three.

Support for Saddam's regime, Franks said, was directly related to the Iraqi people's perception of U.S. commitment to help them out. The more the U.S. became involved, the less the people of Iraq would support the regime. This important argument was based less on solid intelligence from inside Iraq than assumptions about how people *should* feel toward a ruthless dictator. The paucity of U.S. human intelligence sources inside Iraq meant evidence about Iraqi popular opinion or likely reaction to an American invading force was thin. The assumption was that Iraqis would join in if it looked like the U.S. was coming. Whatever the merits, the argument added to the momentum to war—that just the first steps toward war and demonstration of resolve would make winning the war that much easier. And as they all knew, little was more appealing to President Bush than showing resolve.

Incorporating the CIA conclusions about the virtual impossibility of covert action deposing Saddam, Franks said that none of the elements of the opposition were capable of operating with sufficient autonomy to be able to overthrow the regime. The U.S. military would have to be involved if they wanted Saddam out.

Now at slide 13, Franks said that if you accept the assumptions about the degrading of the Iraqi military and you understand the capacity we have to move forces, the necessary time of an invasion could be significantly compressed under the new plan he was developing. Once the president decided, Franks said he would need only about 45 days to deploy the necessary initial force. Then he would conduct air operations for another 45 days. Then at about day 90 they would be ready to begin ground operations. The ground war could take up to 150 days to decisively replace the regime. More force would flow during this phase and it would take about 245,000 troops in all.

In the new plan, he said the focus would be on the slices of regime power—leadership, WMD delivery, the Republican Guard, the Special Republican Guard, internal security.

In the more deliberate old option based on Op Plan 1003, it would take up to six months to build up the force. This would allow simultaneous air and ground operations. Then it would take only 90 days to attack, isolate and remove the regime.

At the 23rd slide, Franks again stressed that under any option he would have to have Kuwait, Qatar, Oman and the United Kingdom for basing and many other countries in the region for overflight rights.

Where do we go from here? This was the question on the 24th and final slide. Franks said he wanted to war-game these options out to make sure he was not selling Rumsfeld a bill of goods. A war game would test the feasibility of all this. He also needed to use the inter-agency process—State, CIA and others—to develop specific tasks and do more detailed planning and study of the various options.

Rumsfeld told Franks to come back to the president in about three weeks to talk about what preparatory actions had to be taken.

Paul Wolfowitz, who was privy to the briefing details, believed that it might be possible to fracture the regime in key areas even before ground operations.

Franks and his planners were skeptical. Past bombing had not brought Saddam to the brink, and Saddam seemed to believe he could weather any bombing campaign.

I'd like you to look at some of these concepts, Rumsfeld said. The secretary seemed to agree on the importance of sufficient force. But what about the strategic vulnerability during a long, drawn-out very ground-oriented campaign? Did they not need a force capable of decisively reaching objectives in a relatively short period of time? If they didn't, they could be caught in the dueling dynamics of ongoing combat operations while they faced a likely decline in international support.

The 90 days is too long, Franks said. The force that I just briefed you on is also too large. He was working the lines of operations to come up with something better. The plan was designed for a unilateral attack by the U.S. They had not yet considered or done the legwork to see what forces other countries might contribute. They didn't even know what might be reasonable to expect from them.

The plan called for just a single front, a ground thrust into southern Iraq from Kuwait, then northward into Baghdad. Franks raised the possibility of a second front in the north attacking from Turkey.

Rumsfeld asked them to continue working the south-only front but to give him some thoughts about how forces might come through Turkey.

Franks had an answer to the astonishing question Rumsfeld had posed the previous month of what could be done quickly, as early as April or May? The minimum ground force to start would still be about 105,000, Franks said. It would take 30 to 45 days to move those forces to the region. So if you think you want to do this in April, you need to let me start moving forces in mid-February. That was in four weeks.

BACK IN TAMPA during this period, Franks realized the issue of time, whether it took six months or three months to get the force to the Middle East, was an enormous hurdle. Some civilians in the Defense Department thought it might be possible to deploy the force in secret. Franks thought if they had five years that might be possible. He didn't know how much time they had to be ready, certainly not years. So large movements of divisions or aircraft carriers—all necessary ingredients for war—were going to be very visible. As part of the influence operations, he decided, they would engage in calculated deception. He called this notion "spikes." They could send more force and get media attention and interest, and then things would go back to normal, nothing would happen and the focus would spike down.

The idea was to play with Saddam's head—to raise and lower

expectations of an attack. They would fly high-volume operations in the Southern Watch. Be very "kinetic," as Franks liked to say, then no war. "I wanted to send Johnny crying wolf over however long a period of time we had," Franks said. Iraq was Johnny; the world was Johnny; the media and public were Johnny.

Rumsfeld liked the idea.

Franks believed there was no way to avoid spikes, so they would just take advantage of them. He wanted to accelerate preparation as much as they could. They ought to have more spikes sooner. They might, for example, move a second aircraft carrier battle group into the Persian Gulf for perhaps five or ten days, fly Southern Watch missions from both carriers, create a spike, then have one of the carriers leave. All this would be followed by no war, hopefully leaving Saddam's brain scrambled.

8

SITTING IN HIS SMALL West Wing office with a structural pillar squarely in the middle, presidential speechwriter Michael Gerson pored over an eight-page outline of the upcoming State of the Union speech he had given the president just before Christmas.

After 9/11, Gerson believed the administration had what he called a "plastic, teachable moment"—an occasion to educate and explain. The world had changed. The president had to tell the country and the world what was going on, what he intended. It was an optimum time to mold and rally public opinion, to underscore once again that America had glimpsed the intentions of the enemy, and that terrorism was now the threat for the next 50 years. But the power of the speech would turn on specifics.

The president had said he wanted an ambitious speech. He would set out the new rules of the game and the direction he was heading in foreign policy. Bush felt, had an intuition, that 9/11 was not an isolated incident. The flood of warnings and the daily Top Secret Threat Matrix report suggested another attack might be imminent.

Gerson wasn't privy to all the most sensitive intelligence coming in, but he had spent enough time with the president in the months since 9/11 to gauge his outlook and his mood. The president was not just talking about opposing threats, he was talking about a reorientation of American foreign and defense policy. This clearly was not like the World War II period, Gerson thought, when an American president could wait for the enemy to attack and then respond. He anticipated that they could lay out this formulation most explicitly for the first time in the State of the Union.

Gerson's friendly manner, with a bit of the nervous, absent-minded professor about him, masks a keen intellect, drive and sharp ear for the memorable phrase. He had majored in theology at Wheaton College in Illinois, alma mater of evangelist Billy Graham, and had been a journalist covering politics for *U.S. News & World Report* in April 1999 when Governor Bush—before he had even declared his candidacy—personally recruited him to be his speechwriter. "I want you to write my announcement speech and my convention speech and my inaugural," Bush had said. Gerson accepted because he wanted to help give the Republican Party a domestic policy message. So it was with some irony that Gerson, now 37, was a wartime speechwriter for a wartime president.

Gerson, who like Bush is a self-described evangelical Christian and "compassionate conservative," admired the way that Bush didn't shy away from injecting his religious convictions and moral conclusions into speeches. Gerson had developed a style, honed in the numerous September 11–related speeches he had drafted for Bush, that fused biblical high-mindedness and the folksy.

He had worked hard on the State of the Union outline, pulling together a lot of research. He had extensive discussions with Rice and her deputy, Hadley, and parceled out some assignments to others on the White House speechwriting staff. He asked David Frum, a respected conservative author on his staff, to come up with a sentence or two summing up the case for going after Iraq.

Frum thought that the relationship Bush was seeking to establish between Saddam Hussein's regime and 9/11 lay in the nexus of states that sponsored terrorism and terrorists who did not have allegiance to one state. He called it an "axis of hatred." He singled out Iraq by name in his proposal. It was a nice phrase with overtones of the World War II Axis powers.

Gerson remembered that when Cheney had joined the ticket in the summer of 2000, he had raised the connection between weapons of mass destruction and terrorism in internal campaign discussions. That was the real axis, Gerson believed. So he changed Frum's phrase "axis of hatred" to "axis of evil," broadening the notion, making it more sinister, even wicked. It was almost as if Saddam was an agent of the devil. The connection between his regime with weapons of mass destruction and international terrorism could put the world on the road to Armageddon.

When Rice read an early draft, she was pleased that the president would be raising the connection between WMD and terrorism. It was an issue that had been put off in Bush's September 20, 2001, speech to Congress because he hadn't wanted to scare the country any more than it already was. Calling the connection an "axis" was clever and calling it an "axis of evil" was most clever, she thought.

Rice and Hadley were aware of the secret war planning on Iraq, and they worried that singling out Iraq as the embodiment of the "axis of evil" connection between WMD and terrorism would appear a declaration of war.

Rice was keeping tabs on what was by then a favorite parlor game in Washington: When does the Iraq war start? She wanted to protect the Polo Step war planning for Iraq, but she didn't want to drop the idea of discussing the general risk of terrorists with WMD. So she and Hadley suggested adding other countries. North Korea and Iran were the clear candidates because both supported terrorism and pursued weapons of mass destruction.

The president liked the idea of the three countries—Iraq, Iran and North Korea.

Hadley had second thoughts about including Iran. The country had a complicated political structure with a democratically elected president, though the real power was held by the religious extremists and ayatollahs. Rice agreed initially and worried that there would be criticism that the president didn't understand that Iran was different, that it had a fledgling democracy movement.

Rice and Hadley proposed that Iran be dropped. Hadley said it would be inflammatory.

"No," the president said, "I want it in." Iran would stay. In an interview later, the president recalled he had specific reasons. "It is very important for the American president at this point in history to speak very clearly about the evils the world faces," he said. "No question about it, North Korea, Iraq and Iran are the biggest threats to peace at the time." Iran was unique, he said, because "there is a freedom movement in Iran and because Iran is relatively open compared to other countries that are run by, you know, theocratic people, because of the Internet, the Diaspora here from the United States and Iran.

"And the fact that the president of the United States would stand up and say Iran is just like Iraq and North Korea—in other words you've got a problem, the Iranians, we know you've got a problem, we hear you got a problem—and the president is willing to call it, is part of how you deal with Iran. And that is to inspire those who love freedom inside the country."

Asked how he thought the Iranians might respond to being called part of an "evil" axis, Bush said, "I doubt the students and the reformers and the liberators inside Iran were displeased with that. I made the calculation that they would be pleased. Up here the president speaks so clearly about the nature of the regime and the harshness and the repression they have to live under. Now, I'm confident the leaders didn't like it.

"Let me make sure you understand what I just said about the role of the United States. I believe the United States is *the* beacon for freedom in the world. And I believe we have a responsibility to promote freedom that is as solemn as the responsibility is to protecting the American people, because the two go hand-in-hand. No, it's very important for you to understand that about my presidency."

I reminded him that in the summer of 2002, before the Iraq War, we had discussed this when he said, "I will seize the opportunity to achieve big goals."

"I don't mean to be grinding on you," he said. "I say that freedom is not America's gift to the world. Freedom is God's gift to everybody in the world. I believe that. As a matter of fact, I was the person that wrote the line, or said it. I didn't write it, I just said it in a speech. And it became part of the jargon. And I believe that. And I believe we have a duty to free people. I would hope we wouldn't have to do it militarily, but we have a duty."

I asked whether such a conviction translated into policy that could seem "dangerously paternalistic" to people in other countries.

"Unless you're the person that happens to be liberated," he said, adding that he wanted to work with other world leaders on this liberation strategy such as the leaders of Britain, Spain and Australia. "Tony Blair, José María Aznar, John Howard all share that same zeal for freedom. It probably looks paternalistic to some elites, but it certainly is not paternalistic to those we free. Those who become free appreciate the zeal. And appreciate the passion."

AS GERSON PROGRESSED with drafts of the State of the Union, he was happy that they had found strong language. By tradition, dangerous countries had been called "rogue nations" or "rogue states." Gerson thought this was too benign and understated the problem, as if they drank too much. "Axis of evil" seemed to echo President Ronald Reagan's provocative declaration in 1983 that the Soviet Union was an "evil empire," a phrase that set the tone for the Cold War showdown in the 1980s as Reagan asserted that there was no moral equivalence between totalitarian Soviet Russia and the United States.

Bush was still baffled about the countries that produced ideologies and people with the goal of killing Americans in terrorist attacks. He wondered how the U.S. could reform such societies, and wanted to advocate the promotion of democracy and women's rights in the Muslim world. No president had said that before. It was part of the change in the president's thinking and the world that Gerson had witnessed since the 9/11 attacks, in his opinion a change as fundamental as the beginnings of the Cold War. So language about promoting democratic and other human values was added to the speech.

In the vice president's suite on the second floor of the Old Executive Office Building, Libby had also been going over early drafts. One version had mentioned Iraq but there was nothing about "axis of hatred" or "axis of evil." Then the phrase appeared in a draft with a mention only of Iraq. He too worried that it would suggest imminent action, and favored adding other nations such as North Korea. Also Syria, with whom the United States had diplomatic relations, but that got nowhere with Rice and Hadley.

It fell to Hadley and Gerson to struggle with language to use about Iran. It would be part of the axis, but it had to be distinguished from Iraq. The language they hit on was: "Iran aggressively pursues these weapons and exports terror, while an unelected few repress the Iranian people's hope for freedom." Hadley felt this was consistent with the administration's policy of reaching out to reformers.

Karl Rove, Bush's senior adviser and political strategist, took no direct part in the decision process for war planning, but he sat in on the speech preparation sessions with the president. He thought that "axis of evil" was a signature phrase, a declaration that U.S. foreign policy had changed, that the country now would have a great mission. It was big, new and different, Rove believed. The war on terror was going to be extended to rogue nations, and the list would be the dominant foreign policy issue for as long as Bush was president. Self-assured, even cocky, Rove, 52, figured that the Axis would be one legacy Bush turned over to his successor. That successor was not known, but Rove was confident the date Bush would be leaving was January 20, 2009, after serving two terms.

Politically, all this was going to complicate the president's life—and Rove's. The first question was, We're in a war, okay, why do you want to cut taxes again? In every other war, the president and Congress had raised taxes. Eventually Bush would want a robust prescription drug benefit in Medicare for the elderly. How could that—and the pursuit of politics as usual—continue in a war? Rove's answer was: with great difficulty. His other answer was that 9/11 had given Bush the leverage he needed in the political system.

Soon after 9/11, Bush had told Rove, Just like my father's generation was called in World War II, now our generation is being called. "I'm here for a reason, and this is going to be how we're going to be judged."

Roughly two-thirds of the American people thought Bush was a strong leader. They might disapprove of his performance as president, disagree with his policies or not like him, but a strong leader could generally prevail with his agenda if he stood up and pushed for it—in other words played politics. That included campaigns, the media, Congress and communications.

With the Axis of Evil statement, Rove believed that Bush was telling the country, "We can't go back to sleep again."

THREE OR FOUR DAYS before the president was to deliver the speech, the White House sent drafts to the State Department for review. Powell and Armitage thought it was too bleak. One line said that 100,000 trained terrorists were still at large. Powell called Rice and suggested the number was insupportable. It was changed to "tens of thousands."

Powell, who felt Reagan had been successful largely because of his optimism and the uplifting drive in his speeches, raised the bleakness of the speech with Bush at the annual Alfalfa Club dinner on the evening of Saturday, January 26. Bush had some uplifting paragraphs added toward the end.

On the drafts that Powell and Armitage reviewed, the "axis of evil" line had the three countries listed. Hmmm, we'll have to explain this one, Powell said to Armitage, but the phrase didn't strike either of them as a problem. Powell thought it was a clever line, but not an "Ich bin ein Berliner." Was it out of character with what he had heard Bush say? No. It's just a State of the Union and it was buried in there. So Powell made no more suggestions.

Nearly two years later Rumsfeld said in an interview that he probably hadn't seen the speech in advance. "I suspect I didn't, but I don't know that." He said it was later in the administration when he started getting presidential speeches in enough time to provide comment or advance reaction. "There's two kinds of seeing something in advance," he noted. "One is when it arrives and it's all done, it's on the TelePrompTer and you need to get prepared to comment on it. The other is where you see draft 5 or 6 and it's going to 15 and you have an opportunity to input." He said he recalled nothing about details in the Axis of Evil drafts, and he added oddly, "That speech was not particularly in my area."

THE STATE OF THE UNION ADDRESS before the joint session of the Congress is an annual, nationally televised ritual that draws a giant audience. Nearly 52 million Americans watched the prime-time speech on Tuesday, January 29, the most for a State of the Union since President Clinton's 1998 address during the height of the Monica Lewinsky sex scandal. As is the custom, President Bush invited a number of distinguished guests, who sat with First Lady Laura Bush in the upstairs gallery. Among them was Hamid Karzai, the new interim leader of Afghanistan who had taken office five weeks earlier.

Bush began by acknowledging Karzai and the successful U.S.-led military campaign that had ousted the Taliban, but his real business was laying out the future. His great objectives, he said, were eliminating the threats posed by terrorists and by regimes that seek weapons of mass destruction. He devoted one sentence to North Korea, one to Iran, and five to Iraq.

"States like these, and their terrorist allies, constitute an axis of evil," Bush said, "arming to threaten the peace of the world. By seeking weapons of mass destruction, these regimes pose a grave and growing danger."

He pledged, "I will not wait on events while dangers gather."

The thrust of these lines suggested that Iraq, Iran and North Korea were somehow in cahoots with one another and working as a trio like the German-Italian-Japanese Axis in World War II. Gerson felt he had to take responsibility for this lack of clarity.

The theme of promoting democracy, the rule of law, free speech, religious tolerance and women's rights in the Islamic world had been watered down in the final version of the speech, though Bush spoke optimistically. "America will always stand firm for the nonnegotiable demands of human dignity."

Bush closed, "Steadfast in our purpose, we now press on. We have known freedom's price. We have shown freedom's power. And in this great conflict, my fellow Americans, we will see freedom's victory."

The president had spoken 63 long paragraphs for 48 minutes. Rice was sure the headline would be about Bush's desire for democracy and political change in the Middle East—something she believed had never been emphasized by an American president before.

THE NEWS MEDIA SEIZED on the "axis of evil" phrase. It was a new concept, subject to interpretation. Were the three countries somehow linked in a way that was not previously known? Was it Bush's war list? He had raised the stakes. The go-get-'em cowboy talk now had put three countries in his sights, most provocatively his father's nemesis, Saddam Hussein. The White House put out word that war was not imminent, and somewhat halfheartedly tried to note that the "axis" was the connection between weapons and terrorism, not among the three designated countries. But the force of the phrase, with echoes to World War II and Ronald Reagan, overpowered everything else.

George Tenet didn't read much into Bush's words. Speechwriters write speeches, that is their job. He didn't see a real shift in focus. The agency was still concentrating on the war on terrorism—in Afghanistan and worldwide.

Rumsfeld's deputy, Wolfowitz, hadn't seen the speech in advance. He was surprised by it, but he believed Bush had driven a stake into the ground. The speech showed that the president had been listening to some of the things Rumsfeld and he had been saying about the connection between weapons of mass destruction and terrorism. He had initially doubted whether it made sense to link the three countries, but without a powerful metaphor no one would have paid much attention. Wolfowitz saw once again how important it was to grab the headlines, and he was reminded that academics didn't get it. Oversimplification was required in a sound-bite culture. Wolfowitz soon saw Axis of Evil as a watershed. Bush had defined the problem in graphic, biblical terms without publicly committing to any particular solution.

In the White House communications shop, Dan Bartlett, the director, was delighted. What a phrase, a mere five syllables! Bartlett, 30, had joined Bush's 1994 campaign for Texas governor out of college and worked for him ever since. He could see that Axis of Evil would become a signature phrase, having a kind of clarity, even daring. The starkness of putting it on the table broke through the clutter. The foreign policy priesthood often argued that diplomacy and policy were about nuance—in other words, clutter. Bartlett scoffed. Not so. Good versus evil worked.

Powell was surprised by the intense focus on the line, and soon realized that it might turn into a to-do list for some time to come. There was lots of grumbling in the diplomatic community; the words were ringing bells of alarm all over the world. So at a senior staff meeting two days after the speech he raised the subject. The words of the president were policy, Powell said. "That's it, we heard it. There is nothing more to discuss or debate." He did not want anyone offering their interpretation or qualification, going out saying, "What the president meant to say was . . ."

ALL THREE COUNTRIES issued denials. "This statement of President Bush is stupid," the Iraqi vice president said. Bush read a report on Powell's senior staff meeting which suggested indirectly that the president might have to back off. He spoke to Rice, who was giving a speech on Friday of that week.

Get out there and reiterate this, he told her. We're serious about it. We're not abandoning it, we're not walking it back.

Rice's speech to the Conservative Political Action Conference (CPAC), a major annual gathering of conservative leaders and activists, had been drafted, so she called her speechwriters with just hours to spare and told them to add strong material on all three countries.

It had to be absolutely clear, she told them, and briefly outlined over the phone what she wanted. The writers scrambled to reformulate the speech, adhering closely to what Bush had said Tuesday night about the Axis countries.

Rice grabbed the revised draft as she was getting in the car, and reviewed it on the short drive to Arlington, Virginia.

"Our nation will do everything in its power to deny the world's most dangerous powers the world's most dangerous weapons," Rice said. She flipped the order of the countries as she outlined one-by-one the threats they believed each posed, listing North Korea first, then Iraq and Iran.

"As the president said, we must not and we will not wait on events while dangers gather," she said.

CHARLES KRAUTHAMMER, a conservative columnist for *The Washington Post*, caught the understory, calling Bush's speech an "astonishingly bold address," and adding, "Iraq is what this speech was about. If there was a serious internal debate within the administration over what to do about Iraq, that debate is over. The speech was just short of a declaration of war."

The president appreciated the impact of Axis of Evil, as he recalled later. "It just kind of resonates." It was way above the normal noise level. "When I edited it, or when I went on the prompter, I don't remember anybody saying, 'By the way, Mr. President, when you say axis of evil, you're fixin' to make headlines.' It was just one of those phrases that caught."

It served a dual purpose for Bush. On one hand, it sounded tough. Since Reagan, no president had so blatantly rattled the sword. On the other hand, the speech blurred the focus by including North Korea and Iran, providing additional cover for the secret planning for covert action in Iraq, and war.

9

RUMSFELD WASN'T WASTING TIME. On Friday, February 1, three days after the State of the Union speech that Rumsfeld later considered "not particularly in my area," he had Franks back at the Pentagon. This was the fifth iteration of the commander's estimate. Franks told him he now had a war plan for Iraq that could be executed as a unilateral U.S.-only invasion. Op Plan 1003 was now called the "Generated Start Plan"—the force for going to war would be fully generated in the region before war commenced.

The timeline, the general explained, would be 30 days for the preparation of airfields and pre-positioning of equipment—"enablers in the theater." Then over the next 60 days they would move the force to the region. After these 90 days the force level would be about 160,000. There would then commence about 20 days of aggressive air operations before the ground assault into Iraq. It would take about 135 days to complete combat operations and move into Phase Four— stabilizing an occupied Iraq. During that phase the remainder of the force would arrive, taking it to about 300,000.

This was the large buildup, smaller than Desert Storm numbers but still a substantial deployment. Franks, however, had halved the period before commencing combat from 180 to 90 days, a big improvement.

"That isn't the trick, that isn't the question," Franks explained. The more important question was at what point during the buildup would they be ready to go to war. His answer was now roughly 45 days into Phase Two, the 60-day force movement period when they would have 105,000 on the ground but not the full 160,000.

I understand the math of all that, Rumsfeld said. When would you want to begin?

Begin? Franks asked. Having learned from the question-master, he turned the tables and asked, What does that mean?

Well, the ground force, the secretary said.

"I don't want the ground force to be the first thing that goes in," Franks said.

No, obviously, Rumsfeld said, we would want to use airpower.

No, sir, the general said, that's not right either. He wanted everything to be simultaneous—or almost simultaneous. That led to a discussion of who or what would go first, or second, even if they were striving for simultaneous action.

They also began discussion of how they might compress the time for the initial force buildup—enabling a "running start"—because of the invisible, covert efforts underway.

The war planning seminar also broached the what-ifs—bad things that could happen. One very bad thing would be the failure to control the areas in western Iraq where the infamous Scud missiles were supposedly deployed. Iraq had shot Scuds into Israel and Saudi Arabia during the Gulf War. That would be a real "strategic dislocator," Franks said, an event so momentous that it would shift the entire strategy and timing. How do you avoid that? One way would be to take control of western Iraq, some 25 percent of the country. The general said that one idea was to bring an armored cavalry regiment of 6,000 to 7,000 troops into the west through Aqaba, Jordan, a port city 300 miles from Iraq's southwestern corner.

Franks said that one of the "high-end" Special Operations Forces commandos, as he called them, had had this reaction: Wait a minute, take what they had learned in Afghanistan. What happens if we introduce SOF in the west before we permit Saddam to know the war has started? Saddam would likely believe war had started only when the first Tomahawk cruise missiles went off in downtown Baghdad, as had happened in 1991.

Rumsfeld had a direct secure line to Franks. They talked regularly, even daily or even several times a day. The secretary continued to pepper the general with questions, constantly raising the bar of expectation. Franks often said, I don't know or I have got to figure that out. Or he said, I don't know *yet*, offering the prospect that he would know sometime, if not soon. Rumsfeld was like a dentist's drill that never ceased.

AT 8:45 A.M. Thursday, February 7, the president addressed the National Prayer Breakfast in the International Ballroom of the Washington Hilton Hotel. September 11 was very much on his mind. "None of us would ever wish on anyone what happened on that day," Bush said. "Yet, as with each life, sorrows we would not choose can bring wisdom and strength gained in no other way. This insight is central to many faiths and certainly to the faith that finds hope and comfort in a cross." In a sense 9/11 had given him his presidency, and he seemed to be arguing that extreme adversity could wind up giving everyone new strength.

"Tremendous challenges await this nation, and there will be hardships," he said.

Later that day, the president and his national security team met in the Situation Room.

Franks presented the refined Generated Start Plan for war with Iraq. It was the first time Bush saw an actual plan that he could order carried out.

Franks had modified the plan slightly from the presentation he had made to Rumsfeld the week before. Under this plan, war with Iraq would still take 225 days. Franks used the term "90-45-90," meaning 90 days of preparation and force movement to the point when war would start, and 45 days of serious bombing prior to the major ground operations. He called this middle period a "diddling phase" of interim kinetics when air operations could be used to fix Saddam and his forces in place while they continued to build to the needed level of ground force. The "45" phase also would include Special Operations work. These forces would jump into and seize the southern oil fields to prevent Saddam from setting them on fire as he had done in Kuwait in 1991. At the end of these 45 days the full force would be there—some 300,000—and it would take another 90 days to complete decisive combat operations to remove the regime.

The final 90-day phase would include two full corps of ground forces—maybe six divisions—plus an additional corps up north, moving through Turkey if that could be arranged.

Franks then displayed a chart called "Timings," broken down by month—March, April, May, June, July, August, September and October, which was the earliest he would technically and comfortably be ready to start combat. This made the timeline of preparatory actions he had briefed in Crawford six weeks earlier more concrete. The top half of the "Timings" chart specified strategic-level issues to consider: when the United Nations would be in session and other diplomatic endeavors; when Congress was scheduled to be in session; what was expected to be going on in Afghanistan, Franks's other theater of active operations. Secretary Rumsfeld and Secretary Powell, these are your issues, he said.

Below the strategic level, Franks had his own schedule—when he would move an aircraft carrier, reposition equipment up from Qatar, move his headquarters forward to the theater.

A third bar across the bottom showed the traditional training cycles of the Iraqi military, presented as a stoplight chart. Franks had used the red, yellow and green chart for the Afghanistan operation, and the president had liked it. Green meant it was good for the U.S., yellow meant it was neutral, and red meant it was bad.

In the period May to September, the Iraqis would be in higher states of readiness because they conducted larger-unit training. This was presented as red on the chart. October and November were yellow, and December-January-February was green because the Iraqi army was in small-unit or individual training and not working as large cohesive units.

Another bar on the chart showed the weather, which was green in the winter months, December to March, then yellow in April, and starting to get red in May during the summer heat. It also showed the normal visibility during each month.

Though October and November were a window, clearly the best times militarily were roughly December 1 through February 2003, Franks said.

Bush agreed. Did that mean that combat operations could not be undertaken in the high temperatures?

"Clearly, no," Franks said, "we certainly can conduct those operations. But if you are asking me my preferences, then I'd rather do it when the weather is more favorable to us than less favorable." For example, they would like to stay away from the windstorms expected in March-April if possible.

We can't always predict the timing, the president said, if it occurs, when it might occur. But I understand where we need to focus attention if we have the luxury of using our own schedule.

Rumsfeld asked Franks, How late could you bump this thing along?

"That's a hell of an elegant question," Franks replied, "but the answer is not elegant. I mean it depends on all those assumptions that you and I like to talk about. If you assume that we're going to have many more spikes in activity, spend more money now and get closer to committing the nation to war, then the timing can be altered." He added that he had made some other assumptions about how long it would likely take the State Department to get basing, staging and overflight permissions from the countries in the region, as well as countries in Eastern Europe. That could change the timing.

Given what they had now, the best time was between November, December and out until about the end of February, Franks said, a year away.

Can you go later? Rumsfeld asked.

"We can go anytime the president of the United States says to go," Franks replied.

But can you go earlier? Rumsfeld pressed.

"We can go anytime the president chooses," the general replied.

"If we had to," the president asked, "could we go earlier?"

"Mr. President, we can go earlier," Franks answered.

What would that mean?

"What it would mean is it would be ugly," Franks said.

Bush laughed. Well, what does that mean?

On the current trend line we're using now to build forces, Franks said, to get our deception the way we want our deception to work the best, the optimum timing looks like November through February. Yes, we can go anytime between now and then, but if we do it early, one or more of these lines of operations is not going to be robust. I mean we're going to be suboptimized somewhere.

They realized that "ugly" meant two things: the war could take longer and U.S. casualties could be higher.

Going later could also create problems. Weather for one.

Rumsfeld said they were working on another scenario. He had asked General Franks, he said, to see if it was possible, by using overwhelming mass and simultaneity of forces, to create enough pressure on the regime to cause it to fracture and crumble very early. Such a massive blow might create unbearable pressure and break the regime in the early period of the war.

The immediate reaction in the Situation Room seemed to be almost, Wow! Was it possible to do it with substantially less force and avoid a war of 225 days?

Franks quickly stepped on that idea. They had to be careful, his requirements were real. The enemy would have a vote; Saddam might not break as we might anticipate, he said. They could not be out on a limb with a smaller force. This had been Powell's point, though Franks did not say so.

Franks said there was still a lot of work to be done. There was a lot of interagency work needed for the Phase Four stability operations after the fighting was over. In addition, he said, if there were going to be a coalition of nations, work needed to begin on that.

He said also that they needed to determine what flight profiles they wanted in Southern and Northern Watch. It could be an opportunity to take out some important targets and substantially improve their position before war. How invasive did they want to be? he asked. He also had to work more on the target sets in Iraq and determine what he wanted them to be, the priorities and ordnance that would be used on each target.

Most immediate, he said, they needed to focus on preparatory tasks. Franks considered this "Phase Zero"—at least one month, perhaps as many as three—for preparing airfields and ports and getting equipment, fuel and other supplies in place. He also explained the notion of spikes—moving in a second carrier battle group, increasing the bombing in Southern and Northern Watch, or conducting an exercise in Kuwait to tweak Saddam, possibly make him think a war was starting, and then back off. Franks planned many, many spikes—feints calculated to deceive.

Bush said he liked the idea of spikes but wondered if fewer but bigger spikes might be more effective. The president also voiced concern about what Saddam might do, a casus belli that would force a U.S. response. He might attack the Kurds or invade Kuwait, for example. How could we make a transition into some response that could be sustained over time?

Franks explained that the capacity to respond would increase through the entire Phase Zero period, as more was done to improve the American position.

Rumsfeld, for the first time, introduced the concept of "shock and awe" to the president. At this point it meant building up so much force and conducting various "spiking" operations and bombing that it might in itself trigger regime change.

The president chuckled a little bit. "Shock and awe," he noted, was a catchy notion. Was it a gimmick? he wondered.

Franks used about 30 slides in the briefing. He said the bottom line was that the preparatory actions needed to continue. They would need to engage the countries in the region to win their support. We need to go back and really begin to put some meat on the bones, the general said. You know, Mr. President, we've been giving you concepts. We've got to be able to put some time and effort into creating something that is better.

The president seemed in neutral. He was not saying I can't wait that long, but he also was not saying, Okay, that's good, we'll hold off.

The meeting had lasted an hour and 10 minutes.

Franks once again felt it had been a great briefing. He had some time before war. By stressing realistic timelines and force needs, he had not even had to address Rumsfeld's question of whether they could be ready in April or May. Clearly Bush absorbed the magnitude of the problem, and the requirement for a robust force. There was no doing this on the cheap.

POWELL, TOO, thought the briefing had gone well. No one seemed trigger-happy. He found some mild comfort that they were no longer discussing the crazy-ass idea of trying to seize the southern oil fields to establish a beachhead or enclave inside Iraq with a force of fewer than 10,000.

On February 12, Powell testified before the Senate Budget Committee. He took a hard line on Saddam, noting that since 1998 the policy of the United States had been "regime change" in Iraq. "And we are looking at a variety of options that would bring that about," he said. And in a formulation intended to calm the waters, Powell added that President Bush "has no plan on his desk right now to begin a war with any nation." War was not imminent.

The next day at a press conference the president said of Iraq, "I will reserve whatever options I have, I'll keep them close to my vest." It was a careful way of not saying anything, leaving all options on the table but not misleading—a cautiousness he would later abandon.

Cheney thought the war plan took too long to unfold. Anything that gave Saddam time might mean he could mine the oil wells or use weapons of mass destruction—attacking American troops with chemical weapons, or his own troops with the intent of blaming the Americans. Or Saddam might retain his unconventional weapons for later use. He needed to be ousted, or at minimum sealed up, with all available speed.

Andy Card, the president's chief of staff, who also was privy to the briefing, concluded that the military was not ready. Franks was talking frameworks and ideas, not much more. It was the best evidence for the need to transform the military, put it in a position so it was ready. Card also worried that Iraq was every general's dream of war: a traditional battlefield, big, complex plans with wheeling corps, thousands of air sorties, and battalions of tanks rumbling across the desert. As General George Patton had said while surveying the battlefield, "I love it. God help me, I do love it."

Card, 54, played an important role for Bush as ever-present backstop. His ticket back to the White House had been the president's father. In 1987 during the Reagan presidency, he had been on the White House staff when Vice President George Bush summoned him to manage his presidential campaign in New Hampshire, the first primary state. The Bush supporters there were divided into three factions that did not get along. Card, who is from neighboring Massachusetts, moved to New Hampshire for a year, spent portions of each morning meeting separately with the leaders of each faction, and during the rest of the day meticulously organized a grassroots campaign. When Bush beat Senator Bob Dole of Kansas in the critical primary, most reporters and political consultants thought it was because of television advertising. Bush senior knew it was because of Card, whom he later brought in as his deputy White House chief of staff and then transportation secretary.

During the Clinton years, Card was the chief Washington lobbyist for the automobile manufacturers and then for General Motors. Bush told his son that there was no more loyal, straightforward person than Card, a structural design engineer by training whose wife, Kathleene, is a Methodist minister. Card considered himself a staffer who was to make sure the president was comfortable with the information he received and the decisions he made.

EARLY IN THE ADMINISTRATION, long before 9/11 and talk of war, Card had a conversation with Bush about the role of the president as commander in chief in making war decisions, what it meant.

"Mr. President," he said, "only you will be able to make the decision to send young men and women into harm's way." The president could and would get advice, even strong recommendations. There might be a war party in the country, in Congress, the media or even his cabinet, as there likewise might be a peace party. But there would be no vote in the National Security Council.

Card recounted for the president how a dozen years earlier, in 1989, he had been deputy White House chief of staff when Bush's father had made the decision to invade Panama to overthrow its leader, Manuel Noriega. The operation was called Just Cause. "I happened to be in the room, the Oval Office," Card said. He had been in charge of the easel used for the briefing maps.

In the Oval Office were Secretary of State James A. Baker III, Secretary of Defense Cheney, White House Chief of Staff John Sununu and General Colin Powell, the chairman of the JCS. There was serious discussion about the implications on all levels, military, diplomatic, Card recalled. "The president asked very tough questions and I remember it came down to do we go or not go." There was no presumption what each would say, but all recommended the war, including Jim Baker. Bush's father and Baker were close friends, had been through a lot, were of the same generation, veterans of lots of policy wars during Reagan's eight years. Baker stood in front of the president's desk and said, "This is a decision that only you can make, Mr. President."

Then everyone left your father alone, Card told the younger Bush. "And I was left to pick up the easel, and the president looks up and I happened to be in his eyesight, but I'm convinced he didn't see me. And I don't know this, but I believe he was praying at the desk.

He was quiet and contemplative. And then he looks up and he said, 'I'm making a decision that will cost young men their lives.' He verbalized it. And then he gets up and he walked out the door. That weighed on me heavily." That was what it was like, that was the loneliness of command.

"I know," the president answered.

10

TERRORISM, ESPECIALLY AL QAEDA, was still the center of Tenet's universe—issues 1, 2, 3, 4 and 5. Iraq was barely number 6. The Iraq Operations chief, Saul, had that ball and was working with his old boss, Deputy DCI John McLaughlin, a mild-mannered veteran intelligence analyst who had risen to No. 2 at the agency.

Saul was also making the rounds with the principals. He had met with Rumsfeld on February 1 to outline a covert action plan to support the U.S. military in regime change operations in Iraq. The DO began having weekly Iraq meetings that month.

Saul was discovering that the CIA reporting sources inside Iraq were pretty thin.

What was thin?

"I can count them on one hand," Saul said, pausing for effect, "and I can still pick my nose."

There were four. And those sources were in Iraqi ministries such as foreign affairs and oil that were on the periphery of any penetration of Saddam's inner circle. The agency had had real trouble getting inside the military, the Republican Guard or the Special Security Organization.

"How come all the good reporting I get is from SIS?" Tenet asked, referring to the British intelligence service.

"Sorry, we'll fix it," Saul said.

Recruiting Iraqis was hard, Saul was learning. The CIA could offer someone from $5,000 to $10,000 a month—big money—to have him commit espionage. The risk was arrest, probably watching his wife and daughter raped in front of him, the murder of his sons, the bulldozing of his house, other unimaginable tortures. What was $10,000 a month in the face of that? The few sources inside beamed out reports, clandestine covert communications. Since the U.S. had no embassy inside Baghdad, the sources had to report by computer, uploading a short-burst transmission to a satellite that immediately came down to CIA headquarters. But it was hair-raising.

Saul repeated: Covert action would not rid the world of Saddam. Only a full military invasion, with intense CIA support, would accomplish that. The only viable way to recruit new sources inside Iraq would be a clear demonstration that the U.S. was absolutely serious and was coming in full force to depose Saddam once and for all.

WITH TENET'S APPROVAL, Saul, McLaughlin and Jim Pavitt, the deputy director for operations, worked on a new Top Secret intelligence order for regime change in Iraq that President Bush signed on February 16. It directed the CIA to support the U.S. military in overthrowing Saddam and granted seven explicit new authorities:

1. Support opposition groups and individuals that want Saddam out.
2. Conduct sabotage operations inside Iraq.
3. Work with third countries—such as Jordan and Saudi Arabia—and support their covert intelligence operations.
4. Conduct information operations to distribute accurate information about the regime.
5. Run disinformation and deception operations to mislead Saddam and the regime's political, intelligence, military and security leadership.
6. Attack and disrupt regime revenues, banking and finances.
7. Disrupt the regime's illicit procurement of matériel related

to its military, especially its weapons of mass destruction programs.

The cost was set at $200 million a year for two years. The leaders of the Senate and House Intelligence Committees were informed secretly. After some disputes in Congress the budget was cut to $189 million for the first year.

Saul would be able to run what he called "offensive counterintelligence" operations to prevent Saddam's security apparatus from identifying CIA sources. But most importantly, the CIA could then work actively with anti-Saddam opposition forces inside Iraq and could conduct paramilitary operations inside the country.

Given the surge in worldwide counterterrorist operations which were being conducted in 60 countries including Afghanistan, the CIA operations directorate was being taxed beyond its capacity, and the talent pool was shallow.

Saul needed 50 officers at once, and he estimated that that would grow to 150 in six months and up to about 360 in the field and at headquarters at the onset of hostilities. He sent out messages seeking volunteers. At least one entire station from the chief on down volunteered. Iraq had been an agency fuck-up for years and many officers—not all, by any means—wanted to help.

Afghanistan had demonstrated the importance of having paramilitary teams inside the country. Solid on-the-ground intelligence and effective lethal operations could not be done from the sidelines. Even though the CIA had a massive effort going on all of Iraq's borders, they needed to be inside.

On February 20, four days after the finding was signed, a CIA survey team secretly entered northern Iraq in the Kurdish area to prepare for the deployment of CIA paramilitary teams that would be called NILE, Northern Iraq Liaison Elements.

ON THURSDAY, February 28, Franks arrived at Rumsfeld's office at the Pentagon bearing two Manhattan-telephone-book-sized Top

Secret binders of nearly 4,000 possible targets in Iraq. The targets, culled almost exclusively from the latest overhead satellite imagery, ranged from serious leadership, security and military concentrations down to Iraqi infantry and armor maneuver companies and air defense units in the field.

Identifying targets for a U.S. air campaign was a leap forward from the abstract war planning of the past few months. In the binders were the details of Franks's slices of regime vulnerability, taking them from starbursts on paper to weapons keyed on buildings and people.

Rumsfeld was surprised and pleased at the large number. Before and during the Afghanistan bombing campaign months earlier, he had complained regularly at NSC meetings about the small number of targets in that primitive country. Often only three or four dozen could be identified. On the third day of bombing in Afghanistan he had memorably declared at his press briefing, "We're not running out of targets, Afghanistan is."

Iraq was a gold mine of targets. Rumsfeld wanted them prioritized. What sort of attack and bombing campaign might have the biggest impact on the regime? What might cause the regime to crumble? They discussed the target sets—command and control targets, communications targets, specific leadership nodes such as Saddam's 50-plus palaces, the key regime paramilitary forces, including the SSO and the Special Republican Guard. Where might they put very rapid, very quick pressure early on that might cause the crumbling to occur? The secretary realized it would take time; he wanted to talk process and see how Franks and his staff would review all these targets and put them into refined categories and target sets.

Discussion turned to the preparatory tasks to improve the military facilities in the region. Rumsfeld wondered what could be done with existing agreements with various host countries that would be routine, and not seen as pointing to war. He also wanted a wish list of all projects that Franks might need.

They spent some time talking about the potential for information operations. For example, how might they get messages to the regular Iraqi army: Don't fight, Don't destroy the oil fields, Don't shoot missiles?

Franks said that the Joint Staff and the NSC needed to get involved and that someone at a senior level of the White House needed to have ownership of information operations because they would involve political statements and set out the causes of war. The tactical IO (information operations) had to match and be linked to what everyone up to the president would be saying.

Rumsfeld agreed that all messages needed to be coordinated. He would talk with Rice and others. Should it reside at the NSC, or should it be in Defense?

VICE PRESIDENT CHENEY told General Franks that he was planning a trip to the Middle East in March and asked what countries he should visit. Who might be ripe for solicitation, pressure, to assist in a war against Iraq? They agreed on at least ten potential countries— Egypt, Oman, U.A.E., Saudi Arabia, Yemen, Bahrain, Qatar, Jordan, Israel and Turkey.

On March 6, Franks briefed Cheney in Washington. The general had a Top Secret paper that he had worked out with Rumsfeld on what was needed from each country. In some cases, it would be active assistance, perhaps even troops, aircraft or intelligence operatives. In others, it would be just basing, staging, transit or overflight rights for the U.S. military. All these Arab or Muslim countries would be publicly against a war, but nearly all privately wanted Saddam out. Their assistance would have to be clandestine to one degree or another. Franks provided Cheney a profile of each leader and intelligence chief. For example, in Jordan where Tenet had extraordinary cooperation, both Franks and Tenet had worked Saad Khair, the head of GID, the Jordanian intelligence service. Both Franks and Tenet also had worked the president of Yemen, Ali Abdullah Salih.

Cheney's mission was to turn up the pressure in each country, to make a sounding of how their leaders felt about Iraq, but not necessarily to sign them up or resolve details about bases, troops, planes, ships, whatever. His message to the leaders was that if the United States were to use force, they would be serious about it.

Cheney was in luck in Jordan where Tenet had virtually bought the GID, less so in Egypt, where President Hosni Mubarak was resistant. On March 15, Cheney flew to the USS *John C. Stennis,* the aircraft carrier stationed in the Arabian Sea with a crew of 5,000. Jets from the giant flight deck were being catapulted off for bombing missions still into Afghanistan.

The vice president told thousands of welcoming crewmen and women what was on his mind. "Our next objective is to prevent terrorists, and regimes that sponsor terror, from threatening America or our friends and allies with weapons of mass destruction. We take this threat with great seriousness. That is our duty as responsible officers of the American government. The United States will not permit the forces of terror to gain the tools of genocide."

On one leg of Cheney's tour it was three countries in a single day, including Qatar, a key ally that would provide staging and a headquarters. It was a blur, and it was hard. Lynne Cheney, the vice president's wife, had a two-hour lunch with the favorite wife of the emir of Qatar.

When do kids start school here in Bahrain? Mrs. Cheney inquired.

This isn't Bahrain, the wife replied.

THE TRIP WAS SOMETHING of a wake-up call for the vice president. The leaders pounded on him not about Iraq, or the threat of Saddam Hussein, or terrorism, but about the Middle East peace process. He kept hearing that the president had better get involved and throw his weight around to set the region on some process to resolve the Israeli-Palestinian conflict. This was a message that Powell had been sending to the White House nonstop. Franks was of like mind. Cheney's other conclusion was that the Middle East was not going in the right direction. Long-term peace was not possible if Yassir Arafat remained leader of the Palestinians.

The vice president had an early morning breakfast with the president on March 21. At about 8:15 A.M., they took questions from reporters in the Oval Office. One asked about what the Arab leaders had said about supporting strong action against Iraq.

Cheney stuck to the cover story. "I went out there to consult with them, seek their advice and counsel, to be able to report back to the President."

Bush stepped in. "I think one other point that the vice president made, which is a good point, is that this is an administration that when we say we're going to do something we mean it; that we are resolved to fight the war on terror; this isn't a short-term strategy for us; that we understand history has called us into action; and we're not going to miss this opportunity to make the world more peaceful and more free. And the vice president delivered that message. I was grateful that he was able to do so. It is very important for these leaders to understand the nature of this administration so there's no doubt in their mind that when we speak, we mean what we say, that we're not posturing. We don't take a bunch of polls and focus groups to tell us what—how to—to what we ought to do in the world."

That day, March 21, and the next, Franks gathered the component commanders of the services—Army, Navy, Air Force and Marines—at Ramstein Air Base in Germany, a large U.S. and NATO airlift installation. These were the on-the-ground commanders who would be in charge of the war. Included was the Special Operations commander, Brigadier General Gary Harrell. In addition, a special covert Task Force 20 had been set to be commanded by Major General Del Dailey.

Franks was poised for war. He was convinced that they were going to do this. By "do this," he meant either Saddam Hussein and his family were going to leave and turn his country over, or the president was going to war. Would Saddam and his family leave? As a practical matter, he concluded that the answer was no.

"Fellas, there's a burglar in the house," Franks told his commanders in a closed session. It was a Special Operations term that meant if you're an airman, you need to go back and be sure that you personally are aware of the target sets and the timing. If you're on the land, you need to be absolutely sure that when you say you can deliver X force on Y day that the transportation will actually permit it, that the timelines that you advertise are timelines with which you can live. In other words, this was not an abstract planning exercise. He conveyed a sense of urgency. Don't advertise something that you can't deliver. "Go to work now." One way or the other, it was going to be done. "Don't let yourself believe that this won't happen."

Franks also offered his vision of the desired operation—smaller, lighter, faster. He said he hoped for a 90-45-90 plan, a 225-day war. He outlined the seven lines of operations and the nine slices of regime power.

Franks did not believe it was important to brief his commanders on all of his contacts with Rumsfeld. But the work with the president was critical to establish that what was on the table had standing with the commander in chief. It would underscore the seriousness. So Franks described in detail each of the briefings he had gone through with Bush, including the post-Christmas session in Crawford and the one-hour-and-10-minute briefing the previous month. In other words, their commander in chief was both behind this planning and involved with the details. To some extent the burglar in the house was George W. Bush.

A DAY LATER, March 23, the JCS began an exercise called Prominent Hammer, a so-called tabletop paper drill without actual movement of forces. It was designed to assess the feasibility of the large Op Plan 1003. If it were executed, would the transportation plan work, and what would the impact be on U.S. forces worldwide? What would it do in Korea where the U.S. maintained a force of some 37,000? What might be the impact on the war on terrorism? U.S. homeland security?

Nothing leaked about the exercise at the time, but two months later *The New York Times* reported on the drill's findings, saying a war on Iraq "would place severe strains on personnel and cause deep shortages of certain critical weapons."

DURING THIS PERIOD Saul went to Tampa to brief Franks on the covert action program the CIA would be undertaking against Iraq.

"You know," Franks said, "I fought these people before." As a brigadier general, he had been assistant division commander (maneuver) of the 1st Cavalry Division in the Gulf War. "I took my measure of them. I'm not worried."

"Okay," Saul replied, "you know your business. That's what you get paid for."

At another meeting with the component commanders, Franks urged them on. "This is fucking serious. You know, if you guys think this is not going to happen, you're wrong. You need to get off your ass."

11

———

IN MARCH, Tenet met secretly with two individuals who would be critical to covert action inside Iraq: Massoud Barzani and Jalal Talabani, the leaders of the two main Kurdish groups in northern Iraq. The two men controlled separate areas of a Kurdish region roughly the size of Maine. The areas were effectively autonomous from Saddam's Baghdad regime, but Iraqi military units were stationed just miles from the Kurdish strongholds and Saddam could easily send them to fight and slaughter the Kurds as he had done after the Gulf War when they had risen up expecting U.S. protection. Saddam had brutally crushed them, killing thousands and prompting over a million refugees to flee to neighboring Iran and Turkey. The Kurds had an extremely hostile relationship with the Turkish government, which historically did not recognize the large minority group or its language.

Tenet had one message for Barzani and Talabani: The United States was serious, the military and the CIA were coming. It was different this time. The CIA was not going to be alone. The military would attack. President Bush meant what he said. It was a new era. Saddam was going down. Of course, Tenet did not know if what he was saying was true, whether war was going to happen. But he had to raise the expectations of the Kurds to win cooperation and engagement. He was about to send some of his paramilitary and case officers into a very dangerous environment. His attitude as the DCI was simple: He would sell fucking tea to Chinamen to make sure his officers got protection.

There was no way anyone, especially tribal leaders, could avoid bumping into Tenet's personality. It is large, passionate, combustible. He gets in faces. It is almost tribal itself. Tenet knew that in that part of the world everyone was selling something. They wouldn't be surprised that he too was selling. It was a world of wanton exaggeration. He needed protections, guarantees and commitments, and he was offering the same. This was survival. And this was another one of the dilemmas he faced—making promises that might not be kept. As some of his predecessors had learned and often said, the agency does not play by the rules of the Marquess of Queensberry, who had introduced gloves and time limits to boxing in the 19th century. CIA covert actions were the dirty side of the ring.

Tenet, however, had a giant lever: money. He could pay millions, tens of millions of dollars in U.S. $100 bills. If Defense Department civilians or officers, or State Department diplomats paid money to get anyone to act or change policy, it could be illegal bribery. The CIA was the one part of the U.S. government that was authorized to pay off people.

Tenet had told Bush that some money was going to be paid on speculation in order to establish relationships and demonstrate seriousness. And that not all of it might look like it had been well spent. It was like chum, small pieces of fish scattered on the water to attract the big ones. In intelligence, you often had to chum far and wide. It was one more thing the president and Tenet bonded over. Bush, one of the biggest political fund-raisers of all time, and Tenet, the U.S. government covert-money man, knew the restorative power of money. So he was asking a lot and offering a lot. Just wait, he told the Kurdish leaders, *it* was coming—the military, the CIA and money.

ON MARCH 29, General Franks marched into hostile territory—the Tank, the secure meeting space of the Joint Chiefs of Staff, the heads of each of the four services. In many respects the Joint Chiefs are an anachronism. Under Title X of the U.S. Code, which deals with the military, the four heads—the chief of staff of the Army, the chief of naval operations, the chief of staff of the Air Force, and the commandant of the Marine Corps—have the responsibility to recruit, train and equip their own services. But the chiefs command no forces in combat. The forces are assigned to combatant commanders such as Franks himself.

Since Franks reported directly to the secretary of defense, the chairman of the Joint Chiefs of Staff was not his boss, and the service chiefs were damn sure not his bosses—though by technical measurements of seniority they all outranked him. In fact, Franks just about considered himself out of the Army. He was a joint war fighter. "I am absolutely purple," he once said, purple being the color that would emerge if you put a uniform from each service in a blender.

The tension between Franks and the chiefs was palpable. The previous year, during the height of the Afghanistan campaign, the chiefs, as is their tendency, were pushing for more of their own in the war—the Navy for one more aircraft carrier, the Army another brigade, and the Air Force another squadron.

Franks one day blew up half jokingly at the chiefs, "You Title X motherfuckers! Let me tell you something. At the end of the day, combatants, and that's either me or the boss I work for [Rumsfeld], are going to put together a joint and combined operation here and it is not going to scratch the itch of any one of the services."

Several of the chiefs remember Franks's outburst as less confrontational and more in a humorous vein, though they vividly remember being called "Title X motherfuckers."

So now Franks had to update them on his Iraq planning. It was a long briefing with 70-plus slides. He tried to present it mostly as a concept of operations, the latest on the Generated Start—probably 180,000 to 200,000 troops or half of Desert Storm.

Franks said he had six months to be ready to execute by October 1 if the president demanded it. But no sooner than October 1.

One of the chiefs thought it was hard to tell how serious this discussion was. Part of it seemed like a drill to scare Saddam. They had a ton of questions.

Franks had, at one point, used five Navy aircraft carriers for the Afghanistan operation, so how many would be needed for Iraq? How do you refresh or rotate the force in a long war? What about presumed weapons of mass destruction? What would the Iraqi response be? What would Israel do if it was attacked? How do you take Baghdad, the capital, with a population of 5 million?

The Army chief, General Eric K. Shinseki, expressed concern about the logistical support for a massive invasion of a country the size of Iraq. How would the force on the ground be sustained? What size of force would really be needed to be successful?

Wolfowitz and the policy crowd thought war with Iraq would be relatively easy, one chief said. Did Franks agree?

Another question was, What do you do with the force between now and then?

Franks tried to answer their questions but the chiefs did not seem happy. The "Title X motherfuckers" had been sidelined since the 1986 Goldwater-Nichols reform legislation, which gave most of the significant advisory power to the chairman of the Joint Chiefs.

THE BUSHES HOSTED British Prime Minister Tony Blair and his family at their ranch in Crawford over the weekend of April 6–7. In an interview with the United Kingdom's ITV Television Network, reporter Trevor McDonald pushed the president about Iraq. "I made up my mind that Saddam needs to go," Bush said. "That's about all I'm willing to share with you."

"Then Saddam must go?" McDonald asked.

"That's what I just said," Bush said testily. "The policy of my government is that he goes."

"People think that Saddam Hussein has no links with the al Qaeda network, and I'm wondering why you have—"

"The worst thing that could happen would be to allow a nation like Iraq, run by Saddam Hussein, to develop weapons of mass destruction, and then team up with terrorist organizations so they can blackmail the world. I'm not going to let that happen."

"And how are you going to achieve this, Mr. President?"

"Wait and see."

McDonald questioned him about the weapons inspectors. Bush said he wanted them back in Iraq. "But this is not an issue of inspectors. This is an issue of [Saddam] upholding his word that he would not develop weapons of mass destruction."

"So whether he allows the inspectors in or not, he is on the list to be attacked?" McDonald asked. "He's the next target?"

"You keep trying to put—" Bush said, then restarted his sentence. "You're one of these clever reporters that keeps trying to put words in my mouth."

"Far from that, Mr. President."

"Well, I'm afraid you do, sir. But nevertheless, you've had my answer on this subject." The prodding took Bush into dangerous territory as he added, "And I have no plans to attack on my desk." Though technically true, it obscured the direct and personal nature of his involvement in the war planning.

FRANKS GAVE RUMSFELD an update on April 11 by secure video, focusing on the specific war preparations that could be taken without attracting much public notice. Since the concept called for a unilateral U.S. attack from the south through Kuwait, they had work to do to upgrade various airfields in the Gulf countries such as Oman, U.A.E. and Kuwait itself. More and more pre-positioned equipment and supplies were moving in, requiring the construction of concrete pads for storage.

In addition, they would need access to vast quantities of fuel as forces would eventually move forward from Kuwait into Iraq. How could the U.S. tap into existing fuel lines that the Kuwaitis would support but would not be known to other nations?

Such initial preparations—and this was only the beginning—
would cost in the range of perhaps $300 million to $400 million. Re-
acting to the sticker shock, Rumsfeld wondered aloud if there were
any way to get other countries to foot some of this bill?

The secretary said he wanted to look ahead. Rephrasing the
president's earlier question, he asked, How would they respond if
Saddam took some action that was a spoiler?

This evolved into a discussion of Operation Southern Watch,
which, with the onset of the U.S. bombing in Afghanistan six
months earlier, had been placed in a holding pattern of sorts. While
poised to respond to provocations, its intent was really to collect intelligence and monitor the no-fly zones. Would it now be possible to
be more intrusive with the intelligence collection? Should they fly
more? Could such operations be a wedge to incrementally improve
the U.S. position before a war?

JUST MORE THAN A WEEK LATER, April 20, Franks briefed the president in a Saturday session at Camp David.

I am feeling a little bit better about the small, lighter, more ac-
celerated concept, Franks said. It seemed to be coming together. Mr.
President, I am probably going to be able to reduce the time about
one-third from what I thought initially. At the end of that period they
would have about 180,000 people deployed. If they did not meet
with immediate success, the force would grow to about 250,000 by
the end of Phase Three, decisive combat operations.

"I'm not yet satisfied with this," Franks said. They had war gam-
ing going on to figure out the time and distance problems. "Don't
take these numbers, Mr. President, to be what we'll execute. This
just happens to be where we are right now."

"It's really important for us that we don't leave ourselves open
in the region," Bush said. He noted that the longer the fighting might
go on, the more susceptible the U.S. would be to the political dynamics in the region. He wanted it done as efficiently and in as short
a time as possible. At the same time, the president told Franks that

he should not let the discussion or his interest in ways to compress time schedules and combat operations lead him to believe that anyone was going to do this with anything less than what was required.

"You tell me, Tommy, what it takes to do this," the president said. "Obviously I want to make sure we do this right and quickly."

Franks saw the problem. Of course, "right" and "quickly" might not be the same thing. Making it quick might, in fact, be wrong. He took this as what he called "a presidential hint" and a very loose one at that.

The general said, "I am going to have to balance risk before I tell you that I have a plan that I'm ready to execute." Key questions, he said, were, "How much force is necessary to be built up over what period of time so that when it begins it doesn't last long?" and, "How long does it have to go before you are decisive and get it finished?"

"Yep," the president said, "exactly right. Tommy, you are my expert. You got to tell me what it takes to do it. Anything you need, you'll have."

At another point Bush added, "If this goes a long time, Dick Cheney says that the region—it's going to be problematic." That was a nice word for disaster. Another presidential hint. The president then added, "It's going to have to go however long it's going to go, but I just thought I'd say that."

LATER BUSH RECALLED that he was indeed trying to send hints. "Very important for a president not to micromanage a war plan to suit, 1. domestic politics and, 2. the international politics. On the other hand, as Tommy planned, I wanted him to understand some of the nuances, or understand issues in a nuanced way. The worst thing a president can do is to say, Oh, no, the war plan must conform to a political calendar.

"It is very delicate for the president to deal with his generals. He must be very careful. They take everything—" the president said, and then restarted, "This is a command structure where when the president says something, it is taken extremely seriously by everybody up and down the chain of command. And so I am mindful of that." So he was sending hints without "jeopardizing" what Franks wanted to do. "Remember this: If a president tries to design a war plan, he puts his soldiers at risk, because I'm a lousy war plan designer."

ON APRIL 24, Franks huddled again with his major commanders, this time in Doha, Qatar. The number of preparatory tasks seemed endless, lots of seemingly small details that if not dealt with could delay or even break part or all of an operation. He had concluded that there were two ways to get things done as a combatant commander: 1. Ask Washington to do it or grant permission for him to do it, or 2. Just do it. Bush clearly had given him extraordinary authority, declaring that the cost would be whatever it was.

Franks told his commanders to inform him as to what they needed, because henceforth they would no longer make financial requests to Washington. So if they needed to do work on a combat vehicle ramp in Kuwait that would cost several million, just do it. Same with extending a runway in Oman. Or pouring concrete in Jordan. Do it.

Later Franks reported to Rumsfeld: The bills are coming. The Pentagon comptroller had the money, Rumsfeld said, so let's go ahead.

ON MAY 9, Franks formally asked his commanders to develop a plan for a second or northern front option for an attack into Iraq through Turkey. He was not convinced that Turkey would go along, so all planning had focused on the southern or Kuwait-only attack. But since cooperation by Turkey was at least possible, Franks wanted it examined. If feasible, the 100-mile Iraq-Turkey border could be used for the introduction of a division-size force of some 15,000 to 20,000 troops. With all the support personnel, Franks initially calculated it might mean a footprint inside Turkey of 25,000 to 30,000. The Turks would be skittish about that. Nonetheless, he figured it was worth a try.

• • •

THE NEXT DAY, May 10, Franks summarized these discussions to
Rumsfeld. The secretary was in search of a clean formulation. What
were all the angles? What could surprise them? What had they overlooked, not anticipated? There were so many variables and un-
knowns. What was it they were not seeing that was in front of their
eyes? Saddam's propensity and ability to provoke in a major way was
a "known unknown." More worrisome were the "unknown un-
knowns" Rumsfeld spoke of so often, the things they might be completely blind to.

The unanswered question that loomed was, Suppose Saddam
forced the U.S. into war before they were ready?

For the time being, all they had in the way of a response were
the Air Force and Navy aircraft already in place. The routine Southern Watch/Northern Watch operations included an aircraft carrier
battle group with about 70 planes plus an additional 120 land-based
Air Force planes. In all that was about 200 aircraft. They called this
the Blue Plan—what would be available on four to six hours' notice
for a come-as-you-are response to buy time.

How could that air component be increased into a graduated series of air operations that would allow enough time for ground forces
to flow into the region for a land attack?

Initial calculations were that a White Level of aircraft—about
450 planes—could be in the region within seven days of a provocation. Then in another two weeks they could build to what was called
the Red Plan of about 750 to 800 airplanes.

This was about half the combat airpower of the 1991 Desert
Storm operation.

Later that day, Franks took his brief on the latest Generated
Start Plan to the NSC principals at the White House. In this briefing
without the president, Franks displayed a map of Iraq and its sur-
rounding neighbors. He reviewed where they stood with the various
clearances with each country—where he thought they would get access or assistance, and where he was not sure.

Since the latest plan, the 90-45-90, called for a 225-day buildup and war, Rice asked if there were a quicker way to do this, to shrink the front end. Time was the vulnerability.

Franks said he was working it. He introduced them to the Blue, White and Red Plans for air operations if Saddam provoked.

Powell had lots of questions about the support that might realistically be expected from some of the countries that were playing two sides—one in public and one in private. The implications for the region were incalculable, so these countries were hedging. Powell wanted to put some additional issues on the table. Looking at the map, he pointed out that there was only a single seaport in Kuwait through which all the combat units and supplies would have to flow. In Desert Storm they had had several.

"Tommy," he said, "you're an expert in this now, and I'm not, but from what I understand . . ." He then praised the planning, the possible tactical play. "Have you thought about the logistics? Can the through-put"—a logistics term for the transit point that Powell intentionally used—"handle this, and do you have what you need and can you get what you need through that one port?"

Franks considered Powell "a little bit of a friend," and the commanding general saw that the former general was wearing kid gloves. It was a reasonable question apparently asked with two purposes: one, to get it out in front of the others and ultimately the president, and two, as a subtle hint to Franks that he ought to watch logistics carefully.

Franks gave a confident answer but insisted, as in everything else, that they were working it hard and did not have all the answers, not even close, not even all the questions.

In addition, Franks surmised that Powell had concerns that were not articulated. Franks was not designing an overwhelming-force operation of the kind Powell had used in the Gulf War, but was moving toward a lighter, quicker plan that was more complex, with lots of moving pieces. Perhaps Powell felt there was too much risk.

Powell believed in maximum military force at the point of decision and he was going to ask questions and offer comments, whether invited or not. What do you think about the sufficiency of the forces involved? he asked.

Franks said he was working toward the right number.

What about the costs?

Franks said that the total operational costs were an unknown at this point because he was still continuing to think about, adjust and shape the size of the force.

On Saturday, May 11, Franks took his map and briefings to Camp David for a long session with the president. He presented the attack plan in a different way, saying it would consist of five fronts. First was a western front where he would send Special Operations Forces to prevent the launching of Scud missiles. Second was a southern front—the main avenue of attack from Kuwait; this would consist of two-plus Army divisions and about two Marine divisions. The third front would be all the information operations. The fourth, a vertical attack into Baghdad. And a fifth would be through Turkey if they won agreement with the Turks.

Franks described the strength of the enemy force. In the north, Saddam had 11 regular army divisions and 2 Republican Guard divisions. In the south, he had 5 regular army divisions and the remaining Republican Guard and Special Republican Guard divisions around Baghdad.

Rice and Card expressed concern about a "Fortress Baghdad" scenario with Saddam hunkering down and forcing ugly urban warfare that could go on and on.

The president also had questions about Fortress Baghdad. Franks thought that the president was echoing an anxiety felt by the others, that he had almost been prompted to ask about it.

There's no way, Franks said, given the 300 miles from the borders of Kuwait, Turkey and Jordan to Baghdad that this guy can be preempted from bringing all his forces into Baghdad if that's what he chooses to do. Especially, he added, if the U.S. decided to attack with a lesser force and do it very quickly. Saddam would have time to move into Baghdad if he wanted. "If he chooses to do that, it's a difficult proposition for us, but at the end of the day, we win."

12

"STOP BOTHERING ME!" the president said to Karl Rove that Saturday, May 11. Rove had alerted him to a story *The New York Times* was preparing on Rove's increasing involvement in foreign policy decisions. It was always best to keep Bush from being surprised by news stories about internecine warfare. Rove insisted he had not provoked the story and was not cooperating with the reporters. "Don't worry about it," the president said. "Condi's territorial," he joked. "She's a woman."

"Mr. President," Rove replied, also tongue-in-cheek, "that's a sexist remark."

Instead of Rice, Rove's recent tussles had been more with Powell, one of the most territorial. Rove's office vetted all the administration appointees, and in three recent instances the State Department had tried to put career people into jobs designated for political appointees. These political appointees were Rove's patronage and his leverage into the departments. He followed them like a hawk. Powell's latest three efforts to circumvent the system were: filling a noncareer slot at the U.S. Agency for International Development (USAID) with a career person; another to a full ambassadorship; and the third to put a Democrat as a scheduler in Armitage's office. Rove sent back the following message: "We're never going to say no to you. . . . What are you going to do for us?"

But the *Times* was not on to any of this. Rove had declined to be interviewed and had responded by e-mail, "I'm not deeply involved in foreign policy!"

On Sunday, the president called Rove to tease him. "I didn't see the story about you." It ran the next day, Monday, May 13, on the front page under the headline: "Some in Administration Grumble as Aide's Role Seems to Expand." The story said Powell was "put off" by Rove's assertion that the war in Afghanistan should be used to benefit Bush politically. But it had few specifics, and had no indication that Rove was in conflict with Rice.

Rove was in his second floor West Wing office about 6:30 A.M. Monday when Powell rang.

"It's a bunch of horseshit," said the secretary of state. "We're friends. And I've always felt we had a good relationship." If anyone understood there were political ramifications that needed to be weighed in everything, it was Powell. "And you're the president's political adviser and you're supposed to advise him."

"Well, thanks," Rove replied. "And I appreciate it, Mr. Secretary."

Rove had figured that State—or Powell—wanted to strike back at the White House, and the best way to do that was to declare everything political, attempt to soften any hard line. He was just collateral damage, he felt, though he maintained he didn't get the reason for the story and frankly didn't care.

When the president, who knew about the tension, saw Rove later that day, he said with some relish to his chief political adviser, "Mr. Secretary, how are you today?"

FOR HIS PART, Cheney knew that the real foreign policy struggle within the administration was not over Rove but Powell. One night he remarked privately that the administration had these intense discussions about the two sides of the Iranian government, that of the democratically elected president, Mohammad Khatami, and the powerful theocratic religious leader, Ayatollah Ali Khamenei. "The debate is whether it's two sides of the same government or whether it's two separate governments," he said of Iran, adding jokingly, "The same question applies to Don Rumsfeld and Colin Powell."

One of the core differences between Rumsfeld and Powell was on the issue of preemptive attacks. Since 9/11, Rumsfeld had been saying categorically that defense was not enough, that the U.S. needed an offense. The battle had to be taken to the terrorists, they had to be attacked, taken out preemptively. Any discussion of employing the military under some theory, and not an immediate threat to U.S. national security, made Powell exceedingly nervous.

On May 29, the former secretary of state in the Reagan administration, George P. Shultz, who was now at the Hoover Institution, a hawkish and well-funded think tank at Stanford University, gave a hard-line speech at the dedication ceremony of the National Foreign Affairs Training Center outside Washington that was named after him. Shultz praised recent remarks by Rumsfeld that the battle had to be taken to the terrorists. He said the right to preempt terrorist attacks extended to threats within the borders of another country. He said this amounted to what he called not just hot pursuit but "hot preemption."

Cheney told his wife that it was Shultz at "his wisest and best."

MEANWHILE THAT WEEK, President Bush had flown to Europe for meetings with German Chancellor Gerhard Schroeder on May 23 and French President Jacques Chirac on May 26. At press conferences in each capital, the president told the two key continental European allies, "I have no war plans on my desk." Bush had now used this formulation three times in public. He was under no obligation to disclose the extensive war planning efforts underway, and it would have been unwise to do so because it would have generated a torrent of speculation and digging by reporters. But in retrospect it no doubt would have served Bush better had he simply repeated his statement of three months earlier: "I will reserve whatever options I have, I'll keep them close to my vest."

That week, in a misleading public statement, General Franks went further. Asked at a news conference in Tampa on May 21 what force would be needed to invade Iraq and how long it would take, the CENTCOM commander said, "That's a great question and one for which I don't have an answer because my boss has not yet asked me to put together a plan to do that." He added, "But beyond speculation that I read much about in the press, my bosses have not asked me to put together anything yet, and so they have not asked me for those kinds of numbers."

Well-wired Pentagon reporters knew Iraq war planning was going on in some way, but sources in the Pentagon, particularly those not privy to the Rumsfeld-Franks sessions, told the reporters that Franks's work amounted to nothing more than a "concept of operations" and did not constitute a "plan." *The New York Times* pursued the Iraq war planning story aggressively. One front page story that spring, Sunday, April 28, with the prescient headline, "U.S. Envisions Blueprint on Iraq Including Big Invasion Next Year," said that the work was tentative and that Bush "has not issued any order for the Pentagon to mobilize its forces, and today there is no official 'war plan.' "

At the same time, Franks was improving his position below the radar, approaching the point where he would soon have two brigades on the ground in Kuwait and pre-positioned equipment for four brigades. Unknown to the reporters, Franks had already told the president that the big plan, Op Plan 1003, could be executed at any time, probably making it the "official" plan, though he was still trying new ideas, juggling with a wide range of force levels, and in no way asking or recommending that it be approved or used.

EARLY SATURDAY MORNING, June 1, chief speechwriter Michael Gerson accompanied the president aboard the Marine One helicopter up the Hudson River to West Point, New York, where Bush was to give the commencement address at the United States Military Academy. Gerson did not usually attend the president's speeches, preferring to watch them on television from home. Their true impact was to be measured there, the way most people heard and saw them. But Gerson believed this was the most important speech he had ever worked on, and he wanted to be there.

Gerson had spent an extraordinary amount of time on the speech, including one long-haul Air Force One flight with the president. They conceived it as a continuation of the theme of Bush's State of the Union Axis of Evil speech in January: that the U.S. was committed to improving the world, making it, as Rice termed it, "safer and better." It grew out of an almost grandiose purpose Bush had found in the presidency since 9/11. Gerson saw his job as translating that sense of purpose into a clear vision.

Gerson recognized the bedrock American hesitancy, even extreme reluctance, to be involved in the world. To change that, the country had to be convinced that both its security interests and its ideals were in jeopardy. The perennial debate in foreign policy between the realism of Teddy Roosevelt's "big stick" and Woodrow Wilson's idealistic goal of "making the world safe for democracy" was sterile in Gerson's view. A president needed realism *and* idealism, and Gerson believed Bush wanted both and to be able to say, in effect, we take power seriously, we take ideals seriously.

In his research, Gerson had gone back to President Truman's 1947 speech proclaiming the Truman Doctrine to assist the free people of Greece and Turkey in their struggle against Communism. He was surprised to learn that Truman had not been a particularly good explainer. The 18-minute Truman Doctrine speech was just boring. In Gerson's view, it had not been Truman or Eisenhower who had explained the necessity of fighting Communism but John Kennedy as a Cold War Democrat in his 1961 inaugural when he proclaimed "the burden of a long twilight struggle." Bush seemed to have clear instincts, and Gerson wanted to give them a structure that would define their historical significance. The goal was no less than to change the American mind-set the same way it had been changed at the beginning of the Cold War.

The Axis speech had identified the possible target countries.

Now Bush would specify the means—"preemption." The argument was as follows: If the United States deferred action, hesitated at striking those who were threats, the consequences might not be immediate. But the prospect of losing half the population of an American city was so horrible to contemplate that it created an urgent duty.

Cheney had been raising these questions about the potential threat of terrorists acquiring weapons of mass destruction since the 2000 campaign, Gerson knew. Since 9/11, it had become Cheney's obsession. He argued that this was the primary national security threat for America in the decades if not the generations to come. Iraq was merely the greatest possible source of connecting such weapons and terrorism.

To meet this challenge, a broad and bold new doctrine of American action in the world had to be explicitly declared. The president told Gerson that he did not want to play what he called "small ball." He had decided that in the future the U.S. would strike preemptively at threats rather than rely on containment or deterrence.

"The war on terror will not be won on the defensive," Bush told nearly 1,000 graduating cadets and their families in West Point's Michie Stadium. "We must take the battle to the enemy, disrupt his plans, and confront the worst threats before they emerge."

The only path to safety was action, he said, "and this nation will act." He bookended the aggressive language with a call for the spread of American values. "Our nation's cause has always been larger than our nation's defense," he said. "We have a great opportunity to extend a just peace by replacing poverty, repression and resentment around the world with hope of a better day." The goal was not only an absence of war but a "just peace" which included moral purposes, democracy, free markets and the rights of women.

Afterward Gerson told a reporter, "You know, this speech is going to be quoted for a long time. You have to pay a lot of attention to this."

"There's no news in that speech," the reporter replied. "You don't use the word Iraq."

Gerson was stunned. Here Bush had laid out the basis of his entire national security and foreign policy strategy.

The speech was the lead story in *The New York Times* and *Washington Post* the next day but was slow to trigger widespread scrutiny. The *Times* said in an editorial that Bush's preemption doctrine represented "a shift with profound implications" and that the U.S. had to take care not to set a dangerous example or get "in the business of unilaterally invading other countries or toppling other governments."

Rumsfeld didn't find much new in the speech. He had been talking publicly about preemption since 9/11, and certainly the war in Afghanistan and the covert war on terrorism worldwide was preemptive to one degree or another. It was a doctrine that went back centuries, a friend reminded him. In the 16th century, Sir Thomas More discussed preemption in his *Utopia,* the idea that when you know there is going to be an attack that will come from a neighbor, you shouldn't just wait for it—you should go and do something. It also just seemed common sense. The underlying intelligence about the threat from another country, the power and quality of information, was the point worth discussing, Rumsfeld believed. What information would you require, and with what degree of certainty, before you launched a preemptive attack?

FRANKS WAS INUNDATED with orders from the Pentagon concerning Iraq. On May 20, Rumsfeld had sent Franks a branch planning order called the "Liberation of Baghdad." It meant he had to do more specific planning to counter or deal with a Fortress Baghdad, a deep worry in the White House, especially for Rice and Card. Four days later, Rumsfeld through the JCS ordered planning for Phase Four stability operations in Iraq after combat operations.

In Rumsfeld's and Franks's nonstop dialogue, they kept returning to the notion of smaller and quicker. They had the big 90-45-90 Generated Start Plan in the can, but neither liked it. It was a placeholder. Instead of shaving and cutting and compressing, as they had been doing for six months, perhaps they needed something entirely new, a fresh start, unencumbered by what was on the shelf. Rumsfeld loved to rethink problems, absolutely adored taking a clean sheet of paper or his dictating machine and beginning again.

Not only did they have to deal with the possibility that Saddam might act provocatively, but suppose that the president, for one reason or another, wanted to prevent Iraq from doing something, wanted to put his preemptive doctrine into practice, and needed a quick option. Say tomorrow? Or next month? Rumsfeld was keenly aware that Bush's presidential speeches were policy. Suppose they had to begin air operations—Blue, White or Red air strikes—and simultaneously were trying to sprint ground forces onto the battlefield to respond to whatever the situation might be?

On June 3, via secure video, Franks presented Rumsfeld with what he called the "Running Start"—beginning war before all the U.S. forces were in the region and ready. The key elements would be using the Blue/White/Red air program to bridge to the movement of ground forces. The questions were the amount, timing, makeup and means of transporting those ground forces.

They returned again to the question of what might cause war because they had no idea what was going on in Saddam's head. It was the supreme "known unknown." The only answer was to be prepared.

Rumsfeld liked the concept of a "running start" and directed that it be pursued. It would have a classic, more sequential style—air first and then ground, but it might be necessary. "Running" nicely captured the fluid world they were working in, filled with possible surprise and what he viewed as the necessity to be ready for any contingency.

On the secure video Franks presented a new concept for dealing with a Fortress Baghdad. He called it "from the inside out," meaning that his forces would aggressively attack and eliminate Saddam's command and control, and also launch against Iraqi divisions closest to the city. This would be designed to preclude large numbers of Iraqi

forces from immediately massing into the center of Baghdad.
Franks's forces would then work from the inside out to the rest of
the country. This would prevent outlying regular army or Republican
Guard divisions from coming back into the city.

On Wednesday, June 19, Franks presented the latest to Bush.
He quickly updated him on the Generated Start. The general said
that if the president notified him, okay, you've got 90 days, he would
feel comfortable beginning the big war plan. If you have time, Mr.
President, and we take advantage of that time, we could generate our
own timeline with a fairly simultaneous and large-scale air and
ground force invasion—the 90-45-90 Plan that would mean a war of
225 days to end the regime.

He assured the president they would win with this plan.

Most important, Franks said, as a result of looking at more
what-ifs, Rumsfeld and he had come up with a new flexible response
option, a kind of running start. This was the short-notice option they
had been groping toward—a shorter time between the president's
decision to attack and the attack itself, the "decision-to-action" time.
They had come up with a rolling start that could begin with the Blue,
White or Red air operations. Franks said he would buy time with
these air operations, which would escalate over time; they would
substantially reduce some of Saddam's capability in and around
Baghdad and keep the Iraqis at bay.

Franks now had two brigades on the ground in Kuwait. It would
take about three weeks to get two additional brigades there. With a
total of four brigades (a division plus) and the Marine Expeditionary
unit nearby, Franks would have a ground force of 50,000—a bare
minimum to push across the Iraqi border as an invasion force. Because he would start deploying more forces at the moment the president ordered air operations, he could get another two divisions into
Kuwait within two to three weeks.

That meant he could have a little over 100,000 for a ground attack within about 30 days.

Bush's response was neutral. He seemed to accept the logic of
another option. He asked Franks to work hard on plans to respond if

Saddam used WMD either against neighbors or U.S. forces. How was the general equipped to preclude it or defend against it, or in the worst case operate in a contaminated environment? The president was keen that Rumsfeld and Franks get on with the interagency support to make sure they completed the preparatory tasks for supplies, basing and fuel in the region. He seemed to be conveying a sense of urgency.

FRANKS MET AT RAMSTEIN in Germany with his component commanders again on June 27 and 28. He told them to shift planning priorities from the Generated Plan to the Running Start concept.

On July 17, Franks updated Rumsfeld on the preparatory tasks in the region. He carefully listed the cost of each and the risk to the mission if they didn't proceed along the timeline which set completion by December 1. Total cost: about $700 million.

The big-muscle movement was for airfields and fuel infrastructure in Kuwait where a massive covert public works program had already been launched. For years the U.S. military had had a joint plan with the Kuwaitis to improve their airfields. Initially Kuwait had agreed to fund these projects but they had deferred the money. So Franks was able to use the existing contracts and construction plans, but pay for them with U.S. funds, so that nothing really new seemed to be in the works, just an acceleration of the old plan. Huge amounts of ramp space were paved at Al Jaber and Ali Al Salem Air Bases in Kuwait for aircraft use, parking and munitions storage.

One initial concern was the logistical problem of transporting fuel from refineries in Kuwait to the Iraqi border so there would be sufficient quantities to move and support a giant invasion. Franks's land commanders initiated a series of contracts with the Kuwait oil ministry to clean out some existing pipelines and create a new fuel distribution capability closer to the camps they were beginning to construct.

All of this was so far below the radar that the Kuwaitis, let alone the Iraqis, seemed not to notice.

Later the president praised Rumsfeld and Franks for this strategy of moving troops in and expanding the infrastructure. "It was, in my judgment," Bush said, "a very smart recommendation by Don and Tommy to put certain elements in place that could easily be removed and it could be done so in a way that was quiet so that we didn't create a lot of noise and anxiety. And were necessary for no matter what the war plan eventually evolved into." He carefully added, "The pre-positioning of forces should not be viewed as a commitment on my part to use military." He acknowledged with a terse "Right. Yup." that the Afghanistan war and war on terrorism provided the excuse, that it was done covertly, and that it was expensive.

Some of the funding would come from the supplemental appropriations bill being worked out in Congress for the Afghanistan war and the general war on terrorism. The rest would come from old appropriations.

By the end of July, Bush had approved some 30 projects that would eventually cost $700 million. He discussed it with Nicholas E. Calio, the head of White House congressional relations. Congress, which is supposed to control the purse strings, had no real knowledge or involvement, had not even been notified that the Pentagon wanted to reprogram money.

ON JULY 28–29, *The Washington Post* and *New York Times* had carried front page stories on Iraq war planning. The *Post* said many senior military officers favored containment, and the *Times* said one option being considered was an "inside-out" attack first on Baghdad. Because this was an incomplete version of Franks's concept of avoiding Fortress Baghdad that he had presented in June, Bush was able to take exception to the reports when he was asked about them at a cabinet meeting on July 31.

"The stated mission is regime change," the president said. "But all this talk from level four people . . . [they] are talking about things they know nothing about. Our intent is serious. There are no war plans on my desk. I believe there is casus belli and that the doctrine of preemption applies. We won't do anything militarily unless confident we can succeed. Success is removal of Saddam."

Rumsfeld told the cabinet, "If it looks untidy in the press, it is. Preemption is an important discussion to have. Problem is that it gets particularized to Iraq."

In a private talk with the president, Rice said the leaks in the media—with a different plan almost every day—had become so "ludicrous" that they were useful.

"Well," she said, "one good thing about this is that I'm sure Saddam is by now totally confused."

13

WITH THE PRESIDENTIAL finding authorizing covert action and allocation of the money, Tenet was ready to send two small CIA paramilitary teams into northern Iraq. He felt emboldened by the agency's success in the Afghanistan war, but, as he was reminded again and again, Iraq was not Afghanistan. His teams would have to transit through Turkey and move covertly into the Kurdish-controlled area of mountainous northern Iraq. Both the Turks and the Kurds posed grave danger to his men, as did Saddam.

Still, a survey team that had been sent in during February to assess the security situation said it was feasible. And Tenet had the necessary money, at least $189 million. This was a big change from his days as DCI in the Clinton administration. He felt that Clinton had always "fucked" the agency on money, that the CIA always seemed last on the list. Once he had to go personally to Clinton's Office of Management and Budget to get $20,000 for communications equipment needed by his people in the field.

The new factor was the absence of doubt at the top. Bush displayed no hesitation or uncertainty. It might be prudent to overrule an earlier decision, step back and debate the merits, but Bush was not that way. Tenet was finding that you paid the greatest price by doubting. There were often a hundred reasons not to act. Some people got overwhelmed by problems and did 50 permutations about why it was insoluble, ending up nowhere. But if you were not afraid of what you had to do, then you would work your way through the problems.

When he took problems to Bush, the president asked, Well, what's a solution? How do you fix it? How do you take the next step? How do you get around this? It was a new ethos for the intelligence business. Suddenly there seemed to be no penalty for taking risks and making mistakes.

So he was going to give it a whack.

IT'S THE WILD WEST, was Tim's * first thought in the second week of July 2002 as he and seven other CIA operatives made the 10-hour overland drive from Turkey into Iraq in a convoy of Land Cruisers, Jeeps and a truck. Tim was in his late 30s, 6-foot-1 with black hair and a boyish, dashing, even movie-star-like smile. He was the deputy in the group but was going to be the designated CIA base chief for Sulaymaniyah in the mountainous region roughly midway between Baghdad and the Turkish border to the north. His base inside Iraq was some 125 miles from the Turkish border, several miles from the Iranian border. CIA headquarters had pulled him out of a station in the region for the assignment. Fluent in Arabic, Tim was a former Navy SEAL. Going back generations, his ancestors had been admirals, but he had left the Navy for what he felt would be the real action as a CIA case officer whose primary job was to recruit spies. In all, eight CIA men went in, four in Tim's team and four headed for a base closer to Turkey.

Winning permission from the Turks had required a half lie. The teams were essentially for counterterrorism, the CIA told the Turks, intending to focus on the threat represented by Ansar al-Islam, a radical terrorist group that violently opposed the secular Kurdish parties and allegedly ran poison laboratories in a village in Iraq close to the Iranian border. The group had links to al Qaeda.

* A nickname.

Tim's team set up its base camp nearby. They were a 45-second helicopter ride from the forward lines of Saddam's military units at his stronghold of Kirkuk.

Living conditions were spare. The team had no air support or medical evacuation capability. It would require 24-hour notice to get any of them out. Tim had a wife and small children, and it was not clear whether the team would be there weeks, months or longer.

Ansar al-Islam's alleged facility was at Sargat, some 25 miles away from the base. The U.S. military called it Khurmal, which was the largest city on the map next to Sargat. The CIA had long-standing but tense relations with the Kurdish group, the Patriotic Union of Kurdistan (PUK), which controlled the area. The PUK leader, Jalal Talabani, headed 1.2 million Kurds who were impoverished but educated and wanted Saddam out. The other Kurdish group, the Kurdistan Democratic Party (KDP), controlled the flow of trucks from Saddam's Iraq into Turkey and was making lots of money. The KDP was not altogether eager for regime change.

Talabani's PUK had ten prisoners from Sargat Tim's group could interview. In interrogations, three prisoners provided what looked like credible information of ties to bin Laden's al Qaeda network. It was verified that the three had been trained at camps in Afghanistan, establishing a pretty clear al Qaeda connection.

Tim put out word that his team would pay cash, a couple of hundred U.S. dollars, for poison samples from Sargat. They were deluged with a parade of locals carrying bottles, canteens, flasks, jars and test tubes. One fellow brought in a clear liquid that he said was highly toxic, but when he spilled it on himself, everyone laughed. Off you go, Tim said. They did not obtain a single sample of real poison.

Tim recruited the cook and his brother from the Sargat facility. The two paid agents provided schematics of every building at the compound that were later verified by overhead satellite imagery.

Tim's core mission was to begin to develop an operational base for covert action to overthrow Saddam. Saul, the Iraqi Operations chief, had issued the oral instructions: I want Saddam's military penetrated. I want the intel service penetrated. I want the security apparatus penetrated. I want tribal networks inside Iraq who will do things for us—paramilitary, sabotage, ground intelligence. Work the relationship with the Kurds. See if it is feasible to train and arm them so they can tie down Saddam's forces in the north.

On the ground in Iraq, there were serious impediments. The Turks insisted on providing man-to-man escorts. So Tim and the other three CIA men were stuck in a little house with four Turks who insisted they also live there. Otherwise they were going to escort Tim and his team out. To compound the problem the Turks hated the Kurds and vice versa. One day the Turks would vent about how sub-human the Kurds were and how they placed no value on human life. That night, the Kurds would say the same thing about the Turks. There was a fight on every issue. Tim said that they wanted to inter-view the prisoners taken by the PUK at once. No, absolutely not. Yes, okay. No, later. No, never. Okay. Everything was a bitter negotiation. The Turkish escorts were also spying on Tim and his team, who were working 18 hours a day. When not obstructing their work, the Turks smoked cigarettes and watched Turkish pornographic videos in their crowded rooms. The scene was half *Animal House* and half what Tim hoped was serious James Bond.

Several weeks into the ordeal, the Turks got a call from their boss, who reported that the Americans were going to bomb Sargat! Turkey would look complicit, the Kurds would go nuts, Turkey would be condemned on the world stage. The wild-rogue Americans are going to start a war. Everyone out! So the minders left, and Tim and the team could start working on regime change. They began inter-viewing refugees and defectors from Saddam's regime who had fled to the Kurdish area.

Two were of particular interest. One was an active-duty Iraqi military officer who had piloted Iraq's French Mirage jets. A second was a mechanic on the MiG-29s. He had extensive data on the col-lapse of the Iraqi air force, which could now essentially perform only kamikaze missions. Iraqi pilots were inventing illnesses on the days they were supposed to fly because they were terrified the inade-quately maintained planes would crash.

Tim's only communications was a secure link back to Saul at headquarters. You might stay there six months, Saul said. Now that you are in, let's not pull you out. The Turks refused to allow any resupply and the conditions were grim, uncertain electrical power and uncertain water pressure. The house was 6,000 feet up in the Kurdish mountains where winter would be bitter. It was a hostile and friendless setting all about—Turks, Kurds, Iranians and Iraqis nearby.

Tim kept probing the defectors, refugees and the PUK leadership, trying to gather intelligence and ascertain who might help and how. The PUK was a hotbed of jealousies and a bazaar of loyalties. They were working with the United States and selling to the Iranians. The highest bidder won. Tim was doling out lots of money and everyone was approaching him. One fellow said he was with Saddam's Special Security Organization but it turned out to be untrue. My brother's cousin, said another alleged defector, saw a mountain and underneath it are hidden all the weapons of mass destruction.

Tim's team established that the Iraqis were running agents into the Kurdish area to find the CIA men and kill them. One of his penetrations of Ansar al-Islam reported that the group was casing the region for Americans who could be ambushed on the roads.

Tim danced, threatened, questioned, begged, cajoled, lied, pushed and attempted to distinguish true from false. Meanwhile, the team was cranking out dozens and dozens of reports based on what they determined to be the best intelligence and transmitting them back to Saul. Tim had to work out a system of sorting. Who would he talk to? How would he spend his time? Who would he pay? How could he test the sources? He started using some Kurds as proxies to go out and meet with potential sources.

One day near the end of August, one of the Kurds who had verifiable gold-plated connections to the PUK inner circle approached Tim. "The PUK isn't treating me as well as they should be," he said. "I really want to help you guys."

Because of the individual's position, Tim invested some personal time. The stories of connections through family and marriage all checked out. A pretty complete picture emerged. Tim started working with the guy, listening, questioning.

"You know there is this large religious group," the man said, "and they're willing to help." It was a group that had been particularly repressed and savaged by Saddam throughout Iraq—north, south, west, along the borders, in Baghdad. The group was strange, fanatical even. But they were hungry for power. Saddam had imprisoned some of their important members. There was a leader who had enormous power and almost unbelievable influence over thousands of group members who had positions in the military and security services. They want payback big-time, the man said. They need assurances. They want guarantees.

It sounded preposterous to Tim. On one hand it smacked of the classic setup; on the other, it was an intelligence case officer's fantasy, a treasure. He had to go the next step, ridiculous as it might seem. "Okay," Tim explained, "here's the way we're going to do this. Before I meet with them tell me what they can do, give me a list of the names of their followers, where they are located."

The man promised. He would deliver. Tim would see. But several days later, near the end of August, the Turks slammed the hammer down hard. Tim's team and the other CIA team were yanked out.

As Tim careened down the treacherous mountains in his SUV on what passed for roads, he could not anticipate that he would soon be back and that he had already set in motion a chain of events that would eventually result in unprecedented and controversial intelligence reports that would wind up in the hands of George W. Bush in the Oval Office. And that the agent reports, dubbed with the CIA crypt DB/ROCKSTARS, would be the triggering event for Bush to start war.

14

A T 4:30 P.M. on Monday, August 5, Franks, carrying 110 slides of
Top Secret/Polo Step war planning, and Renuart, his Black Book
of Death in tow, arrived at the White House Situation Room to brief
the president and the NSC.

The agenda: 1. A very quick overview of the Generated Start
Plan, 2. Update on the Running Start, 3. Introduction of a new con-
cept called the Hybrid, a blending of the Generated and Running
Start, 4. Managing strategic risk, and 5. Iraq targeting primer.

Franks told them the Generated Start Plan was still the 90-45-
90, meaning it was still 90 days to get the forces there before offensive combat operations would begin. They had largely moved beyond
this Gulf War–style concept, but it remained the only executable plan
he had.

But with the alternative Running Start, Franks said, it would be
possible to have a new, more deliberate variation that he called 45-
90-90, largely because the military preparations already underway
would save them time. Transportation of forces and bombing would
begin immediately and simultaneously at the start of the 45 days to
shape the battlefield. Then it would take 90 days more for "decisive
offensive operations" and another 90 days for "complete regime destruction."

In an emergency, a no-notice Running Start would entail commencement of air operations at once via the Blue/White/Red options that gradually built to about 800 aircraft over a week and a half. With the current force posturing, Franks had cut this time in half from his first presentation to Rumsfeld in May. After 20 to 25 days, two brigades could seize the southern oil fields.

Franks turned to slide 16, his new Hybrid concept. It was an attempt to take the best from the Generated and Running Starts and factor in the preparatory actions he had taken up to that point. The Hybrid Plan shrank the front end dramatically, the time allotted to move forces before offensive military operations began.

The Hybrid had four phases:

Phase One: Five days to establish the air bridge, which included involuntarily enlisting all necessary U.S. commercial aircraft to augment the military airlift to the combat region. Then, 11 days to transport the initial forces.

Phase Two: 16 days of air attacks and Special Forces operations.

Phase Three: 125 days of decisive combat operations. At the beginning of the 125 days, they would try to get a division inside Iraq, and within a week another division of ground forces.

Phase Four: Stability operations of unknown duration.

Rumsfeld and Franks made it clear that the beginning of the 11-day force deployment was not a point of no return, but that the flow would be seen and known, and could trigger a move by Saddam.

Displaying another slide, Franks described the advantages of the Hybrid concept. Time could be optimized, the quicker force posturing would improve short-term capabilities in the region, and the increased pressure on the Iraqi regime could enhance diplomacy, Franks said.

So the Hybrid was a 5-11-16-125-day plan. Renuart noticed that Bush's body language, the nods and the forward-leaning attentiveness, suggested he was pleased.

"I like the concept," Bush said.

"Best-seller," Renuart wrote in the Black Book of Death.

We need to have humanitarian assistance on the battlefield from day one, the president said.

Slide 35 was titled, "Examining Things That Could Go Wrong: Strategic Risks." One was an early missile attack by Saddam on Kuwait. The way to mitigate that was to make sure that Kuwait had some counter-ballistic-missile capability, such as the Patriot missiles. More would have to be done to protect Israel.

Franks listed as another risk the possibility of early success. Suppose Saddam walked away or fled, and hundreds of thousands of U.S. troops were flowing into the area? Did they have a legal basis to occupy the country? What if Saddam folded and retreated with his Republican Guard to Baghdad and "circled the wagons"?

Bush once again expressed particular concern about this possibility. Baghdad had more than 5 million people.

Franks reminded them that he had briefed the president three times already on this and was still working the problem.

Yeah, the president said, I know, but some of our guys are still concerned.

Also under "Managing Strategic Risk": What could Saddam do to spoil their preparation? One was to interrupt the oil flow to Iraq's neighbors, especially Turkey, Syria and Jordan.

Powell agreed to address this and talk to the Saudis about providing oil, particularly to Jordan.

Other unanswered questions included: What if Syria attacks Israel? What if Iraq just sort of implodes and someone kills Saddam? What would the U.S. do?

It was pretty much agreed that the U.S. would still have to enter Iraq with the military because they would not know who the new Iraqi leader might be. Could they trust someone new? Probably not. Did they want to deal with that chaos? They would have to continue the flow of forces and put a military force in to maintain stability.

Another question was put on the table: When should they go to Turkey to seek a firm commitment that some U.S. forces could transit through?

We're late already, Franks said. We need to have Turkey commit, but with their national elections coming up, the Turks would not make a decision. Should we go in and ask anyway and risk getting a no? The decision was put off.

Discussion turned to the Phase Four stability operations after combat was completed, not the strategy or the philosophy of occupying a post-Saddam Iraq, but the numbers of troops it would take. Franks noted that if the military attack was carried out, they might have up to 265,000 troops in the country. Over time he would want to draw that down to about 50,000. That would be governed by events in Iraq but he anticipated the drawdown would occur over 18 months after the end of combat.

Lastly, Franks provided an "Iraq Targeting Primer." The imperatives included: 1. The significance of the target, 2. A description of the target and any critical elements, 3. If there was a collateral damage issue in which civilians might be killed, 4. What kind of weapon might be used.

Using an overhead satellite photo of the Baath Party headquarters in Baghdad as an example, he explained: 1. Its significance was that it was their headquarters and Saddam used the party as one instrument of control, 2. The headquarters is a multistory building with extensive communications and security, 3. There is a residential facility nearby that could be damaged, 4. Any number of weapons could be used, including cruise missiles and laser-guided bombs.

POWELL WAS VERY MUCH on edge. The discussions of Iraq were increasingly focused on military planning, a continuing, escalating series of ideas, concepts, detailed sequences, scenarios and worries. The packet of Top Secret slides grew with each of Rumsfeld's and Franks's briefings. Like a proctor at a boys' prep school, Rumsfeld handed out the packets of slides or multicolored sheets and collected them afterward. The president's packet often contained more backup material. Rumsfeld ordered those present not to take notes. He took all the copies back to the Pentagon and had his military assistant lock them in a safe in the defense secretary's suite of offices.

For the first 16 months of the administration, Powell had been "in the refrigerator" or worse, as he and Armitage called his frequent isolation. It gnawed at him when stories appeared in the press suggesting that he was going to resign, what he privately called the "Powell's-on-his-way-out-again mode." Armitage had been pushing hard for Powell to request private time with the president to build a personal relationship. Rumsfeld regularly had such sessions.

Several months earlier, Powell had asked for and received private time with Bush, though Rice sat in on the 20- to 30-minute Oval Office sessions. On one occasion the president invited Powell in alone and the two had about 30 minutes together. "I think we're really making some headway in the relationship," Powell later reported to Armitage. "I know we really connected."

In the days before the latest Franks briefing unveiling the Hybrid concept, Powell had been in Asia making his rounds. He could almost hear the war tom-toms across the ocean. A great deal of momentum was now building. On the long trip back he had started to collect his thoughts on Iraq. Brent Scowcroft, who had been national security adviser to Bush's father during the Gulf War, had declared on a Sunday morning talk show that an attack on Iraq could turn the entire Middle East into a "cauldron and thus destroy the war on terrorism."

Powell basically agreed with that blunt warning. He realized that he had not laid out his own analysis to the president directly and forcefully. And at least he owed Bush his understanding and his views on all the possible consequences of war.

Powell talked with Rice. It was impossible to have a complete policy discussion about Iraq during a meeting that was essentially a military briefing, he said. "I really need to have some private time with him to go over some issues that I don't think he's gone over with anyone yet," he insisted.

Bush invited Powell and Rice to the residence the evening of Franks's August 5 Hybrid briefing. The meeting expanded to include dinner in the family dining room and then continued in the president's office in the residence.

Powell's notes filled three or four pages. War could destabilize friendly regimes in Saudi Arabia, Egypt and Jordan, he said. It could divert energy from almost everything else, not just the war on terrorism, and dramatically affect the supply and price of oil.

What of the image of an American general running an Arab country, a General MacArthur in Baghdad? Powell asked. How long would it be? No one could know. How would success be defined? War would take down Saddam and "You will become the government until you get a new government."

By the time they were in Bush's office, Powell was on a roll.

"You are going to be the proud owner of 25 million people," he told the president. "You will own all their hopes, aspirations and problems. You'll own it all." Privately, Powell and Armitage called this the Pottery Barn rule: You break it, you own it.

"It's going to suck the oxygen out of everything," the secretary continued. So as not to sidestep the politics of it, he added, *"This will become the first term."* The clear implication was: Did the president want to be defined this way? Did he want to run for reelection on an Iraq war?

Powell thought he was scoring. Iraq has a history that is quite complex, he said. The Iraqis have never had a democracy. "So you need to understand that this is not going to be a walk in the woods."

"It's nice to say we can do it unilaterally, except you can't," he said. The geography was formidable. General Franks had said it was imperative that he have access to bases and facilities from allies in the region and beyond. Powell was unusually blunt. "If you think it's just a matter of picking up the phone and blowing a whistle and it goes—no, you need allies, you need access, you need what-not. You need to understand not just a military timeline but the other things that are going to be facing you." He did not feel the downsides had been brought out in sufficient, gory detail.

Saddam was crazy and in a last desperate stand he might unleash weapons of mass destruction. Worse, the U.S., in perhaps the largest manhunt in history, had not found Osama bin Laden. Saddam has more at his disposal, an entire state. They did not need another possibly fruitless, ongoing manhunt. On top of all this, Powell said, such a war would tie down most of the American army.

The president listened, asked some questions but did not push back that much. Finally he looked at Powell. "What should I do? What else can I do?"

Powell realized he needed to offer a solution. "You can still make a pitch for a coalition or U.N. action to do what needs to be done," he said. The U.N. was only one way, but some way had to be found to recruit allies, to internationalize the problem.

Bush said he had loved building an international coalition for the Afghanistan war. What would the Russians or the French do?

Powell said he thought the U.S. could bring most countries along. There was an additional consideration, he said. "If you take it to the U.N., you've got to recognize that they might be able to solve it. In which case there's no war. That could mean a solution that is not as clean as just going in and taking the guy out." In needing and seeking international cover, Powell said, "The international cover could also result in a different outcome." Though the conversation was tense several times, Powell felt that he had left nothing unsaid. There were no histrionics. The president thanked him after two hours, an extraordinary amount of time for Powell without static from Cheney and Rumsfeld.

Rice thought the evening's headline was, "Powell Makes Case for Coalition as Only Way to Assure Success."

In fact Powell had been trying to say more, to sound a warning that too much could go wrong. The Reluctant Warrior was urging restraint, but he had not tossed his heart on the table. He had not said, Don't do it. Taken together the points of his argument could have been mustered to reach that conclusion. Powell half felt that, but he had learned during 35 years in the Army, and elsewhere, that he had to play to the boss and talk about method. It was paramount to talk only within the confines of the preliminary goals set by the boss. Perhaps he had been too timid.

"That was terrific," Rice told him the next day in a phone call. "And we need to do more of those."

Andy Card called Powell and asked him to come over and go through the whole case, notes and all.

Powell felt he had hit a home run. But he was also not sure that the president had fully taken aboard the meaning, the consequences of going to war. Sixteen months later in the office where Powell had made his case, I asked the president about Powell's argument that a military solution would mean he would own Iraq.

"He sure did," Bush replied. "He did say that."

"Your reaction?" I asked, expecting him to articulate an understanding of the case against war.

"And my reaction to that is, is that my job is to secure America," the president said. "And that I also believe that freedom is something people long for. And that if given a chance, the Iraqis over time would seize the moment. My frame of mind is focused on what I told you—the solemn duty to protect America."

I sat there somewhat nonplussed as the president discussed the issues of freedom and security, which were very much beside the points Powell had made. "And he's talking tactics though," I began to ask.

"That's his job," Bush answered, "to be tactical. My job is to be strategic. Basically what he was saying was, was that if in fact Saddam is toppled by military [invasion], we better have a strong understanding about what it's going to take to rebuild Iraq."

That was certainly true, and it was part of Powell's message, but as I listened I glimpsed what Powell had apparently seen—uncertainty that the president fully grasped the potential consequences. Events had rendered a number of Powell's concerns moot by December 2003 when I interviewed the president—Egypt, Jordan and Saudi Arabia appeared stable, oil prices hadn't spiked, and the U.S. had found allies for basing in the region. But Powell was right that the war would dominate Bush's presidency and it was still unclear when or if Iraq could become a stable democracy and U.S. troops could come home. Those facts were very much a part of the president's daily business 16 months after Powell had raised them.

Of the August 2002 period, the president also said, "We had yet to develop our diplomatic strategy. There were certain people in the administration that were hopeful we could solve this diplomatically. And there were some that basically said we can't solve it diplomatically. Therefore let's be realistic.

"Colin felt very strongly that the United Nations was the route to go. And some in the administration had seen how feckless the United Nations had been on this issue and were uncertain as to whether or not the United Nations would be able to get it done." He acknowledged that one of those was the vice president.

THE DAY AFTER Bush's dinner with Powell and Rice, August 6, Franks issued an order to his commanders to make the transition from the Running Start to their new best-seller—the Hybrid concept—a faster war.

That afternoon, the president left for his Crawford ranch for nearly a month-long vacation.

15

———

O N WEDNESDAY, AUGUST 14, Rice chaired a principals meeting without the president, who was in Crawford. They had a working draft of a National Security Presidential Directive, or NSPD, that had been approved by the deputies. It was entitled, "Iraq: Goals, Objectives and Strategy."

With the president on vacation, now was the time for the principals to review the directive line-by-line and make changes so they would have a full consensus to present the president for signature. An NSPD is not the Ten Commandments, though Rice felt it was a good way to make sure everyone was operating with the same instructions.

They met at 8 A.M. and worked for some time, reviewing it line-by-line. The Top Secret document they agreed on stated:

"U.S. goal: Free Iraq in order to eliminate Iraqi weapons of mass destruction, their means of delivery and associated programs, to prevent Iraq from breaking out of containment and becoming a more dangerous threat to the region and beyond.

"End Iraqi threats to its neighbors, to stop the Iraqi government's tyrannizing of its own population, to cut Iraqi links to and sponsorship of international terrorism, to maintain Iraq's unity and territorial integrity. And liberate the Iraqi people from tyranny, and assist them in creating a society based on moderation, pluralism and democracy."

Under the next section, the document listed: "Objectives: To conduct policy in a fashion that minimizes the chance of a WMD attack against the United States, U.S. field forces, our allies and friends. To minimize the danger of regional instabilities. To deter Iran and Syria from helping Iraq. And to minimize disruption in international oil markets."

It stated that the elements of the strategy would include "employing all instruments of national power to free Iraq," including diplomacy, the military, the CIA and economic sanctions.

In seeking regime change the U.S. would be "pursuing our goals and objectives with a coalition of committed countries, if possible, but acting alone if necessary."

Going back decades, U.S. presidents had routinely adopted such an approach in securing national security interests, a kind of coalition-if-possible-alone-if-necessary strategy. Rarely, however, had there been such deep division within a national security team as between Cheney and Powell. Each had a fundamentally different definition of what was possible, and what was necessary.

Another element of the strategy was "to work with the Iraqi opposition to demonstrate that we are liberating, not invading, Iraq, and give the opposition a role in building a pluralistic and democratic Iraq, including the preparation of a new constitution." A further objective was "to establish a broad-based democratic government that would adhere to international law and respect international norms, that would not threaten its neighbors, that would respect the basic rights of all Iraqis, including women and minorities, that would adhere to the rule of law, including freedom of speech and worship."

The final element of the strategy was "to demonstrate that the United States is prepared to play a sustained role in the reconstruction of a post-Saddam Iraq with contributions from and participation by the international community, that rapidly starts the country's reconstruction, that preserves but reforms the current Iraqi bureau-cracy and reforms the Iraqi military and security institutions."

Preserving something can be very different from reforming it. What to keep? What to change? There was a lot of hope that the Iraqis wanted democracy and change. But since no one knew what they might find in Iraq after Saddam, they included both notions.

Powell then said they had to think about how to build a coali-tion, get some kind of international cover at least. The Brits would be with us, he said, but their support could falter in the absence of some international or United Nations–sanctioned coalition. The rest of Europe was unsure, as were U.S. friends in the Middle East.

The first high-profile opportunity for the president to address the Iraq situation formally was a scheduled speech at the U.N. Gen-eral Assembly in less than a month, September 12. Gerson had pro-vided the president an outline for a speech about American values, democracy and human assistance programs—the softer side of Bush's agenda. But Iraq had become Topic A in Washington and the country. Every living former national security adviser or former sec-retary of state who could lift pen to paper or type on a keyboard had weighed in with ideas and critiques.

Powell said that the president had to speak at the U.N. about Iraq. "I can't imagine him going there and not speaking about this," he said.

Rice, who had not wanted a tough speech about Iraq at the U.N., now agreed. In the atmosphere of continuing public and media debate and speculation, to refrain from addressing Iraq might sug-gest that the president was not serious about the threat, or that he was operating in total secrecy. And Bush liked to provide public ex-planations, at least in a general sense, and make news about his own policies.

Powell believed he had Cheney boxed in, and to a lesser extent Rumsfeld. He argued that even if anyone felt that war was the only solution, they could not get to war without first trying a diplomatic solution. It was the absolutely necessary first step. Without the attempt, nobody would be with them—no Brits, no bases, no access or overflight agreements, European and Middle East allies all on the other side. Powell believed he had them, although he sensed that Cheney was "terrified" because once the diplomatic road was opened up, it might work. But the logic of trying was impeccable, Powell believed. *Possibility had now become necessity.*

Cheney harangued about the United Nations. Going to the U.N. would invite a never-ending process of debate, compromise and delay. Words not action.

Powell listened, almost chuckling to himself. Cheney so much did not want to go down that road, so wished to shut it down, but he could not.

"I think the speech at the U.N. ought to be about Iraq," the vice president said, but with one additional element. The U.N. itself ought to be made the issue since it had failed for more than a decade, unable and unwilling to enforce its own resolutions that directed Saddam to destroy his weapons of mass destruction and to permit weapons inspections inside Iraq. The U.N. had to be challenged. "Go tell them it's not about us. It's about you. You are not important." The U.N. was running the risk of becoming irrelevant and a mockery, he said.

Rice liked that. Put the monkey on the U.N.'s back. It had become too much like the post–World War I League of Nations—a debating society with no teeth.

In short order all the principals agreed that they recommend that the president speak about Iraq at the U.N. Certainly he should not ask for a declaration of war. That was quickly off the table, but there was not agreement about what he should say.

LATER THAT DAY, August 14, Franks and Renuart took the now well-worn path to Rumsfeld's office. The purpose was to give a planning update on the Hybrid option, but in fact the secretary wanted to talk about targeting. He was fascinated with the process, eager to understand the crucial relationship between the military value of a target, and the willingness or unwillingness to accept collateral damage to civilians.

Renuart, the air war expert, did a good deal of the talking. In basic terms, each possible target gets an intelligence assessment of its operational value, he said. For example, an Iraqi communications facility would have three uses: as a hub for passing information to Iraqi military forces in the field; for broadcasting propaganda and information to the world; and for linking with worldwide Iraqi embassies where their intelligence agents operated. So it would be an obvious target. But the cost of striking the target would include an assessment of the number of Iraqi civilians who work there. Are they truly civilians or are they tied to some regime structure? What about the daily routines? Not as many civilians would be there at night.

Well, Rumsfeld asked, how do you know how many people are in that building?

Franks and Renuart suggested a hypothetical case where they had overhead imagery of a 10-story building and its parking lot. The analysis suggested that there were about 10 offices per floor, three people to an office, so on any given day during normal business hours, there would be about 300 people. At night, it might be down to caretaker status with only about 50 or less—suggesting a night strike if it was the facility, and not the personnel, they were targeting.

In all, there were at this point some 130 potential targets that might have high collateral damage, which was defined as possibly killing 30 or more civilians.

How sure are we of the intelligence and the analysis? Rumsfeld asked.

The answer was that it varied.

Go back and review and reassess, Rumsfeld directed. He wanted to minimize collateral damage. If it was unavoidable, he wanted them going in with their eyes open.

Franks attempted to explain that it was an ongoing process of refinement, and that the number of high collateral damage targets would go down.

Rumsfeld wanted a complete review—everything put under the microscope again—"refreshed," as he called it.

To destroy the 4,000 possible targets, the generals explained, would require some 12,000 to 13,000 separate weapons. A large building or complex might have 4 to 12 individual "aim points" for individual weapons—bombs or missiles.

Rumsfeld wanted them to work with the intelligence people to make sure collection and analysis of targets were made better and better. In the background was the disaster during the 1999 Kosovo war when the Chinese embassy in Belgrade was bombed because someone at the CIA had an old map. Franks and Renuart went on briefing him for hours.

FROM HIS OFFICE ON 17th Street in downtown Washington, three blocks from the White House, Brent Scowcroft, President George H. W. Bush's national security adviser and Rice's boss when she had been an NSC staffer, was getting bits of intelligence about the Iraq debate inside the administration. Though he was working as a private consultant, few outsiders were as close to the major players in the current Bush administration as Scowcroft.

Scowcroft was troubled because he thought the real threat to the United States was not from Saddam but from al Qaeda. He was baffled that Cheney and Rumsfeld were so focused on Saddam. He had remarked, "The only thing that Osama and Saddam Hussein have in common is they hate the United States. Saddam is an anti-clerical socialist. With all of Saddam's capabilities there are very few terrorist footprints." An associate suggested he write an op-ed piece.

Scowcroft wrote that Saddam's vision of dominating the region was contrary to U.S. interests, but went on to say, "There is scant evidence to tie Saddam to terrorist organizations, and even less to the September 11 attacks. Indeed, Saddam's goals have little in common with the terrorists who threaten us, and there is little incentive for him to make common cause with them.

"There is virtual consensus in the world against an attack on

Iraq at this time," he warned. "So long as that sentiment persists, it would require the U.S. to pursue a virtual go-it-alone strategy against Iraq, making any military operations correspondingly more difficult and expensive." He recommended that Bush should try to get the U.N. monitoring teams back in for rigorous, no-notice inspections.

No one was as close to Bush senior as companion, loyalist and foreign policy soul mate. Scowcroft had coauthored the former president's memoirs. He sent him an advance copy of the article and received no reaction. That meant it was okay.

The Wall Street Journal ran his article on August 15 under the provocative headline, "Don't Attack Saddam."

Scowcroft received two important calls.

"Thanks," said Powell, "you gave me some running room." Scowcroft knew that Powell was careful not to stir up the right-wing Republicans, who didn't think he was a Republican anyway. So Powell always had to lean forward on Iraq without supporting war. Now he was making his move, hoping to be careful yet persuasive. "This is my opportunity," the secretary of state confided, "and I've got to be organized."

Rice also phoned Scowcroft and they had sharp words. Scowcroft's pronouncement made it look as if the president's father had weighed in. At minimum it was a slap at the president.

Scowcroft replied that the piece was no different than what he had said on television 10 days before and no one had complained. "I don't want to break with the administration," he said, apologizing if it had had the impact she described.

There was a deeper concern. Scowcroft realized that Bush senior did not want to leave the impression with the public or with his son that he was looking over his shoulder. It could demean the son, reduce public respect and support, even undermine the presidency. It was also very personal, as Scowcroft well knew.

Neither Scowcroft nor Bush senior wanted to injure the son's self-confidence. So Scowcroft largely shut up in public, though he did not change his view.

• • •

ON THE SECOND FRIDAY of his Crawford vacation, August 16, the president met with the NSC via secure video. The sole purpose was for Powell to make his pitch about going to the U.N. Powell repeated all his arguments.

The president asked for comments from each of the principals. There was support for giving the U.N. a shot, at least in the upcoming speech, even from Cheney.

Fine, Bush finally said, approving the general idea of a speech to the U.N. about Iraq. It should not be too shrill, he cautioned them, or require so much of Iraq that it would look as if they were not serious.

Just before noon, the president appeared at the Crawford Community Center and answered several questions from reporters. He said that he was "aware that some very intelligent people are expressing their opinions about Saddam Hussein and Iraq. I listen carefully to what they have to say." He also said carefully that Saddam "desires weapons of mass destruction," making no suggestion that he possessed them.

The president called Gerson, with Rice on the line, about the U.N. speech. "We're going to do something a little different," Bush instructed. "We're going to tell the U.N. that it's going to confront this problem or it's going to condemn itself to irrelevance, okay?"

Gerson went to work.

POWELL HAD LEFT the secure video NSC meeting feeling they had a deal. He had them—at least Cheney and Rumsfeld, and perhaps even the president. He went to the Hamptons on Long Island, New York, for a vacation. There he met privately with British Foreign Secretary Jack Straw, who had wanted to come over for a day since Iraq was heating up. In Blair's conversations with Bush, it was increasingly clear to the prime minister how committed Bush was to action. Straw had some of the same concerns as Powell. His message was in essence, If you are really thinking about war and you want us Brits to be a player, we cannot be unless you go to the United Nations.

Powell knew this would add to the pressure on Bush, who absolutely had to have Blair on board.

ON AUGUST 20, I interviewed the president in Crawford for two hours and 25 minutes about the response to 9/11 and the war in Afghanistan for *Bush at War*. He talked in sweeping, even grandiose terms about remaking the world. "I will seize the opportunity to achieve big goals," he said. And each move had to fit in the overall purpose of improving the world, making it peaceful, he maintained. "You see it's like Iraq," he volunteered. "Just as an aside—and we'll see whether this bears out—clearly there will be a strategic implication to a regime change in Iraq, if we go forward. But there's something beneath that, as far as I'm concerned, and that is, there is immense suffering." Saddam was starving his people in the outlying Shiite areas, he said. "There is a human condition that we must worry about. As we think through Iraq, we may or may not attack. I have no idea, yet. But it will be for the objective of making the world more peaceful." He did not mention weapons of mass destruction, or any threat Saddam posed to the United States.

"Well, we're never going to get people all in agreement about force and use of force," he said, strongly suggesting that an international coalition or the U.N. was unlikely to solve the rogue-state problem. "But action, confident action that will yield positive results provides kind of a slipstream into which reluctant nations and leaders can get behind and show themselves that there has been—you know, something positive has happened toward peace."

The president gave me a tour of his ranch in his pickup. As we took a walk he brought up Iraq. I had no idea at that time about the extent of secret military planning, the briefings and the various options—Generated Start, Running Start, Hybrid—but he did say that he had not seen a successful military plan for Iraq, and we discussed the importance of patience. The next day he told reporters he was a "patient man" who would carefully weigh the options of achieving regime change in Iraq.

CHENEY SAW HE WAS rapidly losing ground. Talk of the U.N., diplomacy and now patience was wrong in his view. Nothing could more effectively slow down the march to war—a war he deemed necessary. It was the only way. His former colleagues from the Ford and Bush senior administrations were weighing in with a blizzard of commentary—Scowcroft with his cautionary, antiwar message, former Secretary of State James Baker, who urged that unilateral action be avoided. Henry Kissinger, dean of realpolitik foreign policy, had on August 12 published a long, somewhat convoluted piece in *The Washington Post* supporting Bush for forcing the issue of Saddam to a head, but warning about the importance of building support from the public and the world.

The New York Times had made the Scowcroft and Kissinger positions the lead article on their front page on August 16: "Top Republicans Break with Bush on Iraq Strategy." It was a misinterpretation of Kissinger's remarks, which more or less backed Bush. The *Times* eventually ran a correction, but Cheney and his deputy, Scooter Libby, found the article extremely aggravating. The correction would never catch up with the front page headline, and Scowcroft's dissent was indisputable and more potent. It looked as if the march to war was put off.

Cheney decided that everyone was offering an opinion except the administration. There was no stated administration position and he wanted to put one out, make a big speech if necessary. It was highly unusual for the vice president to speak on such a major issue before the president, who was going to address the U.N. on Iraq on September 12. But Cheney couldn't wait. Nature and Washington policy debates abhor a vacuum. He was not going to cede the field to Scowcroft, Baker, a misinterpreted Kissinger—or Powell. He spoke privately with the president, who gave his okay without reviewing the details of what Cheney might say.

At an NSC meeting, Cheney said to the president, "Well, I'm going to give that speech."

"Don't get me in trouble," Bush half-joked.

Trouble is what Cheney had in mind.

"Cheney Says Peril of a Nuclear Iraq Justifies Attack," read the headline in *The New York Times* on the morning of August 27. Powell was dumbfounded. The vice president had delivered a hard-line address to the Veterans of Foreign Wars convention in Nashville and basically called weapons inspections futile. "A return of inspectors would provide no assurance whatsoever of his compliance with U.N. resolutions," Cheney had said of Saddam. "On the contrary, there is a great danger that it would provide false comfort that Saddam was somehow 'back in the box.' "

The vice president also issued his own personal National Intelligence Estimate of Saddam: "Simply stated, there is no doubt that Saddam Hussein now has weapons of mass destruction [and] there is no doubt that he is amassing them to use against our friends, against our allies and against us." Ten days earlier the president himself had said only that Saddam "desires" these weapons. Neither Bush nor the CIA had made any assertion comparable to Cheney's.

Cheney also said that these weapons in the hands of a "murderous dictator" are "as great a threat as can be imagined. The risks of inaction are far greater than the risk of action."

These remarks, just short of a declaration of war, were widely interpreted as administration policy. Powell was astonished. It was a preemptive attack on what the president had agreed to 10 days earlier. Cheney's speech blew it all up. Now Powell felt boxed in. To add to his problem, the BBC started releasing excerpts of an interview Powell had given before Cheney's speech asserting, "The president has been clear that he believes weapons inspectors should return." Stories began appearing that Powell was contradicting Cheney. He was accused of disloyalty, and he counted seven editorials calling for his resignation or implying he should quit. How can I be disloyal, he wondered, when I'm giving the president's stated position?

Ken Adelman, a Cheney friend and former assistant to Rumsfeld at Defense in the 1970s, thought Bush was really delaying too long in deposing Saddam. Two days after Cheney's speech, Adelman weighed in with a blistering op-ed piece in *The Wall Street Journal*. Saddam was a bigger threat than al Qaeda, he wrote, because he had a country, billions in oil revenue, an army and "scores of scientific laboratories and myriad manufacturing plants cranking out weapons of mass destruction."

The problem could not be solved with new U.N. inspections, Adelman wrote. "Every day Mr. Bush holds off liberating Iraq is another day endangering America. Posing as a 'patient man,' he risks a catastrophic attack. Should that attack occur and be traced back to an Iraqi WMD facility, this president would be relegated to the ash heap of history."

It was strong stuff. Cheney did not communicate directly with Adelman on such matters but he passed word to a mutual friend, who called Adelman right after his article appeared to report the vice president's reaction. "Ken has been extremely helpful in all this," the friend quoted Cheney as saying, "and I really appreciate what he has done and it's been great."

A day later, August 29, Cheney spoke to the Veterans of the Korean War in San Antonio. It was the same speech with significant differences. He dropped his assertion that weapons inspections might provide "false comfort," and watered down his criticism, saying that "inspections are not an end in themselves."

Instead of asserting as he had in the first version of the speech that, "We now know that Saddam has resumed his efforts to acquire nuclear weapons," he said simply that Saddam was pursing "an aggressive nuclear weapons program." Some other language was moderated, by eliminating a "very" for example, and about eight paragraphs were removed from the speech.

More than a year later, President Bush referred to this time as "the miserable month of August." He explained, "I remember coming out of August of '02. It was 'the march to war.' All of us—we were really on the defensive. Because we weren't around each other." He was in Texas and the other principals were scattered at various vacation spots. "Every word was picked apart. Cheney gave a speech to the VFW, something I think when you look back on it, when historians look back on it, they're going to wonder what the big deal was. But it created a big furor."

"Powell was upset," I said.

"No," the president said, "I don't know about that. How do I know [he was] upset? I was in Crawford."

16

THE PRESIDENT RETURNED from Crawford to the White House on Sunday, September 1. An unhappy Powell had requested a private meeting with Bush and the next day, Labor Day, he came to the White House for lunch. Rice, as usual, joined them.

Was it not the president's position that the weapons inspectors should go back into Iraq? the secretary asked.

It was, Bush said. Though he was skeptical that inspections would work, he reaffirmed his commitment to go to the U.N. to ask for support. In a practical sense that meant asking for a new resolution. Satisfied, Powell left to attend a conference in South Africa. Cheney's intervention via the two VFW speeches seemed to have been neutralized for the moment.

The president told the principals he wanted to go to Congress to seek a resolution supporting military action against Saddam. Though White House lawyers had told him they believed he had the constitutional authority as commander in chief to act alone, the president wanted congressional authority.

Having spent the better part of a month trying to sort out the international and United Nations issues, which were still not settled, Bush's team only required one principals meeting to figure out the domestic politics. In the discussion, there was a lot of deference to Cheney, who had served in Congress and was president of the Senate.

For the 1991 Gulf War, Bush's father had gone first to the United Nations to get a resolution to use force. Just 45 days before the war it had passed 12 to 2, with Yemen and Cuba voting against and China abstaining. Then only three days before the war, Congress passed its own resolution by a close 52 to 47 vote in the Senate, 250 to 183 in the House.

This time, since it was unclear what role the U.N. would have, if any, Cheney proposed going to the Congress first. In an election year with all the House seats and one-third of the Senate up, he said it was simple. The president should demand quick passage of a resolution so voters would know before the election where every congressman and senator stood on Saddam Hussein and his dangerous regime.

Rice strongly agreed. The politics on the Hill were ripe and mainstream Democrats she knew seemed ready to support a resolution, so the president had maximum leverage. A congressional resolution would strengthen their hand at the U.N. and put the U.S. in the position of speaking with one voice. Going to Congress first seemed self-evident, she said, adding, "How much debate do you need?"

AT NOON ON SEPTEMBER 3, the Tuesday after Labor Day when business in Washington officially resumes, Card gathered a group of senior staffers including Rice, Hadley, Scooter Libby, Dan Bartlett and several others in the Situation Room. It was called the "White House Iraq Coordination Meeting," which would later change to White House Iraq Group, or WHIG. Among those attending was White House legislative affairs director Nick Calio, a well-dressed, slightly graying 49-year-old lawyer and lobbyist whose serious face belies a cheery good salesman. Calio had held the same job for Bush's father in 1992–93—essentially the president's personal lobbyist on Capitol Hill. The selling of regime change in Iraq was about to begin.

Card said the game plan was to ask Congress to vote on a formal resolution authorizing military force in Iraq before the midterm elections. The administration had pretty much blown August. He made clear that September and October were going to be organized, coordinated and focused.

"The president understands the weight of this very large decision," Card said of the prospect of forcing regime change and even starting a war with Iraq. "He wants to involve Congress because he wants more moral authority in moving forward."

Calio had first gotten wind of this back in late May or early June when Rice asked him to carefully feel out some key members of Congress and take their temperature on Iraq. He had researched how members had voted on Iraq issues going back to the 1991 Gulf War resolution. The president's instructions now in the fall were more direct: "Nicky, get the votes."

Judging from Bush's side comments and body language, Calio assumed that the question on Iraq was not if but when there would be a war.

The next morning, September 4, Bush invited 18 key Senate and House members to the White House.

"Iraq is on a lot of people's minds," the president said, "because [Saddam] is a serious threat to the United States and his neighbors and his own citizens." He reminded the lawmakers that Congress had decided in 1998 by an overwhelming vote that regime change was necessary. "My administration embraces that policy even more so in light of 9/11. So I want to have a discussion, want stimulated debate in America through Congress." Adopting Cheney's line, he added, "Doing nothing is not an option.

"Now there are disagreements. When the decision is made, we'll come to Congress for a resolution. I expect Congress to be part of any decision." He said he wanted to hear their suggestions and thoughts and he believed he could answer any reservations they might have.

Democratic Senate Majority Leader Tom Daschle, whose position made him perhaps the most likely important opposition voice, asked several questions about the president's case for war. What's new? Where's the tangible evidence? To whom do we turn logistically without support from the region? "All these questions, if we could address would go a long way," Daschle said.

House Minority Leader Dick Gephardt, the Missouri Democrat, said, "I appreciate your outline, agree with your concern about Saddam Hussein." He added that the American people had to be told about the danger to them. "It's about weapons of mass destruction getting in the wrong hands. They don't see it. We have to do everything in our power to keep WMD from going off. We need to make it graphic."

Gephardt said he and Daschle had talked about this and the president needed to get aggressively engaged if he wanted a resolution to pass.

"Are you saying Nick Calio's falling down on the job?" Bush asked in jest.

Discussion turned to the first President Bush's congressional resolution on the 1991 Gulf War. Calio hoped to use the 1991 resolution as a model.

Senator Don Nickles, the Republican whip, asked, "Mr. President, if we adjourn on October 11 this year, we have five weeks—do you want us to vote before we leave?"

"Yes!" Bush responded, "I want you to have a debate. The issue isn't going away, you can't let it linger."

Senator Carl Levin, Democrat of Michigan and chairman of the Armed Services Committee, asked if Saddam Hussein was deterrable, containable. "The military has deep concerns," he said, suggesting lots of senior officers were hesitant.

"It would be nice if they expressed their reservations to the president rather than just someone in the Senate," Bush said, looking angry.

That afternoon, Rumsfeld briefed senators on Iraq in a classified, closed-door session which over two-thirds of the members attended—an unusually high turnout. Word quickly got back to Calio that it had not gone well, and that Senate Republican Leader Trent Lott was not happy.

Calio ran his 25-person shop in part like an intelligence agency. His executive assistant filed a lengthy "Night Note" summarizing the day's reports from staff who monitored everything on the Hill, including closed-door briefings.

In the "Night Note for September 4," Christine M. Ciccone, a young lawyer who covered the Senate for Calio, reported on Rumsfeld's one-and-a-half-hour briefing. "You have already heard it was a disaster and Lott views it as having destroyed all of the goodwill and groundwork that the president accomplished during his meeting this morning. I found myself struggling to keep from laughing out loud at times, especially when Sec. Rumsfeld became a caricature of himself with the 'we know what we know, we know there are things we do not know, and we know there are things we know we don't know we don't know.' "

Senators had expected that the briefing, coming on the heels of the president's meeting that morning, would begin the process of making the administration's case, she reported. "Instead, Secretary Rumsfeld was not prepared to discuss Iraq issues, was unwilling to share even the most basic of intelligence information, and wasn't having a good day. . . . There is a lot of cleanup work to do here."

Senator Dianne Feinstein, the California Democrat who was on the Senate Intelligence Committee, said at the session that she had worked over the congressional recess on the intelligence issues and had received numerous briefings. "She strongly believes from those briefings," Ciccone reported, "there is no new evidence of Saddam having nuclear devices, and her conclusion is there is no imminent threat." According to the Note, Feinstein "does not believe we are prepared to kill innocent people which will be impossible to avoid because we will be going from mosque to mosque looking for the terrorists, etc."

The fallout was potentially even worse. Ciccone reported that Senators Patty Murray, Democrat of Washington, and Kay Bailey Hutchison, a Texas Republican, had waited for Feinstein at the door and they had left together, and that Kent Conrad, a North Dakota Democrat, had stood and agreed with everything Feinstein had said. Senator Bob Graham, the Florida Democrat and the Intelligence Committee chairman, told *The Washington Post,* "I did not receive any new information." And Nickles, the Republican whip, who was not a hawk on Iraq, used the occasion of a reception in the White House residence that evening to complain directly to Vice President Cheney and the president.

CARD'S GROUP MET AGAIN in the Situation Room on Thursday and Friday that week, September 5 and 6. The White House Iraq Group was coordinating the daily message on Iraq and the "echo"—the effort to reinforce the president's themes and arguments with statements and media appearances by administration officials and friendly members of Congress.

Card thought he had three functions as White House chief of staff. One was what he called the "care and feeding of the president," which was the hardest because it included seeing to Bush's needs and wishes, scheduling him in a way that reflected his priorities, getting authoritative answers and inviting the right people in to see Bush and keeping the wrong ones out. Second was "policy formulation," and third was "selling and marketing."

In an interview with Elisabeth Bumiller, a White House correspondent for *The New York Times,* Card explained that the White House had let the disarray of August run its course because, "From a marketing point of view, you don't introduce new products in August."

The story ran on the front page the next day under the headline, "Bush Aides Set Strategy to Sell Policy on Iraq." Card's Madison Avenue line about "marketing" and "new products" led to a flurry of criticism that the White House was selling war like soap flakes and had waited to wave around the Iraq threat until the two-month election run-up in the hope that the national security threat would benefit Republicans.

• • •

ON FRIDAY, SEPTEMBER 6, Franks and Rumsfeld briefed the president and the NSC on the latest war planning. It included a brief update on the Hybrid Plan. Franks also presented the plan for suppression of Scud missiles that Saddam might have. It would entail an aggressive effort to send Special Operations Forces teams into the areas inside Iraq where they suspected Scuds might be—primarily the south near Kuwait and the west near Israel, areas from which they had been launched in the 1991 Gulf War.

But General Franks had something important to add. "Mr. President," he said, "we've been looking for Scud missiles and other weapons of mass destruction for ten years and haven't found any yet, so I can't tell you that I know that there are any specific weapons anywhere. I haven't seen Scud one."

Some at the NSC meeting thought this was Franks's way of saying he didn't have adequate targeting information—no specific locations of weapons or Scuds so he couldn't attack or bomb specific sites. They thought that Franks was maintaining that he had to have hard intelligence about locations and he just didn't have it. He could not and would not bomb on a surmise.

But it could, and should, have been a warning that if the intelligence was not good enough to make bombing decisions, it probably was not good enough to make the broad assertion, in public or in formal intelligence documents, that there was "no doubt" Saddam had WMD. If there was no doubt, then precisely where were they?

Franks believed that Saddam did, in fact, have WMD, specifically weaponized chemicals. Intelligence officials from other countries had told him they believed Saddam had some weaponized biologicals. Over the years, Franks had seen thousands of pieces of intelligence that indicated that the guy had a terrific capability in WMD. He thought Saddam would use it if the U.S. military invaded, and he was preparing plans and protective chemical-biological suits for his troops fully expecting the worst case. But that's what you do when you are the commanding general, he said. There were many suspected WMD sites that were clearly military installations that he would target. But suspicion is not knowledge.

Rumsfeld was always suspicious of intelligence. His experience was that it generally understated problems, that bad things too often went undetected for years. Later in an interview, the secretary of defense said his generals "recognized that the human intelligence that we had was modest and they also recognized that the nonhuman intelligence was dealing with a very hard target with a lot of underground capability, with a master of deception with a lot of experience in deceiving." He added, "There were some things we knew quite a bit about and a lot of things we knew precious little about." He was comfortable with the fix they had on the large portions of Iraq being patrolled in Operations Northern Watch and Southern Watch, but not much more. The no-fly operations had not located any specific WMD.

The second topic that morning was Fortress Baghdad and Franks's ongoing planning to preclude, if necessary counter, a stand by Saddam's forces in the Iraqi capital. Rice and Card were still deeply worried about the possibility. It would be a military calamity that could mean a long war with high casualties. Rumsfeld later said it was not the president who was persisting on the topic. "The president, he was interested, but not repetitively," Rumsfeld recalled. "He got it the first two or three times. But others were, I think, you know, understandably concerned about it." He added, "I started sending briefers over and anyone who wanted to get the briefing got it. I didn't even bother, I'd heard it so many times."

THAT EVENING the principals met at Camp David without the president to go over the U.N. issues before Saturday morning's scheduled NSC meeting with the president and afternoon summit with British Prime Minister Tony Blair.

Cheney continued to argue that to ask for a new resolution would put them back in the hopeless soup of U.N. process. All Bush needed to say in his speech was that Saddam was bad, a willful, serial violator of U.N. resolutions, and that the president reserved the right to act unilaterally.

But that would not be asking for U.N. support, Powell replied. The U.N. would not just roll over, declare Saddam evil and authorize war. That approach was not salable. The president had decided to give the U.N. a chance and the only practical way to do that was to seek a new resolution.

Powell detected a kind of fever in Cheney. He was not the steady, unemotional rock that he had witnessed a dozen years earlier during the run-up to the Gulf War. The vice president was beyond hell-bent for action against Saddam. It was as if nothing else existed. Powell attempted to summarize the consequences of unilateral action, an argument he felt he had down pretty well. He added a new dimension, saying that the international reaction would be so negative that he would have to close American embassies around the world if we went to war alone.

That is not the issue, Cheney said. Saddam and the clear threat is the issue.

Maybe it would not turn out as the vice president thinks, Powell said. War could trigger all kinds of unanticipated and unintended consequences—some that none of them, he included, had imagined.

Not the issue, Cheney said.

The conversation exploded into a tough debate between the two men, who danced on the edge of civility but did not depart from the formal deference they generally showed each other. It was sharp and biting, however, and they both knew how to score debating points as they pulled apart the last fraying threads of what had connected them for so many years. Powell appeared to harbor a deep-seated anger even though he was getting his way this time. He had always been just one level beneath Cheney in the pecking order. Over three decades he had worked his way up to become the top uniformed military man, chairman of the JCS, and had wound up reporting to Cheney, who had been an improbable pick as Bush

senior's defense secretary when the nomination of Senator John
Tower was rejected by his Senate colleagues. Then as secretary of
state, the senior cabinet post, Powell was again outranked by
Cheney, this time the unexpected pick as vice president. At NSC
meetings, Cheney sat at Bush's right hand, Powell at his left.

Powell was often confounded by Cheney. Years earlier, writing
his best-selling memoir, Powell kept trying to pin down the remote-
ness of the man and had drafted and redrafted the sections on
Cheney, sending them off to Armitage. Not quite right, Armitage kept
replying. Powell finally told Armitage he had found a way to be "relatively truthful but not harmful." In the final version of *My American
Journey* published in 1995, Powell wrote of Cheney, "He and I had
never, in nearly four years, spent a single purely social hour together."
He told of Cheney's last day as defense secretary, when he had gone to
Cheney's suite of offices at the Pentagon and asked, "Where's the secretary?" Informed that Cheney had left hours ago, Powell wrote, "I
was disappointed, even hurt, but not surprised. The lone cowboy had
gone off into the sunset without even a last, 'So long.' "

On Saturday morning, September 7, Bush met with the NSC
and the argument was joined again. Powell said that if for no other
reason than American credibility, they needed to offer a plan to begin
inspections again as part of any reengagement with the U.N. on Iraq.
Procedurally the only way to do this was to seek new resolutions.

Cheney then listed all the reasons inspections could mire them
in a tar pit. First, the inspectors would not be Americans, but lawyers
and experts from around the world who were less concerned about,
and less skeptical of, Saddam. Second, these inspectors, like those in
the past, would be more inclined to accept what they were told by
Iraqi authorities, less likely to challenge, more likely to be fooled.
The end result, Cheney said, would be deliberations or reports that
would be inconclusive. So inspections would make getting to a decision to actually take out Saddam much more difficult.

Thank you very much, the president said. He promised to think
about it.

• • •

THAT MORNING, Tony Blair left London on a transatlantic flight to see Bush at Camp David. The president had invited him to come for a three-hour talk on Iraq and dinner. Blair would be on the ground for about six hours in all—an unusually short stay.

The British prime minister's style was to have ongoing debates with himself and his small circle of advisers, testing, searching, "weighing things up," as one of his advisers said. On Iraq, Blair had traveled several roads. "Look, if Bush hadn't been exercised after 9/11 about these issues," he told his advisers several times, "I would have been worrying about them, and I raised them with him before 9/11." The issues were terrorism, weapons of mass destruction and Iraq. For years, Blair had warned about the threat posed by Saddam.

When Bush had given his Axis of Evil speech earlier in the year, Blair was glad to see that the American president was getting serious about the rogue-state problem. Yet Blair would never have used the Axis of Evil label, this close adviser said. Of the three countries, he was most worried about North Korea, and he believed Iran was close to developing dangerous WMD stockpiles. Iraq was at the bottom of the Axis list for the prime minister, the adviser claimed, suggesting Blair was not at this point as driven about Saddam as Bush.

"Iraq is an American question," that adviser added. "It's not a British question. And it couldn't be anybody else's because no one else had the capability." Britain was not setting the military agenda, needless to say. It was out of the question that Britain would ever go it alone. "We couldn't have invaded Iraq."

Now Bush was pushing extremely hard. For Blair the immediate question was, Would the United Nations be used? He was keenly aware that in Britain the question was, Does Blair believe in the U.N.? It was critical domestically for the prime minister to show his own Labour Party, a pacifist party at heart, opposed to war in principle, that he had gone the U.N. route. Public opinion in the U.K. favored trying to make international institutions work before resorting to force. Going through the U.N. would be a large and much needed plus.

BLAIR AND BUSH took questions from reporters. They said they were committed to ending Saddam's threat once and for all. How or when went unanswered. Bush asserted unequivocally, "Saddam Hussein possesses weapons of mass destruction."

The two with Cheney sat down for a private talk. There was no specific war planning. The issue was political strategy.

Blair said he had to be able to show that he had tried the United Nations. "He's there to make the case for a resolution," Bush recalled later. He told Blair he had decided to go to the U.N., and it seemed he would seek a new resolution.

Blair was relieved.

Bush looked Blair in the eye. "Saddam Hussein is a threat. And we must work together to deal with this threat, and the world will be better off without him." Bush recalled that he was "probing" and "pushing" the prime minister. He said it might require, would likely entail war. Blair might have to send British troops.

"I'm with you," the prime minister replied, looking Bush back in the eye, pledging flat out to commit British military force if necessary, the critical promise Bush had been seeking.

"We want you to be part of this," he told the prime minister. Blair's resolve had made a real impression, he later recalled.

After the meeting, Bush walked into the conference room where Alastair Campbell, the prime minister's communications director, and several other Blair aides were waiting.

"Your man has got cojones," the president said, using the colloquial Spanish for balls.

The president recalled, "And of course these Brits don't know what cojones are." He said he would call the Camp David session with Blair "the cojones meeting."

As a practical matter, by agreeing to Blair's, and Powell's, urging to go to the U.N. to seek a new resolution, Bush had improved his position immeasurably. It meant that no matter what happened, as long as Blair kept his word, he would not have to go it alone.

THE NEXT MORNING, Sunday, September 8, *The New York Times* had a front page story headlined, "U.S. Says Hussein Intensifies Quest for A-Bomb Parts." The story reported that Iraq had allegedly tried to buy thousands of specially designed, high-strength aluminum tubes that could be used in centrifuges to enrich uranium for a bomb. It was an administration charge that would grow significantly more controversial with time. That day the administration blanketed the Sunday morning television talk shows with Cheney, Powell, Rumsfeld and Rice. Each highlighted the danger from Saddam, with Cheney taking the hardest line.

From all her years reading and sifting intelligence, Rice had reached the same conclusion as Rumsfeld: Intelligence generally underestimated threats, rarely overestimated them. On CNN she said, "We don't want the smoking gun to be a mushroom cloud."

ROVE SPOKE WITH BUSH about going to the United Nations. The conservative Republican base did not like the U.N. but Rove agreed it was necessary to try. It could not appear to be a willy-nilly rush to war. The real political problem was the dire impact of the war talk on the economy. They had hosted groups of businessmen in the Roosevelt Room, the large presidential conference room off the Oval Office, and the message they were hearing was simple: Business was not good because people were scared to death about the uncertainties of war. As Rove traveled the country he found that concern palpable.

17

SPEECHWRITER MIKE GERSON probed the president about pre-cisely what he wanted to say to the U.N. Bush did not share Cheney's cynical view that weapons inspections would be useless. At the same time, he did not come close to sharing Powell's comfort with the U.N. Bush said he wanted an outcome—Saddam out and the weapons of mass destruction eliminated. That was the goal, that was the commitment. The commitment was not to the U.N. process. The United Nations devotees believed that everything was fine if a process was going on. No, the president said, he had to have the out-come he wanted.

Rice described to the president how South Africa had elimi-nated its nuclear weapons and subjected itself to a strict inspections process, inviting an exhaustive search of its facilities, dumping mate-rial in parking lots, opening labs and producing detailed records. So there was a model for disarmament that might work.

Fine, Bush said. It was possible. He didn't believe it and he was not abandoning his goal of regime change, but he would try.

As the speech was drafted, Cheney and Rumsfeld continued to pick at the central premise of asking for a new resolution. Playing on Bush's abhorrence of a process solution, they pressed their argument that merely making the request would snag them in a morass of U.N. committees, debates, hesitations, head scratching—in other words, *process.* This would open the door for Saddam to negotiate with the U.N. If that happened, they were finished. Saddam would say whatever was necessary to make it appear that the process was working; then when it got down to the inspections rubber-meeting-the-road, he would stiff everyone.

Asked about his position on the U.N. more than a year later, Rumsfeld said, "We don't vote" in the NSC and added an insight about how he viewed the internal administration debates. "What happens is discussion takes place, pros and cons are considered and we participate in those. The president then begins leaning in a direction. [Then] people say, well, if that's the direction, you need to understand that the alternative direction has these advantages and disadvantages and the one you're leaning toward has this advantage and disadvantage and begin anticipating the problems that can accrue."

Pressed on his personal view, Rumsfeld replied, "My memory on something like that is not perfect and I don't recall whether I wrote memos on it or chimed in at meetings particularly. Clearly there were advantages in going and there were potential disadvantages in going. My impression personally is that, in retrospect, it was the right thing to go and the advantages were in large measure achieved and the disadvantages were for the most part avoided."

Since Bush was going to tell the U.N. either they solve the Saddam problem or the U.S. would, I asked Rumsfeld, "It was really crossing the threshold, wasn't it?"

"It was. It was," Rumsfeld said. But, he added, "It was not the real threshold. The real threshold for me was when people—other countries—started putting themselves at risk on your behalf."

ONE OPTION FOR THE U.N. speech that Rice thought they had to consider, the president later recalled, was issuing an ultimatum that Saddam had 30 days to disarm or the U.S. would lead an attack. That would be a virtual declaration of war. Bush, however, was strongly leaning toward asking for a U.N. resolution. Nevertheless, meetings on the drafting of the U.N. speech continued for days. At one point a request for new resolutions came out of the latest draft. The speech assailed the U.N. for not enforcing the previous weapons resolutions, specifically over the four years since Saddam had forced out the inspectors.

"You can't say all of this without asking them to do something. There's no action in this speech," Powell argued. He knew that the appeal for action would resonate strongly with Bush. "It says, here's what he's done wrong, here's what he has to do to fix himself, and then it stops?" Powell asked in wonderment. "You've got to ask for something."

So the principals fought about what to ask for. What should the "ask" look like? They finally reached consensus that they would simply ask the United Nations to act.

Powell, who was by now somewhat bewildered and beaten down, accepted that. He knew the only way the U.N. acted was through its action arm, the Security Council, and that the only means were resolutions. Calling explicitly for a new resolution would have nailed it, but the call to "act" was for Powell far better than a 30-day ultimatum or war.

On September 10, two days before the speech, Draft #21 landed on Powell's desk with EYES ONLY and URGENT stamped all over it. There was no call for the U.N. to act. The principals committee met. Cheney restated his opposition to a resolution. It was a matter of tactics and presidential credibility, the vice president said. Suppose the president asked the Security Council for a new resolution and the council refused? Where would they be then? If Saddam ever used his WMD, he argued, especially on a large scale, the world would never forgive them for inaction and giving in to the impulse to engage in semantic debates about U.N. resolutions.

Rumsfeld argued for standing on principle, but he posed a series of rhetorical questions, and did not come down hard about the language.

Powell had just about had it with Rumsfeld's familiar technique of speaking in what Powell privately called the "third-person passive once removed." Rumsfeld said things like "One would think" or "One could imagine" or "One might expect" or "Some would say" over and over and over. And no one ever called him on it, including Powell. They just could not have the kind of conversations that led to direct answers about what Rumsfeld really wanted. And Rumsfeld's regard for the State Department was low and getting lower. To Powell, it seemed almost that Rumsfeld was wearing rubber gloves, not wanting to leave fingerprints on policy recommendations.

So Powell and Cheney went at it yet again in a blistering argument.

"I don't know if we got it or not," Powell reported to Armitage, referring to a call for the U.N. to act.

The night before the speech, Bush told Powell and Rice that he was going to ask for new resolutions. He liked policy headlines to come directly from him, so he directed that near the top of page eight in the latest draft, #24, language be inserted which would ask the U.N. for the necessary "resolutions."

Later the president recalled, "I chose the resolution" option. "Blair had a lot to do with it," he acknowledged. He added that before his U.N. speech he also spoke with Australian Prime Minister John Howard, who said, "I'm with you. We need a resolution." Bush recalled that he received the same recommendation from the Spanish president, José María Aznar.

AT THE PODIUM in the General Assembly Hall on September 12, Bush reached the point in his speech where he was going to ask for new resolutions. But the change had not been put into the copy on the TelePrompTer, so he read the old line, "My nation will work with the U.N. Security Council *to meet our common challenge.*"

As he read along with Draft #24, penciling in any ad libs or deletions the president might make at the last minute, Powell felt his heart almost stop. The sentence about resolutions had somehow vanished. The president had not said it—the crucial line!

But as Bush read the old sentence, he realized that the fruit of his war cabinet's heated debate was missing. With only mild awkwardness, he added, two sentences later, "We will work with the U.N. Security Council for the necessary resolutions."

Powell's heart began beating again.

"It was a big speech," the president recalled fifteen months later. "I am coming off the anniversary of [9/11]" the day before. "We were on the defensive. But this speech began to clarify to the American people, first and foremost, what they were reading about" concerning military planning and other strategies for dealing with Iraq. Previously he and the administration had not achieved "clarity" about where they were heading, he said. "And the one other thing about this administration is that we've been able to define an agenda. Now people may not like it, but we've been good about defining agendas so that people understand it. This speech did that. And it had a big effect in America.

"When I walked up there and stood in front of that group, and by the way there's no expressions," Bush continued. The delegates sat mute, almost impolitely so. "It was dead quiet. And I can remember, the more solemn they looked to me, the more emotional I was in making the case. Not openly emotional, the more firm I was in making the case. It was a speech I really enjoyed giving."

The reason he was able to lay down the if-you-don't-we-will challenge to the U.N., he said, was the work and war planning that had been done by Franks and Rumsfeld. "Had we not done that, had we not planned, had I not had that option available, I could not have given that speech," he said. He believed that the military threat was a necessary condition to make diplomacy possible.

The speech was generally a hit. "It had a big impact around the world as well," he noted. The soft-liners liked it because the president was seeking international and United Nations support. Hard-liners liked it because it sounded tough.

Powell stayed in New York to rally support for the policy, especially from Russia and France, who as two of the five permanent members of the Security Council could veto any resolution.

Bush later said, "And I will tell you that there were times when I wasn't sure we were going to get any resolution." He had promised the United States would act if the U.N. didn't. "So I'm sitting there saying to myself, you know, are you prepared to go?"

ROVE GENERALLY MET with Bush in the morning after his intelligence briefing, NSC meeting or calls to foreign leaders. It was usually with Card, Bartlett, the press secretary and some others. Occasionally, he had a few minutes alone with the president, who might briefly vent about something. He reminded the president that all the war talk was drowning out other things and not necessarily to their political advantage.

As the midterm elections approached, he told Bush that the one issue that was a winner was the Homeland Security bill that would set up a new cabinet department as part of the biggest reorganization of the federal government since the creation of the Defense Department. The Democrats were delaying the bill because they wanted to guarantee that government workers could unionize. The president was asking for the authority to make exemptions for national security concerns, which he said every president since John Kennedy had been granted. He went out and campaigned hard, saying that he wanted to defend the country and the Democrats wanted to defend the union bosses. Rove was convinced that the Homeland Security issue and the Senate's delay in voting on or confirming Bush's nominees to federal judgeships would benefit the Republicans in the elections.

SEVERAL TIMES A WEEK Nick Calio arranged for congressmen or senators to attend intelligence briefings or small ad hoc working group sessions, either on Capitol Hill or at the White House, even in the intimacy of the Situation Room. The small-group selling forum worked better than the large sessions. In case anyone was looking around for clues, one of the three red digital clocks marking time around the world was set for "Iraq."

One of the first briefings was given by Deputy CIA Director John McLaughlin, Tenet's No. 2. Afterward Calio urged Tenet to come himself to conduct the briefings. "John can almost scare people he's so balanced," Calio said. They needed to make sales, and McLaughlin was too low-key. They needed a fireball, so Tenet was present at more and more briefings.

Meanwhile the Homeland Security bill was being blocked in the Senate by a filibuster. Calio told the president that they were about to "vitiate" the filibuster.

"Nicky, what the fuck are you talking about, vitiate?" Bush asked. Cheney too wondered aloud what vitiate meant.

The next day Calio brought in a two-page handout of definitions from the Webster's and American Heritage dictionaries describing that vitiate meant to void or render ineffective. Later the White House did exactly that, securing the 60 votes needed to end debate and passing the bill.

On September 19, the president met with 11 House members in the Cabinet Room.

"The war on terrorism is going okay; we are hunting down al Qaeda one-by-one," Bush began. "The biggest threat, however, is Saddam Hussein and his weapons of mass destruction. He can blow up Israel and that would trigger an international conflict."

Delving into elements of the war plan, Bush told the group, "We will take over the oil fields early—and mitigate the oil shock," interrupting himself to issue the stern warning, "Nobody needs to be telling anybody this!"

Bush also shared a tidbit from either the sensitive President's Daily Brief (PDB) or Tenet's daily oral briefing. "This morning in my intelligence briefing I found out that the CIA has a poll stating that 71 percent in France see Saddam Hussein as a true threat to world peace."

No one asked why the CIA reported to the president about French polls. Though the political reaction in France of a new U.N. resolution on Iraq weapons inspections was of concern as the president tried to win international support, it probably did not require clandestine intelligence. A recent French newspaper poll showed 65 percent opposed a war in Iraq even with U.N. backing.

Richard Burr, a North Carolina Republican, said the president should keep saying in his speeches that Saddam gassed his own people.

"I am well aware," Bush said, adding, "He tried to kill my Dad," a reference to intelligence early during the Clinton administration that Iraqi agents had plotted to assassinate Bush senior on a 1993 trip to the Middle East. In response, Clinton had ordered a cruise missile attack on Baghdad.

"Our information gathering is strong. We need to talk to Saddam Hussein's guards," Bush continued. "Unrest in Iraq will help with the rebuilding. Intrusive inspections might spark the Iraqi people."

Bush left the meeting, leaving Calio to wrap up. "We will work in a bipartisan fashion but we want maximum flexibility and we are looking to you all for your help," he urged. "Also remember to speak up when others say discouraging things."

A few hours later, the president released the proposed language of a resolution granting him authority "to use all means that he determines to be appropriate, including force" to deal with the threat posed by Iraq. A front page story in *The Washington Post* the next day said that with the introduction of the resolution, President Bush's "rout of congressional Democrats was virtually complete."

That day, September 20, Secretary Powell testified before the House International Relations Committee in support of the resolution. "I've been known as a reluctant warrior. It doesn't bother me. But the threat of war has to be there," he said. It was an argument that would be adopted by many Democrats who might have been inclined to vote against a congressional resolution. Deterrence and containment of the Soviet Union during the Cold War had been built around the threat of massive conventional and nuclear retaliation. It was a policy that had succeeded and was the model for avoiding war.

Bush was not necessarily asking for war on Iraq. He was merely asking for congressional support as he threatened war. It was Rice's version of coercive diplomacy.

ON SATURDAY, SEPTEMBER 21, *The New York Times* reported in its lead story that Bush had recently received a highly detailed set of war plans on Iraq from General Franks. At a press conference in Kuwait where he was meeting with his field commanders, Franks acknowledged, "We are prepared to undertake whatever activities and whatever actions we may be directed to take by our nation," adding, "Our president has not made a decision to go to war."

In an interview for the *Times* story, the president's spokesman, Ari Fleischer, pointedly departed from previous statements throughout the spring and summer that the president did not have war plans at the ready.

"I am not saying there is no plan on his desk."

BUSH HAD 18 more House members to the Cabinet Room on Thursday, September 26. He opened by saying the last thing he wanted was to put troops in harm's way. "Believe me, I don't like hugging the widows."

Launching into a familiar indictment of the Iraqi leader, he said, "Saddam Hussein is a terrible guy who is teaming up with al Qaeda. He tortures his own people and hates Israel."

The lead story in the national media that day was an erupting war of words between Bush and Senate Majority Leader Daschle, each alleging the other was politicizing Iraq and national security issues.

"Washington is an ugly town," Bush said to the assembled group. "I am well aware of that. This is our duty though."

"If we use force, it will be fierce and swift and fast," Bush said. "First, I promise a good plan. I have been looking each general in the eye and asking them whether or not they see any problems for a regime change. They do not."

He said that nothing could be worse than the present situation. Saddam had two of his own security guards killed to send a message to his inner circle, he maintained. Then, putting the most dire spin on the intelligence, he stated, "It is clear he has weapons of mass destruction—anthrax, VX; he still needs plutonium and he has not been shy about trying to find it. Time frame would be six months" to Iraq having a nuke if Iraq was able to obtain sufficient plutonium or enriched uranium—one of the most difficult tasks.

"People always love a fight, especially in Washington," Bush said, adding, "Yesterday's story in *The Washington Post* was a misquote." The front page story had said, "Four times in the past two days, Bush has suggested that Democrats do not care about national security."

"I never say 'Democrats' in any speech I give," Bush said.

Tennessee Democrat Bob Clement asked, "Have you given up on the U.N.?" and, as an aside, said, "The economy is also unraveling—we have hit a six-year low in the stock market."

"It's four years!" Bush shot back, drawing laughter.

"I haven't given up on the U.N., but sometimes it can be a diplomatic mud pit. I understand diplomacy," he said, and assured them he would not get caught up fighting over the U.N. resolution.

Chris Shays, an eighth-term Republican from Connecticut, said, "Some briefings have left me less confident than before."

The meeting adjourned to the Rose Garden where Bush, in a prearranged move intended to show bipartisan solidarity, made a brief statement with the members standing behind him.

"The security of our country is the commitment of both political parties and the responsibility of both elected branches of government," Bush said, defusing though not retreating from the flap with Daschle.

Restating the new unequivocal charge about Iraq's WMD programs he had adopted three weeks earlier, Bush said, "The Iraqi regime possesses biological and chemical weapons. The Iraqi regime is building the facilities necessary to make more." Ratcheting up another notch, he added, "And according to the British government, the Iraqi regime could launch a biological or chemical attack in as little as 45 minutes after the order were given."

Tenet and the CIA had warned the British not to make that allegation, which was based on a questionable source, and almost certainly referred to battlefield weapons—not ones that Iraq could launch at neighboring countries, let alone American cities. Tenet referred privately to this as the "they-can-attack-in-45-minutes shit."

ON TUESDAY, OCTOBER 1, Bush and Cheney met with a dozen members of the House International Relations Committee in the White House Cabinet Room. "We cannot let history judge us and ask where was George W. Bush and Dick Cheney," Bush said in making his case for action.

Cheney said, "The key things are that we have always underestimated this guy. He has lots of money coming in from oil reserves."

Shelley Berkley, a Nevada Democrat, asked what they would do about Saddam aiming at Israel.

"Super Patriots are a possibility. We have very technologically advanced weapons," Bush said. He turned to Cheney, "What am I allowed to say?"

"Not too much," Cheney replied. "There are launch boxes in Iraq. [We] can fly Predators and preempt strikes."

The president then lit into Saddam. "This guy is a liar. He is playing the international community for a fool. It's like an international mosh pit. Australia, Slovakia, Czech Republic, England— these countries are all on our side. You don't read about this. You read about Germany and this guy winning an election by making me look like a piñata," referring to Chancellor Gerhard Schroeder's anti–Iraq war rhetoric during his reelection campaign.

Bush told the group that when he had spoken to the U.N. in

September, "There were no facial expressions. It was like a Woody Allen movie." There was laughter.

"People out there say you cannot fight in Afghanistan and win in Iraq," Bush continued. "Defeating two enemies is very difficult, but we will do it."

18

S IX MONTHS EARLIER, on May 9, 2002, I had dinner with Senator Bob Graham, the Florida Democrat who chaired the Senate Intelligence Committee, at his townhouse on Capitol Hill. I brought the dinner and he supplied the silverware and plates. It was the second such dinner we had had since 9/11.

In the world of the CIA, secret intelligence and covert action, the congressional intelligence committees were the only outside monitor. Their oversight function was mandated by law, and the chairmen and ranking members of the minority party were supposed to be informed of any significant intelligence activity, failure or covert action. Sometimes the committees were bulldogs, other times lapdogs. Senator Barry Goldwater, the late Arizona Republican, had chaired the Senate committee at a critical period during the reign of CIA Director William J. Casey in the 1980s, and I had found Goldwater a good source of reliable information.

Graham, a small, pleasant but intense man of 65, had served eight years as Florida governor and was in his third six-year term in the Senate. Graham had a family connection to *The Washington Post* where I work. His half-brother was the late Philip Graham, the publisher of the *Post* until 1963 and husband of Katharine Graham. Philip Graham's son, Don Graham, currently is CEO of the Post Company, so Senator Graham thought it best to talk on-the-record and only for my book and not the newspaper. I tape-recorded our lengthy dinner conversations with his permission.

Graham wanted to talk about Iraq and he was deeply troubled. He said he had been briefed on the covert plan, but declined to give details. The circumstances of the briefings—they took place in Cheney's office—particularly bothered him. For the most sensitive covert operations, the White House and the Congress had a long-standing agreement that only eight members of Congress would be informed, the so-called Gang of Eight—the Senate majority and minority leaders, the House speaker and minority leader, and the chairman and ranking member of both the Senate and House Intelligence Committees.

"The theory of this new plan," Graham said, "was that we have failed to achieve the objective of changing a regime and that a primary reason for that failure was that we have relied on intelligence to accomplish this and it can't be done by intelligence alone. It's going to require a little diplomacy, a little economic pressure and maybe a lot of military."

His reaction?

"Well, I am unconvinced that going into Iraq is the appropriate thing to do in the immediate future," he said. "And I'll define the immediate future as being the next two or three years. I believe pursuing this war on terrorism is a very important goal and that this could be the swamp that would keep us from accomplishing that goal.

"The definition of a first-tier terrorist was somebody who was either involved in the events of September the 11th or harbored and provided sanctuary to people involved. And there's not evidence that Iraq fell into either one of those two categories. And so I think it's a stretch to call a war on Iraq another chapter in the war on terrorism.

"Is Iraq a nation that is close to having militarily usable weapons of mass destruction?" he asked. "Again, the answer is most analyses would say that it is some time, like five years, before they are going to be at that point unless they get substantial assistance from outside."

Graham said we ought to monitor Iraq so that "if those numbers appear to be rapidly shortening, then we may—Iraq legitimately would go up higher on the list." He said he had not talked with Bush about Iraq but he had talked to Cheney. "He sort of glides over the issue of terrorism and unites [it with] weapons of mass destruction. He would say that the war that we are now engaged in is not just a war against terrorism, it's a war against terrorism and those states which have the capability of providing terrorists with weapons through which they could escalate the nature of their violence.

"One of these findings is tighter than a Gang of Eight finding," he said, because no staff was allowed. "All the briefings on that take place at the White House and the ones I've participated in have primarily been in [Cheney's] office."

Tenet was present but Cheney did most of the talking. The vice president was intent on Iraq, saying, "We've got to do it because it's the convergence of terrorism and weapons of mass destruction."

Graham asserted that the Bush administration, or at least Cheney, had changed the definition of the war on terrorism. "Now, we're defining a terrorist state as those states which might have the ability to provide weapons of mass destruction, even if they themselves are not engaged in terrorist activities or providing sanctuary."

THE CIA HAD NEVER declared categorically that it believed Saddam possessed weapons of mass destruction. The formal 2000 National Intelligence Estimate concluded that Saddam "retained a small stockpile" of chemical warfare agents—not actual warheads—perhaps up to 100 metric tons, and "might" have precursors for 200 metric tons more. This conclusion was drawn largely from accounting discrepancies between what Iraq had previously told U.N. weapons inspectors it possessed, and what records showed had been destroyed.

The classified December 2000 National Intelligence Estimate on biological weapons concluded that Iraq "continued" to work on development and was poised to, but did not yet have them.

Significantly, in public testimony before Graham's committee on February 6, 2002, on worldwide threats, Tenet had not mentioned Iraq until page 10 of his 18-page testimony, devoting only three paragraphs to Iraq. He said, "Iraq continues to build and expand an infrastructure capable of producing WMD." Its chemical industry was expanding "in ways that could be diverted quickly to CW production. We believe it also maintains an active and capable BW program."

"We believe Saddam never abandoned his nuclear weapons programs," Tenet said, but he made no suggestion that Saddam possessed or was on the verge of building a bomb. "Our major near-term concern is the possibility that Saddam might gain access to fissile material."

After I saw him, Graham and other Senate Democrats pressed the administration to provide a new comprehensive intelligence report or estimate on Iraq. He in particular wanted to see how the CIA covert plan might relate to military plans, diplomacy and the global war on terrorism. What was the exact nature of the Iraq threat? With what kinds of weapons or terrorism? How immediate was that threat? What would war mean to the region and what would the postwar landscape be like? These questions were formalized in a classified letter to Tenet on September 11, 2002, the day before Bush's speech to the United Nations.

Tenet refused the request on the grounds that Graham wanted an assessment of U.S. strategy and policy. That was way outside Tenet's purview. The CIA made assessments and formal National Intelligence Estimates about foreign governments, not its own. Tenet, however, did agree reluctantly to do a rushed National Intelligence Estimate on Iraq's WMD capability. This intelligence work was undertaken in the wake of Bush's and Cheney's high-profile conclusions on the subject—the vice president's August 26 declaration that, "Simply stated, there is no doubt that Saddam Hussein now has weapons of mass destruction," and the president's remark a month later that, "The Iraqi regime possesses biological and chemical weapons."

The National Intelligence Council, a group of representatives

from the key intelligence agencies, began sifting, sorting and assess-
ing the raw intelligence. The council includes the CIA, the National
Security Agency, which does communications intercepts, the Pentagon's Defense Intelligence Agency, the State Department's intelligence bureau, the Energy Department's intelligence arm, and the
National Imagery and Mapping Agency, which performs satellite and
other overhead reconnaissance.

The group had a massive amount of material, much of it old and
not very reliable. Iraq was still one of the hardest intelligence targets.
Saddam had improved his methods of deception and hiding his
weapons programs—whatever they might be—underground. CIA
human intelligence inside Iraq was still weak, and paramilitary
teams like those headed by Tim in northern Iraq had found nothing.

A National Intelligence Estimate is just that, an estimate. During the Cold War it became the document of choice because it was
designed to give the president and his national security team an
overall assessment of the capability and intentions of real threats,
such as the Soviet Union and China. NIEs often include political assessments of the endurance of, say, Colonel Qaddafi in Libya, the direction of the Balkans, famine in Africa, the chances of war on the
Korean peninsula or a nuclear exchange between India and Pakistan.

The format is designed for busy policy makers. So a long NIE of
50 or 100 pages has a kind of executive summary at the front called
"Key Judgments" in which the intelligence analysts would try to give
a bottom-line answer. Would Castro be overthrown? Would Syria attack Israel? Would the Communists win in Nicaragua? Over the decades there had been much criticism of NIEs by policy makers—and
presidents—because the authors hedge and because the "on-this-
hand, on-the-other-hand" reports are littered with maddening quali-
fications. No matter what happened, someone could find a sentence
or phrase in the NIE that had covered such a possibility.

Stu Cohen, an intelligence professional for 30 years, was acting
chairman of the National Intelligence Council when the Iraq assessment of WMD was being prepared. He confided to a colleague that
he wanted to avoid equivocation if possible. If the Key Judgments

used words such as "maybe" or "probably" or "likely," the NIE would be "pablum," he said. Ironclad evidence in the intelligence business is scarce and analysts need to be able to make judgments beyond the ironclad, Cohen felt. The evidence was substantial but nonetheless circumstantial; no one had proof of a vial of biological agents or weapons, or a smoking vat of chemical warfare agents. Yet coupled with the incontrovertible proof that Saddam had had WMD in the past—U.N. weapons inspectors in the 1990s had found it, tested it and destroyed it—the conclusion seemed obvious.

The alternative view was that Saddam didn't have WMD. No one wanted to say that because so much intelligence would have to be discounted. The real and best answer was that he *probably* had WMD, but that there was no proof and the case was circumstantial. Given the leeway to make a "judgment," which in the dictionary definition is merely an "opinion," the council was heading toward a strong declaration. No pablum.

Analysts at the CIA had long discussed the issue of avoiding equivocation. At times, many, including John McLaughlin, felt that they had to dare to be wrong to be clearer in their judgments. That summer McLaughlin had told the NSC principals that the CIA thought they had a pretty good case that Saddam had WMD, but that others would demand more direct proof. The CIA did not have an anthrax sample, and didn't have a chemical weapons sample on hand.

Intelligence analysts and officials worked on the estimate for three weeks. On October 1, Tenet chaired the National Foreign Intelligence Board, the heads of all the intelligence agencies that released and certified the NIEs. No one disputed the central conclusions. Tenet felt he had a group of smart people at the table and that they knew how to craft the estimate properly.

The Top Secret 92-page document that was released said under the Key Judgments, without qualification, "Baghdad has chemical and biological weapons." From that attention-getting assertion, the NIE takes a slow march back down the hill, with muted but clear equivocations. One hint of uncertainty was the second paragraph in the Key Judgments. "We judge that we are seeing only a portion of

Iraq's WMD efforts." It is the kind of statement that might be included in any intelligence report—only a portion of anything is ever seen. In the end, the hedging and backing off telegraphed immense doubt.

The NIE said the intelligence agencies "assess that Baghdad has begun renewed production of mustard, sarin, cyclosarin and VX" but did not say Iraq actually had any, or that they had any sources who had seen any. And the backup was thin. They had clandestine reporting that Iraq "has procured covertly the types and quantities of chemicals and equipment sufficient to allow limited CW agent production." Given the dual use of many such chemicals—for legitimate nonweapons purposes and weapons—the conclusion was speculative.

"Although we have little specific information on Iraq's CW stockpile," the NIE said, suggesting they had a problem coming up with numbers, it stated, "Saddam probably has stocked at least 100 metric tons and possibly as much as 500 metric tons of CW agents— much of it added in the last year."

It was much the same on biological weapons. Some of the intelligence and conclusions come close to contradicting the flat assertions in the Key Judgments. For example, the NIE said, "We judge that all key aspects—R&D, production and weaponization—of Iraq's offensive BW program are active." Active elements of a program do not necessarily mean actual weapons have been made, though it strongly suggests it. Though there was powerful and troubling circumstantial evidence, it did not establish that Saddam "has" the weapons. "We judge Iraq has some lethal and incapacitating BW agents and is capable of quickly producing and weaponizing a variety of such agents." Again, it did not state that Iraq had actual weapons.

The NIE sounded like a weather report on certain topics. "Chances are even that smallpox is part of Iraq's offensive BW program," it said.

Deeper into the NIE the tentativeness grew. "We have low confidence in our ability to assess when Saddam would use WMD," the NIE said. With a string of qualifiers—could, might, probably, more likely and probably again—the NIE laid out scenarios of chemical or biological attacks on U.S. forces, friends and allies.

After a triple set of qualifiers, the NIE addressed Cheney's nightmare—Saddam assisting al Qaeda in a WMD attack.

"Saddam, if sufficiently desperate, might decide that only an organization such as al Qaeda—with worldwide reach and extensive terrorist infrastructure, and already engaged in a life-or-death struggle against the United States—would perpetrate the type of terrorist attack that he would hope to conduct. In such circumstances, he might decide that the extreme step of assisting the Islamist terrorists in conducting a CBW attack against the United States would be his last chance to exact vengeance by taking a large number of victims with him."

Buried still later in the NIE is the statement that there is "low confidence" in this assessment. This followed the statement: "We have no specific intelligence information that Saddam's regime has directed attacks against U.S. territory."

On the issue of nuclear weapons, the NIE said with "moderate confidence" that "Iraq does not yet have a nuclear weapon or sufficient material to make one but is likely to have a weapon by 2007 to 2009."

The State Department intelligence bureau filed an 11-page annex outlining its objections and disagreements with the NIE, particularly on nuclear weapons, saying the evidence did not add up to "a compelling case" that Iraq has "an integrated and comprehensive approach to acquire nuclear weapons."

When the NIE was presented to the Senate Intelligence Committee on Wednesday, October 2, some senators focused on the larger questions the CIA had not addressed. They wanted to know how covert action in Iraq related to military planning, diplomacy and the possibility that an attack on Iraq would trigger a terrorist response against the United States or cause problems in the Middle East. No senator had enough of the picture—military planning details were not provided to the Hill and the CIA plans were highly classified—to frame an effective critique. And the almost daily news accounts of Powell's efforts to secure a new resolution at the U.N. Security Council had shifted the focus to Bush's diplomatic push.

That week some senators were floating alternative proposals for a congressional resolution that would give Bush less than a blank check. Calio let it be known on the Hill in midweek: "Today's the day—we resolve all differences today or we're going without you." The president's chief lobbyist only did that when he already had a comfortable majority. Over several hours that afternoon and evening, Bush and Calio sorted out a final compromise on language. Bush spoke by telephone to Dick Gephardt, who had been seeking a few changes but was generally supportive of the president's course. Having the top House Democratic leader on their side was important.

Rove had several assignments to help win the congressional resolution. He spoke with some House Republicans and acted as a sounding board for some who wanted to send a message to Bush. One assignment was to talk to Senator Chuck Hagel, the Nebraska Republican with an independent streak who was a frequent Bush critic. Rove's argument was that Iraq was an important front in the war on terror. The president needed this resolution in order to give him the maximum leverage to resolve this peacefully and, if not, to have the support to strike militarily.

At 1:15 P.M. on October 2, Bush appeared with dozens of lawmakers, including Gephardt but not Daschle, in the Rose Garden to announce agreement on a bipartisan resolution. Also standing by his side were two key figures from the 2000 presidential contest: Senator John McCain, the maverick Arizona Republican who had been Bush's main primary challenger, and Senator Joseph Lieberman, the Connecticut Democrat who had been Al Gore's running mate against Bush.

The president said that support from the Congress "will show to friend and enemy alike the resolve of the United States." Declaring that "on its present course, the Iraqi regime is a threat of unique urgency," Bush said, "the dictator is a student of Stalin.

"The issue is now before the United States Congress. The debate will be closely watched by the American people and this debate will be remembered in history.

"I urge all members of Congress to consider this resolution with the greatest of care. The choice before them could not be more consequential."

AS PART OF THE EFFORT to win congressional and public support, the president decided to give a prime-time speech laying out the case against Saddam. It was to be delivered in Cincinnati in the Grand Rotunda of the museum at Union Terminal on October 7.

Drafts were flying around furiously. Two days before, the CIA had sent a three-and-a-half-page memo to Steve Hadley and Mike Gerson recommending 22 changes in Draft #6. Some of the recommended changes said that the drafted statements could be strengthened; others recommended certain statements be cut back or dropped entirely.

For example, the draft said that after 1995 Iraq admitted that it had produced 25,000 liters of anthrax and other deadly biological agents. The CIA said the number could be increased to 30,000—the number the president would use.

The draft also said that before the 1991 Gulf War, the best intelligence had indicated Iraq was five to seven years away from developing a nuclear weapon. The CIA recommended changing it to the more accurate 8 to 10 years—the number that Bush would state in the speech. Draft #6 further stated that after the Gulf War, international weapons inspectors had discovered Iraq was much further along in its nuclear program and would likely have had a nuclear weapon within 18 months. The CIA memo suggested that the time frame be changed to two to three years. Bush settled on the formulation "no later than 1993," roughly two years after the discovery.

Draft #6 also contained the line: "And the regime has been caught attempting to purchase up to 500 metric tons of uranium oxide from sources in Africa, a central ingredient in the enrichment process."

The basis for this was an unsubstantiated report from British intelligence that Iraq had recently attempted to buy uranium oxide, known as "yellowcake," from Niger. The CIA was unsure of this for a number of reasons and had shared its concerns with the British. A former ambassador, Joseph Wilson IV, had been sent to Niger to check out the report and had found nothing to substantiate it. The CIA memo recommended that any reference be dropped from the Cincinnati speech, and it was.

The draft said that "On Saddam Hussein's orders, opponents have been decapitated." The CIA said the evidence was that the opponents had been executed, not decapitated. But decapitated stayed in the final speech.

The 26-minute Cincinnati speech was not carried by the top three broadcast networks, but was seen by nearly 17 million viewers on the FOX network and the cable news channels CNN, MSNBC and FOX News.

Bush's core argument was that Iraq "gathers the most serious dangers of our age in one place" and that, "The danger is already significant, and it only grows worse with time."

There was no acknowledgment that they lacked "smoking gun" evidence. Bush instead suggested only a larger risk, one that Rice had publicly raised a month earlier. "Facing clear evidence of peril," he said, "we cannot wait for the final proof, the smoking gun, that could come in the form of a mushroom cloud."

In case anyone missed the point, Bush invoked the Cuban missile crisis of October 1962 when the Soviet Union had installed offensive medium-range missiles in Cuba. Bush quoted President John F. Kennedy saying, "Neither the United States of America nor the world community of nations can tolerate deliberate deception and offensive threats on the part of any nation, large or small. We no longer live in a world where only the actual firing of weapons represents a sufficient challenge to a nation's security to constitute maximum peril."

• • •

THE NEXT DAY, October 8, at least 47 senators were briefed or shown the entire NIE with its key judgment that Iraq "has chemical and biological weapons." Powell spoke with moderate Republican Senator Susan Collins of Maine for 15 minutes, adamantly contending, she later told the *Los Angeles Times*, that "unless Congress passes the authorization for use of force, the Security Council will find a way to sidestep the issue." She added, "I think that's a very valid argument."

On October 10, Calio put out an action item to his staff to tally the total number of members who had been briefed on Iraq. He wanted a readout before the vote, which appeared likely that day. A detailed 11-page spreadsheet of the invitations and meetings was prepared showing he had invited 195 members of the House and all 100 senators to one or more White House–led briefings on Iraq. Calio's staff recorded that 71 senators had accepted and 161 from the House.

That afternoon, after two days of debate, the House passed a resolution authorizing the president to use the U.S. armed forces in Iraq "as he deems to be necessary and appropriate." The vote was a comfortable 296 to 133—46 more than the president's father had in 1991.

In the Senate, Edward M. Kennedy, the Massachusetts Democrat, made an impassioned plea to reject the resolution.

"The administration has not made a convincing case that we face such an imminent threat to our national security that a unilateral, preemptive American strike and an immediate war are necessary. Nor has the administration laid out the cost in blood and treasure for this operation," Kennedy said. He later added that Bush's preemptive doctrine amounted to "a call for 21st century American imperialism that no other nation can or should accept."

Senator John F. Kerry, a Massachusetts Democrat who would soon be running for president, said in a speech on the Senate floor he would vote for the resolution to use force in disarming Saddam because "a deadly arsenal of weapons of mass destruction in his hands is a threat, and a grave threat, to our security." In announcing his support, Kerry stated that he expected the president "to fulfill the commitments he has made to the American people in recent days— to work with the United Nations Security Council to adopt a new resolution . . . and to act with allies at our side if we have to disarm Saddam Hussein by force."

But no Democrat or other critic had been able to gain much traction in the face of the president's repeated declarations about the threat posed by Saddam and the CIA's estimates that Saddam possessed WMD and might be on the verge of becoming a nuclear power.

The vote in the Senate on October 11 supporting the resolution was 77 to 23. Senator Graham of Florida voted against the resolution on the grounds that it was "too timid" and "too weak." He wanted to give the president authority not only to attack Iraq, but also "to use force against all international terrorist groups who will probably strike the United States as the regime of Saddam Hussein crumbles."

Senators Daschle and Feinstein, who had been vocal critics along the way, in the end voted for the resolution, which stated that the president could use the military under the "necessary-and-appropriate" standard to defend against "the continuing threat posed by Iraq." It was a blank check.

19

RUMSFELD KEPT HONING the details of the war plan, pushing the Hybrid Plan closer and closer to something executable, and that covered all bases. He was drilling hard, making sure Bush had detail.

On October 4, Franks presented Bush with a roll-up of the targeting concepts, a more complete briefing on Fortress Baghdad, and a final update on the plan for dealing with Scuds. He also offered some ideas on using Special Operations Forces to support opposition groups inside Iraq. There were briefings for the president on securing and repairing Iraqi oil infrastructure, on collateral damage estimates for hardened and underground facilities in Iraq, and on hydrology—how Saddam might use dams and flooding to destroy critical regions in his country and interfere with U.S. troop advancements.

At an NSC meeting during this period, Rumsfeld was thinking about what could go wrong. He began doodling a list that grew to some 15 items.

"Look," he told the others, including the president, "we better keep this in mind." He then listed all 15.

He came back to the Pentagon, wrote them all out, then sent it around to four of his key advisers, who each added a couple.

On October 15, Rumsfeld summarized it all in a Top Secret three-page memo. "It's an enormous decision," he recalled later.

"One does not do—engage in war lightly, and it was something that you thought about and thought about and thought about. And at a certain point knowing it's not your decision or even your recommendation, my whole focus was less on that than it was on making sure that we had done everything humanly possible to prepare him for what could go wrong, to prepare so things would go right."

Rumsfeld sent the memo to the president and later walked him through it. It began, "The following is an illustrative list of the types of problems that could result from a conflict with Iraq. It's offered simply as a checklist so that they are part of our deliberations."

Among the items:

- Another state could try to take advantage of the U.S. involvement or preoccupation with Iraq.
- Oil disruption could cause international shock waves.
- Iraqi intelligence services, who have a global presence including inside the U.S., could strike the U.S., our allies or other deployed forces in unconventional ways.
- There could be higher than expected collateral damage.
- Fortress Baghdad could prove to be long and unpleasant for all.
- Iraq could experience ethnic strife among the Sunnis, Shiites and Kurds as had happened before.
- Iraq could use chemical weapons against the Shiites and blame the United States.
- Iraq could successfully best the U.S. in public relations and persuade the world that it was a war against Muslims.

The list had grown to 29 items. At the end, the memo stated, "Note: It is possible, of course, to prepare a similar illustrative list of all of the potential problems that need to be considered if there is no regime change in Iraq." This was Cheney's oft-stated point that there was a risk in inaction.

• • •

HAVING HEARD THAT SOME senior military officers were unhappy with the war plan, or even the idea of a war with Iraq, the president and Rumsfeld decided it was time to bring in the Joint Chiefs of Staff.

They had been kept deliberately at arm's length from the planning for Iraq until about two weeks earlier when they had finally been given a briefing. Bush invited them to the White House in October.

Rumsfeld wanted the chiefs to meet only with the president, without General Franks. Wolfowitz, Hadley and Libby were also excluded, though Cheney, Rice and Card attended.

The president asked the four service chiefs for their honest opinion. What did they think of the plan? Could each service do what was asked of it?

Air Force Chief of Staff General John P. Jumper said the air plan was supportable. Saddam's air defense system could be overcome, though he worried that the Iraqis might have the capability to jam the Global Positioning System (GPS) which the U.S. relied on heavily for force tracking, targeting and precision bombing. The air transport system to get forces, equipment and supplies to the region would be stretched, he said, but he believed it could handle the task. General Jumper expressed concern about the availability of precision-guided munitions; the industrial capacity to produce more would have to be at a sustained rate and the smart bombs would have to be used selectively.

The chief of naval operations, Admiral Vern Clark, was also concerned about weapons system production. With the ongoing operations in Afghanistan, he said he also worried about naval aviation and aircraft carrier usage because Iraq would be a second front. But none of this was a showstopper, he said.

Army Chief of Staff General Eric Shinseki was the first to say that he worried that the size of the attacking ground force might be too small. The plan called for a rapid advance on Baghdad. He wondered if the supply system was agile and quick enough for the fast movement. The army would be strung out over several hundred kilometers. Maintaining the supply lines could be difficult. Still, Shin-seki said he supported the plan.

The Marine commandant, General James L. Jones, said the Marines were in good shape, but he had two worries. The Marines were not used to fighting in a contaminated environment if the Iraqis were to use chemical or biological weapons. They had enough chem-bio protective suits for themselves but not enough for any Iraqi civilians, and that was potentially troublesome. Second, he said, urban warfare is hard. Saddam would surely concede the desert to U.S. forces, which could handle anything he might throw at them there, but the urban environment in Baghdad particularly would be different.

"What do you think of the plan for Baghdad?" the president asked.

Jones had not seen the plan so he ducked.

"What do you think of the plan for Baghdad?" Bush pressed.

"I haven't seen the details," Jones said, "but I understand they are being worked out."

After the meeting, Rice would intensify her questions about munitions availability, supply lines, contamination protection for civilians and urban warfare.

On October 29, Franks was again back to brief the president. The session included another update on the means to respond to the use of WMD by Saddam during an invasion, support to civil military operations, and management of the impact of possible WMD on neighboring countries.

NO, NO, NO, NO, the Turkish government had said all that fall to the CIA. Paramilitary teams would not be allowed to pass through Turkey into northern Iraq a second time. Enough pressure was applied and assurances given that finally the Turks agreed but again only with Turkish escorts. Saul passed word of the green light to Tim, who was delighted. He could handpick his own team of ten—six case officers, some of the best Arabic speakers in the agency, three experienced paramilitary officers and a communications specialist. It was the cream. Three senior sergeants from the 10th Special Forces Group from Fort Carson were detailed to accompany Tim's NILE team to go work with the PUK. Another team was assigned to the other Kurdish group, the KDP.

Saul instructed Tim to gather intelligence and recruit agents inside the regime, aid the opposition groups, and prepare for, but not yet conduct, sabotage operations. Gather intelligence on weapons of mass destruction, if possible. Find the weak points in the regime and push. War was coming.

Tim and the other team leader flew to Ankara, the Turkish capital, and appeared before the Turkish general staff. We swear, Tim told the general staff officers, we will do everything we can to keep you in the loop. You will get every single piece of intelligence we collect. You are a full partner in this—an intelligence-gathering mission, a counterterrorist mission. This is not about covert regime change. It was tap dance time, Tim thought. As a case officer trained to recruit agents to turn against their country, it was nothing to lie to the generals. Tall, erect and all-American, Tim and his fellow team leader, who had been named manager of the year by his peers in the Directorate of Operations, believed they had convinced the generals of their sincerity.

Tim and his team of 13 then flew into Diyarbakir in southeastern Turkey, a base for Turkish anti-Kurd operations about five hours' drive from the northern Iraq border. They packed into Land Cruisers and Jeep Cherokees, followed by a truck containing most of their gear. The convoy headed across the border for Kalachualan, a small village which had been PUK leader Jalal Talabani's hideout during the wars with Iraq. It was north of the provincial capital of Sulaymaniyah.

They were carrying tens of millions of dollars in U.S. $100 bills stored in black Pelican boxes, heavy cardboard boxes with hinges that are often sold in art stores. Tim had to sign for his share. In the end he had been advanced $32 million, and he would have to present vouchers to account for it all. Yellow, 3-by-3-inch Post-its signed by the paid agents would suffice, he hoped. When the others lost sight of Tim's vehicle on the way in, they joked that he probably was heading for the Riviera. Tim had found that $1 million in $100 bills weighed 44 pounds and fit neatly into a day backpack.

At the base in Kalachualan, Tim persuaded the Turks not to co-locate with them. There was no way he was going to allow the Turks or anyone to have access to the human agents he hoped to run. His team set up in a building painted lime green which they christened "Pistachio."

Tim quickly hooked up with the man from the PUK inner circle who at the end of August had said members of a repressed religious group wanted to help the CIA and the United States. This man introduced Tim to two brothers whose father was the group's leader, and had almost the equivalent status of the Catholic pope. In a series of meetings, Tim recruited the two brothers. He was still skeptical. The brothers wanted a commitment that President Bush was serious and would send the U.S. military to depose Saddam. "George Bush decides not to do this," one of the brothers said, "we're going to be left out there and all our relatives are going to get killed and all of our followers. If there's any revelation that we're helping you, all our followers are going to get massacred." They were not a hidden, secret society, and Saddam's security forces knew who and where they were.

"I will back you," Tim said. "I'll go to the moon for you, but you must bring me active-duty Iraqi military officers and then I'll make up my mind whether *you're* sincere or not." Sincerity had to be matched in kind. "I'll make up my mind whether we should back you or not."

Okay, the brothers agreed. One day at 2 A.M. they brought a man who had been smuggled into PUK territory to meet with Tim. He was a brigadier general, the head of the Iraqi army aviation staff at one of the principal air bases. Tim and another case officer debriefed the general for two or three hours in the middle of the night before he was rushed back out of Kurdish territory. They didn't know anything about helicopters but they asked him about spare parts, locations, disposition, readiness, fuel, training, communications and whatever, writing it all down to be sent to CIA headquarters where it could be vetted to see if it was real.

After one sensitive question, the general looked at the older brother and asked, "Should I be saying this?"

"You tell them now," the brother directed.

The general complied.

"This is going to work pretty well, isn't it?" Tim said.

After nearly three hours, the brothers said they had to smuggle the general back to his installation near Baghdad.

"Okay," Tim said, "but I'm not really convinced yet. Let's see more."

Several nights later, the brothers brought the head of an antiaircraft battery of French-made Roland missiles who had been assigned to one of the Republican Guard units. Under prodding from the brothers, he provided force disposition, the names of officers and other particulars.

Tim was in disbelief. Previously, the CIA's best source about Iraq might be a walk-in at the American embassy in some South American country who said he had an uncle who is an unhappy Iraqi army general. Direct access to active-duty officers was almost unheard of. The brothers smuggled the officers under carpets in trucks driven across the desert and up over the mountain passes. They said they would not be able to tell in advance who was coming because they had sent word to trusted members of the religious group to send active-duty military officers. And the officers were not told precisely what they were doing until they arrived to be interrogated by Tim and his team.

Next the brothers delivered an Iraqi officer who had carried out 103 pages of war plans for the Republican Guard units north of Baghdad. The officer described attending a secret war game led by Saddam's son Qusay. The plans showed where units would deploy in case of an American paratrooper invasion.

It was a cold, grubby existence for the team. But the Kurds and Iraqis placed much on appearance, so Tim would struggle out of bed for the 2 A.M. sessions, pulling a blazer over his long underwear. He kept well-shaved, didn't grow a beard, but there was grit everywhere and his boots were caked with mud.

The brothers and their father, the Pope, did not want money for each debriefing, but they wanted vehicles and lots of money each month. Tim thought they gave a new definition to avarice.

From headquarters, Saul said that money was not an object. Make sure that you can continue to encourage this flow and ensure that these people are brought out. You can tell them what you need to ensure their continued cooperation.

Tim agreed initially to pay the brothers and their father $135,000 a month. Though they kept pushing on money and upping the stakes, Tim asked them, What do you really want? What is your bottom line?

A seat at the table when the new, post-Saddam government is formed in Iraq, they made clear.

You will have such a seat, Tim pledged. What else and who else have you got?

The brothers provided a list of names and positions that Tim cabled to Saul at the CIA. Sitting in his sixth floor office in the Directorate of Operations, Saul was dumbfounded as he read it over. Not only were there many more in significant military positions, Republican Guard and elsewhere, but the group said they had guys in the Fedayeen Saddam, the thuggish paramilitary group led by Saddam's son Uday, and the Iraqi Intelligence Service and Special Security Organization—all right at the heart of the apparatus that made Saddam's rule possible and until now impregnable.

"Holy shit!" Saul muttered. "If it is 50 percent bullshit, we've still hit a gold mine."

1. President George W. Bush with General Tommy Franks, after the first major Top Secret war planning session on Iraq in Crawford, Texas, on December 28, 2001. "We have made a start," Franks told an aide afterward.

2

2. *Secretary of State Colin Powell, National Security Adviser Condoleezza Rice and Secretary of Defense Donald Rumsfeld. One of Rice's jobs was to "read the secretaries" and referee their frequent tussles. Rice had more access to Bush than anyone.*

3. *Lewis "Scooter" Libby, Vice President Cheney's chief of staff, held three titles in the administration and was a force multiplier for Cheney's agenda.*

4. *Deputy Secretary of State Richard Armitage told National Security Adviser Rice that the NSC system was "dysfunctional."*

3

5

5. *Bush rehearsing his January 2002 State of the Union speech that declared Iraq, Iran and North Korea part of an "axis of evil." White House counselor Karen Hughes and other aides listen. Bush didn't expect it would be such a defining phrase.*

6. *Steve Hadley, the deputy national security adviser, chaired the deputies committee and took on the task of coordinating postwar planning.*

7. *Paul Wolfowitz, the deputy secretary of defense, was one of the intellectual godfathers for ousting Saddam Hussein by force.*

6

7

8

8. *Powell and Armitage, watching the war planning intensify over the summer of 2002, warned of the consequences of war and occupying Iraq, calling it the "Pottery Barn rule": You break it, you own it. Powell was frequently in the "icebox" with the White House.*

9. *Rumsfeld met regularly with Bush in private to review plans, concerns and decisions on Iraq. The invasion plans changed almost monthly for over a year.*

9

10. *White House Communications Director Dan Bartlett (left), Rice and speechwriter Michael Gerson review a State of the Union draft with Bush in the Oval Office. This president made policy in his speeches and often went through two dozen or more drafts.*

11. *Vice President Dick Cheney, in a speech to the Veterans of Foreign Wars at their convention on August 26, 2002, said there is "no doubt" Saddam has weapons of mass destruction.*

12

13. *Senator Bob Graham, the Florida Democrat who chaired the Intelligence Committee, opposed the congressional resolution authorizing the president's use of force in Iraq.*

12. *CIA Director George Tenet called the WMD case on Iraq a "slam dunk."*

13

14. *Rumsfeld and Franks on Capitol Hill with Democratic Senator Carl Levin of Michigan, who also voted against the war resolution.*

14

15

15. British Prime Minister Tony Blair pledged in September 2002 to support President Bush on Iraq. "Your man has got cojones," Bush told Blair's aides after the meeting.

16. Powell and Bush on November 8, 2002, after the U.N. Security Council unanimously passed Resolution 1441 calling for new weapons inspections in Iraq.

17. Spanish President José María Aznar, who supported military action, assured Bush, "You can always see a mustache next to you."

16

17

18. *Cheney, Powell, Bush and Rice during a light moment in the Oval Office.*

19. *Rumsfeld was challenged by Franks during the Afghanistan war—"I'm either the commander or I'm not," the general said—but the two found their way and forged a bold new war plan for Iraq.*

20

20. *Deputy CIA Director John McLaughlin, a cautious analyst whose Top Secret presentation in the Oval Office on Iraqi WMD during December 2002 did not impress Bush as persuasive.*

21

21. *Powell, holding a simulated vial of anthrax, makes the case for war to the U.N. Security Council on February 5, 2003.*

22. *Hans Blix (left) and Mohamed ElBaradei, the chief U.N. weapons inspectors.*

22

23. *The war cabinet meets in the White House Situation Room. Seated at table, from left: George Tenet, White House Chief of Staff Andrew Card, President Bush, Colin Powell, Donald Rumsfeld, Chairman of the Joint Chiefs of Staff General Richard Myers and Condoleezza Rice. (Cheney is not present.) Along the wall, from left: Frank Miller, the director of the National Security Council staff for defense, Steve Hadley, White House Counsel Alberto Gonzales and Scooter Libby.*

24

24. *Bush talks to Russian President Vladimir Putin on March 18, 2003, the day before the war begins, as Rice, Card and Cheney confer.*

25. *James Pavitt, the CIA deputy director for operations (left), Tenet and McLaughlin arrive at the White House with sensitive intelligence reports from the DB/ROCKSTARS on March 18, 2003.*

25

26. Card, Cheney and Rice in the Oval Office. All eventually recommended that Bush approve an attack on Saddam at Dora Farm on March 19, 2003.

27. Saudi Ambassador Prince Bandar bin Sultan, almost a fifth estate in Washington, had unusual access to Bush.

28. *Bush and Cheney meet privately on March 19, 2003. Cheney recommended that Bush order a strike on Saddam. Even if it missed, Cheney said, it would "rattle his cage."*

29. *Watching television in Rice's West Wing office on the night the war began, from left: White House press secretary Ari Fleischer (on phone), Card, Bartlett, Hughes and Rice.*

30. *The war cabinet meets at Camp David on Saturday, March 22, one day after the "shock and awe" air war began. Clockwise around table, from left: Vice Chairman of the Joint Chiefs of Staff General Pete Pace, Chairman of the Joint Chiefs General Myers, Secretary of State Powell, Secretary of Defense Rumsfeld, Vice President Cheney, Deputy Defense Secretary Wolfowitz, Chief of Staff to the Vice President Libby, White House Chief of Staff Card, President Bush, National Security Adviser Rice, CIA Director Tenet and White House Counsel Gonzales.*

31

31. President Bush walks alone on the morning of March 19, 2003, after ordering the start of war. "It was emotional for me. I prayed as I walked around the circle," he recalled.

20

THE TELEVISION MONITOR had a small but highly unusual warning in the corner of the screen: TOP SECRET.

The man sitting at a table in the studio on October 18 before a large, old-fashioned microphone à la Larry King was short and balding, with a big head and large-framed eyeglasses—definitely not out of central casting for a TV talk show or a general. But he wore three stars, the rank of lieutenant general, and spoke in an insistent, high-pitched voice, both brainy and confident. A large banner strung behind him said "Talk NSA." The NSA was for National Security Agency, the inner sanctum of intelligence secrets, which intercepts communications abroad while trying to protect U.S. codes and break foreign ones.

The most secretive and best-funded arm of the vast U.S. spy apparatus—with about $6 billion of the $30 billion total annual U.S. intelligence budget—NSA targets telephones, radios, computers, banking transactions and almost any electron that moved. Its goal is to eavesdrop on the most important communications abroad, unbeknownst to those using the airwaves, phone lines, microwave relays, satellites, undersea cables, computer networks or any other communication device or method. All this is called signals intelligence, SIGINT in the spy world.

Though it is unknown to the outside world, NSA has its own

talk show. "Talk NSA" is broadcast on the secure, Top Secret closed television circuit to some 32,000 employees at NSA and no one else.

Speaking that day was Air Force Lieutenant General Michael V. Hayden, the director of NSA, who had spent 32 years as an intelligence officer with assignments in Europe, Asia and throughout the Pacific. SIGINT battle stations had changed with modern technology, he explained for the camera. It's now the Internet and cell phones, he said, used by everyone from foreign intelligence services to drug traffickers and terrorists. What, he wondered, could he appropriately reveal to all 32,000 people about the gee-whiz operations that demonstrated NSA's ability to track people? The agency was highly compartmented and few secrets spread beyond small units or divisions. Describing a convergence of mathematical theory, physics, miniaturization, high-speed computers, linguistic ingenuity and daring, he provided some examples of the latest techniques and technologies.

Turning to the possible war with Iraq, Hayden had decided to lay it on the line for his workforce, saying something that could not be declared publicly. "A SIGINT agency can't wait for the political decision," he said. Although a formal decision to go to war with Iraq had not yet been made, every instinct and experience told him that war was coming. He had to move resources. He could not wait for President Bush to decide. There was too much to be done. Remaining passive was unacceptable. He had to prepare the agency, and he had been quietly doing so for months. Given the weather in Iraq and the requirement that the U.S. forces would have to wear chemical protective gear, he said, "You can't start a war in Iraq later than March." That was less than six months away. "You've got to do it in January, February or March."

Hayden's declaration would have created a sensation if it had leaked to the news media. Like nearly all of NSA's secrets, however, it did not leak.

HAYDEN WAS NOT GOING to be caught short as he had before 9/11. In important respects, it had been a very bad year for NSA. There was an expectation in the United States, driven by the media, the Congress, even the TV and movie culture, that the country's lead in high technology and investment in its intelligence agencies would provide warning of an attack, even a terrorist strike such as 9/11.

The day before his appearance on the closed-circuit talk show, Hayden had provided Congress and the public with a sobering reality check in testimony before the joint congressional committees on the state of intelligence prior to 9/11.

"Sadly, NSA had no SIGINT suggesting that al Qaeda was specifically targeting New York and Washington, D.C., or even that it was planning an attack on U.S. soil," he said. "Indeed, NSA had no knowledge before September 11th that any of the attackers were in the United States."

It turned out that after examining its vast files and computer storage, NSA had discovered two intercepted foreign language messages on September 10, 2001, in which suspected terrorists said: "The match is about to begin" and "Tomorrow is zero hour."

Those messages were not translated until September 12. Though dramatic in hindsight, Hayden testified, "This information did not specifically indicate an attack would take place on that day. It did not contain any details on the time, place or nature of what might happen. It also contained no suggestion of airplanes being used as weapons." He also noted that more than 30 similar cryptic warnings or declarations had been intercepted in the months before 9/11 and were not followed by any terrorist attack.

Hayden testified that on 9/11 the handful of people working the bin Laden task force in the NSA counterterrorist unit were "emotionally shattered." He did not say in public that they felt they had let the nation down, and that many had been in tears. He also did not say that he now had nearly ten times as many people working in the NSA bin Laden unit than before the attacks.

NSA is geared to provide early warning. The National Security Operations Center (NSOC) is staffed 24 hours a day, seven days a week with about 30 people. Its sole purpose is to monitor and filter the SIGINT so that a so-called CRITIC flash message can be sent to the president to provide essential warning or intelligence within 10 minutes of being processed.

Clues, perhaps even answers, are everywhere in the millions of electronic communications that NSA intercepts every hour. It is a staggering task to make sense of them, sort them and get them out the door to the president, or the military, or the CIA, so they could be acted on.

Hayden had been getting ready for Iraq much of the year. He was not interested in winning close. The first alert for him had been the president's Axis of Evil speech earlier in the year. As a colonel, Hayden had worked on the NSC staff for Bush senior, and had helped write presidential speeches. He knew that speeches, drafts of which were circulated among the various agencies, were a way of ironing out details and reaching consensus. He listened to and read them carefully. Policy was made in speeches, and with someone like George W. Bush, who was plainspoken, they were even more important. The declaration of an Axis of Evil had an unusual clarity and likely meant war, Hayden had concluded.

With his subordinates, he had gone further. "It is my judgment in doing this for [more than] 30 years, I have never seen a condition like this when it didn't end in war. We're going to war."

On July 31, Hayden had NSA conduct a "Rock Drill," an old Army term from the days when a planning exercise consisted of moving around rocks on a map to signify formations. He gathered together all the SIGINT producers who managed the actual listeners and asked how they would tackle Iraq as a wartime target. It was a very technical look at Iraq with lots of maps showing communications targets, and matching them with interception capabilities, methods and equipment, ranging from SIGINT satellites to remote sensors that would clandestinely be placed on borders or inside the country. He was going to have a wartime target list in the hundreds—meaning the NSA would not only try to intercept the senior Iraqi civilian and military leadership, but drill down into smaller military, intelligence and security units.

Hayden directed the NSA staff to prepare a stoplight chart on the quality of SIGINT on the various categories of targets. Green was good, yellow mediocre and red nothing. What had the U.S. military been doing in the last decade? Northern Watch and Southern Watch. So it was green SIGINT on Iraqi air operations, air defense and air command and control. It was yellow, but not a very good yellow, on the Republican Guard and the regular Iraqi army. On Saddam and the political leadership it was red. It was also red on the Special Security Organization and Special Republican Guard.

The bottom line: SIGINT quality and quantity out of Iraq was negligible.

In his testimony to Congress, Hayden had said he had not been able to direct $200 million of NSA money into "new age signals" because it would erode coverage elsewhere. Never again. On his own authority, he had ordered that $300 million to $400 million of NSA's budget be redirected to "Iraq unique" operations and targets. Hundreds of personnel would also be reassigned to Iraq operations. Such was the power of the NSA director. Iraq had reasonably good encryption on some of its circuits, the kind of old-line Soviet coding equipment that NSA knew well and could crack. SIGINT did not get better with time, Hayden knew. It got worse and eventually grew useless. Its value was its immediacy, and he was going to make sure they could give it to people on the battlefield.

He decided that he would for the first time open what he called the "national vaults"—the most sensitive SIGINT—to the ground commanders. A senior enlisted man in his Humvee in battle would have a Top Secret satellite link into the global SIGINT system. Hayden's intention was to have the Iraqi military so thoroughly covered that the man in the Humvee would have more real-time situational awareness about where the Iraqis were than the Iraqis would have about themselves. He would set up a highly classified computer chat room that would link the NSA operators, listeners, other intelligence personnel and military units directly. Its codeword was Zircon Chat. The network could handle up to 2,000 people all linked real-time so an intercept, say of an Iraqi colonel, could be available to the U.S. military on the battlefield. The information could be used to track the Iraqi unit or attack the colonel.

It was going to be knowledge-based war. That would make intelligence more important than ever. Hayden was aware that it placed a tremendous burden on all his people.

Hayden had a dark view of the world. He didn't think it would be possible to preserve the United States as a free society as they knew it by playing defense on the three-yard line all the time. They had to play offense. Hayden had received a Catholic education as a young man and was a student of church doctrine. According to the precepts of his education, particularly his study of St. Thomas Aquinas and St. Augustine, two leading philosophers on the concept of "just war," the U.S. could strike militarily on what he called a "proportional response based upon the evidence available at the time." The targets had to be of sufficient weight to justify the potential loss of innocent life.

Here, in Hayden's estimation, was where SIGINT had improved. As recently as 15 years ago, trusting the SIGINT and making it the basis for action would have been a leap of faith. Now he had linguists—the listeners with the headphones—who followed specific targets for months, even years, in some cases up to five years. The listener almost became a member of the family, could recognize voices instantly and read meaning, tone, inflection, emotion, almost the entire metabolism. So it would not only be the factualness of the literal words, but it could be accompanied by analysis leading to the real meaning and often intent.

A linguist might report, "I've never heard Colonel Takriti so panicked . . . He's unwinding . . . This is happening."

The Iraqi dialect was only one of seven Arabic dialects, so he ordered short courses of four to six weeks for a great many NSA Arabic linguists.

Hayden had reviewed NSA's substantial take from Iraq on Saddam's weapons of mass destruction, the accumulated evidence of programs and concealment. "Massive but inferential," he concluded.

The only parallax that brought all the data points together was the conclusion that Saddam had a hidden WMD program. But it was not a certainty. Discussion of the recent National Intelligence Estimate on Iraq's WMD missed the critical point that these were estimates, full of judgments, not absolute certainties.

One night as he was doing the dishes with his wife, she asked about this and he said, "If it were a fact, it wouldn't be intelligence."

21

POWELL REALIZED THAT HE, the president and perhaps the rest of the world were traveling a road that would come to a fork. One fork would be a new U.N. resolution, weapons inspections and no war. The other fork would be war. It seemed almost that simple.

The secretary's first negotiation after Bush's September 12 U.N. speech was with his NSC colleagues. There was some discussion of trying to get resolutions not just on weapons inspections for WMD, but on Saddam's connections and support to terrorism and on his brutal human rights record. It was clear that few other countries would support such an effort. The terrorism case seemed weak or unprovable, and the issue of seeking regime change because Saddam was a dictator or a particularly brutal despot would not get to first base. It would be both loudly and quietly laughed out of the United Nations, which had its share of countries with one-man rule. WMD was really the only one that had any "legs," Rice said, because at least a dozen resolutions on Iraq's WMD already had been passed and to one extent or another ignored by Saddam.

So the serious discussion was about what to ask for in the new resolution on weapons inspections. Cheney and Rumsfeld lobbied, successfully at first, to put in stringent requirements. The strongest version called for the creation of U.S.- or U.N.-enforced no-fly and even no-drive zones along the routes that U.N. inspectors would travel in Iraq. This would be above and beyond the existing no-fly zones in Operations Northern and Southern Watch. In addition, the draft would give the five permanent members of the Security Council authority to send in their own inspectors along with the U.N. team. Further, it would eliminate all prior exemptions from inspections given to Saddam's presidential compounds and so-called sensitive sites.

If Saddam was found to be in "material breach"—U.N. language for a substantive violation—of any part of the new resolution, it would trigger automatic authorization for the U.S. and others to use "all necessary means" to achieve compliance. "All necessary means" is a U.N. code for war and had been the broad language in the U.N. resolution that authorized the use of force in the 1991 Gulf War. This would all be done in a single resolution.

Powell called it the "maximalist" approach. Cheney and Rumsfeld were hoping that a few provisions would stick when Powell submitted it to the U.N. Security Council. In his darker moments, Powell believed it was so hard-line that it was designed to ensure he would fail. When he offered the first draft, showing it to the Security Council's other 14 members, nobody else was for it. Not the Brits, not the Spanish, not the Bulgarians—the best U.S. allies on the Council. Had there been a vote it would have been 1 to 14, he realized.

Powell reported the complaints to the NSC. On October 23, he circulated a new draft that had been cleared by the president. It softened on the triggering mechanism, no longer authorizing "all necessary means"—war—for any violation by Iraq. Instead, violations would be brought back to the Security Council to "consider" the situation—a term that was vague.

To win a new resolution under U.N. rules, Powell had to get the votes of 9 of the 15 Security Council members. Also any one of the four other permanent members of the Security Council—Russia, China, France or Britain—could veto the resolution. Powell had to get their votes or get them to abstain. In any such negotiation, one country generally emerges as the other side. Since Germany was not on the Security Council, it instantly became clear to Powell that the other side was France. France, Russia and China all had close commercial ties to Iraq and had come out publicly against any unilateral U.S. action to depose Saddam.

As Powell met with his counterparts and burned up the phone lines, he saw that French Foreign Minister Dominique de Villepin, a tall, aristocratic poet-diplomat who had written an adulatory biography of Napoleon, held the strongest feelings against war. It was as if de Villepin and his boss, French President Jacques Chirac, suddenly realized, Wow, we've been given the whip hand. Powell believed that the French and the Russians were in league on this, with France putting up an increasingly vocal counterweight to Powell's effort.

De Villepin insisted on a two-step process. First, a resolution for a new round of inspections. Any violation or "material breach" discovered by the inspectors would then have to be debated by the Security Council. A second resolution would have to be passed to authorize the use of force.

Meanwhile, Cheney insisted that the resolution require Saddam to submit a detailed "declaration" after a resolution was passed. Iraq would have to give a full accounting of all programs to develop chemical, biological and nuclear weapons. Saddam would be given 30 days to do this under Cheney's proposal. It was designed more or less as a trap for Saddam. He would claim he had no WMD and that lie would be grounds for war. Or Saddam would confess he had WMD, proving he had lied for 12 years. As Cheney framed it, "That would be sufficient cause to say he's lied again, he's not come clean and you'd find material breach and away you'd go."

Rice and the others thought it was a brilliant idea, and Powell was asked to sell it to the French, who eventually agreed that the resolution could require such a declaration. De Villepin, however, continued to insist that a second resolution would have to be passed to authorize war.

Bush and Cheney deemed that unacceptable. It would ensure delay, and a second resolution would be harder to get than the one they were negotiating.

To get the French to fall off the need for a second resolution,

Powell decided to pretend to make a deal. Language and alternative language, and alternative language to the alternative language, were flying around. Since de Villepin had agreed that false, inadequate statements in the new weapons declaration by Iraq would be considered a material breach, Powell then got broad language added saying that failure by Iraq at any time to "cooperate fully with the implementation of this resolution should constitute a further material breach." Though this would have to be reported to the Security Council for "assessment," Powell considered it an effective ambush of the French. The language meant that almost anything they deemed Saddam had done wrong would be a material breach. And that, in Powell's reading, would be enough to authorize "serious consequences," the new language for action.

It got so tight and so tense that the final disagreement boiled down to the use of a single word. For about five days Powell and de Villepin argued. As participants remember it, and records indicate, the French position was that a false declaration "and" a general failure to cooperate could constitute a material breach. The "and" meant Saddam would have to fail two tests. Powell's draft said a false declaration "or" a general failure to cooperate could constitute a material breach.

"What we want is better for your purposes," Powell somewhat implausibly argued to de Villepin. "Would you please look at these two words? They are almost identical in terms of meaning and I could argue that you're better off with ours."

De Villepin wouldn't budge.

ON NOVEMBER 1, Powell brought the people who would head the U.N. weapons inspections teams to see Bush and Cheney. Rice and Wolfowitz also attended. They were Hans Blix, a cheery, 74-year-old Swedish lawyer and diplomat who wore dark-rimmed glasses that dominated his large face, and Mohamed ElBaradei, 60, the Egyptian director of the Vienna-based International Atomic Energy Agency (IAEA), which verifies nuclear nonproliferation. The view among the hard-liners, including Wolfowitz, was that Blix was weak and would be pushed around by Saddam.

"You've got to understand, Mr. Blix," Bush said, "you've got the force of the United States behind you. And I'm prepared to use it if need be to enforce this resolution." The president added, "The decision to go to war will be my decision. Don't ever feel like what you're saying is making the decision."

Blix, who had taken over the Iraq weapons inspection commission in 2000 and previously had headed the IAEA for 17 years, said he wanted tough inspections, knew the games Saddam played, and was determined this time to get to the bottom.

Bush seemed somewhat convinced, though Cheney was concerned that Blix, from traditionally pacifist Sweden, would not be tough enough.

POWELL STARTED GIVING ground on the resolution on little things, buried way back in the draft, that he deemed of no consequence. He was on a short leash and he could see that the president was uneasy. To Bush and the NSC, he said, "This doesn't make any difference. Just let me solve it," implying that if left alone he could fix it.

The language of the U.N. is often so vague, overblown, tedious and repetitive that for practical purposes each sovereign country has leeway to interpret resolutions as they wish. Powell realized that what was really important was the headline in some form: Nations Agree on Iraq Resolution. Few would read the actual resolution or understand it. What mattered would be what action or lack of action each country decided upon, but that was down the road.

The French intransigence surprised Powell. Even on the Saturday of his daughter's wedding, 20 minutes before walking her down the aisle, Powell got caught up on a phone call with de Villepin.

The art of a successful negotiation is often to find an endgame in which it gets down to a single issue—in this case "and" versus "or"—and then to capitulate. Powell talked to Rice and said he thought he could get 14 votes of the 15 on the Security Council, perhaps even all 15 if he could give in to the French on the "and." The language would not make that much difference, he argued, but unanimity or near unanimity would make it a victory.

Rice called around to the principals and the president. All wanted to stick with the "or" so Saddam's WMD declaration would be all they would need for war.

It isn't worth it, Rice finally said. Whatever the language in the resolution, they would be in the Security Council arguing over Saddam's weapons declaration anyway. "Let's not hang on ceremony here."

Initially they had thought they could get a U.N. resolution in several weeks, but it was now week seven of negotiations and everyone was frustrated and exhausted. The president and the others finally gave their okay, if Powell was sure. The president, in particular, liked to have something that could be called a victory.

Sometime during the night of November 6 or early the morning of November 7, Powell finally received the final okay from Rice. He called de Villepin, who was on an airplane with Chirac.

"Dominique, we can go with 'and' but only if that's the end of it. There is nothing else to discuss. It is over. And I have to have your approval of that and your president's approval."

"The president is sitting right here with me," de Villepin said. "I will ask him. I think this is it."

Powell waited as they conferred. He thought de Villepin sounded so relieved that either solution would have been acceptable.

"Yes," de Villepin finally said. "Yes."

"Wonderful," Powell replied. "That's a deal with you."

He immediately called the Russian foreign minister, Igor Ivanov. "Igor, I just made a deal with Dominique and it's going to be 'and.'"

"That is a major breakthrough," Ivanov said. "How wonderful! I must hang up and go see the president immediately." He apparently rushed off to talk with Vladimir Putin.

Ivanov called back a half-hour later. Putin approved. "It is wonderful, it is a breakthrough."

No, Powell realized, it wasn't. The seeming compromise was

just getting everybody off the hook. But hey, he thought to himself, you take it where you can get it.

On November 8, U.N. Security Council Resolution 1441 was brought to a vote by the 15 representatives seated around the dramatic circular table. It said that if Saddam continued to violate his disarmament obligations, he would face "serious consequences"— the ambiguous phrase that Powell had got inserted to replace "all necessary means."

All 15 hands went up. The biggest surprise was Syria. Powell never thought that Syria, as the only Arab state on the Security Council at the time, would vote for the resolution. But there was no love lost between the Syrians and the Iraqis, and apparently the Syrians did not want to be isolated. It was read as an important signal of Arab displeasure with Saddam.

"Well done, well done," Bush said in a call to Powell. Later that day, Powell appeared alone at Bush's side in the Rose Garden as the president praised him for his "leadership, his good work and his determination."

Armitage thought the 15 to 0 vote was a stunning development—unanimity on a tough-sounding resolution, suggesting a seriousness about diplomacy by the Bush administration that had not heretofore been evident.

Powell knew he had scored a big victory. He had made diplomacy relevant. Now everyone who had operational responsibilities— the president, Powell, the CIA and the military—had more time. The secretary closely followed the sniping and rumors and negative news accounts of his diplomacy—nearly every day something about Powell screwed up, Powell *is* screwed up, the Pentagon versus Powell, Cheney versus Powell, diplomacy is stuck.

The way he figured it, the 15 to 0 would quell the Powell-is-on-his-way-out stories and whispers for about a month.

He felt he had hoodwinked the French. Though they had won the language, he had gotten them to vote for a resolution that called for "serious consequences." He did not see that payback might be coming.

For his larger, ultimate purposes of avoiding war, however, he may have done too well with the resolution.

LATER PRESIDENT BUSH RECALLED that it had been a very difficult time. He had worried about the "negotiating strategy. I felt like the French were getting the upper hand. In the end, we got a great resolution, and to Colin's credit."

He recalled his attitude, "I am very frustrated with the resolution process. The campaign is happening at the same time." The midterm elections were November 5. Historically the party that holds the White House loses seats in the House and Senate—often many. But the Republicans gained two seats in the Senate, putting them back in the majority, and added six in the House. "We win the elections and win the resolution," Bush recalled. But he said he had a more ambitious goal, which was "a very intrusive inspection regime which Blair and I both were hoping would cause there to be crumbling within the regime."

22

___

O N FRIDAY, NOVEMBER 15, the Saudi ambassador, Prince Bandar bin Sultan, came to the Oval Office to see the president. Cheney and Rice were also there. Bandar had served during four American presidencies. At age 53, Bandar was almost a fifth estate in Washington, amplifying Saudi influence and wealth. He insisted on dealing directly with presidents and is almost family to Bush's father. And he had maintained his special entrée to the Oval Office under this President Bush.

In the Top Secret memo "Iraq: Goals, Objectives and Strategy" that the president had finally signed on August 29, one key goal was "to minimize disruption in international oil markets." The Saudis, with the largest proven oil reserves in the world, are the key to oil markets. They can increase or decrease production by millions of barrels a day, driving prices down or up. Low, stable oil prices are essential to a turnaround in the U.S. economy, which was stalled, and a $5 to $10 per barrel price increase could have a devastating impact.

None of the three Americans in the room, nor Bandar, were unmindful of the impact the economy held in presidential elections. All this gave the Saudis incredible leverage.

Bandar handed the president a private letter from Crown Prince Abdullah handwritten in Arabic and provided an English translation.

"My Dear Friend George Bush: It has been some time since we

had communications. At the beginning I would like to congratulate you for the result achieved by the Republican Party under your leadership, as well your great efforts in achieving an agreed Security Council resolution. There are many things I wish we had an opportunity to discuss face to face. But the most important ones I have asked my ambassador who has been away from Washington for quite some time to discuss with you. I hope he gets his punishment from you as he got it from me." Bandar had not been well and had been away for months. "Please accept my best personal regards and also please convey my regards to your nice wife and to your two dear parents."

As instructed, Bandar then said formally, "Since 1994, we have been in constant contact and touch with you on the highest level regarding what needs to be done with Iraq and the Iraqi regime. Throughout this time, we were looking for seriousness from you that should have been demonstrated in coming together for formulating a joint plan between the governments to get rid of Saddam."

In 1994, King Fahd had proposed to President Clinton a joint U.S.-Saudi covert action to overthrow Saddam, and Crown Prince Abdullah in April 2002 had suggested to Bush that they spend up to $1 billion in such joint operations with the CIA. "Every time we meet, we are surprised that the United States asks us to give our impression about what can be done regarding Saddam Hussein," Bandar said, suggesting that the repeated requests caused them to "begin to doubt how serious America is about the issue of regime change.

"Now Mr. President, we want to hear from you directly on your serious intention regarding this subject so we can adjust and coordinate so we can make the right policy decision." Making a decision on such a sensitive issue is very difficult, Bandar acknowledged, "but at the end we will take the right decision based on our friendships and our interests."

Emphasizing the point, Bandar added, "If you are serious, we will take the right decision to make the right support.

"Now tell us what you are going to do," Bandar read. "If you have a serious intention, we will not hesitate in giving you the right facilities that our two military people can then implement and discuss in order to support the American military action or campaign.

"This will make Saudi Arabia a major ally for the United States. At the same time, it will create a lot of difficulties that I am sure you are very much aware of.

"As you know, we are confident in our internal situation. However, the situation in the Arab and Islamic [world] is quite fluid in a way that it could hurt or threaten our interests and your interests.

"Therefore, to protect those joint interests, we want you in this difficult situation to confirm to us that you will be seriously engaging in solving the Middle East problem. We also expect Saudi Arabia to play a major role in shaping the regime that will emerge not only in Iraq but in the region after the fall of Saddam Hussein."

"Thank you for this," Bush replied. "I always appreciate the crown prince's views. I consider him a good friend. I consider him a good ally, a great ally.

"If I decide to deal militarily with the situation in Iraq, it will mean the end of the current regime—nothing short of that." The president said he wanted to create a new Iraqi government that represented all the different religious and ethnic factions of Iraq. "The main goal is not really the return of inspectors to Iraq, but to make sure that Iraq has no weapons of mass destruction that could pose a threat to the kingdom and/or to Israel." Bush added that when he made up his mind on the military option, he would contact the crown prince prior to his final decision.

Bandar then reminded the president that his father and King Fahd had taken two historic steps together: the liberation of Kuwait in the 1991 Gulf War and the reopening of the Middle East peace process. But neither were completed, and the crown prince and the president now had to finish them by getting rid of Saddam and finalizing the peace process.

Bush said he had discussed this the day before with his advisers and he would like to reiterate his government's commitment to the peace process, regardless of what the prime minister of Israel or oth-

ers around him might say about the Americans' view or position. He
also said he was fully committed to everything he had told the crown
prince at his ranch in the spring. "You tell the crown prince, I give
him my word." Bush went on to criticize Yassir Arafat, saying the
current Palestinian leadership was not useful. Alternative leadership
was needed, he said. Such leadership will emerge if an opportunity is
given to the Palestinian people. He also criticized the Israeli leadership. Sharon is a "bull," he said, "and the alternatives are worse than
him."

The president added, "Changes in Iraq will result in a change of
way of doing things, not only in Iraq but even in Iran."

Bandar expressed annoyance that some in the U.S. government,
particularly the Department of Defense, had tried to contact members of Saudi opposition groups. The president promised to look into
the matter.

Cheney asked what the Saudis wanted to be said publicly.

"We would like everything to be kept confidential and secret between us until further notice," Bandar replied, saying that the Saudis
needed to know the exact details of the military plan. He reminded
Cheney that when he had been secretary of defense and Powell the
chairman of the Joint Chiefs of Staff, they had shown him the secret
military plans for the Gulf War to demonstrate that the U.S. was serious about liberating Kuwait.

Bush then asked to see Bandar alone, and they met without the
others for 15 minutes.

ON TUESDAY, NOVEMBER 26, two days before Thanksgiving, General Franks sent Rumsfeld the MODEPS, technical shorthand for
mobilization deployments of U.S. military forces for war. Franks
called it "The Mother of All Deployment Orders" because it was a
giant request. Almost exactly a year earlier the president had asked
Rumsfeld to begin serious work on the Iraq war plan. This was a first
major step in implementing what they had done.

Franks was requesting that Rumsfeld begin deployment of

300,000 men and women. All would not be needed immediately and likely many would never be needed. The forces would be sent to the region in phases from then through the next spring. It was a big number, including reserves, and under Pentagon procedures they tried to give notice as far in advance as possible to all the units. Franks told the president it was what he would need if you want to start the war on pick-your-date in January, February or March.

The general had been incrementally improving his position in the region with small units, a few ships and aircraft. For example, he now had two Army armored brigades in Kuwait with more than 9,000 personnel and 150 tanks. At maximum there were 60,000 military personnel in the region. But not a lot of this was real combat power on the ground. It included some 20,000 Navy personnel, mostly aboard ships, including two aircraft carriers. The rest were scattered units numbering at most 5,000, except for the Army brigades in Kuwait. For example, the Navy's Fifth Fleet in Bahrain had about 4,000 and the Air Force about 5,000 in Saudi Arabia, not the numbers for an invasion.

But Franks had to give notice to 300,000 personnel—what he might need for the 225 days the Hybrid Plan anticipated from the beginning to the end of decisive combat operations.

After blanching, Rumsfeld said, "We can't do it this way." He saw an immense problem, and he was soon consulting with the president, triggering a bit of a fuss. Notification of the various military units, even if their deployments were months away, would telegraph that 300,000 U.S. military personnel were shipping or flying off to the Middle East. Diplomacy would be over.

Bush made it clear that he did not want a deployment to limit his options.

Dissociate a big deployment or buildup from what Colin is doing on the diplomatic front, Bush instructed. Iraq had agreed to new weapons inspections that were starting the next day. He was increasingly skeptical but could not appear to be pulling the plug. Don't make it look like I have no choice but to invade, he said.

At the Pentagon, after receiving this pretty clear guidance from the president, Rumsfeld went to work. The mobilization and deployment system, formally called the TPFDD (pronounced TIP-fid) for Time-Phased Force and Deployment Data, was focused on notifying units and getting enough ships and airplanes to get those units to the battlefield. Because of the distance to the Middle East, the size of the force, and mass of necessary supplies, ammunition, food and medicine, the issue was the transportation piece.

But the notifications, the assembling of ships and aircraft, the movement of the initial forces all would telegraph to reporters and soon the world that war was coming.

Rumsfeld said they had to find another way to begin the process, to get out the necessary notifications but not use the number 300,000 or anything close to it. "By the way," he said to Franks and his inner circle in his rebuking tone, "did you notice that the holidays are coming up? We're going to affect the lives of 300,000 people and nobody appears to me to have thought about that."

Rumsfeld believed he was lifting up a big rock and finding a big process problem with the entire department that had to be fixed on the fly. The deployment plans were designed like a switch with only an "on" and an "off." There was nothing in between. "We're going to dribble this out slowly," he said, "so that it's enough to keep the pressure on for the diplomacy but not so much as to discredit the diplomacy." He didn't want anyone to be able to say, "Well, you have already made up your mind." So the diplomacy piece was the issue, not the transportation piece.

Franks said the war would be over sooner if he could get the forces there quickly. "If you get the guys identified right now," the general said, "I can truly guarantee you I can compress the major combat phase."

It wasn't going to happen that way, Rumsfeld said. He proposed they break the deployment into modules or pieces. Soon he was examining the TPFDD himself, dipping in and out, finding the pieces or units he wanted. He was going to redesign the switch, transform it into something like a dimmer switch, with gradual, less noticeable deployments.

It took nearly two weeks, and the first major deployment order was issued on December 6. It was going to be slow and Rumsfeld would have to approve each deployment order, perhaps two a week for a long time. This meant some active and reserve units received short notice of less than a week before being activated or deploying, instead of the normal 30 days or more. There was a good deal of grumbling, especially from some Army generals.

Rumsfeld later recalled, "And some of it was criticized. The fact that it took the deployment process and disaggregated it to support diplomacy was never understood out there, and I didn't want to say that's what we were doing so we sat here and took the hit."

AT THE MONDAY, December 2, press briefing, Ari Fleischer laid out why the administration thought Saddam was in a no-win situation. "If Saddam Hussein indicated that he has weapons of mass destruction and that he is violating United Nations resolutions, then we will know that Saddam Hussein again deceived the world. If he declared he has none, then we will know that Saddam Hussein is once again misleading the world." That was because, he said confidently, "We have intelligence information about what Saddam Hussein possesses."

The wisdom of insisting that Saddam make a full and early weapons declaration 30 days after the U.N. resolution was passed seemed evident. He was boxed in. It *seemed*.

Weapons inspections on the ground in Iraq had begun in late November as the U.N. teams traversed the outskirts of Baghdad in their white vehicles. Nothing was found even in a surprise, one-and-a-half-hour search of one of Saddam's presidential palaces.

On December 7, Iraq submitted an 11,807-page weapons declaration that it said demonstrated, and proved, that it had no weapons of mass destruction. Cheney proposed to the NSC that the president declare it a material breach, since the declaration was clearly false, he said, and proved Saddam had lied once again. It should be grounds for war, he said. Why give Saddam another chance? Enough was enough.

As far as Cheney was concerned, going to the U.N. for a new round of weapons inspections was seen by some as a way to avoid war. These included U.N. Secretary-General Kofi Annan, chief inspector Blix, a number of would-be allies, some countries on the Security Council, and certain persons in the State Department, including Secretary Powell. As Cheney sarcastically summarized the stance of these professional diplomats: "Wrap the whole thing up in red tape as it's been done for 12 years previously, pass another resolution, call it good, everybody goes home and nothing happens."

None of the other principals including Rumsfeld and Rice seemed to agree that the declaration on its face was sufficient grounds to abandon inspections and start the war, and the president agreed with them. They would have to study the nearly 12,000 pages. The U.N. resolution required a false declaration "and"—the word Powell had allowed the French to include in the final resolution—a failure to cooperate. On the surface Saddam appeared to be cooperating.

It was just what Cheney feared. They were in the inspections business.

23

R UMSFELD'S STRATEGY OF DRIBBLING out force deployments
was working, generating small news accounts and some curios-
ity, but no big splash. The operating principle was Hide in Plain
Sight. A fourth aircraft carrier, the USS *Harry S. Truman*, had been ordered to the region, for example—a spike in available airpower but
not so unusual as to attract much attention.

As was his custom, Rumsfeld continued to use his press briefings to outline vaguely what he was up to while not billboarding his
exact purpose. He was a master of being honest without being overly
so. For example, during the first week of December he told reporters,
"We've been moving forces around the world. We've got a somewhat
higher presence in the Central Command area today than we did last
week or the week before or the week before that."

Unannounced were plans for the big deployments in incre-
ments of 25,000 to 35,000 that were to come after Christmas, as
would the first big call-up of 20,000 reservists.

Meanwhile, General Franks was steadily improving his position
with smaller deployments of generally only hundreds. In early December he opened a fully operational headquarters in Qatar with
some 600 personnel who had recently been dispatched from his
Tampa headquarters. The old storage depot for pre-positioned equip-

ment he had told the president about in the Crawford briefing a year ago was now a high-tech war room. Dressed in his desert camouflage uniform, he gave reporters a tour of the facility. He and his aides said he could run a war in the same way he could from Tampa.

In Qatar, Franks oversaw a computer and communications war game called Internal Look that was publicly announced and briefed. "This is not a new exercise," a senior official told reporters in a background briefing. "Internal Look was held in 1990, 1996 and 2000." In fact, however, the war game was the first mission rehearsal for an invasion of Iraq using Franks's Hybrid Plan. More than 200 military observers and trainers had arrived from the U.S. to determine if the communications and command decisions moved fast enough in a computer simulation of an invasion.

After the four-day exercise, Franks realized he had more work to do, especially with a ground attack through Kuwait. He wanted the invasion to move much faster, a modern blitzkrieg designed to keep the Iraqis off balance and confuse Saddam's command, control and internal routines. In the exercise, the team of observers and trainers had interjected various problems such as counterattacks, resistance and communications breakdowns. Franks concluded that there was not enough flexibility—what the military calls "adaptive planning," which permits lower-level commanders to change signals quickly because options have been built into their plans.

The ground attack through Kuwait was neither fast enough nor coordinated enough, and Franks decided he would run a second rehearsal if time permitted.

IN HIS ONGOING ROLE as self-appointed special examiner of worst-case scenarios, Cheney had spent a substantial amount of time since 9/11 looking at the potential biological weapon threat to the United States and to U.S. troops overseas. One proposal was to form a kind of "medical NASA," a government arm similar to the national space agency that could do research and produce vaccines. Cheney thought it so important to protect such a program that the administration should propose a way to structure the funding so it could not be taken away by Congress in later years.

Smallpox was a major concern. There was intelligence that indicated that Saddam might want to use the deadly disease as a weapon. The October NIE had concluded there was a 50 percent chance that smallpox was a part of Iraq's offensive BW program.

A huge effort, involving deputies, principals and several meetings with the president, was made to come up with a plan. Studies showed that a smallpox attack in the United States could kill thousands or more and devastate the economy. Smallpox is particularly fearsome for an unprepared population. Since 1972 the risk of infection was so small that regular vaccines had been discontinued. Steve Hadley and others saw the possibility of a smallpox attack as "vulnerability driven." The absence of a vaccination program meant that the United States was unprepared. A new, aggressive program would not be that expensive, and Cheney felt they had a moral responsibility to do something. If there were a smallpox attack that could have been prevented or alleviated and they had done nothing, he felt it would weigh heavily on their souls.

On December 13, in a seven-minute public announcement, President Bush said that U.S. military personnel and other essential civilians in high-risk areas of the world would receive a smallpox vaccine. As commander in chief he too would get the vaccine. "The vaccinations are a precaution only and not a response to any information concerning imminent danger," he said.

What Bush didn't announce was that some 20 million doses of the vaccine would be set aside as a strategic reserve for coalition partners in a war with Iraq. Cheney was particularly worried that if there were war, and Saddam saw he was close to finished, he might use smallpox as a weapon on civilian populations in countries that were hosting U.S. forces. The argument went that if the U.S. did not have a way to reassure allies that it could deal with smallpox, it would be a problem keeping them in the coalition.

There was a lot of head scratching over just how broadly to inoculate, given the possibly dangerous side effects of the vaccine and complex liability issues. The concept of basing a new vaccine program largely on vulnerability baffled many health specialists. But it was hard for anyone, including the president, to say no to Cheney. If there ever were such an attack, the vice president would be hailed as a prophet. Cheney also won agreement from Bush to request $6 billion for a new research and production effort, to be called Project BioShield, for the production of vaccines and treatments for other biological weapons.

THERE WAS ANOTHER problem with the weapons inspections as far as the Bush team was concerned. Blix wanted the CIA at arm's length. The agency provided Blix with information about possible locations of WMD inside Iraq to make the inspections more efficient, and increase the likelihood the inspectors would find WMD. But it was a one-way flow. The CIA had not gained access directly to what Blix was finding and not finding. Blix had said he wanted to be conciliatory to the Iraqis, low-key, nonconfrontational. He did not want what he called an "angry and aggressive" inspections process. Iraqi officials accompanied the inspectors wherever they went inside Iraq.

Therefore U.S. intelligence was going to be pretty much blind about what was really taking place. The CIA does not just spy on potential enemies or unfriendly nations but on friendly nations to learn their true plans, capabilities and intentions. The Godfather's motto of "hold your friends close but your enemies closer" applies to the intelligence business. Since friends can become enemies, and enemies friends, the practice is to spy everywhere possible, including on U.N. officials. Sensitive U.S. intelligence coverage was being conducted on Blix and the weapons inspectors in Iraq because it was critical to the national security that the administration have the best information about what the inspectors were doing. The decision to go to war might hinge on the conduct, findings and outcome of the inspections.

Probably any president, Republican or Democrat, would approve such surveillance, though it was highly sensitive and potentially risky. Spying on U.N. officials and delegates, especially from hostile countries, was a longtime practice. In cases that involve the most important decisions a president might make, all necessary and lawful means tend to be employed to obtain information. Blix and the other inspectors were foreign nationals, and not subject to the anti-eavesdropping provisions that protect most U.S. citizens.

The intelligence indicated that Blix was not reporting everything and not doing all the things he maintained he was doing. Some of the principals believed that Blix was a liar. In any case it looked like the inspections effort was not sufficiently aggressive, would take months or longer and was likely doomed to fail.

THE MORNING OF WEDNESDAY, December 18, President Bush had a private meeting with Spanish President José María Aznar, who supported a military confrontation with Iraq.

With Aznar, Bush scoffed at the Iraqi weapons statement. "The declaration is nothing, it's empty, it's a joke, but we will be measured in response." The president added his private thought that included no ambiguity about what he was going to do with Saddam, "At some point, we will conclude enough is enough and take him out. He's a liar and he's no intention of disarming."

Bush turned to the U.N. process. The notes of the meeting with Aznar show that he did not fully appreciate that Resolution 1441 was subject to interpretation. "If the decision is made to go to war, we'll go back to the Security Council. We won't ask for permission, we will ask for support," Bush said. "That was the agreement with Security Council members. Security Council won't have a veto, but the more countries the easier to achieve a diplomatic objective."

In fact, the five permanent members of the Security Council always have a veto, and the French especially did not think they had made an agreement that Resolution 1441 locked them into war.

Bush added, "War is my last choice. Saddam Hussein is using

his money to train and equip al Qaeda with chemicals, he's harboring terrorists."

Turning to the Middle East, Bush said it was important to move forward on the peace process. "Chirac says that Sharon is pulling the blinds over my eyes." The president then said, "Toro!" He sometimes called Sharon "the bull."

The translator interrupted, "Mr. President, there are two definitions of toro in English," indicating it meant "bull" literally the animal, or "bull" as in bullshit.

Aznar seemed to catch on.

"It's one of the great moments in diplomacy to translate the word toro," Bush said to Aznar and the translator.

AT CIA HEADQUARTERS, Saul, who had day-to-day contact with the operatives, including Tim inside Iraq, was growing increasingly concerned about the mixed message the administration was sending. On one hand Tim and the other case officers were still out on the front recruiting sources with the promise that military action was coming soon. On the other, the president was pursuing diplomatic solutions through the U.N. and weapons inspections. Oh, you're going to negotiate, some sources and foreign intelligence services were saying. You're going to disappoint us again! Every time Bush said that war was his last choice, all the agency's contacts and sources crouched a little lower. War was their first choice, and for some, it was the only choice as they got further and further committed.

Saul was sending regular messages to the seventh floor where Tenet, McLaughlin and the other senior officials resided. "We can sustain this effort up until the end of February," he said at one point. "At the end of February, we're going to start taking losses because the regime is going to start finding things out." They could keep only so many secrets. Saddam's security and intelligence services were ubiquitous, the ferocity of their response to traitors well known. Sources and agents would soon get rolled up. February was the end point. "If you push this much later than that," Saul said, "we're going to get people killed."

At the same time he said, "We can't pull back. If we turn around and pull back, we're not going to have any credibility."

Saul's two paramilitary teams inside Iraq were wondering too. It was the most frustrating thing in the world for them, sitting out on the end of the spear, not knowing when or if this war was going to start. Saul told Tim that he and his team should get out of Iraq for two weeks' rest and relaxation during the Christmas holidays. Go home and be back at the base in early January. It looked as if the war might start in mid-January, and certainly, by God, February, Saul told them. So Tim and his team pulled out for two weeks over the holidays.

In fact, Saul had no idea when a war might start.

THE SAME DAY Bush met with the Spanish president, December 18, he met with the NSC. The CIA wanted to lay out a little more dramatically the problems they were having in recruiting and maintaining sources and agents inside Iraq. Tenet ceded his place at the table to one of his senior covert operatives, Bob,* the mission manager for Iraq who coordinated the work of Saul and his operatives with the analytic work being done. Bob had been the CIA station chief in Pakistan during the Afghanistan war. A small, well-dressed man with a deferential manner and an intellectual bent, Bob gave a status report on the developing agent networks inside Iraq. They had close to a dozen good ones now, but Bob didn't go into detail with the president or the NSC. Instead, he said the number of agents and subagents was growing significantly and their intelligence was getting better. But there were some difficulties.

"Mr. President," Bob said, "we are trying to give conflicting messages to two different audiences simultaneously. There's inevitably going to be some bleed-over. We can't completely compart-

---

* A nickname.

ment one audience by any means from the other. So at the same time that we are trying to do and actively engage in propaganda in a way that will convince the people upon whose cooperation we absolutely depend that war is inevitable, at the same time we're also trying to convince others that, no fooling, the president is quite serious" about diplomacy, the United Nations and weapons inspections.

"Yep," Bush said.

Bob said there were people both outside and inside Iraq with whom the CIA had engaged in a running dialogue. They were saying, we hear you, we understand and we will cooperate with you up to a point, but we'll go no further until we are more convinced, until there is more evidence. So the contradictions in the two-track policy were causing a problem.

"I know I've put you in a difficult position," Bush acknowledged. "I know that this is hard, but this is the course we're on. And we're going to have to keep doing all of these elements at the same time."

As she listened at the table, Rice thought this was a part of a coercive diplomacy—the credible threat of force to achieve a diplomatic outcome. There was indeed some dissonance, but carrying out coercive diplomacy meant they had to live with the contradictions.

DDCI McLaughlin realized that it was a tough position for the agency. The CIA had initiated covert action for a policy that had not been finalized, and yet they had to go ahead with operations and source recruitment as if everything had been decided.

THAT EVENING, December 18, my wife, Elsa Walsh, and I attended a huge White House Christmas party for the media hosted by the president and his wife. The Bushes stood for hours in a receiving line as a photographer snapped pictures with the first couple. When we reached the front of the line, the president remarked that my book *Bush at War* was selling well.

"Top of the charts," he said, and asked, "Are you going to do another book?" He then stretched out his arms and indicated with his body language that there might be a story there, that it should be done.

"Maybe it will be called 'More Bush at War,' " I said.

"Let's hope not," Laura Bush said almost mournfully.

A year later I asked the president about Mrs. Bush's comments. "Yeah," he said, "that reflected her view. Laura understands what it means to go to see family members of the deceased. She understands the sadness and the agony that happens to loved ones because of the death on the battlefield. Death anywhere for that matter.

"But particularly the death on the battlefield," he went on. "And there is a direct correlation between her husband's decision making and that death. She knows that and she knows it's tough. And she also fully anticipated the uproar, the noise, the protestation."

"And she told you this?" I asked him.

"Not really. She told *you* that. And probably by telling you, told me," he said, staring hard. "Laura trusts my judgment and we talked about it some. But, of course, she didn't want to go to war. I didn't either for that matter."

GENERAL FRANKS BRIEFED the president the next day, December 19, reporting on the results of the Internal Look exercise and the latest tweaking of the war plan.

Tell me again about timing, the president said. Despite the U.N. effort, it seemed to Franks that Bush was looking at imminent execution but he wasn't specific.

They covered more what-ifs, the things that could go wrong from Rumsfeld's list. Suppose the Iraqis destroy their oil infrastructure or their hydrology system or power plants? Franks offered more detail on how he planned to attack Saddam's underground facilities and other hardened targets.

Later, Rice asked Tenet and McLaughlin how strong the case was on WMD and what could be said publicly.

The agency's October national estimate that had concluded that

Saddam has chemical and biological weapons had been out for more than two months; the congressional resolutions supporting war had passed by a nearly 3 to 1 margin; and the United Nations Security Council, where a weapons inspection resolution had passed 15 to 0, was engaged in active inspections inside Iraq. Still something was missing.

Even Paul Wolfowitz had commented recently on the inconclusive nature of judgments about Saddam's WMD, according to a *Washington Post* article. "It's like the judge said about pornography," Wolfowitz had told a closed-door meeting of NATO ambassadors, "I can't define it, but I will know it when I see it."

McLaughlin had drawn the short straw to make a presentation to the president and the principals. A cautious analyst, with 30 years of experience in the agency, he was aware that two streams of WMD information that the CIA had were very different. One stream, its importance not to be overestimated in his opinion, was what the U.N. inspectors had developed between 1991, after the end of the Gulf War, and 1998, when Saddam had caused the inspectors to withdraw. During that seven-year period, the inspectors had had physical access inside Iraq. Though never acknowledged, the CIA participated in the inspections secretly, provided tips and intelligence, received full briefings from the inspectors, and advised them on how to locate and destroy weapons. The CIA had obtained ground truth from people with hands-on knowledge. In addition, the CIA had practiced the old Reagan rule of "trust but verify," spying on the inspectors to learn more and make sure U.S. intelligence was getting as full a picture as possible.

During that period, the inspectors had uncovered much more WMD than they had anticipated. The 1995 defection of Hussein Kamel, Saddam's son-in-law and chief of the regime's secret WMD programs, had triggered a seemingly voluntary outpouring of more information and documents from Iraq. In addition, documents on imports and other transactions showed hundreds, even thousands, of tons of chemicals or other raw material that the Iraqis said were for WMD production. The inspectors had destroyed vast quantities of WMD or related equipment and material, all as part of the inspection process.

The second stream of information, obtained since 1998, contained what McLaughlin felt was a dramatically higher level of inference. As he had previously told the principals, the CIA did not have anthrax or chemical weapons samples on hand to prove their case.

In preparation for his appearance before the president, McLaughlin examined reams of material. There was an intercept of a startling conversation involving two people with al Qaeda ties discussing the highly toxic poison ricin. The two had discussed how a sample had been tested on a donkey who had died and then dissolved into chilling laughter. A foreign intelligence service which had provided the intercept was concerned that it might be made public. Others were concerned that making it public might scare people. McLaughlin wasn't sure what it showed. He thought it seemed a little "weird." So he decided not to use it in the presentation to the president.

Another highly classified intelligence file suggested to McLaughlin an intriguing effort by the Iraqis to obtain topographic mapping for all 50 United States. A companion clandestine operation by the CIA had tracked down an Iraqi who had previously worked on his country's Unmanned Aerial Vehicle program and was now living in Australia. The small, comparatively inexpensive UAV drones conceivably could be used to deliver a CW or BW attack anywhere in the world. Aggressively connecting these dots, Wolfowitz was touting this secret intelligence as a "spectacular breakthrough in cracking a procurement network" and "very scary."

The CIA had attempted to recruit the Iraqi who had been living in Australia. He had refused to cooperate unless some 21 members of his extended family were relocated safely outside Iraq. As the agency had dug into the matter it became unclear whether the topographic maps had been acquired intentionally or inadvertently. Anyone could buy them in a map store or on the Internet with a credit

card. The topographic software was not sophisticated. The only significant event, McLaughlin concluded, was that a procurement agent
in Iraq had checked the "yes" box when offered the opportunity to
buy the software.

McLaughlin had enough questions in his mind that he was not
going to include it in his presentation either.

Wolfowitz was flabbergasted at what had been discovered, saying, "The idea that we shouldn't be too worried about a covert Iraqi
UAV program that produces aircraft that are small enough to put in a
shipping container and big enough to drop a quart of anthrax over
Washington, D.C., because he may not have really wanted the map?"
He also thought the Iraqi's refusal to talk unless he could get his
family members out was a perfect opportunity for chief U.N.
weapons inspector Hans Blix to exploit. Under U.N. Resolution
1441 Blix had the broad authority to interview anyone and "facilitate
the travel of those interviewed and family members outside of Iraq."
But Blix apparently had done nothing.

TENET AND MCLAUGHLIN WENT to the Oval Office the morning of
Saturday, December 21. The meeting was for presenting "The Case"
on WMD as it might be presented to a jury with Top Secret security
clearances. There was great expectation. In addition to the president,
Cheney, Rice and Andy Card attended.

With some fanfare, McLaughlin stepped up to brief with a series
of flip charts. This was the rough cut, he indicated, still highly classified and not cleared for public release. The CIA wanted to reserve on
what would be revealed so as to protect sources and detection methods if there was no military conflict.

McLaughlin pointed out that components for biological
weapons were unaccounted for, as were 3,200 tons of precursor for
chemical weapons. Some 6,000 shells were unaccounted for going
back to the Iran-Iraq War in the 1980s.

He flipped to a large satellite photo of a test stand for rocket engines. The stand, as they could see, was clearly larger than would be needed for the small engines of missiles with the permitted maximum range of 150 kilometers.

Another overhead photo showed scarring of the earth at a facility that had been documented as a chemical weapons facility. The scarring "appeared" to be an effort to clean up after a transfer or a spill of chemicals, McLaughlin said.

He flipped to a graphic of a UAV flying a racetrack pattern. Technical collection had established with "absolute certainty," a phrase he did not often use, that the drone had flown in the red circles indicated in the graphic a total of 500 kilometers. In their weapons declaration, two weeks earlier, Iraq had said its UAV had a range of 80 kilometers. The United Nations had limited Iraq to 150 kilometers. The UAV was launched from the back of a truck and had an autopilot. The 500-kilometer range was enough to reach neighboring countries.

McLaughlin was aware that it was probably a rather confusing graphic but one that was quite exciting to intelligence analysts because the flight path could be determined down to the kilometer. The length of time in flight also suggested that the Iraqis had a good deal of confidence in their automated guidance system.

This was a clear weapons violation. The question was why they would be so interested in such a drone. Its delivery capabilities were ominous, but there was no proof of what they intended.

Next McLaughlin presented accounts from several human sources and defectors about large mobile trailers that these sources said were biological weapons production facilities that could move around to evade inspectors.

In his most dramatic example, McLaughlin presented the transcript of an intercepted radio conversation between two Republican Guard officers that he showed on his flip charts.

"Remove," the first officer said.

"Remove," repeated the second.

"Nerve agents."

"Nerve agents."

"Whenever it comes up."

McLaughlin explained that the first officer wanted to make sure any reference to "nerve agents" in radio instructions was eliminated. If Iraq had no biological material, weapons or nerve agents, why were these Republican Guard officers discussing it?

On nuclear weapons, McLaughlin mentioned that Saddam convened a group of Iraq's main atomic scientists, dubbed the "nuclear mafia," quite often and spoke to them in terms that "implied" preparations to resume nuclear weapons research.

He presented yet another intercept in which officers had talked about the concealment of a modified vehicle at the al-Kindi company, a known WMD facility, that was clearly a matter of concern since inspectors were about to arrive there.

When McLaughlin concluded, there was a look on the president's face of, What's this? And then a brief moment of silence.

"Nice try," Bush said. "I don't think this is quite—it's not something that Joe Public would understand or would gain a lot of confidence from."

Card was also underwhelmed. The presentation was a flop. In terms of marketing, the examples didn't work, the charts didn't work, the photos were not gripping, the intercepts were less than compelling.

Bush turned to Tenet. "I've been told all this intelligence about having WMD and this is the best we've got?"

From the end of one of the couches in the Oval Office, Tenet rose up, threw his arms in the air. "It's a slam dunk case!" the DCI said.

Bush pressed. "George, how confident are you?"

Tenet, a basketball fan who attended as many home games of his alma mater Georgetown as possible, leaned forward and threw his arms up again. "Don't worry, it's a slam dunk!"

It was unusual for Tenet to be so certain. From McLaughlin's presentation, Card was worried that there might be no "there there," but Tenet's double reassurance on the slam dunk was both memorable and comforting. Cheney could think of no reason to question

Tenet's assertion. He was, after all, the head of the CIA and would know the most. The president later recalled that McLaughlin's presentation "wouldn't have stood the test of time," but Tenet's reassurance, "That was very important."

"Needs a lot more work," Bush told Card and Rice. "Let's get some people who've actually put together a case for a jury." He wanted some lawyers, prosecutors if need be. They were going to have to go public with something.

The president told Tenet several times, "Make sure no one stretches to make our case."

ROVE SAW THAT the president was "wired up" about Blix. The president knew Rove's attitude toward the Swedes. As the highest-ranking Norwegian-American in the White House—and perhaps the only one—Rove was convinced of the historical duplicity of the Swedes, who had invaded Norway in 1814 and ruled the country until 1905. There was a long-standing grudge and it was a running joke between the president and Rove.

In late December, Rice gave the president another Blix debrief. Not much was getting done. The inspectors were opening warehouses that had obviously been sanitized. In addition, the inspectors were taking time off for Christmas and the other holidays. The sensitive intelligence coverage showed that Blix and his team were not conducting the kind of aggressive no-holds-barred inspections Bush envisioned.

Bush was growing increasingly angry at the process. It was getting worse by the day, he said. The pressure tactic on Saddam was dubious. "I'm not so sure this is going to work," he said. They had set up an inspections system that they hoped would place the burden of proof on Saddam. The Iraqi leader had to declare his weapons, account for them, turn them over, prove he had disarmed. This turned the American notion of justice on its head—the accused had to prove his innocence. The world was not buying it. Maybe war was the only alternative.

"What do you think?" the president asked Rice. "Should we do this?" He meant war. He had never before pressed her for her answer.

"Yes," she said. "Because it isn't American credibility on the line, it is the credibility of everybody that this gangster can yet again beat the international system." As important as credibility was, she said, "Credibility should never drive you to do something you shouldn't do." But this was much bigger, she advised, something that should be done. "To let this threat in this part of the world play volleyball with the international community this way will come back to haunt us someday. That is the reason to do it."

Bush didn't respond.

A YEAR LATER, the president recalled, "I was very concerned about the process, that we'd get wrapped up in a process and Saddam Hussein would grow stronger. I was concerned people would focus on not Saddam, not the danger that he posed, not his deception, but focus on the process and thereby Saddam would be able to kind of skate through once again . . . he would escape the trap again. And would be even stronger. And so there was anxiety about that." He was determined to deal with Saddam and not let him elude them again.

"I would constantly talk to Condi," Bush recalled. He would get updates on the latest inspections and on Blix. "I'm on the phone all times saying, all different times saying, you know, 'What the heck's going on?'

"There was a lot of stress," the president said. "Yeah, I felt stressed." All of the holiday parties at the White House added to the difficulties at the end of 2002. "My jaw muscles got so tight. And it was not just because I was smiling and shaking so many hands. There was a lot of tension during that last holiday season."

Other than Rice, Bush said he didn't need to ask the principals whether they thought he should go to war. He knew what Cheney thought, and he decided not to ask Powell or Rumsfeld. "I could tell what they thought," the president recalled. "I didn't need to ask them their opinion about Saddam Hussein or how to deal with Saddam Hussein. If you were sitting where I sit, you could be pretty clear. I think we've got an environment where people feel free to express themselves."

"Did you ever ask Powell? Did you ever say, Would you do this if you were sitting here?" I asked.

"No," the president said.

One person not around was Karen Hughes, one of his top advisers and longtime communications director. Hughes, who had resigned the previous summer to return to Texas, probably knew how Bush thought and talked as much as anyone. "I asked Karen," the president recalled. "She said if you go to war, exhaust all opportunities to achieve [regime change] peacefully. And she was right. She actually captured my own sentiments."

24

RICE WENT TO HER AUNT'S for Christmas, then to the president's ranch in Crawford, the barren Texas plain where she seemed to have spent a significant part of her recent life. She had a sense that things were changing, that Bush was increasingly seeing that the pressure points—diplomacy, covert action, speeches— weren't going to work. He didn't say anything directly, and she didn't push, since she had already recommended they go to war.

Then on either the Thursday or Friday after New Year's, Rice had a private moment with the president.

"This pressure isn't holding together," the president said to her. The effort to get U.N. inspections on an aggressive track to make Saddam crack was not working. Saddam was getting smarter about how to deal with Blix. The unanimous international consensus of the November resolution was beginning to fray.

The press reports of smiling Iraqis leading inspectors around, opening up buildings and saying, "See, there's nothing here," infuriated Bush, who then would read intelligence reports showing the Iraqis were moving and concealing things. It wasn't clear what was being moved, but it sure looked like Saddam was up to his old tricks and was about to fool the world again. Bush noted that the antiwar protests in European cities and in the U.S. would fortify Saddam and make him think the U.S. would never invade. "How is this happening?" Bush said. "Saddam is going to get stronger."

Blix had told Rice, "I have never complained about your military pressure. I think it's a good thing." She relayed this to the president.

"How long does he think I can do this?" Bush asked. "A year? I can't. The United States can't stay in this position while Saddam plays games with the inspectors."

"You have to follow through on your threat," Rice said. "If you're going to carry out coercive diplomacy, you have to live with that decision."

The president was concerned about the CIA assertion that sources and operations would get rolled up if there was too much delay. The military buildup was in full swing, incremental but real. They couldn't keep all those forces deployed forever. Morale and good logistics support could not be kept high. There wasn't endless time. He was trying to read Saddam. "He's getting more confident, not less," he said. "He can manipulate the international system again. We're not winning."

"Time is not on our side here," Bush said. "Probably going to have to, we're going to have to go to war."

In Rice's mind, this was the president's decision on war. He had reached the point of no return. Many questions remained, including when and how to force an endgame.

Bush was now enveloped in a contradiction: he had privately decided on war, but publicly he was continuing the diplomacy. It was a world of more dilemmas, dissonance and hedging.

ROVE WAS ALSO FLOWN to Crawford for part of the holiday. He had been quietly working on the confidential plan for Bush's 2004 reelection campaign. In fact Rove had been devoted to this project since Bush had been declared the winner in 2000. Rove believed in learning from history, and he had been doing in-depth research on how recent Republican presidents had campaigned for reelection. Nancy Reagan gave him access to Reagan's papers. Rove sent trusted staffers to the Ford Library to see what he had done in 1976. Bush's father opened some boxes for them, and Jim Baker, who had been Bush senior's 1992 campaign manager, gave them his personal papers.

Rove had with him a PowerPoint presentation on the strategy, themes, timetable and an overview plan to win reelection. The essence of the message for the president was: Pay attention man, it's coming.

He found some time alone with the president to brief him at his ranch house. Laura Bush was on the couch reading a book, pretending to pay no attention. Rove could see she was paying complete attention.

Opening his laptop, he displayed for Bush in bold letters on a dark blue background:

PERSONA
Strong Leader   Bold Action   Big Ideas   Peace in World
More Compassionate America   Cares About People Like Me
Leads a Strong Team

On page two:

VALUES
Compassion   Moral Clarity   Responsibility
Opportunity   Ownership

On page three:

ISSUES
Primary: WOT [War on Terrorism]   Homeland   Always Economy
Subordinate: Education   Compassion Agenda   Health
Opportunity   Environment

Rove said that he expected the campaign to be as close as it was in 2000, that the country was as narrowly divided as it was then.

All things being equal, the president asked, when would you like to begin?

Rove noted the first Bush campaign had filed on March 8, 1999, and that it had been difficult to reach their budgetary target, though they did. In a practical sense they had not begun until June 1999. He said he wanted the president to start in February or March of this year and begin the process of raising the money, probably $200 million. He had a schedule. In February, March and April, there would be between 12 and 16 fund-raisers.

"We got a war coming," the president told Rove flatly, "and you're just going to have to wait." He had decided. It was the president's version of Pay attention man, it's coming. War was the only option now. "The moment is coming," he said. The president did not give a date but he left the impression with Rove that it would be January, or February or March at the latest.

"Remember the problem with your dad's campaign," Rove replied. "A lot of people said he got started too late."

"I understand," Bush said. He had been there. But this was decided and this was the way it was going to be. So the early fund-raising was out. He couldn't campaign if he was getting ready to start war. Rove's plans would have to be flexible. "I'll tell you when I'm comfortable with you starting."

Oh, nooooooooo, Rove thought. But he knew there was nothing he could do. With war coming, there was no way he was going to try to convince Bush he needed to go to a fund-raiser in Altoona or anywhere for that matter.

THE PRESIDENT, back in Washington, met with his full cabinet, the 15th such meeting in two years, at 3:30 P.M. on January 6. This was not the group that would make important decisions on war. "If we don't have a case to make, I won't send in the troops," he told the group. Later in a public exchange with reporters, he acted conciliatory about Saddam. "Thus far it looks like he hasn't complied. But he's got time, and we continue to call upon Saddam Hussein to listen to what the world is saying."

Two days later the president met with congressional leaders of both parties. "Sometimes it requires a little muscle to secure good diplomacy," he said. "Before I make a decision I will make that reason known to the Congress and everyone in America."

Later, at 5:20 P.M., he met in the residence with Republican leaders only, and was more candid. "There's a good chance I'll have to address the nation and commit troops to war. It's clear Saddam Hussein is not disarming. I want the process to work before I ratchet up the noise."

On January 9, Franks came to Washington to give the president the latest on the war plan. The main topic was Turkey, which continued to waffle on whether to allow staging of U.S. combat forces. The delay meant Franks's northern front was off the table.

The general also said he was worried about a potential loss of support from Jordan and Saudi Arabia. King Abdullah of Jordan had met that week with the leaders of Turkey, Egypt and Syria to coordinate efforts to prevent a war, though the king was secretly committed to support the war effort. Tenet had a close relationship with the king. The CIA subsidized the Jordanian intelligence service with millions of dollars a year. But the kingdom's population is majority Palestinian and overwhelmingly pro-Saddam. Most of Jordan's oil came from Iraq. Iraq was also running agents into Jordan. Abdullah was in jeopardy, and in Tenet's view had taken on the burden of the century in agreeing to support a war.

Bush asked Franks, If Saddam attacked or did something provocative tomorrow, what exactly could be done?

The answer was an almost immediate air attack using the approximately 400 aircraft in the region, and 15,000 U.S. forces on the ground in Kuwait.

As he reviewed the decision cycle for the Hybrid Plan, Franks said C-Day was when the president would decide to deploy forces. But since they had already been deploying for some time, they had already passed some of the major milestones. Those deployments could continue, and the president did not have to commit to combat operations.

"What's my last decision point?" Bush asked. "When have I finally made a commitment?"

Once you put U.S. Special Forces on the ground inside Iraq for offensive combat operations, Franks replied. These would be the planned operations to protect against Scud missile firings and to protect Iraq's southern and northern oil fields.

Franks said he would be ready to execute in about three weeks. "I'd be ready in early February, but I'd really like the 1st of March," he said.

AT 2:15 P.M. on January 10 Bush and Cheney met privately with three leading Iraqi dissidents in the Oval Office. The president was blunt. "I believe in freedom and peace. I believe Saddam Hussein is a threat to America and to the neighborhood," he said. "He should disarm but he won't, therefore we will remove him from power. We can't make him change his heart. His heart is made of stone."

It was close to a declaration of war.

Rend Francke, the director of a foundation promoting human rights and democracy in Iraq, said, "I believe the Iraqi people can practice democracy if given the opportunity."

The president told them he was interested in their personal stories.

Hatem Mukhlis, who is originally from Tikrit, said, "Saddam killed my father. My family's been involved in politics in Iraq since the '20s. I'm a doctor. All the Iraqis are ready to get rid of Saddam Hussein. The fear is what comes after. The difference is the participation of the Iraqi people. I had democracy in the '50s. My job is to save lives. I'd like to save Iraq and American lives. They're both my people."

"Does the average citizen in Iraq hate Israel?" Bush asked.

"No," the doctor said. "They're so self-absorbed, they're just inward-focused."

Author Kanan Makiya, who wrote *Republic of Fear*, the most credible account of torture and the sadistic nature of the Baath Party and its rise to power, said he was now researching the regime's war crimes. "You're going to break the mold," he said. "You will change the image of the United States in the region. Democracy is truly doable in Iraq. Force for destruction can be turned to a force for construction. Iraqis are a technically able people. They are literate with electricized villages."

"We're planning for the worst," Bush said.

"People will greet troops with flowers and sweets," one said.

"How do you know?" Bush asked.

They all said the information came from people inside Iraq.

On Saddam, one said, "I think Iraqi people themselves will find him and bring him to justice." Another qualified that, saying it was likely they would find Saddam, but not certain.

"What will the Iraqi people need for the future?" Bush asked.

They mentioned currency, medical facilities and immediate humanitarian relief.

"Is there starvation?" Bush asked.

No, but there was malnutrition.

The split between the ruling minority Sunnis and the majority Shiites was not as violent or pronounced as people outside Iraq generally thought, one said. Saddam's method was to divide and conquer.

"What are the elite like?" Bush asked. "Are they well educated? Are there many left or have they been purged like in China?" He then said, "Let's say Saddam Hussein is gone. Now there's a void. What's your vision?"

Cheney, who had said little as usual, interjected, "We need to have a light hand in the postwar phase."

It was important to find the right people now to fill the void, the Iraqis said.

"Will the Diaspora head back?" Bush asked, referring to the Iraqis living out of the country.

Yes, one exile said.

"The democratization of Iraq will be more likely if Iraqis who understand and lived under a democracy fled back," the president asserted. "How long will the military have to stay?"

Two to three years, one estimated.

"How do we deal with the impression the U.S. is bringing a leader in, imposing our will?"

They did not have an answer.

"How do people in Iraq hear things?" Bush asked. "Is it e-mail?"

There were the overseas services of the BBC and the Voice of America, one said. Internet servers were government-owned, so anybody who tried to get onto an Internet service to look up an opposition group would be killed.

One exile said they needed an Iraqi leader modeled on Hamid Karzai in Afghanistan, and a governing council of some sort, plus access to the Internet, entertainment and food.

"We haven't reached conclusions," the president told them, ending the meeting. "I view you and the Diaspora as partners. Your job is to gather the people who want to help and rally their hearts and souls. My job is to rally the world and win the war. I'm not sure my job is to pick" the new leader for Iraq. "I truly believe out of this will come peace between Israel and the Palestinians. Maybe one year from now we will be toasting victory and talking about the transition to freedom."

RUMSFELD DIDN'T WANT to walk into the Oval Office one day and say to the president, "Well, today is the day. From here on the credibility of our country is at stake and we were putting people in jeopardy." So he had been trying to put himself in the president's shoes, attempting to make sure that Bush didn't get so far out in words, body language or mental state that he couldn't get back from a decision to go to war. On the other hand, he felt there was a time when the president should not want to walk back, and really could not. That time would be well before Bush had to decide to put Special Operations Forces inside Iraq, the point of no return identified by

Franks. "I can remember trying to give him as early a clue as possible that that was coming down the road," Rumsfeld recalled.

"There comes a moment as all these things are happening," he added, "when we have to look a neighboring country in the eye and they have to make a decision that puts them at risk. And at that moment the president needs to know that." With the U.S. moving forces at an increasing rate, and the CIA taking more chances, the neighboring countries were increasingly at risk—especially Jordan and Saudi Arabia.

Rumsfeld told the president, "The penalty for our country and for our relationships and potentially the lives of some people are at risk if you have to make a decision *not* to go forward." The only way the damage would be mitigated, he said, is if "there is some very highly visible reason not to go forward, like the capitulation or the departure of Saddam Hussein or something like that." The president was rapidly losing his option of not going to war, Rumsfeld was saying. The real threshold for war was when people and countries put themselves at risk in this way on behalf of the United States. Foreign countries in the region who were supplying sub-rosa assistance to the U.S. were about to make decisions that would put them at even greater risk, he said. More lives would be in danger. The point of no return was approaching.

The president took him aside one day in early January. "Look, we're going to have to do this I'm afraid," he said. Saddam was diddling them. "I don't see how we're going to get him to a position where he will do something in a manner that's consistent with the U.N. requirements, and we've got to make an assumption that he will not."

It was enough of a decision for Rumsfeld. He asked to bring in some key foreign players.

The president gave his approval, but pressed Rumsfeld again, When is my last decision point?

"When your people, Mr. President, look people in the eye and tell them you're going."

25

FROM THEIR ALMOST daily conversations, Cheney had come to realize that the president had made his decision. The vice president believed that other governments would not be willing to step up until they were convinced that the United States meant business. He agreed with Rumsfeld that they had to look people in the eye and say, This is going to happen. They could not leave them high and dry out there with the United States having stirred things up, only to pull back and abandon them to live in the neighborhood with a very bad actor.

Cheney felt that once the president had laid out his objective of regime change, and begun the process of troop deployments and CIA work, then if they didn't follow through, they would be like Clinton—a lot of bold talk and not much action.

One key country that had to be notified and brought along was Saudi Arabia. The prospect of losing its support, a possibility Franks had raised several days earlier, was very troubling. Saudi Arabia was in a particularly precarious position in the Muslim world. Bin Laden had started his al Qaeda movement in large part by charging that the Saudi king, who in the Muslim world is officially and spiritually known as the Custodian of the Two Holy Mosques at Mecca and Medina, had let in the infidels, the U.S. military, before, during and after the 1991 Gulf War. Its continued collaboration with the Ameri-

cans was fueling the extreme fundamentalist movement. Saudi participation in a Gulf War II against Saddam, particularly if it did not
end his rule, was enormously risky.

Cheney wanted personally to communicate a decision to the
Saudis, and he had a memorable precedent for doing so. More than
a dozen years earlier, on Friday, August 3, 1990, just after Saddam
had invaded Kuwait and was threatening to move into Saudi Arabia,
Cheney, then secretary of defense for Bush's father, had summoned
Saudi Ambassador Prince Bandar to his Pentagon office. Joining
them were Powell, then chairman of the Joint Chiefs of Staff, and
Paul Wolfowitz, then defense undersecretary for policy.

President George H. W. Bush had directed Cheney to brief Bandar on the U.S. war plan for protecting Saudi Arabia and driving Saddam from Kuwait. As the group huddled around the small round
table in the secretary's Pentagon office, Cheney told the prince that
they were serious. He produced copies of high-resolution, Top Secret
photographs showing Iraqi divisions pointing at Saudi Arabia. Powell summarized the U.S. war plan, which would include more than
four divisions, three aircraft carriers, plus many Air Force attack
squadrons—a force of between 100,000 to 200,000 at first. "Well, at
least this shows you are serious," Bandar said. Cheney and Powell
wanted permission to deploy the forces through Saudi Arabia, and
Bandar pledged that he would be an advocate with King Fahd.

After Bandar left, Wolfowitz proposed that they start alerting
U.S. forces.

"He blows smoke," Powell said, urging that they wait.

U.S. forces soon deployed into Saudi Arabia.

THIS TIME CHENEY invited Bandar to his West Wing office on Saturday, January 11, 2003. Rumsfeld and JCS Chairman General Richard
B. Myers were also there.

Bandar considered Rumsfeld the toughest secretary of defense
the U.S. had ever had, more so than even Cheney. This, in Bandar's
estimation, was because Rumsfeld had nothing to lose. He was older,

it was his second time in the job, and he already had achieved a great deal. There was a confidence, even an overconfidence, that made him the guy you wanted to lead the charge.

One purpose of the meeting was to convince Bandar that U.S. forces would have to be sent through and from Saudi territory into Iraq. Rescue, communication and refueling support was not going to be enough. Of the five other countries on Iraq's border, only Kuwait and Jordan supported a military operation. The 500 miles of Saudi-Iraqi border were critical. Without it there would be a giant gap in the middle between Kuwait's small 150-mile border with Iraq and Jordan's even smaller 100-mile border.

Sitting on the edge of the table, Myers took out a large map labeled TOP SECRET NOFORN. The NOFORN meant NO FOR-EIGN—classified material not to be seen by any foreign national.

Myers explained that the first part of the battle plan would be a massive air bombing campaign over several days that would use three to four times more explosives than in the 42 days of the Gulf War. The main targets would be the Republican Guard divisions, the security services and Saddam's command and control of his forces. A land attack would follow through Kuwait, plus a northern front through Turkey with the 4th Infantry Division if Turkey approved it. Included was massive use of Special Forces and intelligence paramilitary teams to secure every place in Iraq from which Saddam could launch a missile or airplane against Saudi Arabia, Jordan or Israel.

"You know, Prince, we have assets already in," Myers said, referring to the CIA paramilitary teams.

"Yes, I've been briefed," Bandar said.

Special Forces and intelligence operatives would distribute $300 million to local Iraqi tribal leaders, religious leaders and the Iraqi armed forces.

We've lost strategic surprise after getting stuck in the U.N. process and we are losing the tactical surprise, Myers argued. However, General Franks has come up with ideas that will make surprise largely irrelevant.

The 500-mile Saudi-Iraqi border would have to be covered. Special Forces, intelligence teams and other strikes would have to be launched from there. If there were alternatives, Myers said, they would not be asking the Saudis.

Bandar knew that his country could create a cover for the arrival of U.S. forces by closing a civilian airport at Al Jawf in the northern desert, flying Saudi helicopters day and night as a routine border patrol for a week, and then withdrawing. The U.S. Special Forces could set up a base there that might not attract much attention.

Staring intently at the 2-by-3-foot Top Secret map, Bandar, a former Saudi fighter pilot, asked a few questions about air operations. Could he have a copy of the large map so he could brief the crown prince? he asked.

"Above my pay grade," Myers said.

"We'll give you all the information you want," Rumsfeld said. As for the map, he added, "I would rather not give it to you, but you can take notes if you want."

"No, no it's not important. Just let me look at it," Bandar said. He tried to take it all in—the large ground thrusts, the location of Special Forces or intelligence teams all designated on the map.

For Bandar, there was no way the Saudis could be directly involved in the war if this was only saber rattling, based on hope that Saddam might leave or negotiate a peace. The Saudis would lose bigtime if Saddam survived. If Saddam's head was the price, they would pay it and join in. Bandar recalled President Lyndon Johnson saying, Don't tell a fellow to go to hell unless you intend to send him there.

Rumsfeld looked Bandar in the eye. "You can count on this," Rumsfeld said, pointing to the map. "You can take that to the bank. This is going to happen."

"What is the chance of Saddam surviving this?" Bandar asked. He believed Saddam was intent on killing everyone involved at a high level with the 1991 Gulf War, including himself.

Rumsfeld and Myers didn't answer.

"Saddam, this time, will be out period?" Bandar asked skeptically. "What will happen to him?"

Cheney, who had been quiet as usual, replied, "Prince Bandar, once we start, Saddam is toast."

As Bandar rose to leave, he told Cheney, "This reminds me of our meeting, you and I and Colin."

Cheney laughed.

"But this time no smoke, Mr. Vice President," Bandar said, still apparently smarting from Powell's comment, which was later reported.

Cheney chuckled again.

"I am convinced now that this is something I can take to my Prince Abdullah," Bandar said, "and think I can convince him. But I cannot go and tell him that Myers and Rumsfeld and you told me. I have to carry a message from the president."

"I'll get back to you," the vice president replied.

Bandar left with no doubt that they had made a commitment to him that war was coming, but he had heard big promises before that didn't materialize. He still wanted insurance—to hear it directly from Bush.

Back in Cheney's office, Rumsfeld voiced some concern about the vice president's "toast" remark. "Jesus Christ, what was that all about, Dick?"

"I didn't want to leave any doubt in his mind what we're planning to do," Cheney said. He wanted Bandar to know it was for real, but he didn't plan to be quite as direct with anyone else. After all, he had known Bandar a long time.

In his car, Bandar scribbled out details from what he had seen on the map. When he got home, he took a large blank map of the region that had been supplied by the CIA and began reconstructing the plan piece-by-piece.

THE NEXT DAY, Sunday, Rice called Bandar to invite him to meet with the president the following day, Monday, January 13. The Europeans and their "obstruction" were very much on the minds of both Bush and Bandar. France, Germany and Russia were engaged in a volleyball match in the United Nations, debating the meaning, expectations and timing of the weapons inspections. All three were urging that Blix be given more time.

"Those people cannot help and they cannot hurt," Bandar told Bush. They tried to play bigger than they were.

The assessment was music to Bush's ears. But the president said that he was receiving advice and reports from some in his administration that in the event of war he would have to contend with a massive Arab and Islamic reaction that would put American interests at risk.

"Mr. President, you're assuming you're attacking Saudi Arabia and trying to capture King Fahd. This is Saddam Hussein. People are not going to shed tears over Saddam Hussein, but if he's attacked one more time by America and he survives, he will be larger than life. If he survives and stays in power after you've finished this, whatever it is, yes, everybody will follow his word. If they say attack the American embassy, they will go and attack it."

Before the Gulf War in 1991, Bandar recalled for the president, "Go back to look at what was said to your father—the Arab world will rise from the Atlantic to the Gulf!" Well, that didn't happen then, and it would not happen this time, he said. The problem would be if Saddam survived. The Saudis needed assurance that Saddam was going to be toast.

"You got the briefing from Dick, Rummy and General Myers?" the president asked.

"Yes."

"Any questions for me?"

No, Mr. President.

"That is the message I want you to carry for me to the crown prince," Bush said. "The message you're taking is mine, Bandar."

"That's fine, Mr. President."

Bandar believed it was exactly what Cheney had told Bush to say.

"Anything else for me?"

No, Mr. President.

Now Bandar could return to Saudi Arabia and brief everything he had seen and heard from Cheney and Rumsfeld to the crown prince as if it had come directly from the president. Soon, Bandar had a private session with the crown prince and presented the details and the map.

Crown Prince Abdullah, the 79-year-old half-brother of King Fahd, was the real decision maker in Saudi Arabia. Fahd, who was seriously ill, was only technically in charge. Abdullah was getting conflicting advice and recommendations from his defense, security and foreign ministers—much as Bush was. He wanted to look directly at Bandar. He was anxious and almost spooked, looking for the least possible commitment, the least risk. How would the king have handled this, how would he have dealt with this young American president? What was the mood in America? What were the chances? Were there certainties here?

Bandar tried to stick to the facts.

The crown prince said, "Mum is the word. Just tell nobody until we figure out what to do."

ANDY CARD did not think the decision to go to war was irrevocable just because a commitment had been made to an ally such as the Saudis. Bush could pull back. There would, of course, be consequences, perhaps immense. But if it became necessary, if it was the right thing, they could manage the consequences, and pay the price, no matter how politically expensive. The Saudis and others had been disappointed before. The administration was not locked in. But Card did not get a chance to express his opinion to the president.

WHILE BUSH was meeting with Bandar, Lieutenant General Michael Hayden, the NSA director, met with his agency's top officials in Friedman Auditorium at NSA headquarters for a highly classified "town meeting." The most sensitive and classified intercepts were going to get to the field, he told them. Though he had been working

PLAN OF ATTACK 269

on it for four months, he formally issued what was called a "State-ment of Director's Intent" for a war with Iraq. It said in part, "If di-rected, I intend to conduct a SIGINT and Information Assurance [the protection of secure U.S. communications] operation that will meet the combatant commanders' objectives of shock, speed and awe while also providing policy makers information that is actionable and timely."

Speed and agility would be achieved by "decentralized distribu-tion," Hayden said, meaning intercepts would go immediately to the battlefield. This would be done via the Zircon chat room where intel-ligence and military operations would be fused. There would not be a "traditional hierarchy" but "sharing" and collaboration within NSA, between the large national strategic intelligence assets and tactical intelligence from the theater, with other U.S. intelligence agencies, with allied combat forces and with foreign intelligence services.

"We will push intelligence to those places it needs to be; I ex-pect leaders at every level to actively remove obstacles to dissemina-tion," one of the pre-9/11 problems. Hayden wanted to make sure they were organized so the listeners and analysts would be able "to maintain a sustainable battle rhythm."

ONE OF RICE'S JOBS WAS, as she called it, "to read the secretaries"—Powell and Rumsfeld. Since the president had told Rumsfeld about his decision to go to war, he had better tell Powell, and fast. Powell was close to Prince Bandar, who now was informed of the decision.

"Mr. President," Rice said, "if you're getting to a place that you really think this might happen, you need to call Colin in and talk to him." Powell had the most difficult job of keeping the diplomatic track alive.

So that Monday, January 13, Powell and Bush met in the Oval Office. The president was sitting in his regular chair in front of the fireplace and the secretary was in the chair reserved for the visiting leader or most senior U.S. official. For once, neither Cheney nor Rice was hovering.

Bush complimented Powell for his hard work on the diplomatic front. "The inspections are not getting us there," the president said, getting down to business. The U.N. inspectors were just sort of stumbling around, and Saddam was showing no intention of real compliance. "I really think I'm going to have to do this." The president said he had made up his mind on war. The U.S. should go to war.

"You're sure?" Powell asked.

Yes. It was the assured Bush. His tight, forward-leaning, muscular body language verified his words. It was the Bush of the days following 9/11.

"You understand the consequences," Powell said in a half-question. For nearly six months, he had been hammering on this theme—that the United States would be taking down a regime, would have to govern Iraq, and the ripple effect in the Middle East and the world could not be predicted. The run-up to war had sucked nearly all the oxygen from every other issue in foreign relations. War would surely get all the air and attention.

Yeah, I do, the president answered.

"You know that you're going to be owning this place?" Powell said, reminding Bush of what he had told him at their August 5 dinner. An invasion would mean assuming the hopes, aspirations and all the troubles of Iraq. Powell wasn't sure whether Bush had fully understood the meaning and consequences of total ownership.

But I think I have to do this, the president said.

Right, Powell said.

I just want to let you know that, Bush said, making it clear this was not a discussion, but the president informing one of his cabinet members of his decision. The fork in the road had been reached and Bush had chosen war.

As the only one in Bush's inner circle who was seriously and actively pressing the diplomatic track, Powell figured the president wanted to make sure he would support the war. It was in some way a gut check, but Powell didn't feel the president was making a loyalty check. No way on God's earth could he walk away at that point. It would have been an unthinkable act of disloyalty to the president, to

Powell's own soldier's code, to the United States military, and mostly to the several hundred thousand who would be going to war. The kids were the ones who fought, Powell often reminded himself.

It had taken Bush a long time to get to this point. It had come after 12 years of Saddam's games after the first Gulf War, more than a year of war planning, four months of grueling United Nations diplomacy. It was more than 15 months since 9/11. So it might look like a study in patience. It had not been easy for Powell to buy that patience. He had had to go in and buy it nearly every day. Buy it with the vast national security apparatus that surrounded a president, particularly Cheney, Rumsfeld and the boys over at Defense.

"Are you with me on this?" the president asked him now. "I think I have to do this. I want you with me."

It was an extraordinary moment. The president was asking, almost imploring his secretary of state, his most senior cabinet officer and the most visible administration figure other than himself. There was no salesmanship, just a question: yes or no, up or down.

"I'll do the best I can," Powell answered. "Yes, sir, I will support you. I'm with you, Mr. President."

"Time to put your war uniform on," the president said to the former general. He could wear his diplomatic hat, that was fine, but things had changed.

"He's going to do it," Powell told himself as he left. It was momentous. He had come to realize that this president wasn't one to second-guess himself. He didn't know when Bush reconsidered his decisions, replayed the debates, weighed the arguments. He must, he thought. Powell did it all the time. Maybe late at night, Powell thought. And maybe never? Was it possible? The president spoke so confidently.

Powell figured his job was to continue and finish out the diplomatic track. That might be the answer. The president's conclusion was clear—there was no way to avoid war—but the basis for that was Bush's belief that the U.N. negotiations and inspections were going south. "There may be a way to avoid this," Powell said to himself, imagining he still had time, even though Bush had crossed the river.

Powell knew diplomatic efforts could give the president a problem because they could make him walk back across the river. His rationalization went as follows: His goal was not to "unscrew" the presidential decision, it was to play out the diplomatic hand he held. In his mind, he was not doing this against the wishes of his boss, only against his instincts that diplomacy would not work.

This distinction between wishes and instincts was a delicate and dangerous game. Yet in all the discussions, meetings, chats and back-and-forth, the president had never once asked Powell, Would you do this? What's your overall advice? The bottom line?

Perhaps the president feared the answer. Perhaps Powell feared giving it. It would, after all, have been an opportunity to say he disagreed. But they had not gotten to that core question, and Powell would not push. He would not intrude on that most private of presidential space—where a president made decisions of war and peace—unless he was invited. He had not been invited.

Powell thought Saddam could be contained and would eventually wither. Under the sustained pressure—diplomatic, economic, military and CIA—he might wither faster. Perhaps, contrary to what the president was saying, time was on their side. Saddam had been fully isolated and left friendless in the international community after the passage of U.N. Resolution 1441 in November. It had been a moment of maximum pressure, but the diplomatic pressure was subsiding.

At times, with his closest friends, Powell was semidespondent. His president and his country were headed for a war that he thought might just be avoided, though he himself would not walk away. He had known it would be what he called "a long patrol" when the president had challenged Saddam at the United Nations on September 12, 2002. Powell wouldn't leave the president at the crossroads. He would do so only if he thought all the arguments for war were 100 percent wrong. And they weren't. He wanted the bastard gone as much as anyone.

Another consideration was if the war would be immoral. And Powell couldn't say that either. It was clear that the president was convinced it was both 100 percent correct and moral.

He had not been told to halt the diplomatic track. It was still possible, Powell reasoned, that he could pull a rabbit out of the hat at the U.N. That, he concluded, would leave Bush relieved but unhappy—relieved that all the things Powell had warned him about would not take place but unhappy that the bastard was still there.

Now diplomacy would take on the characteristics of a charade—or the formalized pantomime of the Japanese Kabuki dance to which Powell often referred.

He had not underestimated the extent to which the president had decided that letting the bastard remain was no longer an option. But he probably had underestimated his own usefulness to a president and vice president determined on war.

AFTER HIS MEETING WITH POWELL, the president reported the outcome to Andy Card. "I told Powell that it looks like we're going to have to do this, and I was going to do it," Bush said. "And he said that he would be with me."

Card believed that others, particularly Powell, nurtured a false hope that a diplomatic solution might be found. But not the president, who was now forced to tell others that they were going to have to let it go.

On the other hand—and the chief of staff had to always consider the alternative, that was his job—the meeting might cause Powell to be a little more creative and energetic in trying to find a way back to the road of diplomacy.

At times, Card thought of the president as a circus-horse rider with one foot on a "diplomacy" steed and the other on the "war" steed, both reins in his hands, leading down a path to regime change. Each horse had blinders on. It was now clear that diplomacy would not get him to his goal, so Bush had let go of that horse and was standing only on the war steed.

About a year later, I spent nearly ten minutes reviewing with the president his conversation with Powell, trying to sort out the various recollections. He finally said, "It sounds like you got it right." It was a time of stress, he said, adding, "It was a very cordial conversation. I would describe as cordial. I was here," he said, lightly tapping his own chair in the Oval Office, "he was here," pointing to the main dignitary's chair. "It wasn't a long conversation. I think the log will show it was relatively short." The president was correct. White House records show it had been a 12-minute meeting. "There wasn't much debate: It looks like we're headed to war."

President Bush also stated emphatically that though he had asked Powell to be with him and support him in a war, "I didn't need his permission."

26

BEFORE A MEETING with Polish President Aleksander Kwasniewski the next day, the morning of Tuesday, January 14, Bush's frustration again flared in public as he shifted position on the time remaining to Saddam. While eight days earlier he had said publicly that Saddam has "got time," he told reporters that morning, "Time is running out on Saddam Hussein."

Bush knew he had no better friend on the European continent than the popular, second-term Polish president who had agreed to send troops to the war. The Bushes had hosted Kwasniewski, 47, and his wife for a rare State Dinner the previous July.

"The level of anti-Americanism is extremely high," Kwasniewski said at their private meeting. He had a serious political problem because of his support for Bush.

"Success helps change public opinion," Bush said. "Should we commit troops, we'll feed the people of Iraq." He said it as if that humanitarian gesture might have an impact on public opinion in Poland. He said there was a protocol a country could follow to show the world that it was ridding itself of unconventional weapons—one that South Africa had followed, visibly and aggressively opening up records and facilities for inspections. Saddam had not. "In my judgment it's time to move soon but we won't act precipitously," Bush said, adding, "But time is running out. It's sooner rather than later."

"We will win," the Polish president said, but sounding like Colin Powell, he added plaintively, "but what are the consequences?" After a pause, he continued, "You need wide, broad international support. We are with you, don't worry about it. The risk is the U.N. will collapse. What will replace it?"

These were hard questions that Bush sidestepped, saying only, "We believe that Islam like Christianity can grow in a free and democratic manner."

For Bush, the important things were that Poland would be with him and would supply troops.

THE NEXT DAY, January 15, Bush met with the war cabinet to hear the details of the planned food relief and other humanitarian efforts. This is the best humanitarian relief effort that anybody's ever planned, NSC Middle East affairs director Elliott Abrams told the president and the others. A hard-line conservative State Department official in the Reagan administration, who had pled guilty to withholding information from Congress in the Iran-contra affair, and was later pardoned by Bush senior in 1992, Abrams, 55, was a controversial figure but was valued by Rice and Hadley as a tough bureaucratic workhorse. He had helped plan the relief efforts for the Afghanistan war.

Abrams told the president that Iraq already had food shortages. There were 800,000 internally displaced persons and 740,000 refugees. Some food was being supplied through the United Nations Oil-for-Food Program, which permitted the legal sale of limited quantities of Iraqi oil to buy food. About 60 percent of Iraqis were wholly dependent on the program, and more still partially so. It was estimated that war might displace an additional 2 million. The U.S. was stockpiling food, tents and water for a million, and they were funding other U.N. agencies and nongovernmental organizations (NGOs) that managed the aid distribution to stockpile for another million.

Abrams and Robin Cleveland, a national security specialist in Bush's budget office, told the president that money had to be moved very quietly to these NGOs—in some cases disguising the funds as general contributions—because many of these groups didn't want to appear to favor war. All this would be in place by the end of February. Rumsfeld had been pushing everyone to prepare estimates on the reconstruction needs and costs. That way, they could get the supplemental budget request to Congress on the first day of the war and begin contracting out work.

The exact number of refugees and displaced persons, Abrams explained, would depend on inter-ethnic tensions, violence and reprisals, and WMD scares, as well as the duration and intensity of combat, and the ability to get aid to the populace where they were so they would not leave. The goal was to get in fast as areas came under U.S. control.

Abrams and Cleveland gave Bush an overview of the operations—where the U.S. civil-military operation centers and disaster assistance teams would be located, what the U.N. commission on refugees and the Red Cross would do, how long it would take to get the Oil-for-Food Program up and running again. Though there was consternation about continuing the Oil-for-Food Program, Abrams said they had concluded they had to continue with what was in place, at least at the outset.

The president agreed.

Another key aspect was protecting the humanitarian infrastructure inside Iraq and keeping hospitals and sewage plants from being bombed. Staff-level planners from NSC, Defense and the Agency for International Development (USAID) had gone to Franks's Central Command in November, Abrams said, to offer input on the military plan and specify their no-strike list of sites such as health clinics, water plants and the electrical grid. Beginning in late 2002, they had circulated a phone number and Web site address to U.N. agencies and NGOs who could submit their nominations for inclusion on the no-strike list. The list had grown to thousands and Franks and his staff had incorporated the no-strike nominations into their targeting.

Abrams flashed through several pages of slides on the reconstruction effort, on health care, schools, water, sewage, electricity. There were 250 hospitals in Iraq, 5 medical college hospitals, 20 general military ones. There were 33,000 hospital beds and 9,400 doctors, he said. Another slide listed things that might frustrate relief efforts, such as inter-ethnic fighting or Saddam blowing up the dams.

"This is an opportunity to change the image of the United States," the president said. "We need to make the most of these humanitarian aid efforts in our public diplomacy. I want to build surge capability. I want loaded ships ready to provide food and relief supplies so we can go in very promptly. There are a lot of things that could go wrong, but not for want of planning."

AT THE END OF THE WEEK, Friday, January 17, the president arranged to go to Walter Reed Army Medical Center to visit with some wounded from Afghanistan. It was about as close as he would get to the ugly nitty-gritty of war.

Accompanied by Laura, the president traveled to Walter Reed, five miles directly north of the White House. They first stopped in the room of a soldier in a wheelchair.

"Thank you for your service and sacrifice," Bush said. "Are you from California?" He posed for pictures with the soldier. "We appreciate you, we're proud of you. God bless."

In the next room, a soldier who had lost a leg above the knee in a landmine explosion was in bed. His son was on the bed with him, and his mother stood by. Some of the soldier's fingers had been amputated.

Bush told the soldier that one of his former aides in Texas had lost his leg, and the guy was a runner who learned to run on his prosthesis. "They can make 'em that good these days," Bush added. "You'll be able to run again."

One of the president's assistants saw a look on the soldier's face that said that he didn't believe that the commander in chief's saying he would run again would make it so.

"I'm sorry about your injury," the president said. "Fight on, show your leadership."

"Roger, Mr. President."

The president assured the soldier that he was getting the best care, and asked some questions. When did you come here? Where did you get hit?

"You'll be out there, mark my word," Bush persisted. "You'll be running again."

The soldier still had a grim look of disbelief.

"God bless you," Laura Bush said.

"Thank you for your service," the president added.

Next it was the room of a Hispanic sergeant whose face was severely scarred and deformed, including his lips. He had been injured dismantling a weapon.

"Cómo está," Bush said in Spanish. How are you?

The sergeant could hardly speak, and he was hooked up to a pump of some kind. His mother stood in silence.

"We're proud of your man," Bush said to the mother. "He's serving your country. He'll be fine. He's a strong man." The president presented the sergeant with a Bronze Star. Then he bent down and kissed him on the head, groping for something to shake. The president took the man's left thumb.

The sergeant spoke with difficulty, finally getting it out. "I'd like to stand up for you, sir."

"No, you don't," the president said. "I'm standing up for you. I'm looking forward to seeing you a year from now. You'll be great."

The sergeant was from Houston where the president's parents lived. Bush turned to the mother, "If you see my mother and father, say hello for me."

Walter Reed is among the best hospitals, renowned for its healing and compassionate care. The agony of the battlefield, where medics often had to assign priorities for treatment based on pain and the chances of survival, was filtered out. The high degree of care and nurturing was reassuring to the Bushes. Some 40 minutes later, they were in the second floor lobby of the hospital speaking to reporters.

"Laura and I have just met with five incredibly brave soldiers," he said, "five of America's finest citizens who have been severely injured in the line of duty." He told the reporters how he had thanked them for their service—"noble and strong and good." After describing "the best care possible," he said, "Have a great weekend, and we'll see you next week." The Bushes were off to Camp David, while in Washington that weekend, tens of thousands gathered on the Mall in the largest antiwar protest since the Vietnam era.

Nearly a year later, I asked the president about this visit and its timing, right after the decision to go to war.

"It is my duty to go see those soldiers," he said.

"Are you trying to remind yourself of the consequences of war?"

"No," he said firmly. "I have to go. No, not at all. It's more basic than that. I have the obligation as the commander in chief to go thank them for their service, to comfort them, to make sure that they are getting what they need." His personal attention also would send a message throughout the hospital, he said, reaching the others who were there.

"It's coming at a very interesting moment in your decision," I noted.

"It is," he replied, "but I don't need to steel myself with grief. I mean I don't need to remind myself what grief is about. I've been through September the 11th to grieve with the nation. I am a president who has been through a lot of moments of grief. I have grieved with the widows of Afghanistan . . . saw these kids a year later still longing for their mothers or dads. It's not that I need a lesson on grief."

He added, "You are asking your fellow citizens to be courageous as well. And you are committing them into harm's way. I have a duty as best I can to comfort. I can't comfort everybody, but I can comfort enough for others to know."

FOR SOME TWO MONTHS, since late November, Steve Hadley had been working through the deputies committee—Armitage of State, Wolfowitz of Defense, McLaughlin of the CIA, Libby of the vice president's office—looking at what the transition of power might be in a post-Saddam Iraq once major combat operations were over.

Franks and the military had called this stage the Phase Four "stability operations." Hadley saw it more broadly. It wasn't just achieving stability—political or otherwise. The president wanted to achieve democracy. So Hadley realized they needed a comprehensive postwar plan. It was a long distance between stability and democracy.

Around the first of the year, Douglas Feith, the undersecretary for policy in the Pentagon and a Rumsfeld favorite, came to see Hadley at the White House. Feith, 49, a Harvard graduate with a law degree from Georgetown, is a protégé of Richard Perle, a former Reagan defense official who now served as a member of Rumsfeld's Defense Policy Board, an advisory group. Perle was the most outspoken public advocate for war with Iraq. Feith has a high-pitched, insistent voice. He is articulate and has mastered the language of the management consultant, short, pithy sayings, what he called "big thoughts." He liked to lecture his staff and others in the Pentagon, dwelling on his relationship with Rumsfeld, a methodical, strategic thinker of some originality in Feith's opinion. For example, Rumsfeld advocated what he called the "toolbox approach" to problems, noting that if the only tool you have is a hammer, then every problem looks like a nail. Thus it was essential, as Feith described Rumsfeld's thinking, never to approach problems with only a hammer because life is complex and not all problems are nails.

Feith was not popular with the uniformed military. He appeared to equate policy with paper. His office and files were filled with thick loose-leaf binders seemingly containing every "snowflake"—the term for Rumsfeld's short, terse memos—he had received and everything Feith and his policy shop had churned out in response.

Franks tried to ignore Feith though it was not easy. The general once confided to several colleagues about Feith: "I have to deal with the fucking stupidest guy on the face of the earth almost every day."

Feith's arrival in Hadley's office was important because he had an idea about post-Saddam Iraq. He proposed setting up a planning cell in Defense that would implement policy on the ground in Iraq after the war. It would be best, he said, to lodge this cell in Defense since Franks and the Central Command would have a major role in the post-conflict, but the cell should be interagency from the very beginning. He would have people who could work 24 hours a day, seven days a week. They would take policy-level guidance from the deputies and principals and then implement the plan in Iraq. But the cell would not just plan, Feith said, it would become expeditionary. In the name of efficiency, the people would actually go to Iraq after the military situation permitted and carry out the plans.

Feith took the concept to Rumsfeld, who approved, and he returned to the White House to say such a concept was strongly supported by Rumsfeld. Postwar efforts had been bungled before, Feith argued, and this was the way to do it right.

It was a different way of doing things, first because the planners would be the implementers, second because the State Department would be directly subordinate to Defense. State had been working for almost a year on what was called the "Future of Iraq" project, which had compiled thousands of pages of reports and recommendations from a range of experts on government, oil, criminal justice and agriculture in Iraq.

When the notion of giving the planning and implementing authority for post-Saddam Iraq to Defense was presented to the principals, Powell thought it was logical. In the immediate aftermath of war, only Defense would have the thousands of people, the money and the resources. He certainly had nothing like that at State, though he had some real experts. Defense and the military would be the liberating, conquering, occupying force. With a huge American army running around the battlefield, just for the purposes of unity of command, the job had to go to Defense, he thought. It didn't cross his mind that this was out of the ordinary. It was exactly what had happened after World War II in Germany and Japan.

There was a sense of urgency, and Hadley and the NSC staff had about a week to get a document prepared for the president to sign. It was a rush job. The classified document, National Security Presidential Directive #24, set up the Office of Reconstruction and Humanitarian Assistance (ORHA) in Defense, and was signed by the president on January 20. The document said that if it should become necessary for a U.S.-led coalition to liberate Iraq, the new office would both plan and implement those plans on the full spectrum of issues the U.S. government would face in administering postwar Iraq. That included humanitarian relief, dismantling of WMD, defeating and exploiting intelligence from terrorists, protecting natural resources and infrastructure, rebuilding the economy, and reestablishing key civilian services such as food, water, electricity and health care. The interim authority was to reshape the Iraqi military by reestablishing a reformed, civilian-controlled armed forces, reshaping other internal security services, and supporting the transition to an Iraqi-led authority over time. All the interagency work done by the State Department and others was to be handed over to ORHA.

In the event of hostilities, according to the president's signed order, ORHA was to deploy to Iraq and form the nucleus of the administrative apparatus that would assist in administering Iraq for a limited period of time after the conflict was over.

Rumsfeld and Feith chose retired Army Lieutenant General Jay M. Garner to head ORHA. He had overseen assistance to the Kurds in northern Iraq after the 1991 Gulf War. Powell and Armitage didn't really know Garner.

Powell sent over the "Future of Iraq" study and the names of about 75 State Department Arab experts who had done the study or who could be included in the vanguard going into Iraq. Heading that team were Thomas Warrick, who had supervised the study, and Meghan O'Sullivan, a sanctions specialist whom Powell very much admired.

Later Powell got word that Rumsfeld had kicked Warrick and O'Sullivan out of the Pentagon, ordering them to leave by sundown.

"What the hell is going on?" Powell said in a phone call to Rumsfeld.

Rumsfeld said that as they got into postwar planning, the work

had to be done by those who were truly committed to this and supporters of the change and not those who have written or said things
that were not supportive.

Powell took that to mean that his people didn't support exiles
like Chalabi. In any case, Powell and Rumsfeld got into a giant row
until finally Powell got word that higher authority in the White
House—either Bush or Cheney—had decided that O'Sullivan could
go back to work with Garner, but not Warrick.

Powell wondered if things could get weirder. He identified
seven senior State officials that he wanted to assign to Garner, but
Feith said he wanted outsiders. Feith sometimes criticized the State
Department in private as dovish, calling it "The Department of
Nice." "This is bullshit," Powell said. So he and Rumsfeld got into
another big fight. This time it took a week to resolve. Five of the
seven were eventually assigned. Powell couldn't believe the silliness.

For Cheney, there was a larger question. The president's vision,
which Cheney thought bold, was that they would not just get rid of
Saddam but replace his regime with a democracy. It was a daunting
task, and Cheney thought there were too many in the State Department, the secretary included, who were neither sympathetic nor supportive of the president's goal of democracy in Iraq and trying to
transform the region. These people had argued that a democracy was
too sweeping a change, too hard, something Iraq had never had, a
bridge too far.

In the debates around the table in the Situation Room, the vice
president had argued, "We've got an obligation to go stand up a
democracy. We can't go get some former [Iraqi] general and put him
in charge and say, Okay, now you're the dictator in Iraq. We've got to
fundamentally change the place. And we've got to give the Iraqi people a chance at those fundamental values we believe in."

ON JANUARY 20, Powell attended a United Nations Security Council
meeting where the topic was supposed to be terrorism. Both Cheney
and Rumsfeld had argued that he should not go, but Powell didn't

want to stiff the world organization. In a press conference after the session, French Foreign Minister de Villepin declared, "Nothing! Nothing!" justified war.

Powell was so furious he could barely be contained. Any leverage with Saddam was linked directly to the threat of war, and the French had just taken the threat off the U.N.'s table. He couldn't believe the stupidity. De Villepin was going to make the U.N. irrelevant.

The president recalled, "When de Villepin speaks, it made me realize that Saddam would try to skate even more because he had people that were unknowingly helping him."

Some thought it was a liberating moment for the United States, and even more so for Prime Minister Blair. If the French, who had veto power, had decided that war was not an option, then the whole U.N. process was hopeless. Bush and Blair could argue they had gone to the U.N. and been thwarted by the French.

Following a meeting with economists the next day, January 21, Bush let his frustration boil over. He said Saddam was not disarming and added, "I believe in the name of peace, he must disarm. And we will lead a coalition of willing nations to disarm him. Make no mistake about that, he will be disarmed."

"When?" asked a reporter, caught off guard. "How do you decide when that moment comes that you need to make a judgment?"

"I will let you know when the moment has come," Bush said. There was laughter. Apparently he wasn't declaring war, not yet.

27

A T THE STATE DEPARTMENT, Armitage received a call from the White House communications office saying that they had compiled a 33-page document called "Apparatus of Lies" on Saddam's propaganda. They wanted him to unveil it in public. Card's White House Iraq Group was planning a big rollout of speeches and documents to counter Saddam and the growing international antiwar movement. Millions had marched in European, Arab and Asian capitals.

Armitage read through the document and thought, What bullshit! It was mostly old stories about Saddam's lies stemming from the 1991 Gulf War period, with no clear rationale about why the administration might go to war in 2003. If the United States were to go to war with every regime that told lies, there would be nothing but war.

Armitage told the White House, "This is awful. I'm not going to touch it."

You've got to give a speech, said a White House aide.

Why?

Now was the time, it had been decided, they really needed him out there, Wolfowitz was also going to give a speech. Finally, Armitage agreed. "But the price of me giving it, no clearance on the speech," he said. The White House would not see it in advance; he didn't want a lot of niggling and stupid suggestions. He was finding it harder and harder to keep from being sucked into the White House's propaganda apparatus.

On January 21, Armitage spoke before the U.S. Institute of Peace, a nonpartisan group established by Congress to promote and fund peace efforts. He had worked carefully to balance the hard and the soft. "We must not let the sensible reluctance to fight drive us into wishful thinking." He told them he had recently addressed 4,000 midshipmen at the United States Naval Academy, his alma mater. "I sincerely hope that not one of those young men or young women—or any of our other service members—is sent into harm's way in Iraq. That is what we at the Department of State—and indeed across the government—are working hard to avoid." The next few weeks would tell the story. "And I wish I were here to tell you that I am optimistic." He then recited all the weapons Saddam had that were unaccounted for. He said offhandedly that a document called "Apparatus of Lies" was available in the back of the room. "I commend it to you to the extent that the past is prologue."

ON FRIDAY, January 24, Franks delivered his final war plan, the 5-11-16-125-day Hybrid Plan, to Rumsfeld and General Myers. This is *the plan*, he said. He was no longer planning, though some changes would be made.

The combined 16-day first phase of establishing the air bridge and deploying troops—the "5" and "11"—had been overtaken by events. Rumsfeld had given the approvals to start the air bridge, and incremental deployments of 10,000, 15,000 and 20,000 troops had been going on for some time. By the middle of February there would be a total U.S.-force level of 140,000 in the region, 78,000 of which would be ground forces—Army, Marines and Special Operations Forces.

Because Rumsfeld was the only one in the war planning circle who talked regularly with Bush, he had developed timelines for the president that attempted to project on one sheet of paper what would likely be occurring on the diplomatic and military fronts. A

Top Secret timeline dated January 29 listed the presidential decision day, called Notification Day or N-Day, when Bush would decide on war, as February 22. C-Day, the start of force flow, would follow. Of course, deployments had already begun while the president was ostensibly still deciding, and Rumsfeld, of course, knew that Bush's decision had already been made.

AFTER MCLAUGHLIN'S PRESENTATION on WMD evidence had failed to impress them, Bush and Rice had asked the CIA to put together the best information in a written document—the "slam dunk" case Tenet had promised. Tenet and McLaughlin made it clear they did not want to write a speech for a political appointee or an elected official. That would be crossing the line. They cleared speeches for facts. They also did not want to write a document that had any sales or marketing element. So the result was the driest, most clinical account, with footnotes specifying the sourcing. The text, 40 pages, was sent to the White House on January 22 specifying that it was still highly classified.

The president was determined to hand the evidence over to experienced lawyers who could use it to make the best possible case. The document was given to Steve Hadley (Yale Law '72) and Scooter Libby (Columbia Law '75). They visited the CIA and posed a series of questions which the agency answered in writing.

As far as Libby was concerned, the CIA had made the case that Saddam had WMD and significant terrorist ties. The CIA had been collecting intelligence on Iraqi WMD for decades. There was no doubt where the agency stood: The October NIE had said Saddam had chemical and biological weapons, and Director Tenet had declared the case a slam dunk. Libby believed that the agency, which had the hard job of sifting and evaluating so much information, at times missed or overlooked potentially important material, intelligence that might not be definitive, but could add to the mosaic.

Much had been made in the press of the so-called Office of Special Plans that Doug Feith had set up in his Pentagon policy shop.

Libby thought the fuss ridiculous, created by people who didn't understand the process. The office was essentially two people who were assigned to read all the sensitive intelligence. They had found a few things and Feith had summarized those findings for Libby. It was not given to the president or vice president. For Christ's sake, Libby thought, every single day the CIA chose a half-dozen or more intelligence items to give to the president in the President's Daily Brief (PDB). One paper from Feith or the Office of Special Plans couldn't possibly pollute the intelligence process. The other myth, in Libby's view, was that the Iraqi exile leader Chalabi had a direct channel to pass intelligence to the Pentagon or to Cheney. All of Chalabi's information went to the CIA. They could use it or not as they saw fit.

On Saturday, January 25, Libby gave a lengthy presentation in the Situation Room to Rice, Hadley, Armitage, Wolfowitz, Dan Bartlett and Michael Gerson. Though she had formally left the White House staff, Karen Hughes was there. Karl Rove was in and out of the meeting.

Holding a thick sheaf of paper, Libby outlined the latest version of the case against Saddam. He began with a long section on satellite, intercept and human intelligence showing the efforts at concealment and deception. Things were being dug up, moved and buried. No one knew for sure what it was precisely, but the locations and stealth fit the pattern of WMD concealment. He began each section with blunt conclusions—Saddam had chemical and biological weapons, was producing and concealing them; his ties to bin Laden's al Qaeda network were numerous and strong.

Libby used the intercept of the two suspected terrorists laughing about killing a donkey with ricin that McLaughlin had discarded as unreliable. He said that Mohammed Atta, the leader of the 9/11 attacks, was believed to have met in Prague with an Iraqi intelligence officer and cited intelligence of as many as four meetings. The others knew the CIA had evidence of two meetings perhaps, and that there was no certainty about what Atta had been doing in Prague or whether he had met with the Iraqi official. Libby talked for about an hour.

Armitage was appalled at what he considered overreaching and hyperbole. Libby was drawing only the worst conclusions from fragments and silky threads.

On the other hand, Wolfowitz, who had been convinced years ago of Iraq's complicity in anti-American terrorism, thought Libby presented a strong case. He subscribed to Rumsfeld's notion that lack of evidence did not mean something did not exist. He was taken with possible ties between Iraq and al Qaeda. The absence of firm evidence was to be expected because al Qaeda had tight operational security, so good that some heads of state had wondered to Wolfowitz whether former KGB officers were not training al Qaeda. Some Arab leaders thought it was Israel's Mossad. Wolfowitz had been pushing the CIA to investigate whether former East German security services were involved. He thought it was more than coincidence that al Qaeda, which had been relatively inactive since 9/11, had resumed activity after the president had gone to the U.N. and threatened unilateral action against Iraq. That included the October 12 bombing of a nightclub in Bali that killed 202, the shooting of two U.S. Marines in Kuwait and an attack on a French oil tanker off the coast of Yemen in the span of one week.

The most important response came from Karen Hughes. As a communications exercise, she said, it didn't work. The sweeping conclusions at the head of each section were too much. The president, she said, wanted it to be like the old television series *Dragnet*— "Just the facts." Let people draw their own conclusions.

Rove, who had the Top Secret/codeword security clearances, thought Libby's presentation was very compelling and very strong— also incredibly scary. He was particularly struck by the evidence that Saddam had hundreds of millions of dollars, probably several billion, from illicit oil revenue that could be used to buy WMD. For Rove, it was a potent, deadly combination—a history with WMD, a desire for more, scientists with the know-how, a closed police state and a bunch of money. He was fascinated to see the differences in the approach of Libby with his lawyer's mind, and Hughes with her communicator's mind. He was on Hughes's side. This was a communications problem, not a legal one. Even the best advocacy entailed presenting facts and letting people reach their own conclusions. He, for one, was convinced.

So who then should present the public case? Rice and Hadley pondered that. The case would have to be made to the U.N. so the chief diplomat, Powell, was the logical choice. Hadley believed there were additional reasons to choose Powell. First, to have maximum credibility, it would be best to go counter to type and everyone knew that Powell was soft on Iraq, that he was the one who didn't want to go. Second, Powell was conscious of his credibility, and his reputation. He would examine the intelligence carefully. Third, when Powell was prepared, he was very persuasive.

"I want you to do it," Bush told the secretary of state. "You have the credibility to do it." Powell was flattered to be asked to do what no one else could.

Rice and Hughes told Powell that he should get three days for the presentation to the Security Council—a day each for WMD, terrorism and human rights violations. They seemed to envision a drama equivalent to the Cuban missile crisis in 1962, when U.N. Ambassador Adlai Stevenson displayed satellite photos that showed the nuclear missiles installed in Cuba by the Soviet Union. In one of the most electric moments of the Cold War, Stevenson had asked the Soviet ambassador if he denied his country had put missiles there. "Yes or no—don't wait for the translation . . . I am prepared to wait for my answer until hell freezes over."

"Look," Powell told them, "I can't go up there and stop the world for three days. Adlai Stevenson did not have an Adlai Stevenson week. He had an Adlai Stevenson moment. I can only do this once."

How about two hours each day on each case? Rice and Hughes suggested. They wanted it as long, detailed and boring as possible to demonstrate the depth of the case.

"No way," Powell said. "I'm doing it once."

Okay, it might be three or four hours long.

"No it won't," Powell insisted. "You can't hold these guys for three to four hours." They would fall asleep. In the U.N. everyone had to be given a chance to respond. Powell won agreement that the length and content would be his decision.

AS POWELL WAS PREPARING his presentation, Cheney called.

Colin, the vice president said, look carefully at the terrorism case that Scooter prepared. Give it a good look.

Sure, Dick, Powell said. He generally used the vice president's first name when they were alone. Cheney was not ordering him or trying to direct him. It was just a request to take a serious look.

Powell looked at it. Four Mohammed Atta meetings in Prague. That was worse than ridiculous. He pitched it.

Powell thought that Cheney had the fever. The vice president and Wolfowitz kept looking for the connection between Saddam and 9/11. It was a separate little government that was out there—Wolfowitz, Libby, Feith and Feith's "Gestapo office," as Powell privately called it. He saw in Cheney a sad transformation. The cool operator from the first Gulf War just would not let go. Cheney now had an unhealthy fixation. Nearly every conversation or reference came back to al Qaeda and trying to nail the connection with Iraq. He would often have an obscure piece of intelligence. Powell thought that Cheney took intelligence and converted uncertainty and ambiguity into fact. It was about the worst charge that Powell could make about the vice president. But there it was. Cheney would take an intercept and say it shows something was happening. No, no, no, Powell or another would say, it shows that somebody talked to somebody else who said something *might* be happening. A conversation would suggest something might be happening, and Cheney would convert that into a "We know." Well, Powell concluded, we didn't know. No one knew.

Later I asked the president if he sensed a fever in Cheney. "No," Bush said. "Cheney is a low-key person. He's not feverish. Fever to me is this kind of delirious— He's in control. So, no. I felt a conviction. But no, fever is the wrong word. Whoever said that doesn't know him quite as well as I do, or knows him maybe in a different way."

• • •

ON MONDAY, January 27, Hans Blix gave a tough but balanced report to the U.N. Security Council that covered the first two months of inspections.

"Iraq appears not to have come to a genuine acceptance—not even today—of the disarmament which was demanded of it and which it needs to carry out to win the confidence of the world and to live in peace," he said. Though cooperation was on the whole good, Blix said he had strong indications that Iraq had produced more anthrax than it had declared. "It might still exist."

Blix also had questions about VX nerve gas precursor chemicals. As an example of the accounting nightmare, he noted that an Iraqi air force document indicated that 13,000 chemical bombs were dropped from 1983 to 1988 during the Iran-Iraq War, while Iraq had declared to the U.N. that 19,500 were consumed during that period. "Thus there is a discrepancy of 6,500 bombs." He noted carefully that presumptions one way or the other—guilt or innocence—would not solve the problem and that only "evidence and full transparency may help."

Mohamed ElBaradei, the director general of the International Atomic Energy Agency, said, "We have to date found no evidence that Iraq has revived its nuclear weapons program since its elimination of the program in the 1990s." He noted that his work was in midstream, but he predicted, "We should be able within the next few months to provide credible assurance that Iraq has no nuclear program."

After taking all this in, Rice thought it was possible that they had Saddam on the run, that he might conceivably crack. Would it be like 1995, after his son-in-law defected, and Saddam abruptly admitted he had a biological weapons program? Cheney, for one, said no—he did not for a moment believe Saddam was going to break. More important, the sensitive intelligence on Blix showed some contradictions. Several of the principals thought it showed Blix was again not being straight, even lying. The intelligence showed that Blix did not want his inspectors to be the reason for war and that he feared his January 27 presentation had almost handed the U.S. a casus belli. As a result, Blix was planning to back off in his next report.

Rice told the president she didn't believe Blix was necessarily lying. He was just deeply conflicted.

All this only made Bush more determined on war. All of Cheney's predictions about the U.N. were coming true.

MEANWHILE, I HAD HEARD that Powell was going to present intelligence to the U.N., in part to rebut what the administration had expected Blix to say on January 27. Though Blix's report had been comparatively tough, they were still going to put out something. I wrote a story for *The Washington Post* that ran January 28 under the headline, "U.S. to Make Iraq Intelligence Public; Evidence of Weapons Concealment to Be Shared in Effort to Boost Support for War." I reported on what some administration officials thought was "compelling" and "unambiguous" intelligence that Iraq was moving and concealing weapons, but added, "Sources said U.S. intelligence agencies have not traced or located a large cache of prohibited weapons or ingredients used in the making of chemical or biological weapons. They said the U.S. government still lacks a 'smoking gun.' "

That evening, President Bush devoted the last third of his State of the Union address to a broadside against Saddam. He leaned heavily on the weapons not accounted for from Saddam's previous declarations—25,000 liters of anthrax, material for more than 38,000 liters of botulinum toxin, "enough to subject millions of people to death by respiratory failure," also sarin gas, VX nerve agent and mobile biological weapons labs.

Bush then spoke 16 words that would become notorious: "The British government has learned that Saddam Hussein recently sought significant quantities of uranium from Africa." It was one of his more innocuous accusations, and he accurately attributed the allegation to the British. But less than four months earlier, Tenet and the CIA had excised the sentence from the president's speech in

Cincinnati because the assertion could not be confirmed and was thought to be shaky. Tenet had not reviewed the State of the Union speech, and Hadley had forgotten the earlier CIA warning.

Well-placed officials in the administration were skeptical about the WMD intelligence on Iraq—among them Armitage, some senior military officers and even the CIA spokesman, Bill Harlow, who repeatedly warned reporters that the intelligence agencies were convinced Saddam had WMD but that they lacked "a smoking gun." This skepticism apparently did not make it in any convincing form to the president. The unambiguous pronouncements of the heavyweights Tenet, Cheney and Rumsfeld prevailed.

28

A T A PRIVATE MEETING with Italian Prime Minister Silvio Berlusconi on January 30, the president gave his practiced disclaimer that no decision had been made on military action. But then he stated his true course. Iraq would be disarmed and Saddam would not be allowed to stay in power. "We have put together a lethal military, and we will kick his ass. We will take every step to avoid civilians." Then Bush was back to qualifying. "Should this require troops, I'll be in touch with you. There'll be no surprises." Then he gave the prime minister his pep talk. "This is going to change. You watch, public opinion will change. We lead our publics. We cannot follow our publics."

On Friday, January 31, Bush was scheduled to meet again with Tony Blair at Camp David, but a mix of rain and ice kept them at the White House.

Blair told Bush that he needed to get a second U.N. resolution. He had promised that to his political party at home, and he was confident that together he and Bush could rally the U.N. and the international community.

Bush was set against a second resolution. This was a rare case in which Cheney and Powell agreed. Both were opposed. The first resolution had taken seven weeks, and this one would be much harder.

Powell didn't think it was necessary. He thought a judge would rule that 1441 was enough to move without a second resolution.

There was another complication. The first resolution had passed 15 to 0, so that would be considered the norm. Of course, it was not the norm but a dramatic exception. In 1990, the U.N.'s resolution on the Gulf War had passed 12 to 2, with Yemen and Cuba voting no and China abstaining. Now if they didn't get 15 to 0 on a second resolution, it could be seen as weak.

But Blair had the winning argument. It was necessary for him politically. It was no more complicated than that, an absolute political necessity. Blair said he needed the favor. Please.

That was language Bush understood. "If that's what you need, we will go flat out to try and help you get it," he told Blair. He also didn't want to go alone, and without Britain, he would be close to going alone. The president and the administration were worried about what Steve Hadley termed "the imperial option."

So they were back in the briar patch as far as Cheney was concerned.

"Blair's got to deal with his own Parliament, his own people, but he has to deal with the French-British relationship as well, and its context within Europe," Bush recalled later. "And so he's got a very difficult assignment. Much more difficult, by the way, than the American president in some ways. This was the period where slowly but surely the French became the issue inside Britain."

Bush called it "the famous second resolution meeting" and said Blair "absolutely" asked for help.

POWELL HAD TO DECIDE precisely what he was going to say to the U.N. Libby provided a 60-page version of the case—some 50 percent more than the CIA paper—which he viewed as a kind of Chinese menu from which Powell could select. There were no footnotes, but Libby had provided backup binders from the NSC staff and from Cheney's office.

Powell found much of intelligence murky. He liked to pick up the phone, or look someone in the eye, and talk it out with those who had facts or firsthand knowledge and could make decisions. As Armitage said many times to people around government, "Feed the beast," meaning provide some good information or reliable back-channel gossip that he could pass to Powell. But communications intercepts and satellite photos did not go down particularly well with the beast himself. For Powell, work and life are contact sports. He likes to get his hands on whatever the issue or the people might be. There was no way to interrogate a satellite photo—Hey, what does that dot really mean? What's in that truck?—or penetrate fully the meaning of translated words in an intercept.

The more Powell dug, the more he realized that the human sources were few and far between on Iraq's WMD. It was not a pretty picture. Still, like Bush and the other war cabinet members, he was much influenced by Saddam's past behavior. The dictator had used WMD in the 1980s, hidden them in the 1990s, and if he wasn't hiding anything now, all he had to do was come clean. Powell agreed when Cheney argued, "Why in the world would he subject himself for all those years to U.N. sanctions and forgo an estimated $100 billion in oil revenue? It makes no sense!"

Some CIA analysts and David G. Newton, the U.S. ambassador to Iraq from 1984 to 1988, had warned of falling victim to the "rational man syndrome," projecting what Americans deemed rational behavior on Saddam, who in the past had seemed to specialize in the irrational. Powell was predisposed to believe that weapons were being hidden, and he was briefed on how most of the serious foreign intelligence agencies in the world had also concluded that Saddam had WMD.

Public expectation was building on Powell's presentation. Newspaper stories and cable television were running with it hard: Will Powell deliver a knockout blow? What does he have? What secrets will finally be let out of the box? Will Saddam be exposed? Will Powell have an Adlai Stevenson moment? Will Saddam fold? Will Powell fold?

Powell was well aware that the credibility of the United States, of the president, and his own, were going to be in the Security Council room that day, now scheduled for February 5. Uppermost in his mind was that if he oversold anything, or put out something that was shaky, the Iraqis would rip him a new one the next day. He couldn't leave an open flank.

On Saturday, February 1, Powell went to CIA headquarters and spent most of the day sifting through intelligence, including raw intercepts. The easiest part was figuring out what to discard. There was lots of flimsy stuff, so out it went. He was there late into the evening. The next morning he called Armitage. "What are you doing?"

"I'm just coming back from the gym," Armitage said.

"What are you doing this afternoon?"

"I guess I'm with you."

Please, Powell said.

They descended again on the CIA. Tenet, McLaughlin and other analysts and experts were in and out. Powell said the problem was that he could no longer trace anything because it had been "masticated over in the White House so that the exhibits didn't match the words." Nobody knew where the sources were for specific statements. So he was starting from scratch.

Armitage was skeptical. Saddam had used chemical weapons extensively in the Iran-Iraq War. That was proof he had them in the 1980s. He probably had them now, but where was the rock-solid evidence? And the intelligence on biological and nuclear seemed iffy.

What was the best they had? Powell and Armitage reviewed an intercepted conversation between two senior officers of the Republican Guard that McLaughlin had used in his December trial run. The intercept, from the day before inspections began in November, showed a colonel telling a brigadier general that he had a modified vehicle from the al-Kindi company, which in the past had been involved with WMD. The colonel then contradicted himself, saying, "We evacuated everything. We don't have anything left." It was suggestive, and potentially incriminating, but what he was talking about was not clear. No one could tell from this intercept or any other intelligence. An alternative explanation was that the colonel and the general just wanted to make sure they had complied. Powell decided to use it because it involved senior officers and the "evacuated" quote seemed strong.

Another fresh intercept from the previous week showed a Republican Guard officer from headquarters instructing a field officer about "forbidden ammo." Again it was only suggestive, but Powell decided to use it too.

A third intercept, which had also been used by McLaughlin, was of a colonel instructing a captain to remove the expression "nerve agents" from the wireless instructions, strongly suggesting that he was worried someone might be listening. Powell decided to use it despite the possibility, remote as it was, that the officers were just cleaning up the instruction manual because the nerve agents were gone.

CHENEY AND LIBBY were not giving up on the alleged Iraq connection with al Qaeda, and perhaps the 9/11 plots. Powell just did not see it. That matter finally would have to go to the president.

We don't need to stretch the terrorism case, Tenet said, recalling the president's instructions. They had pretty good evidence that a Palestinian named Abu Musab al-Zarqawi, who had strong al Qaeda ties, was involved with the alleged poison center in northern Iraq where Tim's CIA paramilitary team was operating.

Zarqawi had gone to Baghdad in the spring of 2002 for medical treatment and they thought he had established a base of operations there. The captured assassin of Laurence Foley, a State Department official killed in Jordan in the fall, had said his cell received money and weapons from Zarqawi for the murder. The Zarqawi network was big and dangerous.

There was, however, a big problem. "I can't take you to authority, direction and control," Tenet said, referring to his standard for making a hard case. It meant there was no proof that Saddam or Iraqi intelligence was running things. Libby had argued that operational control was not the only test. The Taliban in Afghanistan did not direct bin Laden. The president's test was if someone harbored terrorists. The CIA could make a case that Saddam had harbored Zarqawi, giving him some kind of sanctuary. Zarqawi was operating in places and ways that Saddam's regime would not have permitted unless it wanted it. So they were technically harboring terrorists. He suggested sticking with the one kernel that was solid.

Tenet understood that Cheney was seized with al Qaeda.

Bush finally backed Tenet 100 percent on this issue in the face of Cheney's pressure.

Powell decided he would lay out the Zarqawi connections in his presentation and he arrived at compromise language. After the WMD case, which would take about 75 percent of his time, he would say there was a "potentially much more sinister" connection between Iraq and al Qaeda. He would present all the Zarqawi links to more than 100 operatives who had been arrested in Europe, including in France, Britain, Spain and Italy.

FOR MONTHS SAUL had been trying to get permission to send one of the CIA's own officers into the heart of regime-controlled Iraq. He had a volunteer, an American citizen who didn't look American, a CIA officer with lots of experience in some of the most hostile environments of the last decade. Final approval for the mission had taken months.

"You are one crazy son of a bitch," Saul told the officer, whom he had known for years. Did he realize what could happen to him if he were captured?

The man was secretly infiltrated in, and he began filing eyes-on reports about Iraqi air defenses that the U.S. military hadn't even known existed, other military installations, and some of the first reporting on the oil-filled trenches around Baghdad that Saddam could set on fire. The mission was one of the CIA's biggest secrets. The operation was briefed only to the president, Cheney, Rice, Rumsfeld and Franks. Every day Saul breathed easier when the agent's reports came in. His arrest could have compromised techniques and a whole bunch of other stuff. The lone ranger filed 130 intelligence reports.

In the mountains of northern Iraq at base camp Kalachualan, Tim and his team had vastly expanded operations. He wanted all agents in place by February 10 because mid-February was the absolute latest the war would start. He had asked the two brothers to produce a specific SSO officer on their list who supposedly had access to the personnel files of the SSO. "Bring this guy here," Tim requested. They brought the man, and the brothers' father, the Pope, attended the interrogation.

"What have you got?" Tim asked the man, who was nervous and almost trembling in front of the Pope.

"Please, this is the CIA and we want you to cooperate with them," the Pope said.

The month has come, Tim said. We are going to overthrow the regime.

Okay, said the man from the SSO.

"Can you prove who you are?" Tim asked.

The SSO man took out a CD-ROM and handed it to Tim. "Here's the personnel files for the SSO."

One of the other case officers loaded the CD-ROM into a laptop computer and up came 6,000 personnel files—names, full background, assignments and many personnel photos. He started looking through the photos. One was of a man who had volunteered to work for the CIA, telling them he was in the Iraqi military. He was SSO, probably a double agent who was being run against them. They decided to feed him some false information.

So rare, so mind-blowing were Tim's informants that the CIA gave them the crypt or secret designation DB/ROCKSTARS. (DB was the designator for Iraq.) Tim was now paying the two brothers $1 million a month for ROCKSTAR intelligence. The brothers seemed to spend the money in about six days, so Tim would offer several hundred thousand more if they provided really good intelligence.

Swimming in a sea of $100 bills, the ROCKSTARS were buying

up weapons on the black market that the PUK was also trying to buy. The Pope, his two sons and their followers were guests of the PUK, and Tim was running their agent network without the PUK's knowledge. The PUK leaders were growing increasingly suspicious as members of the religious group started dressing in military uniforms and running around well-armed. Who are all these religious people playing army? one of the PUK officials asked.

Tim was also doling out millions to the PUK to keep them happy and for the intelligence and security they provided. One day the PUK leader, Jalal Talabani, came to see him.

"Tim, I will need if you can bring me ones and fives and tens because now everything in Sulaymaniyah costs $100." The $100 bills had caused extreme inflation. It seemed even a cup of coffee was going for $100 because no one could make small change.

Tim promised he would try. A million dollars in $100 bills weighed about 44 pounds, so in all tens it would be hundreds of pounds, and in dollar bills thousands of pounds.

The Turks were making resupply difficult, and in order to get money, Tim or other team members had to drive out and back in again themselves, backpacks stuffed. The team was getting jittery and immensely tired of the local food, intestines filled with rice, animal trachea and larynxes, sewed shut and boiled. Their staple was chicken and flat bread.

One of the ROCKSTARS next delivered an Iraqi mobile communications device that was supposed to be sent out for repairs. It was the device used by Deputy Prime Minister Tariq Aziz. It had encryption capability and was part of the SSO communications network. A ROCKSTAR agent had swiped it. Tim had it couriered back to Washington where the National Security Agency was able to exploit it. Soon NSA was listening in to some SSO communications.

The brothers also delivered a key ROCKSTAR, an SSO officer who ran one of the primary telephone switching stations in Baghdad. A burly, mustached figure, he had risen not because of his technical knowledge, but because of his amazing loyalty to Saddam. When they brought him in, the Pope was there. The SSO officer went ahhhh oooooh, literally started shaking and ran over and kissed the feet of the Pope, who told him, "You will cooperate." He soon brought another follower to Tim, the head of an important communications unit for the SSO.

Tim soon learned that communications lines were run or hooked up whenever Saddam changed locations—a rare, possible future clue to the whereabouts of one of the most elusive men on earth.

The ROCKSTAR intelligence was becoming so important that counterintelligence experts at CIA headquarters were assigned to test it in every way possible. Specifics were cross-checked with communications intercepts and satellite and other overhead imagery. Franks and a few others were briefed at CENTCOM where they authenticated it for themselves.

Give us GPS coordinates of these new air defense sites, they said. As a test, the military then flew Northern Watch and Southern Watch missions on the locations, and on closer examination found the air defenses and bombed them. The quantity and quality of intelligence from ROCKSTARS was dwarfing everything else.

By late February, Tim had about 90 agents in the ROCKSTAR network reporting inside Iraq. Each ROCKSTAR had to be smuggled out to give his intelligence. NSA was confident that the Iraqis did not have the capability to intercept satellite phones, so Tim bought about 100 handheld satellite telephones at $700 each from Thuraya, a satellite telecom company based in Abu Dhabi.

Tim handed out phones to 87 ROCKSTAR agents from Umm Qasr in the south to Mosul in the north. The ROCKSTARS could then call in real-time intelligence to a phone bank that Tim's case officers and the brothers manned.

Talabani's PUK had its own direct connection to Washington, and Wolfowitz in particular, via a secure STU-3 phone. Tim did not trust a word the PUK told him about what Wolfowitz supposedly said to them. But he couldn't phone Wolfowitz and say, Hey Paul, did you really tell them this? He was a GS-14 being paid about $80,000 a year, in take-home pay about $4,400 a month or $150 a day. The PUK or anyone might get a sympathetic ear from Wolfowitz or whomever, but Tim was the only person delivering money, by God, and they couldn't piss him off. That was his card. He could insist: He needed more of this—intelligence. Or less of that—conspicuous consumption.

Tim knew the intelligence assets hung by a thinner thread. The primary guy in the PUK with inner circle connections, who had helped recruit the ROCKSTARS, was an alcoholic, and Tim had paid him hundreds of thousands of dollars so he had all the booze he wanted. The ROCKSTARS wouldn't meet with Tim unless the PUK man approved or was there. So Tim found himself acting as an alcoholic counselor. Every Sunday morning it seemed Tim would go sit with him.

The man had a litany of complaints. "I want to quit," he would say regularly. "I hate you." He complained he was not being paid enough. "You don't have any respect for me." Tim had to sit for hours with the man, who was working behind the back of the PUK, which was a kind of blessed organization in his family. Out poured all the resentment and self-loathing, magnified by a huge drinking problem.

Flying by the seat of his pants, Tim showered all the attention he could muster, because if the man walked off or was blown as an intermediary, there would go the ROCKSTARS.

It was not as if Tim was talking to George Tenet. He was out there alone, knowing that anyone he was talking to, including Saul, had only a part of the picture. When was this going to start? What the hell was happening?

AT CIA HEADQUARTERS, Saul continued to be amazed at the successes. NSA provided some tactical SIGINT packages that could pick up radio and other low-power communications, and the ROCKSTARS drove the packages into Baghdad and placed them in critical areas. This gave them a significant new source of intelligence. Everything Tim and his team were now doing had previously been deemed impossible in Iraq. The agency had never run a successful, long-term cross-border operation, never penetrated the IIS, the SSO or the Republican Guard. How long would it last? In intelligence nothing lasts forever, and the really good things tend to die suddenly and unexpectedly.

As Turkey was debating whether to allow U.S. forces to base in their country for a northern front, the Turks shadowing Tim and the other team were becoming more and more difficult. They could close the border at any moment, stranding the teams and cutting off resupply. Once the shooting started, the teams might need enough money for two or three months or more. Saul decided to give Tim and the other team a big money dump—$35 million in cash. That was nearly one ton of $100 bills. It was a pain to smuggle it in, hiding it under MREs (Meals Ready-to-Eat) and other supplies. It took three border crossings to get the $35 million into northern Iraq.

29

O N WEDNESDAY, February 5, just after 7 A.M., several hours before Powell's U.N. presentation was scheduled, Bush met with
20 key members of Congress in the Cabinet Room of the White
House.

"Many of you have heard this before," he said. "It was under
classification. It remains classified until Powell goes at 10:30.
There's more information that we're not certain of." He left the
room, and Rice quickly summarized what Powell was going to say.

Representative Jane Harman of California, the senior Democrat
on the House Intelligence Committee, said it was a "strong case" but
asked, "What's the threat to the homeland?"

Rice responded that Saddam's threat would grow with time.

Representative Nancy Pelosi of California, the House Democratic leader, asked, Would a new regime in Iraq develop weapons of
mass destruction? What about the North Korea problem? She said
they needed a consistent policy. "Can we conclude that the threat is
best eliminated by going to war now? Any fissile material Saddam
Hussein gets is from the outside. It's a global problem, and we don't
have a global solution."

"Handling Iraq isn't a cure-all," Rice answered. If the U.N. can't
solve the Iraq problem with a dozen plus resolutions, she said, "It

will be impotent and we'll have to do it on our own. . . . Iraq is critical to reestablishing the bona fides of the Security Council."

"Is war the best way?" Pelosi persisted.

Rice made it clear that war was the active option. "We tried
sanctions, we tried limited military options, we tried resolutions. At
some point war is the only option."

Representative Ike Skelton of Missouri, the senior Democrat on
the House Armed Services Committee, asked what would be done
post-Saddam.

"Humanitarian teams will accompany military force," Rice said.
"We'll deal with sectarian violence. . . . Need to get the infrastructure up. We don't want to be there forever."

"How long will you be there?" asked Senator Joseph Biden, the
ranking Democrat on the Foreign Affairs Committee.

"We don't know," Rice replied. "It depends on the results. We'll
have help from people inside and outside Iraq."

Republican Senator John Warner, the Armed Services Committee chairman, asked about weapons of mass destruction. "After the
dust settled can cameras find smoking guns?"

"I don't know what we will find exactly, and what period of
time," Rice replied. "Blix says he can't tell you they don't have them."

Senator Carl Levin, the ranking Democrat on Armed Services,
jumped in. "Blix also says he can't tell you they have them. You're in-
consistent."

The danger, Rice said, was that the inspectors would go back in
and not find anything, prompting some countries to call for the lifting of sanctions. "The Iraqis love this game, they're comfortable
with it, they know how to defeat it. We can continue this and the Security Council will split. The inspectors can't disarm Iraq. They can
only verify disarmament."

"If we go in, and don't find caches," Biden said, "we'll have a serious perception problem."

"I believe we'll find them," Warner interjected.

"I don't want to give you a categorical answer," Rice said cautiously, but then added, "He's hiding a lot. I'm quite certain we'll find a lot of it."

After the meeting, Senator Warner told Steve Hadley, "You got to do this and I'll support you, make no mistake. But I sure hope you find weapons of mass destruction because if you don't you may have a big problem."

IT HAD BEEN FOUR VERY, very difficult days for Powell as he sorted through the intelligence reports. So much was inferential, he felt. The intelligence people kept repeating that Saddam had a few dozen Scud missiles. "The Scuds are not anything anyone has seen," he said. As he read, he saw that previous U.N. inspectors had accounted for something like 817 of the 819 Scuds. But there was other information suggesting that some still remained, so he agreed to refer vaguely to "up to a few dozen Scud-variant" missiles.

After the final rehearsal in Washington, Tenet announced that he thought their case was ironclad, and he believed they had vetted each sentence. They had not taken the intelligence any further than it should go. Neither the president nor Powell would be hurt, he said.

"You're coming with me," Powell said. He wanted Tenet sitting behind him at the U.N. as a visible, on-camera validation of the presentation, as if the CIA director were saying each word himself. Tenet was not the only prop. Powell had a sound and light show, audios and visuals to be presented on large hanging monitors in the Security Council chamber. He even had a teaspoon of simulated anthrax in a small vial to wave around.

Millions around the world watched and listened on live television. At NSA headquarters, thousands watched from packed cafeterias and auditoriums that thundered with applause when Powell played the three intercepts, a rare display of their Top Secret work.

Dressed in a dark suit and red tie, hands clasped on his desk, Powell began cautiously. "I cannot tell you everything that we know, but what I can share with you, when combined with what all of us have learned over the years, is deeply troubling. What you will see is an accumulation of facts and disturbing patterns of behavior."

He played the "We-have-evacuated-everything" intercept. He had decided to add his personal interpretation of the intercepts to his rehearsed script, taking them substantially further and casting them in the most negative light. He had told the intelligence officials he was going to do this because he had learned in the Army that meaning had to be explained in clear English. "Note what he says, 'We evacuated everything,' " Powell repeated now, and then offered his interpretation: "We didn't destroy it. We didn't line it up for inspection. We didn't turn it in to the inspectors. We evacuated it to make sure it was not around when the inspectors showed up."

Concerning the intercept about inspecting for the possibility of "forbidden ammo," Powell took his interpretation further: "Clean out all of the areas, the scrap areas, the abandoned areas. Make sure there is nothing there." None of this was in the intercept.

Citing human sources, Powell leveled his most serious charge. "We know from sources a missile brigade outside Baghdad was disbursing rocket launchers and warheads containing biological warfare agents to various locations." He cited satellite photos and other intelligence that suggested a massive housecleaning around old chemical or biological weapons facilities prior to the arrival of U.N. inspectors. "We don't know what Iraq was moving," he said, "but the inspectors already knew about these sites, so Iraq knew that they would be coming. We must ask ourselves: Why would Iraq suddenly move equipment of this nature before inspections if they were anxious to demonstrate what they had or did not have?"

One of Powell's strongest charges was based on several human sources who had provided eyewitness accounts of what they said were biological weapons factories on wheels or in railroad cars. He had detailed sketches of the mobile labs presented on the monitor. He also referred to unmanned aerial vehicles. "We detected one of Iraq's newest UAVs in a test flight that went 500 kilometers on autopilot in the racetrack pattern depicted here"—more than three times the 150 kilometers allowed by the U.N. He said in a menacing tone that these UAVs were a grave potential danger without providing evidence of such. "Iraq could use these small UAVs, which have a wingspan of only a few meters, to deliver biological agents to its neighbors or, if transported, to other countries including the United States," he stated.

Powell characterized Iraqi–al Qaeda links as "potentially much more sinister" and laid out the Zarqawi story and other connections. "Some believe, some claim these contacts do not amount to much. They say Saddam Hussein's secular tyranny and al Qaeda's religious tyranny do not mix. I am not comforted by this thought," he said, adding speculatively, "Ambition and hatred are enough to bring Iraq and al Qaeda together.

"We know that Saddam Hussein is determined to keep his weapons of mass destruction; he's determined to make more," the secretary said. "Should we take the risk that he will not someday use these weapons at a time and a place and in a manner of his choosing, at a time when the world is in a much weaker position to respond? The United States will not and cannot run that risk to the American people."

The secretary's presentation took 76 minutes.

The public undressing of intelligence sources, methods and details was probably more important than their substance, though Powell listed more than 100 specifics. The important element was that it was Powell who made the case. The mixture of understatement, overstatement and personal passion made for riveting television.

Mary McGrory, the renowned liberal columnist for *The Washington Post,* and a Bush critic, wrote in the lead column for the next day's op-ed page of Powell's *"J'Accuse"* speech, "I can only say that he persuaded me, and I was as tough as France to convince." She said that she had been hoping Powell would oppose war, but "The cumulative effect was stunning. I was reminded of the day long ago when John Dean, a White House toady, unloaded on Richard Nixon and you could see the dismay written on Republican faces that knew impeachment was inevitable." She added, "I'm not ready for war yet. But Colin Powell has convinced me that it might be the only way to stop a fiend, and that if we do go, there is reason."

At the White House, Dan Bartlett understood the importance of what Powell had done. He began calling it "the Powell buy-in."

PRINCE BANDAR WAS AT WORK on the French. On instructions from Saudi Crown Prince Abdullah, he went to Paris to see President Chirac.

The French president said there was a basic disagreement and lodged two specific complaints. Bush and the Americans were not respectful of him, and they didn't share intelligence with him.

When Chirac's concerns were reported to Bush, he said he was willing to smother Chirac with both attention and respect. Tenet added that he was receiving information from French intelligence, and that he did not have a problem with the current French intelligence chief.

Bandar met with Egyptian President Hosni Mubarak, who told him that the Egyptians had many intelligence sources inside Iraq. "Our intelligence has confirmed there are mobile labs for biological weapons," Mubarak said. And Mubarak told Bandar about an intriguing message from inside Iraq. "I got an emissary from Saddam saying there are women and children and some people who will be identified to us later who want to come to Egypt. Will you give us a presidential palace?"

Saddam's emissary said that the Iraqis had huge safes that could store $2 billion in cash and gold bullion that they also wanted to bring to Egypt. Mubarak maintained that he had told them that the women and children were welcome. "Any men or officials, you're going to have to make a deal with the Americans, or I'm going to have to call the Americans." Mubarak said he had also rejected the request to allow the $2 billion in cash into Egypt because he would be accused of stealing it. Send it in checks or through a Swiss bank, he said he had told Saddam's emissary.

Bandar reported to Rice that he believed Chirac was going to help, perhaps even support war.

"Are you sure?" Rice asked skeptically.

Bandar said he had three sources. Mubarak and Lebanese Prime Minister Rafiq Hariri both reported that Chirac was heading that way, and his own discussions with the French president had led him to the same conclusion.

AT 11:35 A.M. Friday, February 7, Chirac called Bush.

"I do not share your spirit for why we need war," Chirac said coolly. "War is not inevitable. There are alternative ways to reach goals. It's a question of morality. I'm against war unless it is inevitable and necessary."

"I'm committed to our relationship," Bush responded. "I'm committed to the personal relationship we have and between our countries. You're a consistent man, a compassionate man. I too dislike war. I'm responsible for hugging the families of those who've lost their lives in war. I view an armed Saddam Hussein as a direct threat to the American people. That could explain why we're on different timetables. When the United Nations Security Council says something, it's important that it mean something. Thank you for the intelligence sharing you've been providing."

"I'm positive about the Saudi proposal," Chirac said, referring to the recent suggestion that Saddam be allowed to go into exile, "because it sought to avoid war."

He continued, "If there is a war, we'll work together on reconstruction." Chirac sounded conciliatory. "We will all contribute."

Bush said that food was stockpiled for the Iraqis, and that hospitals would be supplied.

"I fully understand your position is different," Chirac said. "There are two different moral approaches to the world and I respect yours."

When the president hung up, he felt optimistic about the French. Chirac had said there are two moral approaches and he re-

spected Bush's. Was it possible the French would not block a new
U.N. Security Council resolution?

THE SAME DAY, Mubarak's son Gamal came to see Bush secretly in
the White House residence, carrying the same message his father
had given Bandar. Gamal, a top pro-American reformist in his
father's political party, said they had reason to believe that Saddam
might be looking for an opportunity to go into exile and outlined
Saddam's request for safekeeping of family members and $2 billion
in Egypt. A number of countries including Saudi Arabia, Jordan and
Turkey were involved in exile negotiations. What did the president
think?

Despite public statements by Powell, Rumsfeld and Rice the
previous month that exile for Saddam was an option if it would prevent war, the president replied that if Saddam went into exile, the
United States would not guarantee his protection. He also said he
did not look favorably upon those who were looking to offer protection. "If you are looking for assurances from me that we won't do
something," Bush said, "you don't have those assurances." He had
taken a hard line about any country that harbored terrorists, and by
his definition Saddam was a terrorist. But Bush then added ambigu-
ously, seeming almost to offer some tacit encouragement, "There
have been many cases in history where people went into exile and
war was avoided, and we're not ignorant of that fact."

On February 10, Australian Prime Minister John Howard met
with Bush privately in the Oval Office. "We're still in the mosh pit,"
Bush said, "but thanks to your strong resolve we're finally getting
clarity. Either he'll leave or we'll get him. There's a slightly real
chance that he'll leave." Then, envisioning complications with that
scenario, Bush added, "The problem will be whether he's a war criminal and who's harboring him."

Powell was predicting that France would abstain in the Security
Council. "It's really hard to get a yes answer until there's a Kabuki
dance," Bush said, borrowing a favorite Powell expression.

Also on February 10, Rice called Prince Bandar to report that Chirac was going in a different direction. "Your friend in the Elysée has just invited Schroeder and Putin to meet."

Chirac, Putin and Schroeder issued a strong joint statement the same day calling for extended weapons inspections. "Nothing today justifies war," Chirac said. "Russia, Germany and France are determined to ensure that everything possible is done to disarm Iraq peacefully."

So much for Chirac—and Putin and Schroeder.

SOME OF THE DISCUSSION in the NSC had focused on a plan to get Blix's inspectors to "flood the zone," conduct multiple site inspections from the outset instead of a hunt-and-peck approach or a slow buildup. They could also interview Iraqi scientists outside the country to raise the pressure and rattle Saddam. That way Blix might find actual WMD, or Saddam might obstruct the inspectors in such a blatant way that it would create grounds for war.

New, sensitive intelligence on Blix showed that his upcoming second report on February 14 was going to be wishy-washy and vague. He was going to sound positively "Greenspanesque" according to one account, give a carefully balanced update in the manner of U.S. Federal Reserve Chairman Alan Greenspan.

At 8:55 A.M. on Friday, February 14, the president went down to the Situation Room for a briefing on how they would respond if there were a coup in Iraq. Though it seemed almost impossible, they had to have a plan. They didn't want to be caught flat-footed if some Iraqi general seized power from Saddam. The Saudis had been floating the idea publicly. And while a coup might be good news, Iraq could wind up with a new dictator—Saddam-ism without Saddam.

The president and the NSC discussed a formal "Coup Scenario" paper and agreed that if there were a coup, the U.S. would immediately call on the new leader to turn over authority to a duly constituted, publicly supported Iraqi authority appointed by the U.S. There had to be some movement toward democracy. Second, the United

States would ask the new leader to consider inviting U.S. forces in to eliminate the WMD and sever all of the previous regime's terrorist ties. A consensus soon emerged that they would not be able to wait to be invited; U.S. forces would have to move in forthwith. It was sensitive and provocative, but they determined that a coup, with all its imponderables, would not stop the military invasion.

Iraqi opposition forces were planning a meeting in the Kurdish territory of northern Iraq in about two weeks. The meeting was designed to be a deliberate provocation. It would certainly inflame Saddam, and there was the possibility he might attack. He had army divisions just south of the so-called Green Line that divided Saddam's Iraq from the Kurdish-controlled region. The principals agreed that a direct attack on the Kurds would be a mistake on Saddam's part and would increase international opposition to him.

The president was skeptical, but he gave the go-ahead to try.

The NSC was also wrestling with another incredibly sensitive possibility. The intelligence service of a country on Iraq's border reported that it planned to send an emissary to see Saddam, ostensibly for the purpose of negotiation but with the real mission of assassinating the Iraqi leader. The NSC decided that they could not count on, or expect, or directly support the attempt, but it would be great if it happened—with the caveat that they would still have to deal with the issues of democracy, WMD and terrorist links with any new Iraqi leader.

BLIX'S PRESENTATION at the U.N. Security Council later that morning was a scrupulously balanced list of pluses and minuses. His findings were in sharp contrast to Powell's presentation nine days earlier. "Since we arrived in Iraq, we have conducted more than 400 inspections covering more than 300 sites," Blix reported. "All inspections were performed without notice, and access was almost always provided promptly." There was no convincing evidence that the Iraqis had advance warning of the inspections, he said. "The inspections have taken place throughout Iraq at industrial sites, ammunition depots, research centers, universities, presidential sites, mobile laboratories, private houses, missile production facilities, military camps and agricultural sites.

"More than 200 chemical and more than 100 biological samples have been collected at different sites," Blix said. Some three-quarters of those samples had been screened and no prohibited weapons or substances had been found.

"How much, if any, is left of Iraq's weapons of mass destruction and related proscribed items and programs?" Blix asked. So far the inspectors had "not found any such weapons, only a small number of empty chemical munitions, which should have been declared and destroyed." He said that Iraqi documents showed that much had not been accounted for. "I must not jump to the conclusion that they exist. However, that possibility is also not excluded."

Blix noted that many governments were convinced that Iraq still had WMD. "The U.S. secretary of state presented material in support of this conclusion. Governments have many sources of information that are not available to inspectors," he gently chided. "The inspectors, for their part, must base their reports only on the evidence which they can themselves examine and present publicly." He criticized Powell's assertion that Iraq had cleaned up some sites prior to inspections. The two satellite photos of one site were taken several weeks apart, Blix said, and the movement "could just as easily have been a routine activity as a movement of proscribed munitions in anticipation of imminent inspection." If Iraq were to cooperate even more fully, he said, "the period of disarmament through inspection could still be short."

The small television set in Armitage's suite of offices on the seventh floor of the State Department was on as he and his staff wandered in and out watching Powell at the Security Council respond to Blix's testimony. The secretary was angry but by and large kept his cool, though he struck a sarcastic tone at times. He disputed Blix's central conclusion—that disarmament through inspection was possible. "These are all tricks that are being played on us," Powell said. Real, immediate, sincere and unconditional compliance with the

U.N. disarmament resolution would be easy and obvious. "It isn't brain surgery!" he declared. Because the French had proposed more inspectors, Powell said, "More inspectors—sorry. It's not the answer."

"Force should be a last resort . . . but it must be a resort." Powell was fully suited up in his war uniform; the "buy-in" was complete. Saddam's weapons, he maintained, "could kill tens of thousands of people."

30

FEBRUARY 15 HAD BEEN A potential start day for war if the inspections had gone according to plan and exposed Saddam. Now the endgame was not clear. Bush's chief allies—Blair, Howard of Australia and Aznar of Spain—were getting serious heat at home.

"Slow down your troop movements," Bush later recalled telling Rumsfeld. Franks and the military then said they could use a little more time and it seemed to Bush that they were shoving the start date back a bit themselves. Then the president shoved it back further, telling Rumsfeld, "Don, we're accelerating too fast relative to where we need to be because of the diplomatic side."

Cheney detested the idea of a second resolution, though Bush felt the vice president understood the logic, and understood the enormous cross pressures from a variety of fronts—allied leaders such as Blair, the military and the CIA. Cheney heard the phone calls or read transcripts of the calls with these leaders who were in political peril and were asking for the second resolution. "The anxiety came because it was difficult to see us working our way through the process," Bush recalled.

ON SATURDAY, February 22, President Bush hosted Spanish President Aznar at his ranch in Crawford. They had a four-way phone con-

versation with Blair and Berlusconi. All agreed on introducing a second U.N. resolution that would declare that Saddam had "failed to"
comply with the previous Resolution 1441.

The NSC reconsidered the issue of exile for Saddam and decided it should not be foreclosed. So Rumsfeld and Rice again dan-
gled the possibility publicly.

ELIE WIESEL, writer, survivor of Auschwitz and Nobel Peace Prize
winner, came to see Rice on February 27 and the president dropped
by her office. Rice moved to the couch so the president could take the
chair closest to Wiesel.

Wiesel told the president that Iraq was a terrorist state and that
the moral imperative was for intervention. If the West had inter-
vened in Europe in 1938, he said, World War II and the Holocaust
could have been prevented. "It's a moral issue. In the name of morality how can we not intervene?"

"It's very wise of you," Bush said. "The killer sees the protests
of respectable people and thinks they're for him. If the French had
put pressure on him, he'd be gone. I read your views on Auschwitz in
Michael Beschloss's book." In The Conquerors, which focuses on the
World War II decision making of Roosevelt and Truman, Wiesel is
quoted as saying that he wished the Allies had bombed the concentration camps even if the attack killed the Jewish inmates. "We were
no longer afraid of death—at any rate, not of that death."

Bush told Wiesel, "If we don't disarm Saddam Hussein, he will
put a weapon of mass destruction on Israel and they will do what
they think they have to do, and we have to avoid that." The prospect
of a military exchange between Iraq and Israel would be a disaster, no
doubt foreclosing any possibility of Jordan, Saudi Arabia and other
Arab states joining any effort against Saddam.

In the face of such evils, neutrality was impossible, Wiesel said.
Indecision only promoted and assisted the evil and the aggressor, not
the victims. "I'm against silence."

In the days after, Bush routinely repeated Wiesel's comments.

"That was a meaningful moment for me," he recalled later, "because it was a confirming moment. I said to myself, Gosh, if Elie Wiesel feels that way, who knows the pain and suffering and agony of tyranny, then others feel that way too. And so I am not alone."

FRANK MILLER, the director of the NSC staff for defense, had one of the most delicate assignments in the preparations for war. Since August 2002, he headed a group called the Executive Steering Group (ESG), which was created to oversee interagency coordination for Iraq on behalf of Rice and Hadley. A former naval officer and a 19-year veteran of the government's Senior Executive Service, the uppermost tier of civil servants, Miller had worked on nuclear war plans during the Cheney era at Defense.

Miller soon found to his astonishment that one of his chief tasks was coordinating among the various parts of the Rumsfeld Defense Department. The Pentagon's budget office, Feith's policy shop, General Myers's Joint Staff and Franks's CENTCOM staff all operated more or less as independent fiefdoms. In Miller's view, too many senior and mid-level people in Defense were big-idea people who loved concepts, paper and talk, but they were not experienced managers. "They don't do implementation," he reported to Rice and Hadley.

Miller literally had to call representatives of the Pentagon's comptroller, policy office and the Joint Staff to his third floor office in the Old Executive Office Building adjacent to the White House. "Gentlemen, shake hands," he once said, introducing them to each other. "Now, can we work this out?" The issues ranged from nuts-and-bolts logistics such as pouring concrete for new runways to the sensitive matters of prisoners of war and war crimes.

Miller eventually was holding meetings three times a week, forcing the participants to produce charts with red, yellow or green to indicate the progress and status on 21 central issues such as protecting regional allies from Iraqi missile attacks, defining victory, the implications of early Iraqi WMD use against Israel, the consequences of a WMD attack in the theater, the legal basis for occupation, humanitarian relief and the allocation of scarce assets such as Patriot missile units.

Miller formally reported to the deputies committee and moved the paper and policy decisions up to the principals and then to the president if necessary. But he found such chaos that he had to have an off-line meeting each week with Card, Rice, Hadley and Libby to outline problems and blow the whistle so that they could nudge Rumsfeld or others.

Communications between the civilian and military sides of the Defense Department are catastrophically broken, Miller reported. With personal contacts in the Pentagon among the three- and four-star generals and admirals, he realized that the Joint Staff was afraid of Rumsfeld and Feith and did not want to be seen as meddling with Franks's war plan.

Issue No. 16 on Miller's list, for example, was developing a Free Iraqi Force of 5,000 exiles who could fight alongside U.S. forces. Feith wanted to train scouts and eventually a combat brigade to go into Iraq. The JCS had issued a planning order on September 12, 2002, the day of Bush's U.N. speech, but actual training had not begun for another five months. It had been a nightmare finding a training location, vetting the Iraqis to make sure they were not regime sympathizers or spies, and getting money and transportation. A two-star general was put in charge and a central training site finally found in Hungary. Some 800 U.S. military personnel worked for months and spent millions of dollars on the program. But in one of the more dramatic, even comic failures, only 70 Iraqi exiles were trained.

THE MORNING OF MONDAY, February 24, the president attended a secret NSC briefing called "Planning for the Iraqi Petroleum Infrastructure: Issues for Decision." The president and the others had high hopes that the Iraqi oil industry, if freed from U.N. sanctions, could be the fast track for a new regime to reenter the world economy.

Pamela Quanrud, a State Department economist working on

the NSC staff, told the president that a full quarter of the $16 billion generated through the current U.N. Oil-for-Food Program went into a U.N. escrow account to pay reparations to Kuwait and Saudi Arabia for the 1991 Gulf War, and 15 percent went to the Kurds in the north, leaving about 60 percent for the Iraqis themselves. The Oil-for-Food system was governed by a web of U.N. resolutions that they would have to unravel, she said.

The outlook in the event of war was uncertain. Quanrud said they might face a cost of $7 billion to $8 billion to rebuild the oil infrastructure if Saddam blew up the wells as he had done in 1991. Even in a low-damage scenario, first-year revenue would not exceed $12 billion, rising to perhaps $22 billion in the second year, a reasonable amount given Iraq's historic output.

The U.S. would not prejudice future Iraqi government decisions concerning the oil sector, Quanrud said, meaning they would not meddle with existing or future oil contracts or OPEC. Recovery would have three phases. First, the military would secure the oil infrastructure. Then, the U.S. would work with a growing Iraqi civil administration to establish a temporary oil authority and resume production. The oil authority would have an Iraqi chief operating officer and an advisory board of Iraqi and international experts. Finally, once a new Iraqi government took power, Iraqi management would be completely in control.

"Will the majors accept the oil?" the president asked. "Who has title?" He expressed concern about how Iraqi oil would be received in the world market after years of being under the cloud of U.N. sanctions.

The president affirmed the need to enlist Iraqis and Americans knowledgeable about the oil business to help run the sector. "We want to put an Iraqi face on the temporary oil administration," he said, give them full control as soon as possible. The early revenues should go directly to the Iraqis, he added. "Repayment of debt ought to be the last in line." Some of this was held by the Russians, French and the United States, but a good chunk belonged to the Saudis and other Gulf states.

"I'm worried about the adequacy of the oil market," the president stated, expressing concern for the world market's ability to absorb temporary shortfalls during a war in the Middle East. The ripple effect in the U.S. economy could be gigantic, and he asked about the excess production capability of the U.A.E. and Saudi Arabia. Saudi oil policy could be the saving grace. According to Prince Bandar, the Saudis hoped to fine-tune oil prices over 10 months to prime the economy for 2004. What was key, Bandar knew, were the economic conditions before a presidential election, not at the moment of the election.

POWELL HAD FOR some time been questioning the advisability of having only one main seaport and airport in Kuwait as the throughput for forces and supplies. If Saddam were to use chemical or biological weapons on those locations, he could conceivably close down the operation and the supply lines.

Franks had always wanted the option of a northern front, and the British too had suggested that they send their forces through Turkey.

"Are they going to be off-loading at Gallipoli?" Powell asked sarcastically at one NSC meeting, referring to the Turkish peninsula where British and Australian forces launched a disastrous campaign in World War I that left 100,000 dead and is recounted in the 1981 film. "We've seen this movie and it isn't going to happen." Powell thought it was absurd.

Soon the planning shifted to using U.S. forces to go through Turkey. Franks eventually began discussing moving a force of 30,000 to 80,000 through Turkey if all the support and supply troops were included. Rumsfeld sent cargo ships carrying the 4th Infantry Division's tanks to the Mediterranean for eventual off-loading into Turkey.

Such a large force would require changing all the agreements with the Turks, Powell said. "Some 80,000 going through Turkey?

Guys, this is a new Islamic government that can't handle all of this."
The numbers dropped to 40,000, then went up to 62,000.

"I think [the Turks] can handle the overflights," Powell later told the NSC. "I think they can handle the through-put. I think they can handle the air piece. It's when you talk about moving an armored division or mechanized division overland through the length of Anatolia"—Powell liked to use ancient names, this for the portion of modern Turkey in Asia—"with a long huge train behind it, huge numbers of vehicles, going to invade another Muslim country. I will go for that, but that may well be one too many bricks on the scale for the Turks. I don't think we can get it and we're taking a risk at losing it all by going for that. Do you really need it?"

Rumsfeld and Franks deemed it essential.

On March 1, the Turkish Parliament rejected the U.S. request to move troops through their country. Franks later felt that the 4th Infantry Division, which stayed on ships off the coast, turned into an effective deception operation. Using CIA intelligence sources, information was fed to Saddam's inner circle saying that Turkey had secretly agreed to allow U.S. forces to cross their territory and that the Turkish parliamentary vote was a ruse. Franks believed the deception caused Saddam to keep 11 of his regular army divisions and 2 Republican Guard divisions tied down in the north so they would be too late to assist in the fight for Baghdad.

Bullshit, Powell thought.

IN EARLY MARCH, Rumsfeld met in his office with some of his top people—Wolfowitz, Feith, General Myers, Marine General Pete Pace, vice chairman of the Joint Chiefs, even the CIA's Saul, plus his inner circle of Larry DiRita, his top civilian aide, and Lieutenant General John Craddock, his senior military assistant.

How long will the war last? Rumsfeld asked them. He wanted their best estimate. They'd spent more than 15 months on this. How long to achieve regime change?

Well, we're not going to tell you, several replied, because *he* had always told them never to forecast, never provide timetables. Predictions were a felony. "Guesstimates," as they often called them in the military, rarely turned out to be right, and the press often exhumed them down the road. They had learned one of Rumsfeld's key rules. It would almost be as bad as leaking, for God's sake. There was some humor around the table for a moment on this most serious, and critical, of questions.

No, no, no, Rumsfeld said insistently. He wanted answers on this. This was a private meeting. They all trusted each other, had to.

General Myers said somewhat optimistically that he thought it would take the U.S. forces about two to three weeks to get to Baghdad, and 30 days in all. Later, in an interview, Myers said he didn't want to discuss his prediction because it was Rumsfeld's poll. "He's the pollmaster there," Myers said. "He's the Gallup guy."

General Pace, the vice chairman, said later that it was an unusual question from Rumsfeld. It was "the only time he ever asked me what I really, really thought. We had a lot of information that a lot of the divisions were going to capitulate. As best I can recall, what I told him was that if the intel we had was right, it was going to take less than a month. If it was not right, it could take us two to three months, depending upon the kind of fight back we had. But I said you don't know until you start doing stuff what's really going to happen."

Franks said weeks, not months.

Saul said three weeks. DiRita was specific, 13 days. General Craddock said 21. Wolfowitz said seven days.

When the others looked to the secretary, Mr. Gallup, for his estimate, he said, Not on your life! You think I'm crazy? He wasn't going to play, though he had written everyone's number down on a piece of paper which he placed in a desk drawer. They ranged from 7 days to 30, reflecting a lot of optimism among those who supposedly knew the most.

The president later said the estimates never made their way to him. "Rumsfeld's too cautious to do that, by the way. He's too smart.

Rumsfeld's not going to come in the Oval Office and say, 'Mr. President, this will be over in nine days.' " And he guessed correctly that Rumsfeld never gave the others his prediction. "I know Rumsfeld. I know him well. I'm not surprised." Franks too never gave him an estimate, he said. Even in his own mind Bush said he did not make a calculation. He indicated that he "suspected" it would be weeks, not months; however, "I was prepared for the worst."

FRANKS HAD TOLD SOME of his staff that he thought there would be fewer than 1,000 casualties on the U.S. side and probably only several hundred. The president said that he had heard this, but that he had had another worry. "I was more worried about Saddam using weapons of mass destruction on his own people. Not on us. On his own people. And we would be blamed for human catastrophe in the world."

But there were not supposed to be any enemy body counts. It was one of the poisons from Vietnam. The Vietnam vets, now in the upper ranks, were inoculated. They had learned the lessons. General Pace had served in the Vietnam jungle as a young Marine officer.

"Not once in this building have we ever reported a number," Pace, a normally mellow man, said later in his Pentagon E-Ring office, referring to enemy body counts. "Probably because guys like me from Vietnam know what happens when you start counting. You completely skew the way people think, the way folks on the ground operate. What we want the people on the ground to understand is that we want to get the job done with the least amount of killing, but with whatever is needed to be done to protect our own guys. And asking for body counts . . . causes people to focus on 3-to-1, 5-to-1, 7-to-1."

Pace seemed to shudder at the recollection of the time 35 years ago when Defense Secretary Robert S. McNamara and the generals thought they were winning if the kill ratio of North Vietnamese to U.S. was high enough. "The purpose was not to go kill X number of people, the purpose was to remove a regime. If you could do that without killing anybody, you win. If you have 1,000 people killed and you haven't done anything to replace the regime, you lose. So numbers don't count."

Even to ask the question of a commander is trouble. "If 'How many did you kill?' is the question, then the message I've given him was, Oh, I wasn't supposed to get the city, I was supposed to kill people. Not the right answer."

Franks, nonetheless, would later give a confidential body count estimate to the president and the principals.

FEITH WAS WORKING on the postwar planning and lots of paper was flying around as usual. For more than a month, he had been working on a paper entitled, "U.S. and Coalition Objectives."

On March 4, Feith came to the White House and gave a secret briefing to the president and the NSC. The full PowerPoint briefing listed these objectives:

- Iraq's territorial integrity is maintained and the quality of life in Iraq is improved visibly.
- Iraq is seen to be moving toward democratic institutions and serves as a model for the region.
- The U.S. and coalition maintain freedom of action to carry out the global war on terrorism and WMD capture and destruction activities.
- Obtain international participation in the reconstruction effort.
- Obtain the support of the Iraqi people.
- Obtain the political support of the international community, including the regional states, preferably through a U.N. Security Council resolution.
- Place as many Iraqi faces in positions of physical authority as quickly as possible.
- Accomplish the above urgently.

A key challenge would be making the correct trade-off between maximizing legitimacy through international institutions versus maximizing efficiency. They had to decide what level of participation the Baath Party would be allowed in a post-Saddam order. The existing Baath bureaucracy was experienced and efficient. Feith said he hoped to gain as much legitimacy from the participation of the Iraqis as from the international side.

Feith displayed organization charts. It was a lot of abstract political science, and the president didn't have much to say other than to remark that he wanted to see information on how they would deal with the military and intelligence services.

RUMSFELD AND FRANKS met with the president and the NSC the morning of Wednesday, March 5, in the Situation Room. The multicolored slides and briefing papers, all marked Top Secret/Polo Step, began with a single page that said in large letters that were more than a quarter-inch high:

PRE-DECISIONAL DRAFT

The term had been on most of the classified war planning papers because the Pentagon lawyers believed the designation would allow them to protect the documents from being disclosed to Congress or under the Freedom of Information Act. The argument was that "pre-decisional" documents were a part of internal deliberations and not subject to disclosure. It was a legal dodge that some other veteran government lawyers thought probably would not withstand a court test.

Franks had a total U.S. force level of 208,000 in the region that included a ground force of 137,000. All Navy forces were in place, and ground and air were falling into place. Some 50,000 more troops, almost all ground forces, were slated to come in during the next two weeks, though Franks said he could start the war at any time the president directed. Coalition forces, mostly British, would number about 44,000.

Rumsfeld had one of his timelines that he called "notional," meaning it did not have real dates associated with each event because the president had not given a start date. But it provided a likely sequence for a two-week period. One of the first actions would be engineering work on the Kuwait side of the border, cutting massive amounts of barbed wire so the U.S. and coalition forces could cross into Iraq. Rumsfeld felt strongly that they had to issue a public ultimatum to Saddam giving him a 48- or 72-hour period to step down. This ultimatum was identified as a "center point" on his timeline. The timeline showed no major combat during this ultimatum period, only Special Operations Forces activity.

Negotiations with Turkey over basing had meanwhile reopened, and Franks had to decide what to do with the 4th Infantry Division, which was now waiting on 27 ships offshore.

The president asked if they were prepared to deal with possible sabotage of bridges and oil wells by Saddam's forces. CIA sources in Iraq and foreign intelligence services felt they were covered, he was assured.

"We really don't know," Rumsfeld said, once again expressing skepticism about intelligence. "People may be lying to us," he said. "Their seriousness with us will depend on their judgments about how serious we are." Implying that the intelligence people were stringing some sources or agents along, he said, "At some point things change and the diddler can turn into the diddlee." The implication was that the deceiving or diddling of others might reap a harvest of lies in return, but it was a Rumsfeldism that left several shaking their heads.

Why wait two days after the expiration of the ultimatum to begin air operations? the president asked.

Franks said they needed the two days to get Special Operations Forces across the border into all regions of Iraq to take down border observations posts, stop any Scud attacks and secure the oil wells.

Rice asked, If an execute order from the president was built around this timeline, would that lock us in?

Powell said he was still trying to get a second resolution.

"No, it won't lock us in," Rumsfeld said. "We need to be flexible around diplomatic work." He said the timelines could be moved later but it would be hard to move them earlier.

Franks said that they now had identified 24 high-collateral-damage targets that could result in the killing of 30 or more civilians if struck. A very sophisticated process had been developed to evaluate each. Franks had satellite or other photos of all 24, but he said he didn't feel comfortable with the overall intelligence on a number of them.

"I'm not picking targets," Bush said. In the Vietnam War, President Johnson had spent hours reviewing and approving targets. "I want you to tell us about targets you think you have to hit to secure victory and to protect our troops."

Franks continued briefing on the high-collateral-damage targets. He flashed the photo of the Special Republican Guard barracks in Tikrit, Saddam's hometown 100 miles north of Baghdad and his strongest base of support. The military value was high, he said. It had been struck during the Gulf War. Franks showed the six different aim points on the building where six bombs or missiles would be programmed to hit. They believed, but were not certain, that the barracks also served as a command and control facility, so more than 30 civilians might be killed. He did a similar review of the other high-collateral-damage targets, though he suggested that Bush not dwell on any of them unless he had a question.

"Oh, I see there's a school here," the president said of one example.

"That's why we're going to hit the target at night," Franks replied. "There won't be any kids in school at night." Franks cited another example for a proposed daytime strike on a facility because most civilians in that neighborhood would be at work.

"We reserve the right to come back to you," Rumsfeld said to the president, "if we think there are any other targets we feel are necessary to hit that may represent high collateral damage."

Franks wanted to know precisely what kind of public warning they should issue to the Iraqi military not to use WMD.

The president said he wanted it to be strong and to be issued both in the region and outside. He would be willing to include such warnings in his own statements, he said.

At the end they went over the schedule of briefings that the president would want in the course of the war—how often they would meet and at what time of the day. Rumsfeld agreed to work it out with Card.

After the briefing, Card felt that they had just seen the Vietnam legacy staring them in the face. Only after Vietnam would the military consider briefing a president on targets in such detail. It was almost an obligatory "cover-your-ass" by the military. Card raised the issue with the president when they were alone. The two are one year apart in age. Card had gone from high school to take an oath to be in the Naval ROTC; Bush went from college to take an oath to be in the Air National Guard. Neither was predisposed, in Card's view, to wearing the tie-dyed T-shirts of the antiwar movement, but they were both aware of the trap that can be set, and had been set, for politicians who try to play warrior.

The realities of the Defense Department today, Card told the president, were that they did not want to own any problems. They wanted a political figure to own them. Laughing, Card said, "That, for the record, was for the Defense Department's records to say, 'You knew.' "

"Yeah," the president said. "Yeah, I know."

AFTER LUNCH ON MARCH 5, Bush met with a personal envoy who had been sent by Pope John Paul II to argue against war. There would be civilian casualties, and it would deepen the gulf between the Christian world and the Muslim world, said the envoy, Cardinal Pio Laghi, who had served as the Vatican ambassador to the United States and was an old Bush family friend. It would not be a just war, it would be illegal and it would not make things better.

"Absolutely," the president rejoined, "it will make things better."

• • •

AT A PRIME-TIME TELEVISED news conference the next night, March 6, the president repeated his case that Saddam was not disarming. "Iraqi operatives continue to hide biological and chemical agents to avoid detection by inspectors," he claimed. He said, "We're still in the final stages of diplomacy," and added, "We're calling for the vote" at the U.N. on the second resolution. "It's time for people to show their cards."

The president carefully threaded his way, implying there would be war but not saying so. Near the end, in a verbal slip almost suggesting a royal we, Bush said, "I've not made up our mind about military action." Cheney, Powell, Rumsfeld and Rice knew otherwise.

While not acknowledging a contradiction, the president nine months later explained his thinking in an interview. "I'm now realizing that a failure at this point in time, of policy, would create a much stronger Saddam. Which means I haven't done my job. My solemn obligation as a matter of fact made it harder to do my job. And so it was an anxious time. Not a time of doubt. I was sure of my decision to get there in the first place. It was the tactics, it was the road—it was just so winding and hazardous. It was like we were navigating through this very difficult terrain."

The president was increasingly under attack by conservatives because the war had not yet started. Ken Adelman, who had been pushing for war for more than a year, launched a broadside in USA Today on March 7. "Give Saddam Hussein a last, last, last, last, last chance. Oh please," he wrote. The administration had "made a whopping mistake waiting too long already. . . . We frittered away time. Waiting emboldens France to act like an important country."

Rove went up to the Congress on his rounds. The message: Saddam's a danger, go get him, stop stalling. One group of House conservatives told Rove over lunch that the president was moving too slowly and the situation was going to get away from him. He had regular lunches with William Kristol, editor of the conservative magazine *The Weekly Standard,* the *Post* columnist Charles Krauthammer and several others from that crowd. Their message to Bush: Stop being a weenie and go do it. Rove passed all this to the president, who said, "I'd rather be criticized as moving too slowly than moving too fast." But, as Rove knew, the president was going to go.

Though Bush maintained he did not read the editorial pages of newspapers, he became aware of the rising storm. "I began to be concerned at the blowback coming out of America: 'Bush won't act. The leader that we thought was strong and straightforward and clearheaded has now got himself in a position where he can't act.' And it wasn't on the left. It was on the right."

31

"LOOKS REALLY GOOD. This is going to happen," Saul once again reported to Tim at Kalachualan base in the northern Iraq mountains. Tim and his CIA team felt they were stranded, lost both in place and time. Yes, no, yes, no, yes—it added up to maybe. The cold and the uncertainty gnawed at them. Tim had 87 ROCKSTARS out there, some already reporting on their Thuraya phones. He had set up a communications center atop a snowy mountain about 10,000 feet up, three 1970s trailers and some old Quonset huts wrapped in plastic and tied with ropes. They christened it "Jonestown."

The plastic whipped and blew all over in the intense wind, letting water seep in. Temperatures hovered below freezing. Jonestown was an unbelievable dump, the sound of the wind and flapping plastic was like a demon trying to beat them off the mountain. The two brothers agreed to come each day to Jonestown to take the phone calls from the ROCKSTARS reporting on their Thurayas from all over Iraq. They were late risers, reporting for duty about 2 P.M. and staying until 4:30 or 5 A.M. Tim had three of his case officers and two Special Forces guys up there for security, basically living at Jonestown. They listened to the reports coming to the brothers in Arabic and then relayed them on a secure radio down the mountain.

Tim's base, Pistachio, was three miles down the mountain in the foothills, a winding, switchback drive that took 15 minutes

through a no-man's-land. They were inundated with reports, "Pistachio, this is Jonestown, we have information that . . ." They tried to
take the phoned-in reports and turn them into intelligence reports as
fast as possible for transmission to CIA headquarters. Then there
were the transmissions back up the mountain: "Jonestown, this is
Pistachio, can you . . ." Tim always wanted more detail—clarification, verification.

At Jonestown they had a high-tech 7-by-7-foot screen that
would display the exact location of each call coming from inside Iraq.
The brothers were petrified that Saddam's security service had a similar capacity or could direction-find Jonestown's location. Tim was
pretty sure the Iraqis couldn't find them. But he knew the Iraqis
could probably find some of the ROCKSTARS dispersed throughout
Iraq.

The brothers and the Pope were nervous, certain Saddam would
have them killed as soon as the war started. The PUK Kurds were
angry and were harassing members of the group, even beating up
some of them for buying all the black market weapons. Out of these
awful conditions, the flow of intelligence was getting better and better. A bodyguard for Saddam's son Qusay became a ROCKSTAR and
began phoning in. SSO officers who were specialists in communications for the regime leadership joined up. At times, Tim thought he
had the Iraqi equivalent of the Rotarians running intelligence for
him—dutiful but weird.

The Pope and the brothers were putting maximum pressure on
their followers for good, inside stuff. One startling report came in
from a would-be ROCKSTAR. Well, Saddam has submarines painted
red and white and they're patrolling underneath the Tigris River. The
report had to be translated from the Arabic. Candy-striped submarines? Tim asked. Did he mean submarine or boat? With a pro-
peller? What exactly did the guy mean? It turned out to be bullshit.
In the sea of rumor and gossip, Tim and the case officers had to filter
everything.

Then one day a call came in from one of the ROCKSTARS that
wasn't right. The man was speaking under duress. Then a different

voice said something like, "We knew you were CIA." The phone went dead and stayed dead. One of the ROCKSTARS had been caught by some element of Saddam's security service. Then the ROCKSTAR appeared on Iraqi television. He had clearly been beaten and tortured. "I have been caught. I'm a bad person," he said. "I'm a traitor." Someone in a uniform waved a Thuraya phone before the camera, saying anyone caught with one of these was a dead person and all his brothers and his father would be killed too. A Thuraya phone was now a death sentence. Kalachualan base never again heard from 30 of the 87 Thuraya phones.

ON SATURDAY, March 8, Rice checked in with David Manning, Blair's national security adviser. Blair was being pummeled for his support of Bush and his Iraq policy. The British press referred to him as "Bush's poodle." Blair had made the problem worse by asserting that his was the moral position. In an interview with *The Guardian* newspaper the previous week, he had compared himself indirectly to Churchill. "A majority of decent and well-meaning people said there was no need to confront Hitler and that those who did were war-mongers," he said. Asked why he was following Bush with such devotion, he answered, "It's worse than you think. I believe in it. I am truly committed to dealing with this, irrespective of the position of America. If the Americans were not doing this, I would be pressing for them to be doing so."

Rice found herself learning British politics. There were 413 from Blair's Labour Party and 166 Tories in Parliament, giving him a huge edge. The Tories supported a war in Iraq, but a defection of 150 or more Labourites would leave the Tories with the temptation or opportunity to join the Labour defectors to bring down Blair's government in a vote of no confidence.

"He's prepared to go down if necessary," Manning told Rice. The general sense was that if one of Blair's ministers bolted, he could survive, but if it was two ministers, a vote would be dangerously close.

The next day, Sunday, March 9, Rice discussed Blair's situation with the president.

"Do you think he could lose his government?" Bush asked.

"Yes."

"Would the British really do that?"

"Remember Churchill," she said, noting that he had lost his government after winning World War II.

From Bush's perspective, Blair was the guy who had stuck his neck out, who had the "cojones" to be strong and steady. If his government went down, Bush would not only lose his chief ally but it would strengthen Saddam. Imagine the headlines! Plus, Bush reasoned, he would be blamed. It would be a double whammy.

The president was very worried. He called Blair for one of their regular conversations. They explored the possibilities, which other countries on the Security Council they could get to support them with a second resolution.

"If they don't vote with us," Bush said, "what I want to say to you is that my last choice is to have your government go down. We don't want that to happen under any circumstances. I really mean that." If it would help, Bush said, he would let Blair drop out of the coalition and they would find some other way for Britain to participate.

"I said I'm with you. I mean it," Blair replied.

Bush said they could think of another role for the British forces—"a second wave, peacekeepers or something. I would rather go alone than have your government fall."

"I understand that," Blair responded, "and that's good of you to say. I said, I'm with you."

Bush said he really meant it that it would be okay for Blair to opt out. "You can bank on that."

"I know you do," Blair said, "and I appreciate that. I absolutely believe in this too. Thank you. I appreciate that. It's good of you to say that," the prime minister repeated in his very British way. "But I'm there to the very end."

• • •

MAKING THE ROUNDS of the Sunday television talk shows, Powell expressed optimism that the U.S. and Britain could get a majority on a second Security Council resolution. On NBC's *Meet the Press*, he said there was "a strong chance, and I'm encouraged that we might get the 9 or 10 votes needed." But only Spain and Bulgaria had committed to the U.S.-British resolution, leaving Powell at least five votes short, though he was on the phone with three African nations he expected to get.

Dueling headlines appeared in the next morning's papers. *The Washington Post* said, "Powell Optimistic About U.N. Support; 'Strong Chance' Seen for Majority Backing," and *The New York Times* declared, "Urgent Diplomacy Fails to Gain U.S. 9 Votes in the U.N."

AT THE USUAL 8:55 A.M. NSC meeting on Monday, March 10, Frank Miller, the NSC staff director for defense, briefed on the latest plans for post-Saddam Iraq. "Those who ran Saddam's Iraq cannot work for us and cannot run the future free Iraq, but we need to keep the state running," he said. U.S. intelligence estimated that there were about 25,000 top people from the Baath Party, and Miller said all should be removed from government posts and other positions of power and influence. They comprised just over 1 percent of the 2 million government employees in Iraq, so removing them would not leave public institutions without leadership, he said.

Miller said they needed to preserve records and detain key war criminals. Justice and police personnel were believed to be professionally trained and could be used by the temporary government the coalition would set up. "A successful establishment of rule of law in the immediate post-conflict environment is critical to ensuring stability, allowing for relief and reconstruction, and rapidly rebuilding Iraqi society."

The president said, "We need to convince the people in Iraq that we trust them." He wanted some government ministries to be placed under Iraqi control as soon as possible. "The people in Iraq have suffered under Saddam Hussein," Bush said, "and they will have some resentment toward those Iraqis that were outside the country during Saddam's rule." He didn't want to select the new rulers, he said, effectively putting the nail in the idea that Chalabi would take over, and deferring the notion of an early provisional government. "We've got to hold our fire on getting the details set until we've learned more," he said.

Powell proposed that they get a separate U.N. resolution as a kind of legal umbrella over the Iraqi interim authority.

That could help, Bush said.

Next, Treasury Secretary John Snow outlined the plan for establishing a new currency in Iraq. There were two currencies: the Swiss dinar in the north, and in the south the Saddam dinar with Saddam's picture plastered on the front of each bill. After the takeover, Snow said, they would want to make sure no more Saddam dinars were printed, and existing stashes would be seized to prevent hyperinflation. Once Saddam was gone, they would have to pay people to keep the economy going, he said.

Snow's favored option for an interim replacement currency was the American dollar. In the first Gulf War, U.S. banks had frozen nearly $1.7 billion in Iraqi assets, and under the Patriot Act the president could seize the money permanently. It would take more than three 747 jets to transport the currency to Iraq.

Bush approved the interim U.S. dollar plan but wanted to make sure people in Iraq, pensioners particularly, would get a raise of some sort, yet not so much as to distort the economy. Instead of Saddam on their currency, Iraqis would soon get former American presidents Washington, Jackson, Lincoln and Grant as well as early American heroes Hamilton and Franklin.

THAT AFTERNOON, Bush met in the Oval Office with Rice, Hadley, Card, Bartlett and Gerson. The fate of the second proposed U.N. resolution was still uncertain, but the president was going to have to say something publicly about it. How would they frame the reaction to a U.N. vote? Bush could issue an ultimatum to Saddam to get out of Dodge—a favorite expression in the Bush family—or he could just announce the beginning of military action because Saddam had not complied with the first resolution, 1441.

The president had made it pretty clear that it would be an ulti-matum. He asked Rice what was going on at the U.N., and again ex-pressed impatience with the drawn-out, disorderly process. The Brits, Chile and Spain all had proposals floating. After much back-and-forth, Gerson was told to work on two speeches: one assuming a veto of the second resolution by the French at least; another that as-sumed a reaffirmation of 1441.

But at the core of the dithering over the U.N. resolutions was Blair's fate. It was very much on Bush's mind. If Blair's government fell, it would be a real disaster they all agreed.

At the Pentagon press briefing the next day, March 11, Rumsfeld indicated that the British might not participate if there was war. "That is an issue that the president will be addressing in the days ahead, one would assume," Rumsfeld said.

"What the fuck are you doing?" an official from the British em-bassy in Washington immediately asked Rumsfeld's office. It was in-sulting. The British army had 45,000 troops in the region—nearly half the British ground force. Every British news organization would soon be calling around to the Pentagon, the embassy and 10 Down-ing Street asking, What does that mean? Are the Brits pulling out?

Rumsfeld issued a personal clarification saying he had "no doubt" that the British would give their full support to any attempt to disarm Iraq. "In the event that a decision to use force is made, we have every reason to believe there will be a significant military con-tribution from the United Kingdom."

On March 11, Rice issued to the principals "A Summary of Con-clusions," classified Secret, that codified what had been agreed upon at the NSC that morning. That way any of the principals could come back and request revisions if the memo did not reflect what they believed had occurred. The summary laid out how an Iraqi interim authority would be set up as soon as possible after liberation. It would include Iraqis, Kurds and opposition exiles. A Baghdad conference would be convened "to broaden the base," as had been done after the Afghanistan war, to name interim leaders and "to assist in the establishment of a new democratic government." The document summarized the briefings given to the president on currency, oil and reformed bureaucracy.

AT 7:15 A.M. Wednesday, March 12, the president and Gerson huddled over two drafts—both ultimatums. The third alternative—a simple announcement of military action—had not yet been written. Bush said it was important to have that draft now as well.

Card and Rice came in to see how they were doing.

"This needs to end," Bush said. The U.N. was ridiculous. Maybe the best outcome would be no second resolution. Just hang the military action on Resolution 1441. Maybe he ought to issue the ultimatum to Saddam—in the next day or two. Rice seemed to favor just announcing action, no ultimatum. The ultimatum speeches did not write very well and they contained a potential contradiction: Both drafts said the United Nations didn't have the courage of its collective convictions, but of course it already had acted with Resolution 1441.

Blair says he is still in trouble in Parliament, the president told them, and is worried about a vote of no confidence on the war. Blair had been voicing deep concern in their almost daily phone conversations. Still, Bush told them, "I don't think he's going to lose office."

Vice President Cheney and Karl Rove were supposed to contact Tories in Britain to argue that they should support Blair and war.

AT THE NSC MEETING later that morning, Doug Feith briefed on the post-invasion plans for dealing with the Iraqi foreign ministry and the military and intelligence services. On the foreign ministry, he said the goal was to "purge the ministry of senior Baath leadership and intelligence officers." Iraq's 56 embassies abroad would have to be dealt with. They should ask host governments to expel the ambassadors and suspected intelligence officers, and freeze Iraqi bank accounts.

Okay, the president said, who's going to do it?

Powell said he would.

On the Iraqi Intelligence Service, Feith said it had to be completely dismantled in a way that was transparent to the Iraqis and the world. Could they preserve the Special Republican Guard? The answer was no. The Republican Guard? No. The SSO? No.

When they got to the regular army, the answer was maybe. Feith outlined his plan: Downsize the armed forces, demilitarize the society. Create a depoliticized armed forces that would be subordinate to political control, a civilian control that would represent Iraq's ethnic and sectarian composition. He said the special militias, such as the Fedayeen Saddam, would have to be dismantled and its members demobilized.

The interim authority would be running prison camps for formations of surrendered Iraqis at the company, battalion and maybe even brigade level, Feith said. The plan was to "not immediately demobilize all the people and put them on the street, but use them as a reconstruction force." He said that three to five regular army divisions would form the nucleus of a new army.

What they didn't plan for was the possibility that hundreds of thousands of soldiers would just go home, that the workforce to rebuild the country would melt away.

LATER ON WEDNESDAY, March 12, Blair called Bush for an update.

"If we don't have the votes," Bush said, "pull it down. We're through." He had had it with the resolutions.

"Would you try one more time?" Blair asked, referring to the key votes of Mexico's Fox and Chile's Lagos.

"Of course," Bush said, "I'd be glad to do that."

Bush called Fox. "Vicente, I'm insisting there be a vote tomorrow in the U.N. Can we count on your vote?"

"Exactly what's the language like in the resolution?" Fox asked.

"Vicente, we've debated this issue long enough. The security of the United States is on the line. I want your vote."

Fox said he would get back to him. Later, during dinner, Rice called Bush to say she had received a phone call saying that Luis Ernesto Derbez, the foreign minister, was now in charge of the Mexican policy because Fox had to go into the hospital for back surgery.

"Interesting," Bush said. He called Chilean President Ricardo Lagos, a distinguished leader in Bush's view, so he was polite. No threats.

"Can we count on your vote?" Bush asked the 65-year-old Socialist leader.

"Are you sure it's time to bring up the vote?"

"It's time to bring up the vote, Ricardo. We've had this debate too long."

"But we're making progress," Lagos replied.

"That's only because we've got a couple of hundred thousand troops. If those troops weren't there, there'd be even less progress diplomatically. And Saddam Hussein could care less. Any progress you think is being made is illusionary." Bush then stated his predicament clearly. "And I'm not going to leave our troops there. They're either going to go in, and remove him, or they're coming home, Ricardo."

This was a sobering thought. For both practical and political reasons, bringing the troops home without solving the Saddam problem was unthinkable for Bush. It was similar to the position his father had found himself in during January 1991 with 500,000 military men and women in the Middle East. "We have to have a war," Bush senior had told his advisers several weeks before launching the Gulf War. Once again a President Bush, this time with over 200,000 troops in the Middle East, had put himself into the position where he had to have a war.

Bush asked Lagos, "Ricardo, what's your vote?"

No, the Chilean president replied.

"Thank you very much," Bush said.

Bush called Blair and described his talks with Fox and Lagos. "You have to consider these two conversations," Bush said. "This is not positive news. It's over."

32

WHEN THE PRESIDENT met with Irish Prime Minister Bertie Ahern the morning of Thursday, March 13, the inevitable topic of the French came up. Bush told Ahern that, "Chirac has pushed it to the point where there's a huge anti-French backlash in America. He's the butt of the jokes. He's taken it too far." The problem, Bush said, was that this wasn't just about Saddam Hussein—it was about the ascendancy of power in Europe. This could have been resolved peacefully if Germany and France had shown more willingness to confront Saddam. Instead, the Iraqi leader had picked up signals from the two leaders, Bush maintained. It had led him to think he could get away with defying the U.N. as he always had.

Bush said that Chirac was a "bully," especially to the East European nations. That created a backlash and wound up helping Tony Blair, the president maintained, because the French seemed so dogmatic.

Later that day, Bush met with his advisers and expressed a strong interest in having a summit with Blair to show solidarity. In part it was to fill the void. War was certain, but the diplomatic circus hadn't ended. What could he do? He did not want to just sit around. It was a miserable period, filled with uncertainty. But Blair's people were concerned about the prime minister leaving the country for even eight hours because of the Maggie Thatcher precedent, when in 1990 she had gone abroad to a conference and returned only to be ousted as party leader. Blair didn't want Bush to give a speech or issue an ultimatum. He, Blair, had to pick the right moment to call for a parliamentary vote. So any speech from the American president would not be until Monday at the earliest. Whatever would serve the British, Bush decided.

AT 10 A.M. Friday, March 14, Bush announced agreement on a "road map" for peace in the Middle East in the Rose Garden. It was another concession to Blair, who had pressed him to not delay the peace plan until the Iraq issue was resolved.

Shortly after noon at the White House press briefing, Ari Fleischer announced a summit with Blair and Aznar in the Azores, "to review this diplomacy as it's brought to its conclusion."

Later that day, Hadley gave Gerson a Top Secret document that had the bullet points to include in the ultimatum speech. It was a result of a principals meeting, and it had been heavily driven by Rumsfeld, who wanted only a 48-hour ultimatum.

PRINCE BANDAR made an appointment to see the president to convey an urgent message from Crown Prince Abdullah. The Saudi leader still hoped for a last-minute solution to avoid war, still wished to overthrow Saddam covertly. But the delay, the U.N. dancing, was worse than war in the Saudis' view. The effort to help Blair was hurting America's friends in the Middle East. King Abdullah of Jordan was beside himself. "Let's go," he was telling the Saudis, "I can't take this." The Saudi crown prince's message was simple—the apparent indecision was unfavorable for everyone in the region. What was it, war or no war?

When Bandar was shown into the Oval Office, Cheney, Rice and Card were there. Card was surprised at Bandar's appearance. The ambassador's weight often fluctuated and that day the buttons on his jacket were straining. He seemed tired, nervous and excited. He was sweating profusely. It was quite a scene.

"What's wrong with you?" the president asked Bandar. Don't you have a razor, something to shave with? The prince normally wore a well-trimmed beard and now his face was an unkempt thicket.

"Mr. President," Bandar said, "I promised myself I would not shave until this war starts."

"Well, then, you are going to shave very soon."

"I hope so," Bandar said. "But I think by the time this war starts, I will be like bin Laden." He then indicated a long beard of a foot or two.

Bush bristled. He did not like being taunted and did not think the allusion was funny. Bandar knew Bush hated any suggestion that he was indecisive. "I'm telling you, you are not going to wait too long," the president said.

Bandar said he had heard that the war had been set to start on March 3, then nothing. Next it was supposed to be March 10, but it didn't happen then either. Now Bush was supposedly going to issue an ultimatum to Saddam.

"Don't even start," the president directed.

"Crown Prince Abdullah—"

"Don't," Bush snapped. "I know. I'm going. I'm serious."

"Mr. President—"

"Look, I'm telling you! Don't even go there. I am going, Bandar, just trust me."

"Well," Bandar said, "then I guess, okay . . ."

"After the ultimatum, how long do you think it will be before we start the war?" the president asked.

"You asking *me*?"

"Yes," the president said.

"You know how long."

"Give me your guess," Bush inquired sharply.

Bandar said 72 hours.

"Wrong!"

Cheney was fidgeting in his chair and seemed to want to telegraph reassurance to Bandar, as if to say, "Relax, my man is going to
do it." Rice wore a poker face, as did Card.

"All right," Bandar said.

BANDAR THEN WENT to see Rumsfeld. It was their third meeting
since the effort to get the second U.N. resolution had begun. Rumsfeld seemed nervous. His biggest fear was that Saddam would make
a last-minute offer asking for just a few more days; then the Russians
and French would argue that that was reasonable.

"Mr. Secretary," Bandar said, "I feel as panicky as I did in 1991."
The situation eerily resembled the eve of the Gulf War, when Saddam
could have made the simplest concession, perhaps simply promise to
order his army out of Kuwait. At that point the United Nations and
the U.S. might have had to delay the war. Though Saddam almost always did the stupid thing, didn't see a chance to delay war by playing
the diplomatic card, Bandar nonetheless said, "I am very worried the
same thing could happen."

"Well, you met with the boss this morning," Rumsfeld noted.
"What do you think?"

"I think the temptation is there around him, Don," Bandar said.
"But I think your man and my man has made up his mind."

Rumsfeld said, "It wouldn't hurt if you reconfirmed that."

AT 7 A.M. Saturday, March 15, Saul picked up his secure phone at his
home in the Washington area. He had been up and stumbling around
on his computer for several hours. The CIA Iraqi operations chief
was finding it hard to sleep these days.

"They blew it up!" the caller from CIA headquarters reported to
his chief. "We're waiting for confirmation from imagery."

"Keep me posted," Saul said.

"Don't get excited because we don't have confirmation."

Saul waited. Reaching this moment—or *maybe* reaching this moment—had taken several months of discussion and debate with Franks and his staff. When could the agency begin active sabotage inside Iraq? In December, Franks had been worried that sabotage might trigger an Iraqi response that Franks was not ready to deal with. Saddam might find sabotage on any scale a provocation and begin his own military operations while Franks was supposed to be giving diplomacy a chance to work. But finally the okay had been given.

One of the CIA teams in the north had given the Kurds explosives, and provided a technical officer to train them in their use. The target was the Mosul-to-Baghdad rail line, a key link over 200 miles long. The instructions to the Kurds had been to blow the line, then call the railroad company and say, "We've blown up the rail. Don't send any trains through." That was clear enough and it was part of Bush's insistence on reducing civilian casualties.

About 9 A.M. Saul got the next call from the operations officer.

"Okay, we got the imagery. They blew up the rail." The hit was about 20 miles south of Mosul.

"Good."

"And they didn't make the call."

"Oh, fuck," Saul said. "What does that mean?"

"Well, we've got a derailed train." Oil tankers were all over the place and some passenger cars had derailed.

Saul had gone through the CIA's contra war in the 1980s when the agency had been supposed to overthrow the leftist Sandinista regime in Nicaragua. He remembered when the agency mined the harbors, setting off a firestorm in Congress, which hauled in CIA Director Bill Casey and other agency operatives and raked them over the coals. "Well, at least, it's Saturday," Saul said to himself. "I've got Sunday to prepare my testimony on the Hill Monday morning. I'm going to be called in." Saul phoned Deputy Director for Operations Jim Pavitt, the head of all the agency's covert and clandestine activities.

"Jim, the first operation's happened."

"What happened?" Pavitt inquired.

"We derailed a train. We got oil tankers all over the place.

There's a big-ass oil stain. There's passenger cars. We don't know if we have casualties or what."

Saul heard an ominous silence, a full dead stop on the other end, and figured that Pavitt was just going to whale into him.

"Well, I guess these things happen in wartime. Keep me posted," Pavitt said.

Saul called his guys. "Go for it! He didn't care. Go!" The word went out: Commence operations.

It had been a troop train and there were casualties. The Kurds rubbed it in, tossing pamphlets in the area: People Rise Up! Liberation Is At Hand!

Several dozen additional attacks were launched. Official vehicles were blown up. Baath Party headquarters was hit. So was IIS headquarters. From north to south, Saddam statues, paintings and posters were defaced. There were nighttime drive-by shootings of government buildings. Security and IIS guards were posted to major Saddam monuments, pulling them from other duties. "Overthrow Saddam" and "Down With Saddam" pamphlets were handed out in the theater where the Baath Party had been instituted.

A rocket-propelled grenade was fired at another train transporting fuel on the Baghdad-to-Syria line. In Kirkuk, near the border of the Kurdish-controlled territory, some 20,000 protesters marched on the Baath Party headquarters calling for Saddam's downfall. Anti-Saddam vandalism and graffiti were all around. Basically it was a big "Fuck You."

But there was a lingering problem, Saul realized. Now that everything had started, God forbid the president would pull back and stop, because the CIA no longer could.

THE SABOTAGE was not really designed to weaken the regime, merely to focus it inward and create the impression of an insurgence inside Iraq, which Saul as well as everyone knew was not true.

On the intelligence-gathering front, Saul felt they had made more substantial progress. The high point was, of course, the

ROCKSTARS. He had some other penetrations of the tribal networks inside Iraq, maybe two dozen in all if the ROCKSTAR network
were included. He counted about a dozen penetrations of the security apparatus and another dozen of the Republican Guard and regular army, again if the ROCKSTARS were counted.

The agency had provided some intelligence to Franks on the location of the few remaining surface-to-surface missiles and antiaircraft positions that had been confirmed by overhead imagery. They
would be struck when war commenced.

There had been a good number of other penetrations. Several
Iraqi engineers in the oil fields had agreed to help the CIA and were
able to provide real-time reporting on any effort by Saddam to rig the
wells with explosives. A CIA paramilitary team was planning to accompany the lead U.S. military units that would cross the Kuwait-
Iraq border and stay in communication with the engineers in the
hope of preventing an oil field catastrophe.

A ROCKSTAR recruit was the head of security in the Iraqi port
of Umm Qasr. Iraq is landlocked except for a small bay at the end of
the Persian Gulf where Umm Qasr is located. For over three months
the agent had provided details on the placement of mines and security forces so that U.S. Marines might be able to virtually walk in and
seize the port.

Senior officers in key Iraqi military units, up to six divisions,
had agreed to stay out of the fight, surrender and turn over all their
forces. This created high hopes for a so-called capitulation strategy
in which the surrendered units could be used for stabilization efforts
inside Iraq after the war.

Another of the agency's Iraqi sources in the Gulf region had
provided the names of Iraqi intelligence operatives in a half-dozen
countries who were members of two-to-four-man teams that had
been directed to conduct terrorist attacks at U.S. facilities in those
countries when the war started. The names and details were specific.
The CIA had tracked down the operatives and wrapped up the teams.

Saul believed the agency was running some potentially effective
deception operations against Saddam. Normally the CIA would run

double agents—someone the CIA knew was really working for the other side—for the narrow purpose of trying to see how Iraqi agents communicated. "Let's stop this horseshit," Saul had directed. The double agents identified through the CD-ROM SSO personnel file could be more useful if they were fed false information about how and when war was coming.

Several double agents were provided information that the war would be Desert Storm II with a massive, extended force buildup. In another example, one or more suspected double agents who had walked in volunteering to spy were quizzed about border crossings on the Iran-Iraq border and debriefed extensively about Iran. This was designed to create the impression that an attack might come through Iran, a notorious enemy of Saddam.

Other misinformation was spread that the U.S. would attack with a two-division thrust from Jordan into Iraq.

Yet another double agent was provided with phony U.S. war plans that had been elaborately forged to show that the main attack would be a massive air assault on Saddam International Airport in Baghdad. The Special Republican Guard moved tanks and armored personnel carriers onto the tarmac to block the expected attack.

One of the most imaginative operations was designed to show that the United States was trying to foment a coup and had penetrated the Special Republican Guard, which protected Saddam. An agent who the CIA knew was a double was given a risky assignment. He was handed a large rock and shown communication gear that had been buried inside the rock. He was told it transmitted short, low-power burst transmissions to an overhead satellite that another paid agent would be regularly sending out. He was told to plant the rock in a specific place near the housing area or barracks of the Special Republican Guard. The CIA built a concealment area in the double agent's car and paid him a small amount of money. He placed the rock near the barracks. The transmission device had been compromised in the past, but the CIA was confident that the Iraqis could not break the code. The device was preset to broadcast at times when hundreds of Special Republican Guard members went to and from work—suggesting that one of them was secretly communicating by sending burst transmissions to the rock.

A report from another foreign intelligence service later said that the Special Republican Guard commanders had been called in and warned that someone in their midst was plotting against Saddam. Anyone caught plotting would be executed. Documents obtained after the war showed that Saddam had been briefed on the alleged CIA operation and the Iraqis had conducted an investigation to find the traitor.

Other covert actions included getting countries to freeze Iraqi bank accounts abroad. Iraqi intelligence often paid recruits not with cash but by offering a U.N. Oil-for-Food contract. The recruits could make $1 million from such contracts, and attempts were made to get the money frozen in Lebanon, Jordan and Switzerland. In one case, some $650 million was frozen.

Efforts to stop the illicit procurement of alleged WMD material as directed in the presidential intelligence order of February 16, 2002, were not very successful. The idea was to take computers being shipped from abroad and secretly program them to malfunction in suspected WMD facilities. But the computers somehow wound up in the Baghdad telephone and communications system, which went down intermittently before the war.

AS I HAD BEEN interviewing various officials and sources during the buildup to war, three separate sources said confidentially that the intelligence on WMD was not as conclusive as the CIA and the administration had suggested. This was troubling, particularly on what seemed to be the eve of war. I spoke with Walter Pincus, a colleague at *The Washington Post,* who had written extensively about the weapons inspections and intelligence in Iraq. Pincus said that he had heard precisely the same thing from a number of his sources. So I drafted the following five paragraphs for a possible news story and hand-carried a copy to Pincus and the national security editor at the *Post:*

"Some of the key U.S. intelligence that is the basis for the conclusion that Iraq has large caches of weapons of mass destruction looks increasingly circumstantial, and even shaky as it is further scrutinized, subjected to outside analysis and on-the-ground verification, according to informed sources.

"A senior Bush administration source briefed last month on the intelligence said it was 'pretty thin,' and might be enough to reach the legal standard of 'probable cause' to bring an indictment but not enough for conviction.

"Intelligence from overhead satellite photography and imagery, another senior administration official said, provides vivid pictures of Iraqis moving material. 'We've seen them bury things,' this official said, 'dig them up, open the doors, and take away what was in it in special containers. We've seen a lot.'

"Asked if the U.S. intelligence knew what was in the special containers, the official said, 'No. But they sure are careful about it.'

"The official said that the administration did not want a smoking gun—irrefutable proof. 'The whole intent of 1441 and the way it was written was that it keep the burden off of us.' "

I also gave Pincus a copy of a letter that Tenet had written to Senator John Warner, the Armed Services Committee chairman, saying that the intelligence agencies had given the U.N. weapons inspectors "detailed information on all of the high value and moderate value sites" that were suspected of having connections to WMD.

Pincus and the national security editor both thought my draft version a little strong. I agreed. Though the sources were excellent, they were only saying the evidence was skimpy. None were asserting that WMD would not be found in Iraq after a war. Pincus rightly wanted to focus on the inability of the U.S. intelligence agencies to provide specific information about amounts or locations of WMD in Iraq. He wrote a story that was published Sunday, March 16, on page A17 headlined, "U.S. Lacks Specifics on Banned Arms." I was listed as having contributed to his story.

Even now I cannot disclose the identities of the sources. But I did not feel I had enough information to effectively challenge the official conclusions about Iraq's alleged WMD. In light of subsequent events, I should have pushed for a front page story, even on the eve of war, presenting more forcefully what our sources were saying. Several of these sources, I know, did voice their reservations within their various organizations but they also did not have enough to robustly challenge the conclusions that had already been reached. I have no evidence that the reservations of these particular sources reached the president.

33

ANDY CARD HAD SUGGESTED that the Bush, Blair and Aznar mini-summit be held in Bermuda. But that was too far for Blair and too close to the United States. Another White House proposal was for Bush to go to London. Blair's aides balked—the American president in London at that time would have been a provocation for massive protests. They had finally settled on the Azores, a group of Portuguese islands in the North Atlantic closer to London than Washington. The prime minister of Portugal, José Manuel Durão Barroso, who also supported war, served as the host. The four leaders huddled with their top aides for a closed-door session at an airbase on Terceira Island on Sunday, March 16.

Bush began by summarizing why they were there. "Maybe lightning will strike," he said, "and Chirac will agree with our co-sponsored resolution, but there won't be any negotiations." That would mean a delay of "a week or two weeks or three weeks." He made clear his position that war would start in a matter of days, not weeks. If there were a delay, he said, "Public opinion won't get better and it will get worse in some countries like America."

Chirac had taped an interview for the CBS television show *60 Minutes* to be aired that night, and someone handed the British prime minister a summary of Chirac's remarks. Blair told the others that

Chirac was calling for U.N. weapons inspectors to be given another 30 days in Iraq.

Forget it, Bush said, it's a delaying tactic. It added a clarity to what he already believed. France would grasp at any straw to postpone war. The other leaders seemed to agree.

The four reviewed the long-running diplomatic efforts, which they agreed had been pretty much exhausted. They were in accord that they ought to give diplomacy another 24 hours, though a breakthrough was unlikely, and then pull down the second resolution formally at 10 A.M. Eastern Time the next morning.

There was some discussion about whether they had legal authorization to go to war. They went point by point through 1441 and concluded that the "serious consequences" gave them the authority for war if there was noncompliance, and surely Iraq in their view had not disarmed.

"I'm going to have to give a speech," Bush said. "I'm going to have to give Saddam Hussein an ultimatum." Saddam would have 48 hours to get out of Iraq with his sons. "That's what I'm going to do, okay?" He wasn't consulting. He was informing. "So everybody knows," he added.

They turned to the possibility that France, Russia or some other Security Council member would introduce a counter-resolution to delay "serious consequences" and force a vote. That could be a real problem. All they could do, they agreed, was get on the phone and head off the undecideds, get their commitment to oppose a counter-resolution and vote no if necessary.

Blair stiffened. "If another country tried to introduce a new resolution for the sole purpose of delaying us," he said, "we'd have to regard that as a hostile act diplomatically."

This brought them back to the French. "I'd be glad to veto something of theirs," Bush said, "really glad."

The diplomatic planning was over. "You know," the president said, "we're going to, we have to keep planning for a future postwar Iraq, and we all agree on the five basic principles. Territorial integrity has to remain. We need immediate, we need to be ready with humanitarian aid to get it in there immediately to head off any food or displaced persons crisis." The U.N. would continue its Oil-for-Food Program. "More than half of Iraqis get their food there and it has a ton of, lots of wealth of the Iraqi people through prior sales of the Oil-for-Food Program in escrow. The U.N. has got to be ready to step in to use that wealth to help people out.

"We have to build an international consensus for Iraq, a new Iraq, at peace with its neighbors, and we'll go back to the U.N. for another resolution after the war. The U.N. can help with many issues but should not run the country." He made it clear that the coalition would be in charge. They then worked over the joint statements that would be released later that day.

"GERSON, ARE YOU TRYING to avoid attention?" the president said to his chief speechwriter as he left the meeting. That's exactly what Gerson was trying to do. He had accompanied the president on the 4,600-mile round-trip so they could work on the ultimatum speech, which was still highly secret and not yet final.

"Do you have a copy of the speech?" Rice asked Gerson. He did, but it had his notes, edits and other chicken scratches on it.

"That's okay," she said, "I'll take it." She then handed it to Blair. Gerson was a little bug-eyed. It was about as close-hold a document as there might be, setting the final timetable for war. At the same time, he realized that every word of Bush's speech could have a tremendous impact on British politics, perhaps immediately, since a vote of confidence in Parliament was pending. Gerson noticed that Alastair Campbell, Blair's communications and strategy adviser, was reading the copy and jotting notes.

AT 5:30 P.M. Bush and the other leaders began a news conference in the community activity center ballroom at the Lajes Field Air Base.

The prime minister of Portugal welcomed everyone and tried to

frame the message. "This was the last opportunity for a political solution," he told the reporters, "even if it's one in a million."

Bush took the floor. "We concluded that tomorrow is a moment
of truth for the world," he said, declaring that Resolution 1441's
"logic is inescapable: The Iraqi regime will disarm itself, or the Iraqi
regime will be disarmed by force." He got ahead of himself as if war
was a certainty and Saddam was out, saying, "We'll push as quickly
as possible for an Iraqi interim authority," and quickly added, "if military force is required."

In his turn, Blair framed the issue somewhat differently—"the
key point, which is our responsibility to uphold the will of the United
Nations set out in Resolution 1441 last November."

The coalition had designated itself the enforcement arm of the
United Nations Security Council. The leaders were, in effect, issuing
an ultimatum to the U.N. and its process at the Security Council. It
highlighted the problem of a preemptive war and seemed to lay bare
the paradox of coercive diplomacy. The reporters noticed. One asked,
"Aren't we going to war here?"

Bush said that the decision was Saddam's.

Another reporter noted in the middle of a convoluted, multipart
question, "There's no possible way out through the United Nations
because a majority does not support a war action." No one contradicted him.

So would there be a vote on the second resolution?

"I was the guy that said they ought to vote," Bush said. "France
showed their cards. . . . They said they were going to veto anything
that held Saddam to account. So cards have been played, and we'll
just have to take an assessment after tomorrow to determine what
that card meant." Bush said he wanted to talk about the U.N.'s importance. "In the post-Saddam Iraq, the U.N. will definitely need to
have a role. And that way it can begin to get its legs, legs of responsibility back."

He did not say in public what he had said in private to the other
leaders, that the U.N. "should not run the country."

• • •

GERSON FINALLY GOT his speech copy back from the British. They wanted the president's speech to be more conditional, with the phrase or concept "*if* war comes" liberally sprinkled throughout. Though it would imply war, it should not be a war speech. A kernel of hope for a peaceful solution had to remain. Gerson didn't have any problems with the suggested changes. It was the kind of mood he was in at that point. He was going through some personal turmoil about the coming conflict.

As a deeply religious Christian, Gerson was conscious that it was the Lenten season, the 40-day period of penance and prayer in preparation for Easter. His son and he had given up sweets for Lent. He was fasting for two days, and he was praying that something would happen to avoid war.

Blair had to leave early to get home and tend to politics and rebellion in his party. Card thought he was filled both with resolve and angst. It wasn't confident resolve. He was nervously firm, Card believed. Rice thought it was still very touch-and-go with the British. As she stood watching the British depart, she said, "Gee, I hope this isn't the last time we see them."

ON AIR FORCE ONE, Bush and Rice agreed it now was just a matter of managing the politics of the U.N. and not pulling the plug before Blair had his vote in Parliament. Hughes and Bartlett joined them and they went over the speech line-by-line. It was some 30 paragraphs. So it would run about 15 minutes. The British suggestions were acceptable, and Gerson went back to one of the plane's computers and carefully put in the changes.

The speech recalled the past 12 years of diplomacy, and laid the fault on Saddam. "Our good faith has not been returned," Bush was to say and insist, "We wanted to resolve the issue peacefully."

"If we must begin a military campaign. . . .

"Should Saddam Hussein choose confrontation, the American people can know that every measure has been taken to avoid war," the speech now said. "If Saddam Hussein attempts to cling to power . . ."

On the other hand, it was a war speech and it gave little ground. It raised starkly the possibility of a nuclear attack. "The Iraq regime continues to possess and conceal some of the most lethal weapons ever devised." Terrorists with "nuclear weapons obtained with the help of Iraq" could kill "hundreds of thousands of innocent people in our country or any other."

The speech also invoked 9/11. In one to five years, the threat from Saddam would multiply, it said. "We choose to meet that threat now, where it arises, before it can appear suddenly in our skies and cities."

It also contained a reflection of Bush's post-9/11 speeches, namely that some may believe it is an age of terror, but through his actions Bush would make it an age of liberty. Gerson knew well that that had been the president's consistent theme since 9/11: The United States was going to control what goes on and not be controlled by the decisions of others. It took a poke at the French, declaring, "These governments share our assessment of the danger, but not our resolve to meet it."

When Gerson was finished with his corrections, he joined the president and the others, who were about 10 minutes into the Mel Gibson film *Conspiracy Theory*. Bush loudly summarized the plot, and during the rest of the movie made fun of it as fairly predictable.

When it was over, Bush handed Gerson a few more stylistic edits on his copy.

At 7:42 P.M. Eastern Time, hours later over the Atlantic, Bush called Australian Prime Minister John Howard, the key ally who was not at the summit. Australia would be contributing 2,000 troops.

"We're going to wait till morning," Bush told him. Powell was going to work the phones overnight. "Colin's going to kind of take the temperature of the allies, the Arab countries at the U.N., and we'll see where we are. If nothing's changed, we're going to pull down the resolution. I'm going to give a speech that night, we're just going to give Saddam the ultimatum."

Is this going to be the declaration of war speech?

"No, it's an ultimatum speech."

Howard was worried about Australian public opinion, and said he needed one last official word from Bush before the war started. "Otherwise, it would look to the Australian people like Bush just started the war without even telling his biggest allies."

"No, no," Bush said, "this isn't the last call you're going to get from me."

34

IN WASHINGTON THE NEXT DAY, Monday, March 17, Rice was on the phone to the national security adviser of India at 7 A.M. The Indian prime minister, Atal Bihari Vajpayee, had sent a letter to Bush two days earlier, offering to host a summit of the five permanent members of the U.N. Security Council—Russia, France, China, the U.K. and the United States—to work out their problems. The U.S. had repeatedly urged negotiations on India in its dangerous disputes with Pakistan since both countries possessed nuclear weapons. So Vajpayee's offer had to be rejected carefully.

"Great idea," Rice said politely, "but we don't see the point now." Thanks for your concern and help. "We appreciate the prime minister's efforts, but at least one country had made it clear." France would veto. "Therefore, we just don't see the usefulness of such a meeting."

The president was focused on heading off a counter-resolution in the U.N. It could gum up the works and detract from the legitimacy now invested in 1441. In a call to Aznar, Bush asked for help with President Lagos of Chile. He had failed to win Lagos's support for the second resolution the previous week, but Aznar had more influence. "Can you call Lagos and urge him not to try any last-minute maneuver?" the president asked. Maintaining the stalemate in the Security Council was critical now.

Aznar said he would call Lagos, and added his own request, "Look, it would really help me enormously if you would call Juan Carlos. Just check in." King Juan Carlos I is Spain's head of state and, though largely a figurehead, he is popular and held sway in the nomination of the country's president. Aznar wanted him to be satisfied.

"Great idea," Bush said.

In a 15-minute call, Bush and Blair coordinated efforts to make sure there was no counter-resolution. They agreed that the Russians would have to be talked to at various levels.

Blair said the prospects for the upcoming vote in Parliament looked better, but it was still tough for him right now. "I think I can win," Blair said. "I'm concerned about the margin of victory. I don't want to depend on Tory votes. I want to win my own party strong. I know I'm not going to win them all, but I don't want the Tories to be able to say without us, you would have lost, and I'm working hard on the Labour Party to make sure I get a very clear solid majority of the Labour votes."

At 8:55 A.M. Bush met with the NSC. Powell reported that nothing had changed overnight. The French were not going to bend.

The president told Franks that he might have to execute what was now called Op Plan 1003 V within 72 hours. "I'm not giving you the go order yet, but you have to be ready," he directed. "Do all the last-minute things you need to do."

THE PRESIDENT CALLED in Ari Fleischer. Go out at 9:45 and say that our allies have conferred again this morning and we have withdrawn the resolution, he instructed his press secretary. There would be no vote at the U.N.

So at 9:45 A.M. Fleischer appeared in the press room and said: "The United Nations has failed to enforce its own demands that Iraq immediately disarm. As a result, the diplomatic window has now been closed. The president will address the nation tonight at 8 o'clock. He will say that in order to avoid military conflict, Saddam Hussein must leave the country."

Half the press corps flew out of the room to file. Fleischer had never seen anything like it in his more than two years as White House press secretary. He thought, "How else can I get rid of them that easily?" The stampede was mostly from the back of the room. The wire services and TV guys in the front rows could stay to try to squeeze more out of Fleischer, knowing their news organizations were monitoring and would send out or broadcast the bulletins.

Afterward, Bush paid his debt to Aznar and spoke to the Spanish king for four minutes. "Your Majesty, here's what's going on. We're going to pull down the resolution and I'm going to speak to the American people." The king cordially thanked him for calling.

At 11 A.M. the president called the prime minister of Bulgaria, Simeon Saxe-Coburg Gotha. The Bulgarian leader, who was going to permit overflight rights and send a team of several dozen experts in chemical and biological warfare defense to the region, voiced concern about appearing on a public list of coalition members.

"What do you mean?" Bush asked. "You're going to send people in, everybody's going to know you're going to be there, but you don't want to be on the list?"

The prime minister expressed unease.

Rice jumped in to clarify, "You're not saying you're not sending the guys, right?"

"Oh, no, no, no, we're sending the guys."

That's all Bush wanted. He wanted as many in the coalition as possible, small as their contributions might be. In terms of public notice, he said, "It's fine. Do whatever you have to do."

Rice then talked by phone to Russian Defense Minister Sergei Ivanov to tell him Saddam was going to get 48 hours, and the diplomacy was over. "We would hope that you don't introduce a new resolution," she urged gently, and asked about rumors that Igor Ivanov, the foreign minister, had a movement afoot to elevate the next meeting of the U.N. Security Council to a ministerial level. She worried that it would force Powell to show up so they could take some whacks at Bush and him, or that Powell would be the only foreign minister absent. "Please don't send Igor to the U.N.," she insisted.

"I can't say for sure he won't go," Ivanov replied, "but I do promise that if he does he's not going to make it a big political exercise. He's not going to use it as an opportunity to bash or embarrass you."

Rice said they had reports that the Iraqis had acquired night vision goggles and GPS devices from the Russians.

"Don't worry, we'll look into that. Of course we wouldn't sell them that stuff." The former Soviet Union used to sell such equipment to them, he noted. "It could just be old equipment. You might be getting your signals mixed up." He then started talking about having Rice visit Russia.

Rice called U.N. Secretary-General Kofi Annan. "If there's a war, in the postwar situation the U.N. will have a vital role to play," she said. The word "vital" was one that the British had insisted upon, but it was undefined. "We'll work with you on that," she said, leaving the "that" also undefined.

Her next call was to Putin's chief of staff, Alexander Voloshin.

"Please don't send Ivanov to the U.N., please don't try to elevate this to a foreign ministers meeting," she said, adding a new twist. "If you do, Powell's not going to go, we don't see the point in it."

Voloshin hemmed and hawed. "We'd love to have you come to Moscow."

That morning, Bush had the first of two full TelePrompTer sessions to read through the entire speech. The first half went smoothly, but as he got to the action sentences—"Saddam Hussein and his sons must leave Iraq within 48 hours. Their refusal to do so will result in military conflict, commenced at a time of our choosing"—he had a kind of catch in his throat.

Gerson knew that one of the reasons to practice a speech was so the president could experience the emotions of the words the first time. Then, on second practice, he could drive through them, and on the third control them, and himself. He still got a chill when he heard the words, even though he had written them and heard them practiced.

At 2 P.M. Bush called Australian Prime Minister Howard to go over what he was going to say that night.

"George," Howard said, "if it comes to this, I pledge to you that Australian troops will fight if necessary."

Bush called Israeli Prime Minister Ariel Sharon. "Ariel, I told you in the Oval Office I would give you 72 hours' notice. I'm giving it to you now."

"We've got it," Sharon said, and thanked the president. The call took about three minutes.

At 4:45, Bush did a second read-through of his speech in Cross Hall, the formal, red-carpeted corridor on the first floor of the White House where he would deliver it live in three hours. Afterward, when Gerson walked up to the podium, Bush rolled up the text and playfully slapped his speechwriter over the head with it. Bush, as is usual in such moments, was loose, even momentarily over the line.

THE PRESIDENT HAD PROMISED to keep the Congress informed and he had two meetings with the leadership scheduled for that evening. Rice and some others, including Cheney and Fleischer, were giving him a pre-briefing in the Oval Office to review who would be attending. It was a normal routine, but little had to be said. They were well aware of the extraordinary dimensions of what was going on. "The hardest part," Bush told them, "was making the decision that force may need to be used." That had been six months earlier when he went to challenge the U.N. on September 12, 2002, declaring that the U.N. had to solve the Saddam problem or he would. "The decision today to use it was not the hardest."

Bush greeted the Senate and House leaders in the Roosevelt Room—House Speaker Dennis Hastert, Democratic leader Nancy Pelosi, and Senate Democratic leader Tom Daschle. Senate Majority Leader Bill Frist came in late.

"We came to the conclusion that it was impossible to do because of the French," Bush explained, referring to the second resolution. "We all agreed it was time to move forward. We did everything we could in the U.N." He described his speech, the 48-hour ultima-tum. "We will remove him from power, which was the law in 1998, which some of you may have voted for," he noted, adding that Sad-dam might take the offer and leave.

"Please say you have intelligence that says that," Pelosi re-marked.

No, Bush said. "We have a lot of intelligence to tell you that he's in complete defiance."

About 6:15 P.M. Bush expanded the meeting to include the for-eign affairs and intelligence committee chairs. "The Iraqi generals are war criminals," he told them and added a new and significant twist. "If Saddam Hussein leaves, we'll go in anyway. That way we can avoid ethnic cleansing. We'll go in in a peaceful way, and there'll be a list of country after country after country all who are solidly with us in this coalition." Going in was important to get the WMD and to deal with the Baath Party leadership.

Bush continued. "Turkey will be with us eventually. Erdogan is learning," he said, referring to Recep Tayyip Erdogan, the new demo-cratically elected prime minister. "We'll win without Turkey. It would be nice to have Turkey. The issue is how to make sure they don't go into northern Iraq."

At 6:26, Bush excused himself to prepare. Cheney and Rice stayed to answer questions.

Bush held a conference call with Homeland Security Secretary Tom Ridge, Powell, Tenet, FBI Director Robert Mueller, Attorney General John Ashcroft and several others to confer on what was being done about domestic terrorist threats. A decision was made to raise the national terror alert by one level to Orange/High in antici-pation of reciprocal attacks on the U.S. in the event of war.

Back in the Roosevelt Room, Senator Warner asked if diplomacy was at an end and if anybody thought Saddam would leave.

"The odds are against it," Cheney said. He noted the 4th In-fantry Division would have been helpful if it had been there weeks ago, if it had been permitted to go in from Turkey, but it had helped pin down the Iraqis, he said, repeating Franks's claim.

Senator Joseph Biden, the senior Democrat on the Foreign Relations Committee, wondered about the future U.N. role.

"I think we'll be greeted as liberators," Cheney said, ducking the question, "but there are scores to be settled. It's a tough neighborhood. We'll provide security."

Rice said they would set up an interim Iraqi authority to govern. "We want to put the administration of Iraq in the hands of Iraqis ASAP."

Cheney said he had talked personally with the Turkish leaders. "In no uncertain terms, we don't want them in." He had delivered that message. "I think they'll behave. We've got to keep a lid on the Kurds too." Even friends were dangerous.

"Israel played no role, is not part of the coalition," Cheney said, "but we are working closely with them on their reaction."

Senator Pat Roberts, Kansas Republican and chairman of the Senate Intelligence Committee, said that he thought 48 hours was a lot of time.

"I can't talk about that type of thing, yet," Cheney said. He said that homeland security was important. Recalling the first Gulf War, when he was secretary of defense, he said that Saddam and his intelligence service had tried to mount attacks in the U.S., but it was almost comical they were so pathetic.

"We don't expect difficulties with Iran," Rice said.

Democratic Senator Robert Byrd of West Virginia then read from prepared remarks, basically opposing Bush and what he was about to do. "I stand four square behind our military. I will support appropriations for our troops. People need to know costs and reconstruction plans, but there are unanswered questions. I don't support a blank check with grandiose plans." He warned of mission creep and threats here at home. Finally he chastised the president and vice president for not engaging enough with the Congress.

WELL BEFORE 8 P.M., Bush was in the Red Room adjacent to the Cross Hall. He was peeved. One TV network had filmed him playing in the backyard of the White House with his dogs, Barney and Spot, throwing a stick to the dogs. He had just been relaxing. The network had been running the footage much of the day.

"Isn't this a violation of the rules?" the president asked Bartlett and Fleischer. Yes, it was. The media, which had unusual access around the White House, was not supposed to film the backyard. The agreement was that it was strictly off-limits. The endless recycling of the footage seemed to be on his mind: the president playing with his dogs, particularly on this of all days. It was a message he didn't want to send.

Gerson was off to the side listening to the conversation. He didn't see any damage. Walking and playing with dogs is what Americans did, but he didn't say anything.

"Gerson," Bush said, defusing things, "you're being too quiet." He walked over to his speechwriter. "Are you nervous?"

"Yes, I am," said Gerson.

Bush told him a story about his father's first televised presidential campaign debate in 1988 with the Democratic nominee, Massachusetts Governor Michael Dukakis. One of my brothers and I were real nervous and just couldn't watch it, he said. So we went to the movies, just because the debate and all that was riding on it was too much. But the movie didn't distract us, he said, and we kept coming out in the lobby and finding a phone to see how the debate was going. We finally left the movie and went home and Dad called and asked, "How'd I do?" Oh, just terrific! we both said.

"One minute," someone called, and the president took a moment to compose himself.

Gerson knew it was the speech that mattered. It contained the heavy lifting. The announcement of military action, expected in several days, would be oddly anticlimactic.

"My fellow citizens," the president intoned at 8:01 P.M., "events in Iraq have now reached the final days of decision." As he began, Bush displayed a slight awkwardness that is not uncommon for this president. But his words and the setting amplified the moment. The nation had grown used to these evening presentations, had seemingly even grown used to him as their president. Gerson thought it was one of Bush's better into-the-camera performances.

Tom Shales, *The Washington Post*'s television critic, later wrote that Bush had a "funereal solemnity and an aura of mournful regret" in the 15-minute speech and "not a trace of bravado."

BUSH BEGAN TUESDAY, March 18, with some diplomatic handholding. He called the new Chinese president, Hu Jintao, at 7:48 A.M. to congratulate him, and assure him that the Iraq situation would not adversely affect U.S.-Chinese relations, and to thank him for China's effort in seeking a peaceful solution to the situation in North Korea.

Later the president spoke with Putin, and described how France's actions had generated significant anti-French sentiment in the U.S. "There's nothing I can do about this. The American people are mad and rightly so. I thank you for not inflaming Russian sentiment against America or personally attacking leaders you disagree with. It helps me with American public opinion toward Russia. It helps keep our relationship strong."

Putin, who had enough troubles of his own, essentially said, boy, I'm not going to do anything like that. If Igor Ivanov, his foreign minister, went to the U.N. it would be only to talk about weapons inspections, Putin said. "Ivanov will not try to score propaganda points."

They agreed that the U.N. should be involved in post-Saddam Iraq, and Putin pushed Bush on whether he would attend the summit scheduled in St. Petersburg, which is Putin's hometown, for the city's 300th anniversary celebration.

"I certainly hope I can make it," Bush said somewhat coyly.

AT THE SENIOR STAFF MEETING that morning two announcements were made: White House tours for the public would be suspended, and medical teams would be on hand for stress management.

In the Oval Office, budget director Mitch Daniels told the president they would need some $73.3 billion in a supplemental appropriation from Congress for fighting the war and boosting homeland security.

"We need a strategy to keep it lean," Bush said, "to keep pet projects off of it."

Rice spoke with her counterpart in Canada, who said, sorry, we can't be a part of this, but promised to keep their rhetoric at a low boil—just enough to satisfy Canadian public opinion but without being belligerent or provocative.

This was Blair's day of reckoning. His one-hour speech in Parliament that day was called one of his most effective and passionate even by some of his leading critics.

"In this dilemma, no choice is perfect, no cause ideal," Blair said. "But on this decision hangs the fate of many things."

At 1:30 P.M. Bush called Blair to say, "Tremendous speech."

"I know now I've got the votes to win the resolution," Blair said, "because the whip counters have been up all night working away. And the only question is the margin, but I'm confident."

They talked about the need to give Russia, France and Germany a way back into the fold.

IN NORTHERN IRAQ came the familiar call, "Pistachio, this is Jonestown!" heralding a report from a principal ROCKSTAR agent, an SSO officer who was running part of the communications links that Saddam used as he moved between palaces and other locations.

The agent had learned that Saddam's communications used a certain cable set and the status board emitted a beep indicating where the Iraqi leader was located. But by the time the location was relayed to CIA headquarters it was usually 45 minutes to an hour old, and Saddam would be gone. Significantly, imagery confirmation often came after the fact the next day, showing the movement of security vehicles.

As Tenet got these reports he realized they were getting close to having a real-time fix on Saddam's location—a longtime goal previously thought impossible.

The principal agent had recruited a ROCKSTAR subsource named Rokan who ran security at Dora Farm, a complex southeast of Baghdad on the bank of the Tigris River that was used by Saddam's wife. Dora Farm had the SSO codeword *Umidza,* meaning "slaughterhouse" or "house of butchery." On March 18, Rokan reported to the principal ROCKSTAR that Saddam was at the "slaughterhouse." Tim asked for more detail and verification. It turned out that Rokan had a Thuraya phone and he could be geo-located on the video display at Jonestown. Rokan was indeed right at the farm where he said he was.

Rokan said he had better get off the phone. The person on watch at Jonestown started screaming. "You will stay on the phone!" It was not a very calm conversation. At another point one of the brothers told Rokan, "Under penalty of death you must be on this phone every two hours." The brothers liked to think of themselves as omnipotent, and when one of the ROCKSTARS didn't call or answer his phone, they took it as a serious personal affront. They didn't want to show weakness in front of Tim and the CIA.

Tim tried to sort out what he had. It was more than promising— the proven SSO source, his associate Rokan and the geographic match at Dora Farm.

Tim sent a report to Saul saying that there was a possibility that Saddam or his family was at Dora Farm or might be coming. In any case, there were definitely communications and other activity that suggested a high-level visit. He could tell at long last that war was close because Jim Pavitt, the head of the agency's clandestine arm, had sent a cable to all stations and bases stating, "In the very near future and absent some unlikely and extraordinary turn of events, our nation will embark on a dangerous mission to disarm Iraq and remove Saddam Hussein from power."

TENET WENT TO THE WHITE HOUSE at 4 P.M. to see the president and Rice. He had been keeping Bush updated on the ROCKSTARS and how they were getting the CIA closer to locating Saddam. Now, he said, several ROCKSTARS were reporting with increasing detail and granularity the possibility that Saddam or his family was at Dora Farm or soon would be. It was more than tantalizing, Tenet said, as the ROCKSTARS increasingly provided new information that cross-checked with locations and other intelligence.

BUSH HAD NEVER paid such close attention to a debate or vote in a foreign legislature as the one going on that day in the British Parliament. "What's the vote count?" he had asked a number of times during the day. Finally at 5:15 P.M.—10:15 P.M. London time—the Parliament voted. Blair won by 396 to 217. Though he had lost a full third of his own party's vote, the Tories voted for war. A second vote on a government-sponsored resolution scored an even wider margin, with fewer Labour dissenters. It looked like Blair and Co. had cleverly played up the expectations of a possible defeat so that victory was even more dramatic.

At 6:15 P.M. former Secretary of State Henry Kissinger, now age 79 and out of office for 25 years, came to see Rice for 15 minutes. He happened to be in town. He restated his view that the longer the waiting went on, the more people would question the resolve to go to war. You can't cock the gun as you have and not pull the trigger, he said. Rice agreed.

PRINCE BANDAR FELT in the dark. He had not been given a heads-up on the ultimatum speech the night before. That was very troubling. Bandar had always found Bush an open man, stating clearly what he felt—black or white, love you or hate you, good or evil. Bush's private statements the previous Friday had been reassuring—"I'm going . . . I'm serious . . . Trust me . . ."—but not definitive. Bandar prided himself in receiving clarity from the top. He had seen too many people, American presidents included, reverse course for reasons that were not appreciated or known in advance. Nothing happened until it happened, and even then Bandar often had doubts. He asked Rice if he might see Bush and went in before 7 P.M. for 11 minutes.

"Mr. President, I just hope you haven't changed your mind," Bandar said to Bush, "now that you have issued the ultimatum."

"Look, Bandar," Bush said, "I cannot tell you much, but I promise, you will be the first one to know"—the first foreign government. "But don't worry. Just have faith in me, trust me."

Bandar was almost frantic. "Look, I trust you, but for God's sake, it's too late now for anybody to back off!"

35

BUSH BEGAN BUSINESS on Wednesday, March 19, at 7:40 A.M. with a 20-minute call to Blair on the secure phone. Both leaders were in high spirits. Bush congratulated Blair on the vote.

"Not only did you win, but public opinion has shifted because you're leading," Bush said, expressing his deep conviction that people and nations will follow in the "slipstream," as he has previously called it, of leaders who take strong stands and define their missions. "That is why the vote happened the way it happened. It's the willingness of someone to lead."

Bush and Blair referred obliquely to the possibility that something might change in the war plan. Even on the secure phone line they talked in code.

The president said, "I heard from my intel people that somebody on the ground, one of our people, had witnessed a guy who spoke out against Saddam and had his tongue cut out and was left to bleed to death in public."

"Jesus," Blair said, "that's awful."

At Bush's intelligence briefing that morning, Tenet said that he might have something really good later on, but he wasn't going to say anything more. He didn't want to raise expectations on the day the president was going to order the war to begin. It was unusual for

Tenet to be so vague, but Bush knew the ROCKSTARS were getting close to Saddam.

Card noticed that Tenet was excited, almost effervescent. Tenet was never undermotivated but this was unusual, Card thought. Very unusual.

Bush and Card lingered over Blair's lopsided victory in Parliament that somewhat mirrored the Senate and House votes that had given war authority to Bush by a wide margin.

The president's mind, however, had already moved downstairs one flight to the Situation Room where he was going to give the go order to Franks and the troops.

A short time later, as he met with the NSC in the Situation Room, Bush asked, "Do you have any last comments, recommendations or thoughts?"

No one did.

Then a secure video link came up with Franks and nine of his senior commanders. It is likely the first time a president was going to speak directly with all his field commanders on the eve of war.

Franks, who was at Prince Sultan Air Base in Saudi Arabia, kicked it off by explaining that he was going to have each commander brief the president.

"Do you have everything you need?" Bush asked the first, Lieutenant General T. Michael "Buzz" Moseley, the Air Force commander who was running the air operations out of Saudi Arabia. "Can you win?"

"My command and control is all up," Moseley said. "I've received and distributed the rules of engagement. I have no issues. I am in place and ready." He was careful not to promise outright victory. "I have everything we need to win."

"I'm ready," said Lieutenant General David D. McKiernan, the Army ground commander. "We are moving into forward attack positions. Our logistics are in place. We have everything we need to win."

Vice Admiral Timothy J. Keating said he had 90 ships of the U.S. Navy plus 59 coalition ships. "Green across the board."

Bush repeated his questions to each of the other commanders. The answers were all affirmative, and got shorter each time.

"The rules of engagement and command and control are in place," Franks said. "The force is ready to go, Mr. President."

In a little set piece that he had prepared, the president said, "For the peace of the world and the benefit and freedom of the Iraqi people, I hereby give the order to execute Operation Iraqi Freedom. May God bless the troops." At this point, the war plan called specifically for 48 hours of stealth operations, and this invisible component would go to a new stage about this time—9 A.M. Eastern, 5 P.M. in Iraq—as the first Special Operations teams crossed the border from Jordan into western Iraq to find and stop any Scud missiles.

"May God bless America," Franks replied.

"We're ready to go," the president said. "Let's win it." He raised his hand in a salute to his commanders, and then abruptly stood and turned before the others could jump up. Tears welled up in his eyes, and in the eyes of some of the others.

The president moved rapidly out of the room, returning to the Oval Office with only Card, who stuck to him like Velcro.

"They're ready," he said to his chief of staff, "and that was just execution."

He went through a door in the Oval Office outdoors for a walk by himself.

Bush later recalled that moment. "It was emotional for me. I prayed as I walked around the circle. I prayed that our troops be safe, be protected by the Almighty, that there be minimal loss of life." He prayed for all who were to go into harm's way and for the country. "Going into this period, I was praying for strength to do the Lord's will. . . . I'm surely not going to justify war based upon God. Understand that. Nevertheless, in my case I pray that I be as good a messenger of His will as possible. And then, of course, I pray for personal strength and for forgiveness."

After his walk, the president made a series of secure phone calls to leaders of coalition countries saying in essence, "We're launching!"

Karl Rove, Dan Bartlett and Ari Fleischer were next in the Oval Office. Card wanted to make sure those who knew didn't say anything or tip off the others in the administration. It was lockdown mode, Card figured, but for those who were in the know, the adrenaline was flowing. He could see it in Bush and feel it in himself. Rove stayed behind, and the president told him he had ordered war.

"PISTACHIO, PISTACHIO, this is Jonestown," came the call to Tim at Kalachualan base in northern Iraq. Jonestown had just received a report from the ROCKSTAR who handled communications for the SSO that added to the intelligence about Dora Farm. Calling in on his Thuraya phone, the source said he had just heard from another ROCKSTAR who had gone down to help with communications at the farm and had noticed a significant security detail. They were stocking food and supplies. It looked like a family gathering. Tim relayed this to Saul at CIA headquarters.

Saul was not disseminating a lot of the ROCKSTAR intelligence because it was not crucial to the military planning, which he thought was basically done. He worried that too much dissemination might compromise the prized network. Sometime after 10:15 A.M. he reviewed the latest overhead imagery of Baghdad. Lo and behold, under the palm trees at Dora Farm were 36 frickin' security vehicles! It was a huge number, it was not for one or two people. The farm was used by Saddam's wife Sajida, and Saul knew that Saddam had used it.

BUSH MET WITH SECRETARY RIDGE and New York City Mayor Michael Bloomberg at about 10:30 A.M.

"We're on the verge of war," the president said, "and since New York City is a potential top target, it's important we visit." He praised the city's efforts at preparedness, but advised the mayor to focus on the main potential targets of the terrorists. "Keep your eye on tunnels, bridges and the Jewish community."

At 11:30 A.M. Washington time, a second Special Forces commando team launched into Iraq, this one from Saudi Arabia.

The president met with top advisers on energy matters at 1:05 P.M. in the Roosevelt Room. The meeting included Cheney, Powell, Rice and Card. The questions focused on the international flow of oil. What additional disruptions could take place in the marketplace? Venezuela, which was in political turmoil, had already drastically cut back production. Should the president use the strategic petroleum reserve?

Bob McNally, an energy expert on the White House staff, reported that crude prices had already fallen from $37 a barrel to $31. That was good news. A rapid increase in price would hike costs for businesses and consumers across the board.

The Saudis had pledged to stabilize the crude oil market by increasing output and putting crude into tankers that were pre-positioned in the Caribbean or heading there.

When they looked at oil worldwide, McNally said, the crude oversupply was 1.5 million to 1.9 million barrels a day. That dramatic oversupply was driving the price down.

Energy Secretary Spence Abraham said the Saudis would cover for any loss of oil from Iraq by upping production to 10.5 million barrels a day for 30 days—an extraordinary pledge. In December, the Saudis had been supplying only 8 million barrels a day, and in February fewer than 9 million.

Secretary of Commerce Don Evans said that about two-thirds of the Iraqi oil fields were located close together, and it was not clear from intelligence how many had been wired to explode.

The president, displaying technical knowledge gained from his earlier oil business career, said that if explosives were rigged on the top of the well, the fire would be relatively easy to extinguish, but if an explosion were set off deep down in the pipes it could take forever to put out those fires. "If they blow up their oil fields it will be more than one month. If they really blow them, it will be years."

• • •

SOMETIME AFTER 12:30 P.M.—8:30 P.M. in Iraq—Tim received a ROCKSTAR report that Rokan had actually seen Saddam, who had left the slaughterhouse about eight hours earlier to attend meetings but would be back to sleep at Dora along with Qusay and Uday. It was 100 percent sure that Saddam "must" be returning. Tim knew that in the context the "must" meant maybe, but he had to report what he had been told. He felt he had no choice when he was referring to the one person they wanted to nail. He dispatched a report to Saul that their principal agent says Rokan has seen Saddam, who is coming back to sleep at the farm. It was a judgment call, but Tim said it is 99 percent certain. Nothing is 100 percent. The whole situation was murky, but these were two-sentence reports, with no room for nuance.

AT 1 P.M. at least 31 teams of Special Operations Forces entered Iraq in the west and north.

"They're on the ground, they're in," Card said in an aside to the president.

"They should be," Bush replied. It was almost too quiet. He and Card were anxious to see if Al-Jazeera or CNN or any news organization had picked up some movement.

At 1:45 the president spoke with Aznar for 20 minutes.

"We have to kind of speak in code," Bush said on the secure line. "Things are changing. You may not see much but it's a difference pace."

Just after 2 P.M. there was still no leak.

Card checked with the Situation Room.

"The Poles are in," he reported to the president. "They've got the platform." A Polish special forces team had gone in early and captured one of the key targets—an oil platform in the south.

Bush spoke briefly with Polish President Kwasniewski.

"The Aussies are in," Card reported. An Australian commando team had moved into the west.

At 3:06 P.M. Bush spoke with Danish Prime Minister Anders

Rasmussen. Rasmussen said that a parliamentary resolution was going through that would enable Denmark to commit a submarine and a naval escort to the war.

"I'm not going to be speaking tonight," the president said, "but you know I'll keep you posted."

TENET, MCLAUGHLIN, Saul and several other CIA operatives had raced over to the Pentagon with Tim's intelligence report and satellite photos.

Rumsfeld had been following the ROCKSTAR intelligence and felt it merited the attention of the president. The odds were that the group was not being duplicitous; people were putting their lives at risk. But like most intelligence, it was imperfect. Rumsfeld talked with Franks, who thought Dora Farm was a good target, and the secretary asked that he make sure they were ready to attack it.

About 3:15 P.M. Rumsfeld called Card. "We've got some developments, and I want to come over and talk about them."

Card passed Rumsfeld's request to the president, who phoned Rice. "Don Rumsfeld just called," Bush reported, "and he wants to come over with George Tenet. Says it's something major that they want to talk about, and he's coming over. Get down here."

Tenet phoned Steve Hadley. "I'm coming," the DCI said cryptically, "I'm not going to say a word on the phone. I want to do it with Don in the presence of the president. Nothing before that."

Rumsfeld, McLaughlin, Tenet, Saul and two other CIA men arrived in the Oval Office and went into the president's dining room.

"We've got two guys close to Saddam," Tenet said. He quickly summarized about the security guy, Rokan, at Dora, and then the other ROCKSTARS who had gone down to help with communications. Tenet produced satellite photos that showed the location of the farm near Baghdad at a bend in the Tigris River. There were several houses on the farm. "Saddam and the two boys have been here, and might come back if they're still not there." The CIA was in direct communication with both sources.

Bush questioned them about the sources. Who were they? How good were they?

Saul explained that a key to the ROCKSTAR network was the SSO officer in communications who worked with the two eyes-on sources at Dora. The SSO man's contacts and recruits into the network had turned out to be very good. In terms of Iraqi sources we are running, Saul told the president, we judge him to be one of the better, more reliable sources. He had been one of the first ROCKSTARS to come to Kalachualan base. They had been running him for months and a lot of his reporting had been confirmed, especially through SIGINT.

"This is really good," the president said. "This sounds good."

"Well," Saul said, "we'll never get 100 percent confidence but the organization has proven reliable." At this point, they had one source, Rokan, on the specifics of Saddam being there or about to return. "Right now," Saul said, "it's about 75 percent certain."

A decapitation strike on the top regime leaders now appeared possible. They contemplated the impact of taking out Saddam and his sons. Who would make the decisions inside Iraq? Everyone was so used to directions from the highest level. The best-case scenario was that it might even break the regime, make war unnecessary. That was unlikely but possible.

What kind of weapons would you use? the president asked.

General Myers, who had joined the group, said Tomahawk cruise missiles, and he proposed a strike package of 15 to 17.

Bush was skeptical. He asked, Who is in which building? Where would Saddam stay? Do the sons have kids? Where is the wife? Is Saddam with his wife? Are we sure it is not just where he put all of the kids to stay?

IN NORTHERN IRAQ, Tim threw a blazer over his long underwear and put on his muddy boots. It was the ritual of respectability with the Kurds. No matter how grubby, the brothers up at Jonestown would be in coat and tie. He hopped in his Cherokee and drove himself up the treacherous three miles from Pistachio to Jonestown to be on the scene where the ROCKSTAR reports were coming in. It was snowy and he worried about rolling the Jeep, but he raced to the top. The atmosphere at Jonestown was frantic with the brothers screaming, "Don't hang up! Stay on, stay on the phone! Don't hang up!" Click. Tim decided the best thing to do was scream back at the brothers.

"The fate of your nation hangs on you," Tim yelled, "and I'm going to pull it all away from you and if you let me down now, you're not going to get the seat at the table."

The principal source phoned in a report cobbled together from what his two subsources at Dora Farm were telling him: Uday and Qusay were at the farm for sure, and Saddam was expected back at about 2:30 A.M. or 3 A.M. Iraqi time. The sources on the scene also reported details about the houses. Additionally there was a *manzul* on the compound, the report said. *Manzul* could be translated as "place of refuge" or "bunker." Tim chose bunker. The report provided some details about the "bunker"—distances from the main houses, and its thickness in so many meters of concrete under so many meters of earth. Tim frantically took this and sent back to CIA headquarters a flash message summarizing the information.

The president had more questions. "Is it going to disrupt Tommy's plan?" he asked. They had spent over a year on that plan. What would be the impact? Would it blow the whole element of surprise? The Special Operations Forces that had gone in already were supposed to be covert. Would this expose them? "Go ask Tommy," he directed Rumsfeld.

General Myers eventually reached Franks.

"What do you think about taking a shot at this Dora Farm target?" Myers asked.

Franks had been watching the time-sensitive targets carefully and he had known the night before that the CIA had been getting closer to Saddam, perhaps at Dora Farm. It looked like a target for a Tomahawk cruise missile and Franks had ordered the Navy to program some missiles on the target. "Let the lads work it all night," he had said, and then told them they were not going to shoot. It was still during the 48-hour ultimatum period the president had given Saddam and his sons to leave. Franks felt pretty strongly, and had counseled Rumsfeld, that they not take a shot during that period. It was a kind of grace period. Franks considered it the higher moral ground not to take a shot at someone who might, improbable as that was, be leaving out the back door.

Can you do it in two hours? Myers next asked.

Franks said they could. The Tomahawks were ready to go.

SOMETIME AFTER 4 P.M.—now past midnight in Iraq—the latest ROCKSTAR report arrived in the Situation Room and was taken immediately to the Oval Office.

"They say they're with him right now! Both of the sons are there," Tenet said. Their wives were there. The families were there also. Saddam was expected back at 2:30 to 3 A.M.—in less than two hours. There was a bunker and one of the ROCKSTARS had paced off where it was, had gone inside and taken rough measurements.

Hadley asked Saul, "Can you show me where the bunker is?" Saul wasn't sure, but they took the overhead photos and Hadley tried to draw a sketch. McLaughlin was soon doing an improved amateur engineer drawing.

Powell was the only principal missing, and at about 5:15 the president told Rice, "You better call Colin."

"Colin, get to the White House!" she said, reaching Powell at the State Department. She was abrupt and offered no explanation. When Powell arrived in a matter of minutes, they summarized for him. He tried to hang back because it was primarily a military matter. Soon he was going through the pros and cons—collateral damage, failure to hit Saddam. "If we've got a chance to decapitate them, it's worth it," he finally said.

Rumsfeld strongly recommended a strike, and Cheney agreed though he seemed to be holding back.

Bush filled the time with questions, at one point asking, Were they really sure what they were looking at was what they thought they were looking at?

"It's as good as it gets," Tenet said. "I can't give you 100 percent assurance, but this is as good as it gets."

Bush was still worrying about the women and children. This could be a kind of baby milk factory, he said, recalling an incident from the 1991 Gulf War when the Iraqis had claimed a suspected biological weapons plant that was bombed was really for the production of baby milk. "They would bring out dead women and children," Bush said, "and the first pictures would be of civilian casualties on a massive scale of some kind." Could Iraq use this as a public relations exercise? he asked. It could engender sympathy for Saddam. Dead babies, children and women would be a nightmare. That sure would get things off on the wrong foot.

Rumsfeld and Myers said it probably didn't matter what they hit in the first strike because the Iraqi propaganda machine was going to say that the United States killed a number of women and children anyway. And if necessary the Iraqis would execute women and children and say the United States did it.

That was indeed the downside. But the others—Cheney, Rumsfeld, Tenet, even Powell—seemed taken with the upside, a shortcut to victory.

Myers raised a serious problem. If there was a bunker at the Dora compound as they now suspected, the cruise missiles would not penetrate. They would need the bunker-busting 2,000-pound bombs to get that deep. Myers was sent off to talk to Franks.

FOR A MOMENT, the group weighed the downsides. They had promised to defend Israel, and the full defense of Israel was not ready. What were the other consequences? Suppose the Iraqis used a strike as a pretext to set the oil wells ablaze? Suppose they fired Scud missiles into Israel or Saudi Arabia? The consequences of an early attack were immense. The plan called for the air campaign to begin in two days.

At about 5:40, Cheney came out for a break and summoned Libby. The vice president explained what had come in. "It seems like pretty good intelligence, but like all intelligence, it could be a setup," Cheney said. "But there is not enough time to make a full judgment."

Libby went back into the Oval Office with Cheney.

Bush went around the room and asked, Would you do it?

"I would do it, Mr. President," Card said. It was too good a chance not to take. Rumsfeld too was strongly in favor.

Powell thought it was a hell of a lot of very specific information that seemed not bad, though it was a little curious that the CIA sources on the other end of the satellite phones could have acquired so much.

"If we've got a chance to decapitate them, it's worth it," Powell recommended again.

Rice and Hadley had some more questions about the sources, but both favored an attack.

MYERS REACHED FRANKS on a secure phone. Could he load up a stealth fighter with a pair of EGBU-27 bombs, the bunker busters, for the attack?

"Absolutely not," Franks said. "We don't have the F-117 ready to go." The F-117A Nighthawk, the stealth single-seat fighter jets, typically carried two of the bombs when fully loaded.

Franks checked further. The Air Force had been following the intelligence and the night before had readied one F-117. The Air Force squadron in Qatar had that day received word that the bombs could be dropped in pairs safely, though it had never been tried before.

Franks asked what the probability was of a single F-117 getting through and delivering its pair of bombs? Though stealthy and radar-evading, the F-117 would have to go in prior to the suppression of Iraqi air defense, weak as that was. The plane would be going in cold. The answer came back that the Air Force could only say there was a 50 percent chance of success.

Prepare two bombers, Franks ordered, figuring that would improve the chances.

In Qatar, the Air Force squadron was able to load a second F-117.

Franks sent word to the Oval Office that it would be possible, but he needed a final decision to go by about 7:15 P.M. in order to get the F-117s in and out of Iraqi airspace well before dawn.

RUMSFELD, MYERS AND CIA men were running in and out of the Oval Office to find secure phones at West Wing locations. Card was concerned that the window of opportunity was closing. Did they really understand the intelligence? Was it necessary to change the weapons? Myers was trying to find out how long it would take the F-117s to be loaded, take off, then fly from Doha to Baghdad and back. How many tankers do they have to have to refuel the planes?

"Where is the sun?" someone asked. When would the sun be coming up in Iraq?

Another question arose. If it was approved, should the president go on television that night and make his speech announcing the beginning of the war—a speech now scheduled for Friday?

"Look, this is an ongoing operation," Cheney said. "We didn't announce that the Special Forces were going in. We didn't announce the Poles were taking over the platform. We didn't announce the Australians were heading toward the dam. We don't have to announce it yet. You don't announce it until you are ready to announce it."

Rumsfeld seemed to half agree. "If someone should go, maybe it should be me," he said, but he then added, indicating Bush, "Or maybe it could be you."

Powell raised the CNN effect. The attack would be seen *instantly*. Reporters stationed at the Rashid Hotel in Baghdad were close enough possibly to see it or hear it. Dozens of cruise missiles and bunker buster bombs. The press was spring-loaded to proclaim, "It started! It started!" Antiaircraft fire and tracers would be flying all around. The war was going to begin with this event.

"If lives are in jeopardy," the president said, "I've got to go announce it."

Cheney reminded him that lives were already in danger and there had been no announcement.

Should I wait until the next morning? the president asked. That would give Franks another 12 hours before any announcement.

Bush called in Karen Hughes and Dan Bartlett to the Oval Office. He told Saul to sum up the intelligence.

Then, the president said he was probably going to order the attack. "How do we do this?" he asked Hughes and Bartlett. "Do I go on television?" Should he inform the public before, during or after? Should the secretary of defense do it? Everyone turned to Hughes. They knew how much Bush relied on her.

"No, you need to do it, Mr. President," she said. "The American people shouldn't hear it from the press, they shouldn't hear it from somebody else. They should hear it from you. And you should tell them what and why." If they hit civilians or women and children, the president had to be ahead of the curve. She added her trademark observation, "We can't sort of be catching up."

Bartlett agreed with Hughes, but Cheney still had reservations. What would this mean for Israel, Turkey, Saudi Arabia? Do we have our defenses ready for Israel? We promised Israel we would defend them. Tommy's plan has a defense, but the plan wasn't fully implemented yet.

Powell could not understand that they would start a war and not get out front with a presidential announcement.

"I promised people I'd let them know when the war begins," Bush said. "And if lives—the war is beginning tonight, lives will be in jeopardy, I have to tell the American people that I've committed American forces to war."

Cheney didn't seem happy.

"They have to hear it from me," Bush said. "I'm doing it." This would be starting the war, he said. "Let's not kid ourselves."

At about 6 P.M. Card called Gerson. "Is it ready?" Card asked. There was only one speech left to give.

"In about five minutes I can have it ready," Gerson said.

"I want you to meet me outside the Oval Office at 6:30 with several copies of the speech."

Gerson went down to the Oval Office and sat in one of the two chairs outside.

Card soon emerged. "We'll be with you soon enough. Just wait," he told him. Card took the copies of the speech, leaving Gerson to cool his heels. Obviously something was up but Gerson had no idea what. Tenet and his people were running in and out making secure calls.

Inside the Oval Office, the president went around the room again, asking if all the principals agreed, almost pushing each to the wall. They did.

Bush turned to Saul. "Well, what do you think?"

Saul's head was spinning. He had never been involved in a discussion like this, let alone been asked his opinion. He was worried about the pilots of the F-117s. His intelligence was now going to put American lives directly at risk. The planes would be going in with no electronic countermeasures, no fighter escort, no advance suppression of Iraqi air defense. "I have to apologize that we have to present you with this very tough decision," Saul said to the president. "I really feel sorry for you having to make it."

"Don't," Bush said. "That's what I do. I'll make the decision."

"Well, sir," Saul said, "then I would say launch."

THE PRESIDENT KICKED everyone out of the Oval Office but Cheney.

What do you think, Dick?

"This is the best intelligence we've had yet on where Saddam's located," Cheney replied. "If we get him, it may save a lot of lives and shorten the war. And even if we don't, we're going to rattle his cage pretty seriously, and maybe disrupt the chain of command. That's well worth the effort in and of itself." Now he was unequivocal. "I think we ought to go for it."

The others came back in. Finally, at 7:12 P.M., the president said, "Let's go." It was three minutes before Franks's deadline.

Powell noted silently that things didn't really get decided until the president had met with Cheney alone.

Myers went to the secure phone to inform Franks.

RUMSFELD EMERGED and said to Gerson, "I was just butchering your speech."

The president called out, "Gerson, come on in." Hughes and Bartlett were standing there.

"We're going after them," Bush explained.

"I don't understand," Gerson said.

"The intelligence is good," Bush replied, explaining that it showed they had a shot at Saddam and his sons. "Let's hope we're right," he added, choking up.

Rumsfeld's "butchery" of the speech was simple. He wanted the president to say that this was the "early stages" of military operations, and again in the second paragraph refer to the "opening stages" of war.

"I want to see you over in the residence when you're ready," Bush said to Gerson and Hughes, directing that the changes be made.

The two went up to Gerson's second floor office and made the changes in a few minutes. Gerson was glad they were going to restore a line that had been cut from Monday's ultimatum speech. Referring to Saddam and his alleged weapons of mass destruction, the line now read: "We meet that threat now, with our Army, Air Force, Navy, Coast Guard and Marines, so that we do not have to meet it later with armies of firefighters and police and doctors on the streets of our cities." Gerson felt it was the most vivid way to put it. The implication of avoiding another 9/11 would be clear.

Rumsfeld read the speech word-for-word to Franks over a secure phone to make sure he had no objections or suggestions. He had none.

Rice placed a quick call at 7:30 P.M. to Benjamin Netanyahu, the Israeli finance minister, about another matter. He said he already knew about the war and wished it would be fast and "bloodless."

She woke up Manning, the British national security adviser.

"David, there's a little change in plans. And I'm sorry to say this, but I think you better wake the prime minister and tell him."

BUSH WENT TO THE RESIDENCE. Card sat with him in the Yellow Room. Are you comfortable? the chief of staff asked. Are you ready to give the speech? He wanted to separate the two—the decision to go after Saddam and the speech.

Yes, the president said, he was ready on both counts. Though he had asked all in the war cabinet, including Card, if they would do this, and each had said yes, he asked again. "You would do this?"

"Yes," Card said, "this is the right thing to do. Absolutely. Take this chance."

How long have the F-117s been up? the president asked. When do they get there?

The next report said they were in Iraqi airspace. There would be no more preliminary reports because they would be on radio silence over Iraq.

HUGHES, BARTLETT AND GERSON went over to the residence. Unsure if the president wanted to see them or just receive the speech, they asked the usher to check. If Bush was having dinner, they did not want to interrupt. The usher soon came back and escorted them up to the Treaty Room, Bush's private office. Gerson thought Bush was subdued and a little pale. For the first time he looked to Gerson a little bit burdened by all of this. The president took the speech and began to read it aloud: "My fellow citizens, *at this hour* . . .

"American and coalition forces are in the early stages of military operations to disarm Iraq, to free its people and to defend the world from grave danger."

He read through the 10 paragraphs and said it was fine. He had no changes. He walked them to the elevator.

Quietly, as if to reassure himself, Bush said again, "The intelligence is good."

RICE CALLED PRINCE BANDAR. "Can I see you at 7:45?" she asked.

"Condi," Bandar said, "we have to stop meeting like this—this hour. People will talk."

Normally any meeting after 6:30 P.M. was a kind of codeword, meaning that Bandar would be seeing the president. And 7:45 was really late, about an hour before Bush normally went to bed. Bandar had booked an entire small Arabian restaurant in Georgetown that night to dine with his wife, family and some friends. He told his wife to go ahead. He arrived in the West Wing lobby and noticed a photographer. Odd. When he was finally ushered in at 8:28 P.M., Rice stepped to her outer office to greet him. Flash!

Bandar jumped, saying, "I hope he works for you."

"Yes, yes, don't worry."

They were about to sit down as the photographer snapped again, and when they sat a third time.

"The president has . . ." Rice began.

". . . asked me to tell you," Bandar interrupted, completing her sentence, "that we are going to war."

It was obvious—the expiration of the ultimatum and the photographer. "I've been meeting you in this office for two years and I've never had a photographer in here. I'm not retiring to take goodbye photos. You're not retiring. Have you told anybody else foreign other than me?"

No, Rice said, though the Israelis already knew.

"Then that photo is important to me," Bandar said. "In the record I am the first foreigner to be told."

About 9 P.M. hell will break loose, Rice said. "And your friend, the president, insisted that you be informed immediately."

"Tell him the next time I see him . . ." Bandar began, but some

20 years in Washington kicked in—deep suspicion. "Next time I see him, *if* the war has started, I will be shaved." Both laughed.

But the levity lasted for only a moment. Bandar believed that he could sense a weight in the air. Rice, direct and usually jovial, had a look that almost said: Hold your breath, off we go, nobody knows what is going to happen in about 45 minutes, how the world will change, good or bad.

"Where is the president now?" Bandar asked.

"He is having dinner right now with the first lady and then he decided he wants to be alone."

"Tell him he will be in our prayers and hearts," Bandar said. "God help us all."

Rice's phone rang at 8:29 P.M.

"Yes, yes, Mr. President," she said. "No, I told him . . . He's here . . . Yes, he is with me. I told him. Well, he said you're in his prayers."

"He said thank you," Rice reported after hanging up. "Just keep praying."

Bandar, who thrives on his access to the American president, rationalized that if Bush had said, "Come on over," or if he had chatted on the phone, the moment could not really have been as heavy as Bandar thought. Had the whole truth hit Bush? It didn't matter who did what to whom. Bush was responsible whether it was massacre, defeat, humiliation—or glory. Only the owner of the decision could describe it. So Bandar excused himself and left. The walk from the West Wing to his car outside seemed 1,000 miles. Cool air hit his face and he suddenly began to sweat, then there was a little shiver.

How different it was from the 1991 Gulf War. This time they were telling Saddam they were after his head. Under the rules of mortal combat, Bandar judged that if Saddam were worth anything, chemical, biological whatever would be flying within an hour—on Israel, on Jordan, on Saudi Arabia, on anyone. He would surely use them. His chest almost collapsed. He was very happy to have finally finished the bastard, and yet there was a sense of history turning into something they could not imagine or foresee. He got into his car and told them to take him home. Calling his home, he issued orders,

"Anybody who is in the restaurant come on back home. Anyone who is at home, don't leave. Anyone who is on the road, turn around, call the house and meet me there."

He had arranged a code to alert Crown Prince Abdullah if he learned early, a reference to the Roda—an oasis outside Riyadh.

"Tonight the forecast is there will be heavy rain in the Roda," Bandar said from his car phone to Saudi Arabia.

"Oh, I see," said the crown prince. "I see. Are you sure?"

"I am very sure," he replied, adding that the Americans had great capabilities, satellites and so forth, to predict the weather.

"Tell me again."

Bandar repeated.

The crown prince took a deep breath. "May God decide what is good for all of us." Then he asked loudly, "Do you know how soon the storm is going to hit?"

"Sir," Bandar said, potentially blowing operational security if any foreign embassy or anyone else with the capability was listening in, "I don't know, but watch TV."

"IT'S BEEN A VERY LONG DAY," the president recalled of that day. "I get upstairs, and I can't sleep. Because I've got about an hour and a half now." He didn't want to speak until the bombers were off their targets. "I was trying to take a little nap." Once more, he called Rice.

No news.

He tried to sleep or read or find something to do and couldn't so he called Rice again.

"Mr. President, we've just got a report from the person on the ground. A convoy has pulled into the complex."

"Is that convoy full of kids?" Bush asked. It hit him that there was no turning back now. The bombers were going in first, followed immediately by 36 cruise missiles. They had doubled the Tomahawk attack package. The Tomahawk cruise missiles, which had been launched to the Dora Farm target more than an hour earlier, had no self-destruct mechanism so they were going in no matter what.

"No," Rice replied, "he thinks that it looks like the kind of convoy that would bring Saddam Hussein."

About an hour later, the president came down to the Oval Office and did a read-through. He was wearing his game face now, Gerson was glad to see. The transformation from the burdened man was pretty amazing. After the dry run, Bush went to his study off the Oval Office.

FLEISCHER WAS HANGING around knowing that the extraordinarily long meeting meant something, especially with all the running around by the principals and the presence of even a few unfamiliar faces. He had never seen so many phones in the Situation Room. So he was going to be careful. Normally at the end of the day he would put a so-called lid on, telling the White House reporters that there would be no more news that night.

Finally, Card took Fleischer into his corner office.

It's going to start tonight, Card said. These are the early stages. We have a target of opportunity and are sending a stealth fighter to go after it.

"Are we sending anything else in?"

"I told you everything you need to know," Card replied. The attack would be south of Baghdad. Iraqi antiaircraft batteries would soon be going off.

Rice, Card, Bartlett and Fleischer gathered around the TV in Rice's office. At 9:30 reports came that air raid sirens had gone off in Baghdad. Antiaircraft fire soon followed.

"Go out," Rice told Fleischer.

Fleischer was at the podium at 9:45: "The opening stages of the disarmament of the Iraqi regime have begun. The president will address the nation at 10:15."

MYERS REPORTED TO HADLEY that the F-117s had successfully dropped their bombs, but the pilots were not yet out of hostile territory. Hadley went to the study off the Oval Office where the president was getting his makeup, and relayed the report to Bush and Rice.

"Let's pray for the pilots," Bush said.

At 10:16, the president appeared on television, the stock flags and family photos in the background. He said the "early stages" of the military campaign against Saddam had begun, without offering any details. "More than 35 countries are giving crucial support," he said. "A campaign on the harsh terrain of a nation as large as California could be longer and more difficult than some predict." It was a time of "grave danger" and "peril."

"Our forces will be coming home as soon as their work is done," he said. "This will not be a campaign of half-measures."

When he was done, he asked Rice how the speech had gone. One of the better ones, she told him.

Hadley called Myers, who reported at about 11 P.M. that the pilots were out of hostile airspace and on the approach to land. Rice called the president.

"The pilots are out of harm's way," she said.

"Well, thank God for that."

BEFORE 8 A.M. local time in northern Iraq, midnight in Washington, Tim sent a report saying that the principal ROCKSTAR reported that Saddam and his two sons were at Dora Farm when the bombs and missiles hit, but he did not know their status. Tim did not want to report again until he was pretty sure they had gotten Saddam. About noon—before dawn in Washington—he sent another cable. Again he had to report what the ROCKSTARS said, but he was uncertain because he was just getting snatches from ROCKSTARS fleeing the scene. Rokan, their source, had been killed by a cruise missile. One of Saddam's sons, it was unclear which, had come out shouting "We've been betrayed" and shot another of the ROCKSTARS in the knee. The other son had emerged from the rubble bloody and disoriented but it wasn't clear whether it was his blood or someone else's.

Saddam had been injured, according to a ROCKSTAR eyewitness, and had to be dug out of the rubble. He was blue. He was gray. He was being given oxygen. He had been put on a stretcher and loaded into the back of an ambulance, which then did not move for half an hour before departing the farm across a bridge.

Around 4:30 A.M. Tenet called the Situation Room and told the duty officer, "Tell the president we got the son of a bitch."

They didn't wake the president. And by the time Bush arrived at the Oval Office about 6:30 A.M., Thursday, March 20, they weren't so sure. It looked as if Saddam might have survived.

At 11 A.M. Bush called Blair. "Thank you for understanding that plans change," Bush said. "My opinion is that if the military comes with an option and highly recommended it, then everybody adjusts to the plan. And that's what happened."

Blair was in an expansive mood. He had led his reluctant nation to war, and the immediate prospects looked quite good. "I kind of think that the decisions taken in the next few weeks will determine the rest of the world for years to come," Blair said. "As primary players, we have a chance to shape the issues that are discussed. Both of us will have enormous capital and a lot of people will be with us."

EPILOGUE

ON MARCH 20, the first full day of the war, General Franks reported that Special Forces were in partial control of the vast western desert area—25 percent of Iraq's territory, which enabled them to prevent Scud missile firings—as well as the southern oil fields. A total of 241,516 U.S. military personnel were in the region, joined by some 41,000 from the U.K., 2,000 from Australia and 200 from Poland. The ground force, U.S. and coalition, numbered 183,000, most of it poised to move north from Kuwait into Iraq, and then the 250 miles to Baghdad.

During the nearly 16 months of war planning, Franks had continuously shrunk the period of air operations that would be conducted before ground forces invaded. The Hybrid Plan had initially called for 16 days of bombing before the invasion, based on the traditional view that U.S. air superiority should soften up and destroy as much of the enemy as possible before a land assault. Franks had whittled down the air-only phase to five days, then to his current plan of just nine hours of "shock and awe" bombing and missile strikes—beginning at 1 P.M. Washington time on Friday, March 21—before the major ground incursion that was scheduled for 10 P.M. Friday night.

This was possible because Franks had good intelligence on where all the Iraqi tactical formations were located. Satellite and other overhead photography, communications intercepts and human intelligence coming from CIA sources such as the ROCKSTARS showed them that Saddam had not positioned his forces to counter a ground assault. Incredibly, given the publicity about the force buildup, Franks had come to realize that it was still possible to achieve significant tactical surprise.

There were two other factors at play. Franks had learned that Saddam had moved some howitzers and tanks into the oil fields. It was a strategic imperative that the U.S. fully secure those oil fields. Second, the president had already started the visible part of the war with the strike on Dora Farm.

Franks now proposed an even more radical change—to push the start of the ground war up by 24 hours, ahead of the air war. He was prepared to commence the ground attack at 10 P.M. Thursday, as dawn broke in Iraq. "Just as if someone had given me a vision, I had put my ground forces on a 24-hour alert to be able to go first," he said. The air campaign would begin as scheduled at 1 P.M. Friday, after nightfall in Baghdad.

Rumsfeld approved. He had been pushing to make the ground and air campaigns more concurrent. The president was informed but he considered it a tactical decision that Rumsfeld and Franks, not he, should make.

Wolfowitz was delighted, thinking this would counter the image of American war making in the Middle East as one of massive bombing campaigns, with its inevitable collateral damage, to make it easier for American ground troops. Why begin with an ugly air campaign if you could achieve a strategic success, he reasoned.

At 5 P.M. Thursday, Cheney and Libby went to see Bush in the residence. Rice and Card were there. Rumsfeld gave an upbeat summary of the plan over the speakerphone. Cheney said it was vital that the United States be seen as strong now, and he raised an earlier discussion he and Libby had had about the importance of winning decisively. World War I, he said, had been settled with an armistice and some Germans felt they had not been beaten. In this war, it was crucial they make certain there would be no ambiguity about victory.

• • •

AT 6 A.M. Iraq time on Friday, March 21, the 1st Marine Division crossed the Kuwait-Iraq border, followed shortly by the Army's 3rd Infantry Division. The ground assault pushed some 60 miles into Iraq. Resistance was light. The first casualties were four American and eight British troops who were killed in a helicopter crash.

The president had no key decisions to make that day, and he spent most of his time being briefed and talking to coalition leaders. He told Blair, "I would say we have 40 percent of the country easily and 85 percent of the oil fields, and those are two unbelievable accomplishments for day one." In a call with Aznar, Bush recounted how he had given the order for war in a video teleconference with Franks and the commanders two days earlier.

"Never feel alone at moments like that," Aznar said. "You know there are many of us who are with you."

"I understand that completely," Bush said.

"Every time that you sit down remember that we are with you. You can always see a mustache next to you," said the mustached Spanish leader.

ON SATURDAY, March 22, Franks updated the president and the war cabinet at Camp David via video teleconference. He said the lead column of the 3rd Infantry Division was now 150 miles into Iraq. In a later call to Blair, the president reported, "The body language of Tommy and all the commanders is pretty positive. They are pleased with the progress, pleased that no WMD has been shot at us, and we are looking and we'll find the stuff." There were some defections of Iraqi military but not mass surrenders so far, Bush said, and the U.S. wasn't taking prisoners of war. "Thousands are just taking off their uniforms and going home."

"Yes, they are just melting away," Blair said.

"Just melting away," Bush echoed.

• • •

AT HIS SPRAWLING, high-tech headquarters in Doha, Qatar, Franks monitored battlefield progress on a large plasma screen that depicted both the red-colored enemy forces and his blue-colored forces in a real-time visual representation. This Blue Force Tracker included indicators for small, medium and large blue coalition units. Several days into the war, as his ground forces were moving toward Baghdad, all the blue tracking designators seemed suddenly to merge into what looked like a giant blue blob or massive concentration. To Franks that represented an ideal target for a biological or chemical weapons attack by Saddam.

"We've got a fucking disaster on our hands," Franks exploded. "It's got to be fixed or I'll relieve everyone!"

A WMD attack would be what Franks termed a "strategic dislocator," halting his drive to Baghdad. "We have to disperse this fucking formation as quickly as we can because we are presenting a target of opportunity to the enemy at exactly the wrong time." One helicopter from Iraq's meager air force with a gallon of chemicals or biologicals could stop them cold. "I want every plane and helicopter destroyed on the ground immediately!" he ordered. He soon calmed down when he realized that the blue forces were not as close together as the plasma screen had seemed to indicate.

ON MONDAY MORNING, March 24, Putin called Bush. "This is going to be awfully difficult for you," the Russian president said. "I feel bad for you. I feel bad."

"Why?" Bush asked.

"Because there's going to be enormous human suffering," Putin said.

"No," Bush said, "we've got a good plan. But thank you for your concern."

As they talked, Bush realized that Putin, who was engaged in a bloody war with Chechen rebels, was expressing concern about the personal toll on him.

"Well, thanks for calling," Bush finally said. "You're awfully kind to do that."

He later recalled, "It was a genuine call. It wasn't a told-you-so. It was a friendship call. And I appreciated it." He added, "That's the only call I got along those lines, by the way."

Rice thought the call was odd, and a day or so later she gave Bush an article by a retired Russian general who had visited Baghdad and written that of course Bush would win the war, but to do so he would have to carpet-bomb Baghdad.

The president recalled that he was distressed that it was not understood that the United States had found a way to wage war that as much as possible spared civilians, avoided collateral damage and targeted the leaders and their means to fight and maintain power. Wars of annihilation, carpet-bombing and fire-bombing cities should be a thing of the past, he believed.

OVER THE NEXT WEEK, U.S. and British forces met with resistance from unconventional militias such as the Fedayeen Saddam commanded by Saddam's son Uday. Foul weather and sandstorms also slowed progress. Some generals, including the senior U.S. Army ground commander, Lieutenant General William S. Wallace, made remarks suggesting that the war would be longer, perhaps even take months. It became a dark period for Bush and the team with the Army stalled, dozens of Americans killed, some taken prisoner and the news coverage negative.

In a meeting with a group of veterans in the Roosevelt Room on Friday, March 28, the president said, "I'm not paying attention to the press. It looks like—I don't know what it looks like. I get my information from Tommy Franks." He added, "The important thing is to win the peace. I don't expect Thomas Jefferson to come out of this, but I believe people will be free."

The next day, meeting with the NSC, Bush touched again on these themes. "Only one thing matters: winning. There's a lot of

second-guessing regarding the post-Saddam world. Our job is to
speak to the American people, tell them how proud we are of the soldiers; to the world, to tell them that we will accomplish this mission;
to our European allies, thanks for your help; the Iraqi people, we will
be coming to liberate the entire country." He added, "Don't worry
about the carping and second-guessing. Rise above it, be confident,
remember your constituencies."

"We can't let the press get us to comment on every battlefield
development," Powell said. "Stay focused on the big picture."

"It's not a matter of timetable," Bush repeated, "it's a matter of
victory."

ON WEDNESDAY, April 2, Rumsfeld reported to the NSC, "We've got
116,000 men in Iraq, 310,000 men in the theater." Some 55 percent
of the bombing that day would be directed at three key divisions of
the Republican Guard, Saddam's loyal main fighting force. Half the
Tomahawk cruise missile inventory had been shot. The lead elements of the 3rd Infantry were 10 miles from Baghdad and U.S.
forces had opened a small second front with paratroopers in northern Iraq. CENTCOM reported to the president that two Republican
Guard divisions were now combat-ineffective.

Bush spoke again to Aznar. "We are losing one part of the war
and this is propaganda," he said. Iraq was using mobile vans to keep
state TV on the air, though Bush told him they were being found and
destroyed. The president had become a kind of morale officer to the
world leaders and recounted to Aznar a recent conversation with
Franks. "I said, Tommy, do you have everything you need? And he
said, Yes, Mr. President. And I said, Tommy, how do you feel? And he
said we are on the way to victory. I know Tommy very well. We are
from the same part of Texas. I know when he is telling me the truth
and when he is putting some Texas B.S. on me, and in this case he's
telling the truth."

Bush told Australia's John Howard that after a week of bad
press things were looking up. "I think everybody has a nice little

bounce in their step these days. There's a kind of sine curve to this operation. We had initial euphoria and then the guessing stage and now back up to the working stage. It is a predictable pattern, but now we are on top of the wave. The way I would describe the psychology inside Iraq is that Saddam has his fingers around the throat of the Iraqi people and he has two of his fingers left and we are prying them loose."

He went on, "Every speech I give I remind them of the atrocities of the regime just to make the point that they act like terrorists. The lawyers are saying that we should not say it because of the connotation." He was not supposed to prejudge people who might eventually be tried as war criminals. "I can say it is terrorist-like activity," he said and added, "Lawyers, they're dreadful."

THE MORNING OF WEDNESDAY, April 9, Franks gave the president and the NSC an update by secure video. "Had a good week. The troops are focused, the morale is good, the locals are remarkable," he said. City by city he listed the current situation: In the south, all the enemy formations are destroyed. Basra, there's occasional sniper fire. In Nasiriyah, local leaders are emerging. In the central region, we've destroyed 90 percent of the equipment of the Iraqi forces. In the north, the regular army is fixed and battered, at only 50 to 60 percent strength.

What was striking were the omissions—there was no talk of Fortress Baghdad, no refugee crisis and no use of chemical or biological weapons.

At one point Franks said, "There are 30,000 Iraqi casualties estimated."

Rumsfeld had been trying to make sure they did not provide numbers. He later recalled, "I remember leaping in and suggesting that that person probably really doesn't know that number and that my impression would be that it would not be helpful that people walked out of the room with that number in their heads."

"In other words, we had just been mowing them down as we're

coming in," the president commented later in an interview. He said he had asked if they were civilians or soldiers, and had been told they were soldiers. I mentioned that some generals estimated that 60,000 Iraqi military were killed, but no one knew because they didn't find the bodies. "That's what I asked," Bush said. "Where are all the bodies? And they answered: With the uniformed divisions they bury the bodies immediately. In the Muslim tradition I guess."

At the end of the briefing, Bush brought up post-Saddam Iraq. Since Saddam had spent 20 to 30 years ruining his country, it would take awhile to rebuild it. The reconstruction shouldn't be compared to an American or a Western European city at the outset. "We still have a lot of work to do. Don't let the celebrations fool you."

That day, April 9, was the symbolic end of Saddam's rule. His government collapsed as the U.S. Army occupied the banks of the Tigris River, and U.S. Marines swept into downtown Baghdad and helped a group of Iraqis topple a 20-foot statue of Saddam, using an armored vehicle with a chain and pulley to wrestle it down. The prolonged effort was captured live on worldwide television. Watching some of the coverage between meetings, the president noted how small the crowds seemed to be. But across the city, thousands of Iraqis took to the streets to rejoice. It seemed to be the sweets and flowers that some had predicted.

At 11:27 A.M. Bush spoke with Aznar. "The strategy is paying off," the president said, "but you won't see us doing any victory dances or anything here because of the northern third of the country—Mosul, Kirkuk and Tikrit are still in enemy hands. We've still got work to do inside Baghdad, find high-value leadership." Two days earlier, they had bombed a restaurant where they believed Saddam and his sons were, though they had not yet seen proof that any had survived the first night's attacks. "I personally believe we've killed Saddam Hussein twice. I think we killed the real guy the first day and yesterday we killed the fake." As to WMD, the president said, "There's a massive amount of tunnels and caves. We have to control expectations on that. It's going to take a while to dig out the rubble and find where he stored the stuff."

The next day, April 10, Ken Adelman published an op-ed article in *The Washington Post* headlined, "Cakewalk Revisited," more or less gloating over what appeared to be the quick victory, and reminding readers that 14 months earlier he had written that war would be a "cakewalk." He chastised those who had predicted disaster. "Taking first prize among the many frightful forecasters" was Brent Scowcroft. Adelman wrote that his own confidence came from having worked for Rumsfeld three times and "from knowing Dick Cheney and Paul Wolfowitz for so many years."

Cheney phoned Adelman, who was in Paris with his wife, Carol. What a clever column, the vice president said. You really demolished them. He said he and Lynne were having a small private dinner Sunday night, April 13, to talk and celebrate. The only other guests would be Libby and Wolfowitz. Adelman realized it was Cheney's way of saying thank you, and he and his wife came back from Paris a day early to attend the dinner.

When Adelman walked into the vice president's residence that Sunday night, he was so happy he broke into tears. He hugged Cheney for the first time in the 30 years he had known him. There had been reports in recent days of mass graves and abundant, graphic evidence of torture by Saddam's regime, so there was a feeling that they had been part of a greater good, liberating 25 million people.

"We're all together. There should be no protocol, let's just talk," Cheney said when they sat down to dinner.

Wolfowitz embarked on a long review of the 1991 Gulf War and what a mistake it had been to allow the Iraqis to fly helicopters after the armistice. Saddam had used them to put down uprisings.

Cheney said he had not realized then what a trauma that time had been for the Iraqis, particularly the Shiites, who felt the United States had abandoned them. He said that experience had made the Iraqis worry that war this time would not end Saddam's rule.

"Hold it! Hold it!" Adelman interjected. "Let's talk about *this* Gulf War. It's so wonderful to celebrate." He said he was just an outside adviser, someone who turned up the pressure in the public forum. "It's so easy for me to write an article saying do this. It's much tougher for Paul to advocate it. Paul and Scooter, you give advice inside and the president listens. Dick, your advice is the most important, the Cadillac. It's much more serious for you to advocate it. But in the end, all of what we said was still only advice. The president is the one who had to decide. I have been blown away by how determined he is." The war has been awesome, Adelman said. "So I just want to make a toast, without getting too cheesy. To the president of the United States."

They all raised their glasses, Hear! Hear!

Adelman said he had worried to death as time went on and support seemed to wane that there would be no war.

After 9/11, Cheney said, the president understood what had to be done. He had to do Afghanistan first, sequence the attacks, but after Afghanistan—"soon thereafter"—the president knew he had to do Iraq. Cheney said he was confident after 9/11 that it would come out okay.

Adelman said it was still a gutsy move. When John Kennedy was elected by the narrowest of margins, Adelman said, he told everyone in his administration that the big-agenda items like civil rights would have to wait for a second term. Certainly it was the opposite for Bush.

Yes, Cheney said. And it began the first minutes of the presidency, when Bush said they were going to go full steam ahead. There is such a tendency, Cheney said, to hold back when there is a close election, to do what *The New York Times* and other pundits suggest and predict. "This guy was just totally different," Cheney said. "He just decided here's what I want to do and I'm going to do it. He's very directed. He's very focused."

"I want you three guys to shut up," Lynne Cheney said, pointing at Cheney, Wolfowitz and Adelman. "Let's hear what Scooter thinks."

Libby, smiling, just said he thought what had happened was just "wonderful."

It was a pretty amazing accomplishment, they all agreed, particularly given the opposition to war. Here was Brent Scowcroft, the pillar of establishment foreign policy, vocally on the other side, widely seen as a surrogate for the president's father. There had been Jim Baker insisting on a larger coalition of nations. And Lawrence Eagleburger, secretary of state in the last half-year of Bush senior's administration, on television all the time saying war was only justified if there was evidence that Saddam was about to launch an attack on us. Eagleburger had accused Cheney of "chest thumping."

Someone mentioned Powell, and there were chuckles around the table.

Cheney and Wolfowitz remarked that Powell was sure someone who followed his poll ratings and bragged about his popularity. Several weeks earlier in a National Public Radio interview, Powell had said, "If you would consult any recent Gallup poll, the American people seem to be quite satisfied with the job I'm doing as secretary of state."

He sure likes to be popular, Cheney said.

Wolfowitz said that Powell did bring credibility and that his presentation to the United Nations on WMD intelligence had been important. As soon as Powell had understood what the president wanted, Wolfowitz said, he became a good loyal member of the team.

Cheney shook his head, no. Powell was a problem. "Colin always had major reservations about what we were trying to do."

They turned to Rumsfeld, the missing brother. Both Cheneys told some affectionate stories going back to the late 1960s when they had hooked up with Rumsfeld.

Adelman recalled the torment of writing speeches for Rumsfeld during his first stint as secretary of defense. "I was working on one speech, the 12th version or something, and getting back his rewrites— his chicken scratches—his printing, he can barely write. And I looked at it and took it to him and said, 'Don, you can change what I write and you can change what you yourself write or want to say, but goddamn, I've given you a great Pericles quote. You can't change Pericles.' Don then took the draft and put some more chicken scratches on it. I looked at it, and he had retained his rewrite of the great Athenian general, and penned in, 'as Pericles should have said.' "

Cheney said he had just had lunch with the president. "Democracy in the Middle East is just a big deal for him. It's what's driving him."

"Let me ask," Adelman inquired, "before this turns into a love fest. I was just stunned that we have not found weapons of mass destruction." There were several hundred thousand troops and others combing the country.

"We'll find them," Wolfowitz said.

"It's only been four days really," Cheney said. "We'll find them."

PRESIDENT BUSH did not take his own advice to avoid victory dances and not be fooled by celebrations. On May 1, the former Texas Air National Guard jet pilot donned a flight suit and landed on the aircraft carrier USS *Abraham Lincoln,* which was at sea just off the coast of San Diego. In an address to the nation from the flight deck, he proclaimed, "Major combat operations in Iraq have ended." Though he was technically correct and did caution, "We have difficult work to do in Iraq," there was no doubt that it was a victory speech. As Bush spoke a large banner hung in the background: "MISSION ACCOMPLISHED."

Speechwriter Gerson had pulled out all the rhetorical stops. "The tyrant has fallen, and Iraq is free," the president said from the sunbathed deck. It was "a noble cause" and "a great moral advance" that he linked to Normandy and Iwo Jima, Franklin Roosevelt's Four Freedoms, the Truman Doctrine, Reagan's challenge to the evil empire and his own war against terror that began on 9/11. "In the images of falling statues, we have witnessed the arrival of a new era." The war on terror would not be endless. "We have seen the turning of the tide."

In May 2003, General Garner was replaced by L. Paul "Jerry" Bremer III, the head of the Coalition Provisional Authority, who was to oversee the rebuilding of Iraq and the eventual transition to democracy.

For Bush's team there was little time for the empty feelings that often follow the conquest. Though in many respects the war was a stunning military victory, the aftermath soon became a continuum of violence and uncertainty.

Franks was the first to retire. A number of his subordinate generals and others thought he had blown the stability operations. The Office of Reconstruction and Humanitarian Assistance, initially headed by Jay Garner, was not made subordinate to Franks but was given equal status. Franks, with all the troops and experience, was not in charge. He did not argue or fight for it. "I have a war to fight," he said many times. He believed he had pushed Rumsfeld, Wolfowitz and General Myers on the postwar plans as much as he could, arguing that they could not just pay lip service to issues. He had said that the decisive combat operations would go very fast, that they needed to focus on the aftermath. But Rumsfeld and the others had been focused on the war.

When major combat was over in May, Franks was exhausted and took a leave. Rumsfeld wanted him to become the Army chief of staff, a promotion in name only. The combatant commander is king, and Franks certainly did not want to become one of the Title X motherfuckers. He left the Central Command in July and retired from the Army in August. He told friends that he made $1 million giving speeches in his first several months of retirement, and he signed up to write a memoir for which he received a multimillion-dollar contract. He told publishers that he had no criticism of Rumsfeld, who was his buddy and friend. No way was he going to offend his No. 1 patron. His book would be a serious memoir, not a gossipy exposé.

POWELL SPENT the next months more often than not on the defensive. To those who thought he should have been a more forceful advocate against war, he replied that he had taken his best shot. He had not misled anyone, he told associates. He had argued successfully in August and September 2002 that the president adopt two tracks— plan for war and conduct diplomacy through the United Nations. The president could travel those two tracks only so long before he would reach a fork in the road, and one fork was war. "He's the president," Powell told associates, "and he decided and therefore it was my obligation to go down the other fork with him."

As the war planning had progressed over the nearly 16 months, Powell had felt that the easier the war looked, the less Rumsfeld, the Pentagon and Franks had worried about the aftermath. They seemed to think Iraq was a crystal goblet and that all they had to do was tap it and it would crack. It had turned out to be a beer mug instead. Now they owned the beer mug.

Visiting Iraq in the fall of 2003, Powell saw the mass graves and heard the testimony of witnesses to the torture and oppression. He was delighted that Saddam and his whole rotten regime were gone. It was the saving grace. Certainly the decision to go to war was not 100 percent wrong. History, after all, had not yet determined whether it was right or wrong.

Armitage was growing increasingly restive. He believed that the foreign-policy-making system that was supposed to be coordinated by Rice was essentially dysfunctional. That dysfunction had served well as long as Powell and he could delay war. But that effort had ultimately failed. Later in 2003, whenever there was a presidential speech or an issue with the White House, particularly on the Middle East, he would say to Powell, "Tell these people to fuck themselves."

Powell's response was to soldier on.

Months after the war, Rice asked Armitage about his all-too-apparent distress. The NSC system is dysfunctional, he told her bluntly, and the deputies committee was not carrying its load. Policy was not sufficiently coordinated, debated and then settled. She needed to be a good, knock-down-drag-out fighter to be a strong security adviser and enforce discipline.

Rice said that she was dealing with genuine heavyweights, as Armitage well knew. Cheney, Powell and Rumsfeld were not shrinking violets, and the president wanted to make sure each had his say.

In early October, the president gave Rice new authority and responsibility for coordinating the tremendous task of stabilizing and rebuilding Iraq.

On October 12, 2003, *The Washington Post* published a long front page story headlined, "Rice Fails to Repair Rifts, Officials Say; Cabinet Rivalries Complicate Her Role." The story by Glenn Kessler and Peter Slevin, the paper's two chief State Department reporters, reflected Armitage's critique precisely, though no current administration officials, including Armitage, were quoted by name.

Rice expressed her concern to Powell, who defended his deputy. "You can blame Rich if you want," Powell said. "Rich had the guts to go talk to you directly about this, so I don't think he is the source." What Armitage had said reflected a general feeling around Washington and in the foreign policy establishment, Powell said. "We are not knitted up and we don't go about these things well. And whether you like it or not, that's a view that is heard around town. And I'm sorry it comes back to the NSC for not making it happen." Powell thought Rice was more interested in finding someone to blame for the public airing of the problem than in fixing it.

CHENEY CONTINUED to be Powell's bête noire. At meetings of the principals, in Powell's view, Cheney improved on his technique of not betraying his position by insisting he either didn't have one, or could change his mind in 30 minutes. Powell finally decoded the technique. He concluded that he had to listen carefully because Cheney's disavowals generally turned out to be positions Cheney was not going to change his mind about.

Relations became so strained that Powell and Cheney could not, and did not, have a sit-down lunch or any discussion about their differences. Never.

Powell thought that now that Bush and the administration had to live with the consequences of their Iraq decisions, they were becoming dangerously protective of those decisions. There was no one in the White House who could break through to insist on a realistic reassessment. There was no Karen Hughes who could go to Bush and say, Pay attention, you're in trouble. Powell believed it was the hardest of all tasks to go back to fundamentals and question your own judgment, and there was no sign it was going to happen. So he soldiered on once again against the current.

RUMSFELD HAD BEEN the overall manager, the withering interrogator, the defense technocrat who had given the president the plan of attack. Cheney called it Rumsfeld's "up-to-his-eyeballs kind of management." Powell, who had seen a fever in Cheney, never detected that in Rumsfeld. If Bush had decided against war, Powell was sure that Cheney, Wolfowitz and Feith would have wrung their hands and probably would have gone nuts. But not Rumsfeld.

Franks, too, knew Rumsfeld's drive but also detected a detachment, as if at times he was outside the room looking in through a window.

When I interviewed Rumsfeld in the fall of 2003, I asked if he wanted a war.

"Oh goodness no," he said, "no one with any sense wants conflict."

Did you recommend going to war?

He paused. "It's an interesting question. There's no question in anyone's mind but I agreed with the president's approach and his decision. Whether there ever was a formal moment where he asked me, Do I think he should go to war, I can't recall it."

The president later said he had not asked Rumsfeld.

But Rumsfeld said the president did ask other key questions that fit with his own definition of his job as secretary. "I can remember him asking me, Do I have confidence in General Franks? Do I have confidence in the war plan? And do I have confidence in these pieces?" This all appealed to the war technician in Rumsfeld. "He had to develop confidence that this institution which is his instrument—the country's instrument—had thoroughly examined these things." And the president then had to decide who he wanted to give a long leash to and who a shorter leash. "He functioned as a superb executive in process of this," Rumsfeld said. He didn't micromanage. "This president has a lot of the same quality that Ronald Reagan did where he'd look out, way out to the horizon and plant a standard out there and then point toward it."

Since the burden of the decision to launch a preemptive war is a huge one, I asked if the president ever discussed this with him.

"No," Rumsfeld said.

"Were there ever any—?"

"Never," Rumsfeld said. "He carries his responsibilities very well." The president did not worry decisions to death because he had invested the time up front to examine and determine what he wanted and why, Rumsfeld said. Somebody who has not, he said, "tends to be uncomfortable with the decisions and can be blown off the wind—blown by the wind and change their mind and be worried and anguished. And his worry and investment was before the fact, not after the fact."

TIM, THE CIA base chief in northern Iraq, realized that he had lived every operation officer's dream. He had been out on his own—no State Department, no military, nothing—only himself and money.

On March 24, 2003, five days after the start of the war, Tim made his way down to Dora Farm. The place had been picked pretty clean. It looked like the remnants of a flea market, people were still carting stuff away. There were craters and clearly the place had been attacked. He searched everywhere. There was no bunker nor any hint of one. He found a subterranean pantry for food storage attached to the main house. Perhaps that was what his ROCKSTAR agents had been referring to. It was baffling and mysterious. Was it possible that *manzul* was neither a place of refuge nor a bunker, but a pantry?

Tim eventually tracked down some of the ROCKSTAR agents who had reported that night. Two said that their wives had been captured by Saddam's agents and tortured by having their fingernails pulled out. Another maintained that his house had been bulldozed. There was some evidence to support these claims, but Tim was unsure.

Soon Tim was reassigned to CIA headquarters to work undercover on other issues. Saul and other superiors asked him and the team members to put down the sequence of events of the day and night of March 19–20, 2003. They wanted a very briefable, immaculate package. The more Tim searched his memory and the few documents, he realized that much was cloudy. Everyone had been stressed. The ROCKSTARS on the ground had not wanted to disappoint, and had obviously been worried about being captured or killed.

Tim made a series of efforts to write down in a meaningful way what had happened. He tried a version. Did he have 40 percent? Or 62 percent? Or 83 percent? he wondered. What percentage of the truth was available? What had slipped away? What had been untrue? He tried several more times. It wasn't black or white, and it certainly wasn't a straight line. Was he getting closer or further from the truth? He never produced a definitive version. The biggest unanswered question was, Had Saddam and his entourage been there that night?

ON OCTOBER 2, 2003, David Kay, Tenet's handpicked weapons expert who supervised the 1,400-strong Iraq Survey Group, gave an initial public report on the first three months of their search for WMD inside Iraq. He said they had made "remarkable progress" but the selective destruction of computer hard drives and documents hindered their work. He presented a strong case that Iraq had violated the U.N. resolutions in ways not realized before the war. But the headline was his statement that, "We have not yet found stocks of weapons."

RICE WAS BECOMING more and more of a believer in the importance of long-term outcomes. She felt it was important to be patient for the real outcome in Iraq, not just about WMD but about a political settlement. And that might be quite a bit later. She found some comfort in the fact that the president was holding firm and thinking about the long term. Visiting Japan in October 2003, Bush had told Prime Minister Junichiro Koizumi, "If we hadn't gotten it right in 1945 and helped build a democratically prosperous Japan, our conversation—between a Japanese prime minister and a president of the United States—could never take place. One day, a president of Iraq and a president of the United States are going to be sitting there trying to solve some problem and they're going to say they're glad *we* created a democratic and prosperous Iraq."

THE VIOLENCE and the insurgency inside Iraq continued, and hundreds of U.S. military personnel and Iraqis were killed.

My first interview with President Bush for this book took place Wednesday afternoon, December 10, 2003, in the president's office in the White House residence for more than one and a half hours; the second was the following afternoon in the Oval Office for more than two hours. Rice and Bartlett were present during the interviews.

I had submitted a 21-page chronology listing specific meetings, decision points or turning points that I wanted to ask about. The president said that he had had a chance to review some of his own records before we talked. The focus of my questions was the decision to go to war, and his detailed answers and recollections about specific events and turning points have been fully reflected in the narrative. More general questions and answers have been left for here.

We spent some time discussing Vice President Cheney. In addition to saying that he didn't think the vice president was feverish about al Qaeda or Iraq, the president said, "He doesn't want to be viewed as a hero or a villain. He wants to be viewed as a loyal vice president. Which he is. And you know, he's got opinions. People appreciate his opinions because Dick's the kind of person who doesn't necessarily talk a lot. But when he does talk, he gives the impression that he is a thoughtful person."

I said that Cheney had emerged as kind of a Howard Hughes, the reclusive man behind the scenes who would not answer questions.

"That's what I told him," Bush said. He indicated Cheney should get out and do more interviews. By being silent, Bush said, "There's a danger that you'll either be a heck of a lot more powerful than you are, or a heck of a lot weaker than you are. And it's neither."

Detailed questions "frightened" and "scared the heck out of him," the president said. The vice president's tendency to be circumspect was admirable, he added. "That's why I love Cheney." He later added that "Cheney is scared to death of" any false impressions from material that might be taken out of context or hyped. "Cheney doesn't want to be in the middle of any sharp elbows."

Bush continued, "I know Cheney well. And he's by the way a very good vice president.

"He wants to be anonymous from that perspective and he should be. On the other hand, he was a rock. I mean he was steadfast and steady in his view that Saddam was a threat to America and we had to deal with him."

He added, "He sees this book coming out in an election and again he's just, he's worried about it, just to be frank with you."

We turned to the question of doubts. I quoted what Tony Blair recently had said at his party's annual conference: "I do not at all disrespect anyone who disagrees with me." Blair had also said he had received letters from those who had lost sons in the war who wrote that they hated him for what he did. I quoted Blair, "And don't believe anyone who tells you when they receive letters like that they don't suffer any doubt."

"Yeah," President Bush replied. "I haven't suffered doubt."

"Is that right?" I asked. "Not at all?"

"No. And I'm able to convey that to the people." To those who had lost sons or daughters, he said, "I hope I'm able to convey that in a humble way."

I asked about his father in this way: "Here is the one living human being who's held this office who had to make a decision to go to war. And it would not be credible if you did not at some point ask him, What are the ingredients of doing this right? Or what's your thought, this is what I'm facing."

"If it wouldn't be credible," Bush replied, "I guess I better make up an answer."

"No, no," I said. "I'm being hard and direct because . . ."

"No, no, no," the president replied. "You should be. Look, I talk to him of course. I cannot remember a moment where he said, 'Don't do this' or 'Do this.' I can't remember a moment where I said to myself, maybe he can help me make the decision. Because you got to understand, this decision is not like all of a sudden there is a threat to Kuwait. And boom. This is part of a larger obligation that came to be on September the 11th, 2001. This is part of a large and a different kind of war. It's like a front."

"Did you say to him, 'Dad, how do I do this right? What should I think about?' "

"I don't think I did," he replied.

"Did you have any discussion about it?"

"I'm confident—sure we did. I'm trying to remember. It is incredible history to have a father and son fight a war in the same theater. That's never happened before. Maybe it has, no it hasn't. Of course the Adams boys." The son of John Adams, the second president, was John Quincy Adams, the sixth president. "John Q. never went back to war. But it's a different war. See, it's a different war.

"I'm not trying to be evasive. I don't remember. I could ask him and see if he remembers something. But how do you ask a person, What does it feel like to send somebody in and them lose life? Remember, I've already done so, for starters, in Afghanistan.

"The discussions would be more on the tactics. How are we doing, How are you doing with the Brits? He is following the news now. And so I am briefing him on what I see. You know, he is the wrong father to appeal to in terms of strength. There is a higher father that I appeal to."

The president conceded it would be a "fantastic" moment in history. "But I'm not hiding it. I just can't remember a poignant moment. I'm confident it happened, that he would say, 'Hey son, this must be incredibly stressful for you. I just want you to know we love you and hang in there.' " He said that his father no doubt tried to provide reassurance. "It was less, 'Here's how you have to go take care of the guy,' and more 'I've been through what you've been through and I know what's happening and therefore I love you' would be a more accurate way to describe it."

I mentioned that one of my bosses at *The Washington Post* had suggested a tough question on weapons of mass destruction. "Was the president misled . . ."

"No," the president said.

". . . by the intelligence or did he mislead the country?"

"No," he said. "The answer is absolutely not."

"What happened?"

"What do you mean by what happened?"

In terms of the WMD and the "slam dunk" case that Tenet had promised.

If the large number of violations of U.N. resolutions reported by David Kay in October 2003 had been known before the war, the president said, it would have established material breach and provided a cause of war. "But I think it's way too early to fully understand the complete history." The intelligence was hard enough for the U.N. to pass several resolutions and "hard enough" for former President Clinton to decide to strike Iraq in 1998 when 650 bomber or missile sorties were launched.

"But we have not found any weapons of mass destruction," I said.

"We have found weapons programs," Bush said, "that could be reconstituted."

"Could be, I agree," I said.

An actual weapon could be built very quickly, he said. "And so therefore, given that, even if that's the very minimum you had, how could you not act on Saddam Hussein? That's my answer."

I said that after 9/11 he had been the "voice of realism," telling the country after the catastrophic attack that it would be a long and difficult war. From my travels, I said, many people, including his supporters, were saying he was less the voice of realism for not saying and acknowledging that the weapons had not yet been found.

"I don't want people to say, 'Aha, we told you so.' I want people to know that there is a process that's ongoing," he said, adding that not one person had suggested to him that he make such an acknowledgment. "But you run in different circles than I do. Much more elite."

"It's really lots of business groups," I said.

"The realism," the president said, "is to be able to understand that nature of Saddam Hussein, his history, his potential harm to America."

I said I was trying to address the simple fact that no WMD had been found. "We haven't found bubbling baths."

He chuckled.

"But the status report," I said, "for the last six or seven months, is we haven't found weapons. That's all."

"True, true, true," he said. He contended that they had found enough. "The person who wants the president to stand up and declare that publicly is also the person who wants to say, 'Shouldn't have done it.' And there is no doubt in my mind we should have done this. Not only for our own sake, but for the Iraqi citizens." He said Kay's initial report was justification enough that Saddam was dangerous. "I'm probably sounding incredibly defensive all of a sudden," he added coolly. The failure to find "the bubbling vat" did not render Saddam "benign."

I said I was asking these questions because I wanted to show in the book what he thought the status of the WMD search was.

"Why do you need to deal with this in the book?" he asked. "What's this got to do about it?"

I said that I had to cover the aftermath of the war. This was a key question.

The president said he wanted to make sure that his acknowledgment that no weapons of mass destruction had been found so far would not be published in *The Washington Post* until the book was released. "In other words, I'm not going to read a headline, 'Bush Says No Weapons.' "

I promised that he would not, though less than two months

later he would effectively make that acknowledgment, saying on February 8, 2004, on NBC's *Meet the Press*, "I expected there to be stockpiles of weapons" and "We thought he had weapons."

Did he feel there was any miscalculation about how long it would take to stabilize and pacify Iraq after the war?

"No," he said, "I think I was pretty well prepared for a pretty long haul." Many positive things have occurred, he said. He noted that the Iraqi oil fields had been successfully protected, mass hunger avoided, and a new currency introduced, which was itself "an impressive feat," he said. "The major issues that we'd thought we'd be confronted with just didn't happen."

The violence, he said, was mostly in about 5 to 10 percent of Iraq. "It's dangerous because there are still enough thugs and assassins there that can do you in. . . . But it's still tough. There's still loss of life." He said he was optimistic about the outlook. "It's just a matter of time. It's a matter of a society evolving. It's a matter of a sovereignty issue evolving"—when the government would be turned over to the Iraqi people. He said the liberation was "changing a mentality." Iraqis would soon "be on the front line of the police work" and would be the ones to go after the assassins, along with Iraqi troops. He complained that some of the positive things in Iraq did not get coverage in the American media.

"What matters is the emergence of a free society where people realize their lives are better off. And where they work through their traumas so they can seize the moment." Summarizing at the end of our first interview, he said of the war and the aftermath, "It is the story of the 21st century."

He continued about his own brief visit to Iraq two weeks earlier. "And when I went there in Thanksgiving, I went to thank the troops, but I also went to say to the Iraqi people, seize the moment, this is your country." During a successful transition to self-government, the key would be minority rights for those groups and tribes that were not Shiites and "a clear understanding that vengeance and jealousy won't rule the day."

The president said he believed the record would show that he,

Rumsfeld, Franks and the other military people developed a war plan that carefully targeted Saddam, the Baathist leadership and inner circle, and their means to retain power. The war was precisely directed at them and that apparatus—military, security service, secret police. As much as possible average Iraqis were spared. It would be a blueprint of historical significance that, he said, "will enable other leaders, if they feel like they have to go to war, to spare innocent citizens and their lives."

Telling that story was one of the chief reasons the president said he had agreed to be interviewed in depth about the war, and why he wanted Rumsfeld and others in the administration to answer my questions. "But the news of this, in my judgment, the big news out of this isn't how George W. makes decisions," he said. "To me the big news is America has changed how you fight and win war, and therefore makes it easier to keep the peace in the long run. And that's the historical significance of this book as far as I'm concerned."

The president reminded me that back in his private office he keeps a brick brought back by the Special Forces unit that had conducted the first U.S. military raid into Afghanistan after 9/11. It was from the compound of Taliban leader Mullah Omar. It was a reminder, he said, that when he put boots on the ground and ordered direct ground engagement, U.S. military personnel would die. It was not the antiseptic war of shooting cruise missiles that protects U.S. military personnel. "If you shoot Tomahawks from submarines, you don't put anybody in harm's way," he said.

"A president must be steel to deal with the casualties that inevitably come from a strategy aimed to win the war," Bush said. "And I mean there will be death, and particularly if you are aiming to free an entire nation of people. There will be death." In Iraq, with nearly 200,000 U.S. military personnel on the ground, he said, "I knew there would be casualties. And that brick reminds me of that."

Two days later, December 13, the U.S. military captured Saddam Hussein, unshaven and apparently disoriented, pulling him from a hole near a farmhouse outside Tikrit. The next day, Sunday, the president addressed the nation. "The capture of this man was crucial to the rise of a free Iraq," Bush said. "It marks the end of the road for him and for all who bullied and killed in his name." He added, "A dark and painful era is over," but cautioned, "The capture of Saddam Hussein does not mean the end of violence in Iraq."

THE FAILURE to find WMD and the continuing violence and instability inside Iraq—the fact that the war was not really over—was giving pause even to the true believers, none more so than Wolfowitz, who for many years had been an outspoken and persistent advocate for ousting Saddam.

Wolfowitz found himself asking with some frequency whether the war had been worth it. The question arose most painfully at the funeral of Army Lieutenant Colonel Chad Buehring, who was killed on the floor right below Wolfowitz when his hotel in Baghdad was attacked in late 2003, and during the dozen or more times he visited wounded servicemen at military hospitals. He tried to show his gratitude for their courage and sacrifice. The stories of those killed or wounded illustrated how the real price of war fell disproportionately.

But despite his anguish over the ongoing violence, Wolfowitz held firmly to the belief that the war was justified and worthwhile and that the decision was an act of personal courage by the president. After 9/11 he had been convinced that terrorism was no longer a manageable evil. Both its intersecting worldwide networks and its state sponsors must be attacked. Saddam's regime had long deserved to be overthrown, but after 9/11 his removal was important enough to risk American lives directly.

Wolfowitz visited Iraq three times in the nine months after the end of major combat operations and found a resilience and sense of mission among the troops that almost took his breath away. One colonel told his men that what they had done equaled what their grandfathers had accomplished in Germany and Japan, or their fathers in Korea. For Wolfowitz, Saddam's Baathist party was a Nazi-like organization of gangsters and sadists. Removing it from power not only removed a threat to the U.S. but was an opening to a better world.

As a military campaign, the war had been brilliant, he thought. It had been accomplished with fewer American casualties than anyone could have dared to hope, without involving Israel. There had been no use of WMD, no destruction of the Iraqi oil fields, no outside intervention by Turkey or Iran, and no significant ethnic conflict in the north among Kurds, Turks and Arabs. If someone had predicted this before the war, he would have thought it wildly optimistic.

Much had been accomplished on the positive side for Iraq and the Middle East, he believed, though the healing would take time. Freedom is a universal human aspiration, he believed, not just an American one. The United States had to support moderate Muslims and the talented people of Iraq in building free institutions. Despite predictions, he had seen democracy spread in East Asia, and the world had seen what happened in Eastern Europe in the last 15 years. So 10 or 20 years from now, Wolfowitz was confident this war would be seen as an essential stage in the march toward human freedom, democracy and the defeat of terrorism from which Americans would benefit.

SENATOR BOB GRAHAM, the Florida Democrat who in 2003 made a brief run for the Democratic presidential nomination, thought the war in Iraq was one of the most serious errors of American foreign policy since World War II. It was as if the United States had gone to war against Mussolini's Italy in 1941 instead of Hitler's Germany. Graham believed that the Hitlers of terrorism were al Qaeda and Hezbollah, extremists backed by Iran. Both posed greater threats than Iraq; both had the capability and the will to attack and had a covert presence within the U.S., he believed.

The Iraq War had taken the focus particularly off of al Qaeda, which he believed had regenerated itself and was now more dangerous. The result was that the United States was more at risk than before the war.

On the WMD issues, Graham thought the CIA had used bad intelligence and then the administration, the president included, had manipulated and hyped it. He believed Tenet should have resigned or been fired, and was surprised that Bush had taken no action to attempt immediate reform of the CIA. He felt the president should have stood up and taken responsibility for the errors. In the 2004 election, he hoped the American voters would agree with him and remove Bush from office.

AT THE BEGINNING OF 2004, Cheney was confident that the Iraq War would be seen as a history-shaping event. He was unrepentant about his analysis of terrorism and his assertions about Saddam. The great threat to the nation was al Qaeda armed not just with box cutters and airline tickets but with a nuke in the middle of an American city. The administration had been accused of not having connected the dots before 9/11. How could they afford to ignore the dots after 9/11? It was just that simple.

Cheney believed that given the intelligence reporting about Iraq–al Qaeda links over so many years and the intelligence evidence on WMD, no one in his right mind sitting in Bush's position as president could have ignored it. Cheney still thought the 2002 NIE was pretty good.

Overall, he thought Bush had figured out how to focus on what was essential and important, where to spend his time. The president didn't waste time on trivia. Over the nearly 16 months leading up to war, he had zeroed in on the military plan. Cheney had watched the president's questions ripple down through the Defense Department and the military, once telling an associate, "They know they're going to have to come answer tough questions from the Man."

Cheney also was convinced that Bush had an abiding faith that if people were given freedom and democracy, that would begin a transformation process in Iraq that in years ahead would change the Middle East. There was a moral dimension. One of Cheney's favorite military historians, Victor Davis Hanson, has argued that leaders and nations can become "accomplices to evil through inaction." Bush had acted. What the president had done, Cheney thought, was much more significant and tougher than what he had seen up-close in the other administrations he had served—Ford's and Bush senior's.

There was so much focus on the aftermath and criticism of the postwar planning. Cheney thought it wouldn't matter in the end. It would be noise to history as long as they were successful in what they were trying to do. Outcomes mattered. He thought history would treat Bush very well, though he acknowledged that the jury was still out.

KARL ROVE had come to love Cheney. Nearly all presidents have had to deal with vice presidents with real or imagined political futures. Even Bush senior, the super-loyal vice president, broke publicly with Reagan several times when he deemed it politically necessary, such as when the Reagan administration was negotiating with Panamanian leader Manuel Noriega and Bush had distanced himself from dealings with the unsavory strongman.

But Cheney had made it clear he did not aspire to the presidency. It was almost an unheard-of luxury to not have the vice president nipping at the president's heels, Rove realized. Cheney did not seem worried about covering his own ass, an amazing phenomenon in politics. His advice was not tainted by any political self-interest that Rove could identify. Cheney didn't always win with the president, though his depth of knowledge was often unmatched. He had a sense of Washington, though in Rove's view, it was not always accurate. Cheney's filters were his personal biases and attitudes. One that Rove noticed was his obsession with al Qaeda, "a real fever" as Rove too called it, agreeing with Powell.

Cheney remained nervous about being in the same place as the president, and he continued to worry that al Qaeda would strike and decapitate the government. So he was still at times going off to undisclosed locations or absenting himself. On a few occasions Rove and the president had discussed the news stories that Cheney was really pulling the strings and running things behind the scenes. Some of the White House communications people worried about this. Bush laughed. Both of them had seen how deferential Cheney was. "Yes, Mr. President," or "No, Mr. President." It was no different when the president and Cheney were alone.

When the president wasn't around, Cheney often referred to him as "The Man," saying that "The Man wants this." Or, "The Man thinks this." Cheney was a forceful, persistent advocate, but the president decided. The clearest evidence of that was Cheney's strenuous objection to going to the U.N. to seek new weapons inspection resolutions. The president had gone against his advice. Cheney had saluted.

Rove argued that the politics of the Cheney-is-in-charge thesis worked in their favor. First, anyone who believed that was long lost to them anyway. Second, Rove wanted them to keep talking about it, throw the campaign into that briar patch. He believed the ordinary person wouldn't buy it. Here 67 percent were saying Bush was a strong leader and that included a third of the people who disapproved of his performance in office. A strong leader would not kowtow to his vice president, and Bush did not look meek in public.

BY EARLY FEBRUARY 2004, Rove could see that Iraq was turning into a potential negative. The violence on the ground continued. The U.S. military had more than 100,000 troops there and would require that many or more for some time. American soldiers were being killed at too high a rate, and they hadn't reached a political settlement. Turning the government over to the Iraqis looked shaky. The failure to find any weapons of mass destruction, and Bush's and Tenet's public acknowledgments that the intelligence might have been wrong, were potentially big setbacks.

Previously, Rove had claimed he was salivating at the prospect that the Democrats would nominate former Vermont Governor Howard Dean in the 2004 presidential race. But Dean had imploded and Senator John Kerry, the Massachusetts Democrat, had won 12 of the first 14 Democratic primary contests and it looked like he was headed for the nomination. Politics is a game of recovery, adaptability and optimism. So Rove had a new line.

"The good news for us is that Dean is not the nominee," Rove now argued to an associate in his second floor West Wing office. Dean's unconditional opposition to the Iraq War could have been potent in a face-off with Bush. "One of Dean's strengths though was he could say, I'm not part of that crowd down there." But Kerry was very much a part of the Washington crowd and he had voted in favor of the resolution for war. Rove got out his two-inch-thick loose-leaf binder titled "Bring It On." It consisted of research into Kerry's 19-year record in the Senate. Most relevant were pages 9–20 of the section on Iraq.

The record was that Kerry had been all over the map. Sounding like a method actor who believes his lines, Rove offered some readings from the Kerry record.

"Iraq has developed a chemical weapons capability," Rove quoted Kerry saying in October 1990, according to the *Congressional Record*. Saddam has been "working toward" development of WMD or "had all those abilities," Kerry had said in January 1991. (Of course, this turned out to be true as the U.N. weapons inspectors discovered after the 1991 Gulf War.) In 1998, as a member of the Intelligence Committee, Kerry said that Saddam was "pursuing a program to build weapons of mass destruction" and in October 2002, he said, "I am prepared to hold Saddam Hussein accountable and destroy his weapons of mass destruction." And, "The threat of Saddam Hussein with weapons of mass destruction is real. . . . He has continued to build those weapons."

Rove's eyebrows were jumping up and down as he read. "My personal favorite," he said, quoting Kerry on March 19, 2003, the day the war started: "I think Saddam Hussein's weapons of mass destruction are a threat, and that's why I voted to hold him accountable and to make certain that we disarm him."

"Oh yeah!" Rove shouted. And that had been on National Public Radio! He had it all on tape. So here is a member of the Senate Intelligence Committee saying that Saddam had the stuff. And the Bush campaign argument would be as follows: "You're looking at the same intelligence the president is and arriving at the same conclusion, and if you accuse him of misleading the American people, what were you doing? Are you saying, I was duped?"

Of course, when the aftermath of the war turned sour, Rove noted, Kerry started backing away, arguing that he had voted not for war but only to give the president the power to threaten war. More starkly, Kerry had said on *Meet the Press* in August 2003 that the congressional resolution "we passed did not empower the president to do regime change, we empowered him only with respect to the relevant resolutions of the United Nations." Well, Rove and the rest of the country knew that the resolution clearly gave the president approval to use the military in Iraq.

Rove was gleeful. "It's on tape!" he said, "and we've done testing on it, and you put out there, literally you take the footage of him saying some of this stuff and then have him in the exchange with Chris Matthews saying I'm antiwar and people say, 'What a hypocrite!' "

Kerry would have, and did have, answers. His main response was that Bush did not press hard enough or long enough with the U.N., that he did not build a legitimate global coalition, that he did not plan for the aftermath, and was too eager to go to war when Saddam was isolated and weak.

But Rove believed they had Kerry pretty cold on voting to give the president a green light for war and then backing off when he didn't like the aftermath or saw a political opportunity.

Whatever the case, Rove sounded as if he believed they could inoculate the president on the Iraq War in a campaign with Kerry. It remained to be seen, but Rove was certainly going to try.

POWELL AND ARMITAGE were still concerned about the influence of exile leader Ahmed Chalabi, the head of the INC. Though the president had declared that he was not going to put his finger on the scales and help select new leadership in Iraq, Chalabi, as a member of the Governing Council, had made it appear he had Bush's support. He had sat near Laura Bush during the president's State of the Union address on January 20, 2004, but afterward the president said he wasn't happy that someone had given out the seat. At times, Powell thought Chalabi was the biggest problem they had in Iraq. From the reports Armitage received from Iraq, most Iraqis thought Chalabi was a knucklehead. And though it was denied by others in the administration, Armitage believed that Chalabi had provided hyped WMD intelligence that had made its way to Bush and Cheney before the war. It was his understanding that the CIA and Congress were going to investigate Chalabi's role in the intelligence fiascos.

For Armitage soldiering on had its limits. Powell and he were fighting the good fight, attempting at every possible turn to soften the appearance—and reality—of unilateralism and arrogance in Bush administration foreign policy. But Armitage didn't think that either Powell or he came off as soldier of the year or even the month.

A newly appointed assistant secretary of state who had worked for one of the conservative think tanks in Washington had come to see Armitage his first day on the job. "I think with my contacts I'll really be able to fix the relationship and act as a bridge between Defense and State," the new man said.

"You're on our team," Armitage told him, realizing that he was ripping the poor man's head off. "You don't bridge shit. I've known all those fuckers for 30 years. You ain't bridging shit." After about three weeks on the job the new man came to see Armitage again.

"Well there, how we getting on?" Armitage inquired.

"Oh, fine, sir."

"It's a lot harder than you thought, isn't it?"

"I had no idea," the new man said. "It's mind-numbing." He then went on to detail how "the motherfuckers" at Defense had been trying to obstruct the efforts with the U.N.

A close friend of Armitage's from Congress told him that he and Powell had really failed. They had become the enablers, providing cover and an appearance of reasonableness so Cheney and Rumsfeld

worked their will. Armitage didn't think his friend from Congress
was wrong. In moments of his own despondency he looked back on
his three years at State and could find redeeming moments only in
his personal relationship with Powell as they had tried to solve problems with diplomacy, not war.

Armitage found two significant lingering difficulties from the
Iraq War. Though he believed they would put down the insurgency
and win in the end, the U.S. military was going to pay for ten years or
more. The Army, in particular, was stretched too thin. They were
fighting three wars really—Afghanistan still, Iraq and the continuing
global war on terrorism. It was not logical nor was it possible, in Armitage's view, that this could be accomplished with a force of the
same size that existed during the Clinton administration in peace
time. But that was what the Bush administration was attempting.

The second problem was political. Armitage did not see what
could come to pass in Iraq or elsewhere in the remaining eight
months before the presidential election that would alter the perception that Bush was in a jam. Armitage's Republican friends in the
Senate, who in late 2003 thought they could win two or three more
seats in November 2004, were now worried that control of the Senate, and even the White House, might go to the Democrats.

ON WEDNESDAY, January 28, 2004, David Kay, who had recently resigned as head of the Iraqi Survey Group, told the Senate Armed Services Committee that, "We were almost all wrong, and I certainly
include myself." He said that 85 percent of the work was done and he
did not expect ever to find WMD stockpiles in Iraq. "It is going to
take an outside inquiry," he said, to investigate the intelligence failure on WMD. He argued that it was "important to acknowledge failure" and that the Congress and the public would only have the
necessary confidence in any intelligence that reached the president
and top officials if there were such an inquiry.

Pressure mounted from both Democrats and Republicans for
an independent investigation. Bush initially said no, but then he,

Cheney, Rice and others in the White House quickly grasped the necessity—and the opportunity. So they decided to seize the initiative and proposed an independent bipartisan commission to be appointed by the president. They would include two conditions. First the commission would look at WMD and intelligence problems more broadly, not just in Iraq but at proliferation in Iran, North Korea and Libya. Second, the commission would not report until some time after the presidential election.

Cheney called around to some members of the Senate and House intelligence committees, arguing the key point that an inquiry during a presidential election season would be a travesty and that it would instantly politicize the intelligence issues. By acting quickly and getting ahead of the curve, as Karen Hughes so often urged, the White House shaped the news. "Bush to Back Probe of Iraq Data, Officials Say," read the headline in *The Washington Post*, which broke the story on Sunday, February 1. The reporters noted, "Bush's shift in position represents an effort to get out in front of a potentially dangerous issue that threatens to cloud his reelection bid."

On Monday, February 2, after a cabinet meeting, a reporter asked the president, "Do you think that the country is owed an explanation about the Iraq intelligence failure before the election so that voters have this information when they elect a new president?"

"First of all, I want to know all the facts," Bush said, noting that they were not all in, and he did not answer the question.

POWELL WAS SURPRISED that Kay had not gone quietly. Tenet had told him that Kay was going to remain a senior adviser to the CIA and that the agency would "keep him on the farm." Well, Kay had bolted from the blazing barn. Powell spent some time going through the transcript of Kay's Armed Services Committee testimony. It certainly showed that Saddam had the intent and the capability to produce WMD. But the absence of actual stockpiles of biological and chemical weapons was a big problem, and could not be dismissed.

Perhaps it was his old military mind, but if the data on which he had made a decision changed, Powell figured he had, at a minimum, to acknowledge that he would have rethought the decision if the new data had been available. Now that Kay was saying with as much authority as anyone possessed that they had been "terribly wrong" on the stockpiles, the administration had to face the new reality. There was an entirely different set of facts regarding one of the key reasons for war.

After the cabinet meeting on February 2, Powell, carrying a fully annotated transcript of Kay's statement, met with a group of editors and reporters from *The Washington Post* for an interview. I did not attend.

Powell defended Bush's war decision, saying "It was the right thing to do."

If Tenet had said before the war started what Dr. Kay has now said about there being no actual stockpiles, one questioner asked, would you still have recommended the invasion?

"I don't know," Powell replied, "because it was the stockpile that presented the final little piece that made it more of a real and present danger and threat to the region and to the world." He added, "The absence of a stockpile changes the political calculus. It changes the answer you get."

The secretary's remarks were the lead story in the *Post* the next day: "Powell Says New Data May Have Affected War Decision."

Powell knew the White House held its breath any time he was out talking to the media and that Rice read the newspapers very early in the morning. She would get excited over any news that did not conform with the president's position. Rice had already discussed Powell's comments with the president when she called him that morning.

Both the president and she were "mad," she told the secretary of state. Powell had "given the Democrats a remarkable tool." The president had taken the public position that the jury on WMD was still out, that he wanted to know the facts. Now Powell was out with a new line. He had made stunning headlines throughout the world once again.

Even when Rice was passing him a message from the president,

Powell did not particularly enjoy being dressed down by someone 17
years younger who held the job he had had 15 years earlier. "Look
what else I said," he replied. "It was great." But he just did not think
when they were faced with an entirely different set of facts regarding
one of the key issues in the decision to go to war that he could deny
he would at least reconsider.

Both Powell and Rice knew that Powell had never made an overall recommendation on war to the president since he had never been
asked. That had not come up at the *Post* interview.

Rice's message was clear: Get in line.

At 10:45 that morning as Powell was leaving the State Department for the White House to meet with the president and U.N.
Secretary-General Kofi Annan, he was asked by reporters about his
remarks to the *Post*.

He did not repeat them. He stated that Saddam had had the intention and maintained the capability to develop WMD. "The bottom line is this: The president made the right decision," Powell said,
and he added three more times that the president's decision was
"right." He made an extraordinary statement that even if they had
had "other information"—presumably something like Kay's assessment—before the war, it would not have changed the war decision.
"It was something we all agreed to and would probably agree to it
again under any other set of circumstances."

For Powell, several things were clear from the president's demeanor, his style and all that Powell had learned about Bush. The
president was not going to toss anyone over the side, not Powell, not
Tenet. The president also made it clear that no one was to jump ship.
Kay's precedent highlighted the dangers of that.

The president was stalwart that they absolutely had done the
right thing in removing Saddam. The war cabinet had all signed on.
They were a team. The larger message was clear: Circle the wagons.

IT HAD TAKEN a long time for Tenet to come to grips with the enor-
mity of his problem. A month after major combat had ended he was

not worried that they had not found WMD. They would find it for sure, he thought, though it might take months. By September 2003, after failing to turn up anything for nearly six months, his position was that it would take ten years. He felt their intelligence had been good and even if given the chance he would not change their estimates. By November, Tenet was arguing that they might never get the answer on WMD. The looting and document destruction inside Iraq had been so extensive that the Iraq of March 18, the day before the war began, no longer existed.

The WMD issue pulsed in the background for 10 months until Kay's resignation and declaration that they had all been wrong. This put Tenet in a bind. He and the CIA took pride in their hard-nosed analysis and conclusions. The bar was very high, and being wrong was not acceptable. Tenet had been privately very critical of news stories that had been wrong or overreaching about a possible quagmire in the Afghanistan war in late 2001. "There's never any price," he had said, when the media is wrong. He said that if the CIA director had given out equivalent bad information the president should "fire your ass."

But no one at the CIA was paying a price or being held accountable for what seemed to be a mistake, and Tenet was the one who had assured Bush that the case on WMD was "a slam dunk."

The agency was now scrubbing all the intelligence, trying to figure out what had gone wrong, even using reverse engineering techniques by taking the apparent reality of no WMD and attempting to determine how each piece of intelligence could have been wrong or misunderstood.

Tenet agreed with his deputy, John McLaughlin, that they had to dare to be wrong in order to be clear. He went further. He believed the CIA has what he calls "a duty to warn," a responsibility to point out potential danger. Perhaps a tendency to overstate the dangers had grown out of the investigations after 9/11 that had pointed to the failure to connect the dots about al Qaeda. No one, Tenet especially, wanted to be caught understating a potential threat.

"I'm not a fool," Tenet told associates in one breath, and in the next said the failure to find WMD was "weird." He knew his head could go on the chopping block. The Senate and House intelligence committees were investigating, and their leaders had said publicly they would issue highly critical reports.

Tenet decided to launch a defense. On February 5, 2004, the one-year anniversary of Powell's WMD presentation to the U.N., he made a rare public speech at Georgetown University.

"We are nowhere near 85 percent finished," he said of the WMD search, directly disputing Kay's public statement. "Any call I make today is necessarily provisional. Why? Because we need more time and we need more data." He said that they had discovered that Iraq had research and development, intent and capability to produce chemical and biological weapons. Halfway through the speech he acknowledged they had not found biological or chemical weapons.

The CIA was reviewing and examining everything in order to improve its performance, and had discovered that one of their sources had "fabricated" information, Tenet said. He noted that the CIA's human spies had provided the information that had led to the capture of some top al Qaeda leaders, including Khalid Sheik Muhammad, the mastermind of the 9/11 attacks, and had played a key role in uncovering the secret nuclear proliferation network of Abdul Qadeer Khan, the father of the Pakistani nuclear program who had helped Libya, Iran and North Korea with their nuclear programs. During the ongoing investigations and reviews, they would have to be careful, he warned. "We cannot afford an environment to develop where analysts are afraid to make a call, where judgments are held back because analysts fear they will be wrong."

In a sense, Tenet was asking that there be little or no price to pay for being wrong. Given the aftermath of 9/11 and the ongoing al Qaeda threat, the CIA had adopted a mentality of warning-at-any-cost. For years the problem had been getting the attention of the policy makers and the public. Of course, it was one thing to be wrong about warning of an attack on the United States. Tenet and all the senior officials in the CIA were certain al Qaeda would attack again. Deputy Director for Operations James Pavitt told associates in early

2004, "We'll still get hit again. We'll still get a massive hit of some kind. Absolutely. Absolutely." But, he added, "If five years passes, six years, seven years passes and we don't have one, I will be perfectly satisfied and comfortable having been wrong." But being wrong about information that Saddam possessed biological and chemical weapons—the basis for war—could hardly leave anyone satisfied and comfortable.

As Tenet went over the intelligence again and again, he acknowledged to associates that the CIA and he should have stated up front in the NIE and in other intelligence that the evidence was not ironclad, that it did not include a smoking gun.

"HOLY SHIT!" Powell said to himself as he read a copy of Tenet's speech. Here was the CIA director saying that the aluminum tubes they had previously been so confident were for use as centrifuges for enriching uranium were possibly for regular artillery shells. Powell remembered that he had challenged them on this before his U.N. presentation a year ago. John McLaughlin had gone into a long recitation about the thickness of the walls of the tubes and the spinning rates, arguing they had to be for centrifuges. Now Tenet was saying, "We have additional data to collect and more sources to question," and his agency "may have overestimated" the progress Saddam was making on development of nuclear weapons. Powell felt let down.

Tenet was also backing away from previous assertions of certainty on the alleged mobile biological labs. The CIA had earlier said it had five human sources for the claim, Powell remembered. Now Tenet was saying there was no consensus: "And I must tell you that we are finding discrepancies in some claims made by human sources about mobile biological weapons production before the war."

Powell let out another holy shit! He knew very well that Tenet had told the president "in brash New York language," as Powell once put it, that the case on WMD was a "slam dunk."

The president was the most visible manifestation of someone who had bought in. Powell was the second most visible, and he real-

ized he was expendable. He knew that Tenet felt bad, and that as director he was looking out for the CIA. But this was a real mess. Powell found himself now asking the most intense and penetrating
questions about anything the CIA said or told him.

Powell did not share Armitage's concern that the two of them
had been enablers for the Cheney-Rumsfeld hard-line policies. When
he sorted out all the issues Powell felt that the State Department had
done a good job and did not get sufficient credit for some of its successes such as improved relationships with China and Russia.

Whenever anyone suggested that Powell should have pangs of
conscience on the war, Powell said he had done everything in his
power. In August 2002 he had nearly broken his spear, laying before
the president all the difficulties of a war—the potential consequences
and downsides. It was at a time when he thought the president was
not getting the whole picture. He had warned the president. It was
the president's decision, not his. Now the United States owned Iraq.
Bush owned it. But Powell felt he had done his job.

AFTER TENET'S SPEECH, the president had one message for his intelligence chief. "You did a great job," Bush told Tenet in a phone call.

For Rice, the process of going to war had been hard, and, she
thought, it should be hard. The aftermath was troubling, particularly
the failure to find WMD.

She knew that intelligence is not fact. From all her years dealing
with intelligence, going back to her time watching Russia on Bush
senior's NSC staff, she was keenly aware that they relied on intelligence when they didn't know something. Though the CIA's intelligence on Iraq WMD was among the most categorical she had ever
seen, intelligence has limitations as the basis for policy. It is more
suggestive, reflecting possibilities and shadows rather than certainties. She had personally quizzed the agency's national intelligence
officer on the conclusions about the Iraq WMD, asking at one point
if the assertions were a fact or a judgment.

"It is a judgment," the officer had said.

As national security adviser, Rice did not dare try to influence the CIA's National Intelligence Estimate, but given her closeness and status with Bush, if anyone could have warned the president to moderate his own categorical statements about WMD, it was Rice.

But Cheney had effectively preempted that issue on August 26, 2002, when he declared that there was "no doubt" Iraq had WMD. And the president had soon followed with his own statements of certainty even before the CIA's October NIE was issued.

As the WMD controversy grew in 2004, the president expressed his concerns to Rice. To air all of the CIA's problems could have two negatives that he wanted to avoid. First, the controversy would lead to congressional investigations like the Church and Pike Committees in 1975–76 that revealed CIA spying on U.S. citizens, drug testing and assassination plots on foreign leaders. He did not want a new witch hunt, mindful of the history of investigations that he believed had demoralized the workforce and made the CIA risk-averse for a long time. Second, Bush did not want a future president hampered if there was a need to take preemptive action against another threat.

At 1:30 P.M. Friday, February 6, the president appeared in the press briefing room to announce what was now old news. He said he would appoint a nine-member commission to look at American intelligence capabilities and the intelligence about WMD worldwide. It was to determine why some prewar intelligence about Iraq's alleged WMD had not been confirmed on the ground. Bush praised the people who work for the intelligence agencies as "dedicated professionals engaged in difficult and complex work. America's enemies are secretive. They are ruthless and they are resourceful. And in tracking and disrupting their activities our nation must bring to bear every tool and advantage at our command."

Then the president added, "Members of the commission will issue their report by March 31st, 2005."

ONE THEME that emerged repeatedly in all the hours I spent interviewing the president and the hundreds of hours I spent interviewing others close to him or involved in the Iraq War decisions is Bush's conviction that he made the right decision.

In the second interview with him, December 11, 2003, the president said he had once told Rice, " 'I am prepared to risk my presidency to do what I think is right.' I was going to act. And if it could cost the presidency, I fully realized that. But I felt so strongly that it was the right thing to do that I was prepared to do so."

I asked if, as I had heard, he had said at one of the meetings in the run-up to war: "I would like to be a two-term president, but if I am a one-term president, so be it."

"That's right," the president replied. "That is my attitude. Absolutely right." He noted that things could have gone wrong on the ground, in the run-up, or they could have become trapped with endless U.N. weapons inspections.

"And if this decision costs you the election?" I asked.

"The presidency—that's just the way it is," Bush said. "Fully prepared to live with it."

That day, after two hours, we stood in the Oval Office and started to walk out. Darkness was beginning to settle in outside. The upcoming presidential election would perhaps be the most immediate judgment on the war, but certainly not the last. How would history judge his Iraq War? I asked.

It would be impossible to get the meaning right in the short run, the president said, adding he thought it would take about ten years to understand the impact and the true significance of the war.

There will probably be cycles, I said. As Karl Rove believes, I reminded him, all history gets measured by outcomes.

Bush smiled. "History," he said, shrugging, taking his hands out of his pockets, extending his arms out and suggesting with his body language that it was so far off. "We won't know. We'll all be dead."

ACKNOWLEDGMENTS

Simon & Schuster and *The Washington Post* once again have supported me completely by giving me the time and an unusual amount of independence to pursue this book.

Alice Mayhew, who has been my editor at Simon & Schuster for the past 32 years through 12 books, once again devoted her usual focus and unmatched skill to the project, ensuring we published as fast as possible once we had the story. On deadline, Alice is a force of nature full of ideas, questions and edits both small and large.

Leonard Downie Jr., *The Washington Post*'s executive editor, and Steve Coll, the *Post*'s managing editor, provide both the backing and flexibility for in-depth, book-length projects. Don Graham, the *Post*'s chief executive officer, and Bo Jones, the publisher, are first among media executives who understand journalism and the importance of trying to get to the bottom of a story.

Bill Hamilton, the *Post*'s assistant managing editor for enterprise (meaning everything) and one of the best people in the newspaper business, devoted several weeks helping with the editing and excerpting the book for the *Post*. Special thanks for his thoughtful guidance.

A book has the advantage of using all that has gone before. This book is based on my own reporting, though I am certain that I have used material that sources have told me about or information reflected in records that has appeared earlier in some form in another publication or news account. I owe an immense debt to everyone who has written about or reported on the lead-up to the Iraq War, its conduct and its aftermath. They have by and large done a great job. The hundreds of reporters who were embedded with military units in the region during the war warrant special mention. More than a dozen lost their lives, including Michael Kelly and David Bloom.

My colleagues at the *Post* provided much assistance, not only in their excellent daily coverage but informally with many suggestions and ideas. Those reporters include Walter Pincus, Dana Priest, Thomas E. Ricks, Karen DeYoung, Mike Allen, Dana Milbank, Vernon Loeb, Bradley Graham, Glenn Kessler, Peter Slevin and Barton Gellman. Liz Spayd and Michael Abramowitz, who run the national staff, were as always gracious and helpful.

Much significant background and understanding was also provided by *The Washington Post* foreign staff. This group of remarkable reporters, so ably led by Phil Bennett and David Hoffman, includes Anthony Shadid, Rajiv Chandrasekaran, Rick Atkinson and countless others.

Olwen Price transcribed many interviews, often under extreme time pressure, and she has our sincere thanks.

Joe Elbert and his photo staff at the *Post*, still the best, provided many of the pictures in this book. Special thanks also to Michael Keegan and Laris Karklis for the map.

At Simon & Schuster, Carolyn K. Reidy, the president, and David Rosenthal, the publisher, made sure the people and systems were in place to get this book on the bookstore shelves as fast as 21st-century publishing permits. Thanks to Roger Labrie for many assists. I also thank Jack Romanos, the president and chief executive officer; Elisa Rivlin, the general counsel; Victoria Meyer, the executive director of publicity; Aileen Boyle, the director of publicity; Jackie Seow, art director and jacket designer; Linda Dingler, director of design; and Mara Lurie, the production editor who so skillfully managed a fast-track schedule.

A special thanks to John Wahler, the production manager, for his care and expertise with all details—small, medium and large.

Mark Malseed and I give special thanks to Fred Chase, who assisted us and copyedited *Bush at War* in 2002, for coming again from Texas to copyedit this manuscript and give us a clear-eyed read and innumerable important suggestions.

The core of this book comes from more than 75 sources. Most agreed to provide information as long as their identities were not revealed. To all those unnamed and named I offer my thanks and gratitude. Many spent hours, some a dozen or more, with me engaging the subject.

I was also helped immeasurably by the reporting and analysis in *The New York Times, The Wall Street Journal, Newsweek, Time, U.S. News & World Report,* the *Los Angeles Times, The New Yorker, National Journal,* the Associated Press and many other news organizations. The Web site of the nonprofit group GlobalSecurity.org is an invaluable resource on military, intelligence and national security matters.

Robert B. Barnett, my agent and attorney, again provided steady and wise advice as counselor and good friend. Because he represents prominent Democrats such as former President Bill Clinton and Senator Hillary Rodham Clinton and prominent Republicans such as Karen Hughes and former Senator Bob Dole, he did not see the book until it was printed.

Thanks again to Rosa Criollo, Norma Gianelloni and Jackie Crowe.

My two daughters, Tali, who is a reporter for *The San Francisco Bay Guardian,* and Diana, who is in first grade, graciously endured the process of reporting and writing this book.

Elsa Walsh, my wife and my best friend, once again provided support, advice and wisdom on this, the ninth of my books during our 15 years of marriage. The intensity of writing books about subjects in the news that are unfolding and changing almost daily places an unusual strain on family life. Elsa adjusts with astonishing grace, only half joking that for the past year life has been "All Iraq all the time." For this, much else and the good life she has created for our family, this book is dedicated to her.

INDEX

Abbott, Steve, 29
Abdullah, Crown Prince of Saudi
    Arabia, 228–31, 266, 268, 312, 347,
    348, 396
Abdullah, King of Jordan, 257
Abraham, Spence, 381
Abraham Lincoln, USS, 412
Abrams, Elliott, 276–78
Adams, John, 421
Adams, John Quincy, 421
Adelman, Carol, 409
Adelman, Ken, 18, 164–65, 333, 409–12
Afghanistan, 5–8, 62, 92, 141, 260
    al Qaeda in, 5, 12, 26, 37, 53
    opposition forces in, 20, 64
    Taliban in, 5, 37, 53, 67, 92, 301
Afghanistan war, 3, 5–8, 31, 37–38, 53,
    62–67, 118, 128, 133, 137, 151,
    162, 191, 207, 342, 421, 434
    bombing in, 5, 12, 54, 110, 112, 121
    boots on the ground in, 5–6, 26,
    425
    CIA paramilitary teams in, 5, 6, 46,
    59–60, 67, 71, 109
    as cover for Iraq war plans, 62, 63,
    137
    as first target in war on terrorism,
    25–26, 50, 93, 410
    laser guidance in, 41, 54
    lessons of, 30, 41, 54, 55, 64, 97–98,
    99
    quagmire in, 26, 37, 438
    U.S. Special Forces in, 5, 6, 54, 59–60,
    425
    wounded from, 278–80
Agency for International Development,
    U.S. (USAID), 127, 277
Ahern, Bertie, 346

Air Force, U.S., 54, 118, 378, 392
    Dora Farm strike and, 388–89, 391,
    393, 397–98
    Iraq war planning and, 42, 113,
    118–19, 124, 207, 232
Al Jawf, 265
Al-Jazeera, 382
al-Kindi company, 249, 299
al Qaeda, 107, 186, 246, 262, 427
    in Afghanistan, 5, 12, 26, 37, 53
    Ansar al-Islam's ties to, 140, 141
    attempt to link Saddam and Iraq with,
    26, 40, 119–20, 159, 188, 199, 241,
    289–90, 292, 300–301, 311, 428
    East Africa bombings of, 26, 30
    intelligence on, 45–47, 215, 438
    nuclear or dirty bomb threat linked
    to, 45–47
    as threat, 4, 12, 24, 165, 428, 429,
    439–40
Annan, Kofi, 235, 367, 437
Ansar al-Islam, 140–41, 143
anthrax, 5, 189, 197, 201, 246, 247,
    293, 294, 309
anti-Americanism, 275
anti-Communism, 131
antiwar protests, 253–54, 280, 286
"Apparatus of Lies," 286–87
Aqaba, 97
Arafat, Yassir, 112, 231
Armitage, Richard L., 20, 91, 127, 150,
    226, 283, 298, 317
    aftermath of Iraq War and, 432–34,
    441
    "Apparatus of Lies" and, 286–87
    in deputies committee, 20, 280–81
    Libby's contact with, 50, 289–90
    news media and, 38–39, 50

Armitage, Richard L. (*cont.*)
    Powell's relationship with, 20, 39, 50,
        79, 149, 176, 183, 299, 415
    Rice critique by, 414–15
Army, U.S., 17, 36, 55, 413, 434
    in Iraq War, 378, 392, 403, 405, 406,
        408
    in Iraq war plans, 55, 59, 113,
        118–19, 126, 151, 207–8, 232, 234,
        287
Ashcroft, John, 369
Atta, Mohammed, 289, 292
Augustine, Saint, 218
Australia, 89, 183, 190, 314, 319, 324,
        362–63, 368, 382, 389, 401
"axis of evil," 87–95, 131, 177, 216
"axis of hatred," 86–87, 90
Aziz, Tariq, 303
Aznar, José María, 89, 183, 240–41, 319,
        366
    in Azores summit, 347, 357–60
    Bush's phone calls with, 364–65, 382,
        403, 406, 408
Azores summit, 347, 357–61

Baath Party, 70, 148, 259, 329, 339, 351,
        369, 425, 426–27
Baghdad, 10, 108, 148, 187, 389,
        426
    CIA activities in, 70, 301, 354
    in Iraq War, 401, 402, 404–6
    in Iraq war planning, 77, 83, 98, 119,
        126, 148, 205–8, 301, 325, 326,
        353; *see also* Fortress Baghdad
    Saddam's command and control in,
        11, 14, 134
    Special Republican Guard protection
        of, 56, 71, 126
    Zarqawi's operations in, 300
Bahrain, 58, 111, 112, 232
Baker, James A., III, 105, 163, 411
Bali, bombing in, 290
Bandar bin Sultan, Prince, 263–69,
        312–15, 324, 375–76
    Bush's meetings with, 228–31,
        266–68, 347–49, 376
Barroso, José Manuel Durão, 357,
        359–60
Bartlett, Dan, 94, 168–69, 185, 289,
        312, 340–41, 361, 371, 380, 419
    Dora Farm strike and, 390, 392, 393,
        397
Barzani, Massoud, 116–17
Bay of Pigs, 68
BBC, 164, 260
Belgium, 62
Belgrade, Chinese embassy bombed in,
        159
Berkley, Shelley, 190

Berlusconi, Silvio, 296, 320
Biden, Joseph, 308, 370
bin Laden, Osama, 25, 38, 53, 141, 150,
        159, 215, 262, 289, 348
    NSA task force on, 215
    nuclear or dirty bomb threat linked
        to, 45–47
    as threat, 4, 12, 24
biological weapons, 29, 30, 294, 366
    anthrax, 5, 189, 197, 201, 246, 247,
        293, 294, 309
    Cheney's examination of, 237–39
    mobile labs for, 294, 310, 312, 440
    of Saddam, 13, 48, 173, 190, 194–99,
        203, 220, 238, 245–49, 288, 289,
        293, 299, 310, 312, 317, 324, 333,
        387, 395, 404, 407, 435
Black Book of Death, 7, 145, 146
black market weapons, 303, 336
Blair, Tony, 89, 161–62, 227, 337, 393,
        420
    in Azores summit, 347, 357–61
    Bush's meetings with, 119, 174,
        177–79, 296–97, 346, 347,
        357–61
    Bush's phone calls with, 338, 343,
        345, 365, 373, 377, 399, 403
    fears about fall of, 337–38, 341, 342,
        346–47
    U.N. route and, 162, 177–79, 183,
        285, 296–97, 319, 320, 358
    vote for war and, 375, 378
Blix, Hans:
    intelligence on, 239–40, 293–94
    reports by, 293–94, 315–18
    weapons inspections and, 223–24,
        235, 239–40, 247, 250, 251, 253,
        254, 267, 293–94, 308, 315–18
Bloomberg, Michael, 380
Blue Plan, 124, 125, 134, 135, 146
Bob (CIA operative), 242–43
botulinum toxin, 294
Bremer, L. Paul (Jerry), III, 412
Buehring, Lt. Col. Chad, 426
Bulgaria, 339, 366
Bumiller, Elisabeth, 172
Burr, Richard, 187
Bush, Barbara, 279
Bush, George H. W., 17, 23, 70, 90–91,
        168, 216, 276, 279
    assassination attempt against,
        187
    Bush, Jr.'s relationship with, 160,
        420–22
    defense secretary appointed by, 27,
        175–76
    in elections, 104, 255, 256, 371
    Gulf War and, 1, 9, 149, 168, 170,
        263, 267, 344, 420, 421

Panama invasion and, 105–6
Scowcroft's relationship with, 149,
    159, 160, 411
Bush, George W.:
absence of doubt in, 139–40, 420
Afghanistan war and, 3, 5, 6, 26, 30,
    53, 66, 151, 162, 191, 421, 425
Afghan war wounded visited by,
    278–80
"axis of evil" and, 87–95, 131, 177,
    216
Aznar's meetings with, 240–41, 347,
    357–60
in Azores summit, 347, 357–61
Bandar's meetings with, 228–31,
    266–68, 347–49, 376
bipartisan solidarity of, 189, 200
Blair's meetings with, 119, 174,
    177–79, 296–97, 346, 347,
    357–61
Blair's telephone calls with, 338, 343,
    345, 365, 373, 377, 399, 403
body language of, 44, 50–51, 73, 146,
    169, 243–44, 260, 270
in cabinet meetings, 137–38, 256
Card's role for, 104–6
"The Case" for WMD and, 247–50
Cheney's pro-war speeches and,
    163–66
Chirac's relationship with, 312,
    313–14
coercive diplomacy and, 73, 184, 188,
    243, 360
congressional members' meetings
    with, 169–70, 171, 186–91, 257,
    307, 368–69
congressional war resolution and,
    167–72, 187–88, 200–204
conservative criticism of, 333–34
Crawford briefing and, 52–66, 79–80,
    114, 237
at Crawford ranch, 44, 52–66, 80,
    153, 154, 161, 162, 165–66, 253–56
decision to go to war made by,
    260–62, 268–74, 288, 436–37, 441,
    443
delay in war start date and, 319,
    333–34, 347–49, 357, 375–76
Desert Badger and, 64–65
diplomatic efforts of, 4, 73, 151, 153,
    189, 200, 232, 241, 243, 254, 257,
    271, 273, 319, 333, 347, 358,
    413–14
Dora Farm strike and, 383–99, 402
in election of 2000, 18, 23, 27–28, 79,
    86, 254, 255
in election of 2004, 150, 254–56, 428,
    435, 443
energy issues and, 381

Franks's briefing of, 53–66, 79–80,
    98–103, 114, 121–22, 126, 130,
    135–36, 145–50, 173–74, 205, 208,
    237, 244, 257–58, 329–32, 407–8
on freedom, 88–89, 93, 152, 258, 276,
    405, 424, 428
hints made by, 122–23
Homeland Security bill and, 185,
    186
humanitarian issues and, 147, 156,
    162, 259, 275–78, 313, 327,
    358–59, 384, 387, 405
importance of showing resolve and,
    81, 116, 152, 320–21, 406, 418–19,
    437
intelligence briefings of, 46, 47,
    52–53, 68, 73, 117, 140, 144, 185,
    186–87, 253, 374–75, 377–78,
    383–85, 391, 392, 394, 422, 433
intelligence failure investigation and,
    434–36, 442
intelligence order signed by (Feb. 16,
    2002), 108–9, 139, 354
Iraqi dissidents' meeting with,
    258–60
Iraq War and, 144, 377–99, 402–8,
    412–17, 420–29, 436–37
Iraq war plan evaluation requested by,
    1–4, 7–8, 30, 31, 35
Iraq war plan problems and, 205–8
ITV interview of, 119–20
in JCS meeting, 207–8
lack of combat experience of, 78
legacy of, 90, 165
length-of-war estimates and,
    326–27
Middle East peace process and, 112,
    230–31, 241, 260, 347
morality of, 86, 132, 272, 313–14
no-fly zone enforcement worries of,
    13–14
in NSC meetings, 40, 98–103, 114,
    161, 164, 173–74, 176, 234–35,
    242–43, 315–16, 322–24, 328–32,
    339–40, 365, 378–79, 405–8
nuclear or dirty bomb threat and, 46,
    47–48
optimism of, 91, 93, 313–14
patience of, 162–63, 165, 271
point of no return of, 258, 260–61
post-Saddam planning and, 230,
    258–60, 281–84, 322–24, 328–29,
    339–40, 342–43, 358–59, 360, 372,
    406, 408, 418–19, 424, 432–33
Powell's relationship with, 79, 149,
    167, 226, 251–52, 436–37, 441
preemption doctrine of, 34, 132–33,
    134, 137–38, 203, 417
as president-elect, 9–12, 18, 19

Bush, George W. (cont.)
  press conferences of, 65, 103, 113,
    129, 161, 162–63, 178, 256–57,
    279–80, 333, 359–60
  process solution abhorred by, 180–81
  religious beliefs of, 86, 379, 398
  reluctance to go to war of, 3, 188,
    240–41, 244, 252
  Saddam ultimatum and, 330, 341,
    342, 347, 358, 359, 361–63,
    365–72, 375
  September 11 attacks and, 3, 24–27,
    53, 60, 85–86, 89, 90–91, 98, 131,
    162, 169, 177, 184, 270, 280, 362,
    392, 410, 412, 421, 422, 425
  "shock and awe" and, 102
  Spanish of, 178, 241, 338
  stress of, 165, 251, 274, 333
  as strong leader, 91, 430
  target selection and, 331, 332, 405
  tax cuts and, 28–29, 90
  Tenet's relationship with, 67, 68, 117,
    440, 441
  U.N. resolutions and, 167, 175,
    178–84, 186–87, 189, 221, 222,
    224, 226, 227, 229, 333, 338,
    340–45, 357, 358, 363, 364–66,
    368, 430
  vaccines and, 238, 239
  war funding and, 137
  weapons inspections and, 36, 39, 120,
    160, 164, 167, 180, 186–87,
    223–24, 227, 230, 232, 234–35,
    241, 243, 250, 251, 253, 254, 270,
    271, 333, 430
  Wiesel's meeting with, 320–21
  WMD claims of, 92, 93, 164, 186,
    189–90, 195, 294–95, 333, 362,
    408, 422–24, 428, 430, 442
Bush, George W., speeches:
  "axis of evil" in, 87–95, 131, 177,
    216
  in Cincinnati, 201–2, 294–95
  to Congress, 87, 92–93
  preemption doctrine in, 132–33,
    134
  Saddam's capture in, 425–26
  September 11 in, 86, 98, 362, 392,
    412
  State of the Union, 85–96, 131, 177,
    294–95, 433
  ultimatum, 342, 347, 358, 359,
    361–63, 365–72, 375, 392
  to U.N., 156, 157, 161, 163, 174–75,
    180–85, 190–91, 272, 290
  war announcement, 390–94, 397,
    398
  war victory, 412
  at West Point, 130–33

Bush, Laura, 52, 65, 92, 244, 255,
    433
  war wounded visited by, 278–80
Bush at War (Woodward), 162, 243
Byrd, Robert, 370

cabinet meetings:
  July 31, 2002, 137–38
  January 6, 2003, 256–57
  see also war cabinet
Calio, Nicholas E., 137, 168–71,
    185–87, 200, 203
Campbell, Alastair, 178, 359
Camp David, 25, 119, 121–22, 126,
    174–79, 280, 403
Canada, 373
Card, Andrew H., 25, 104–6, 185, 207,
    268, 322, 332, 342, 402
  Azores summit and, 357, 361
  Bandar's meeting with, 347–49
  "The Case" for WMD and, 247–50
  Dora Farm strike and, 388–91, 393,
    397
  Fortress Baghdad and, 126, 133,
    174
  Powell's diplomacy and, 152, 273
  start of war and, 378–83
  White House Iraq Group and,
    168–69, 172, 286
Card, Kathleene, 104
Casey, William J., 192, 350
Central Command (CENTCOM), 2, 7,
    14, 277, 406, 413
  in Gulf War, 49–50
  Iraq war planning and, 61, 62, 63,
    304, 321–22
  Rumsfeld's visit to, 36–37, 40
  Tampa headquarters of, 7, 36–37, 40,
    76–78, 83–84, 130
  see also Franks, Gen. Tommy
Chalabi, Ahmed, 19–20, 284, 289, 340,
    432–33
chemical weapons, 29, 30, 46, 366
  in Iran-Iraq War, 293, 299
  of Saddam, 13, 48, 104, 173, 190,
    194–99, 203, 206, 222, 241,
    245–48, 288, 289, 293, 299, 310,
    317, 324, 333, 395, 404, 407, 431,
    435
  VX nerve gas, 189, 198, 293
Cheney, Dick, 19, 27–30, 47, 48, 49,
    186, 220–24, 289, 414, 428–30,
    433–35
  al Qaeda-Iraq link and, 199, 292,
    300–301, 419, 428
  background of, 27–28, 29, 49, 78
  Bandar's meetings with, 228–31,
    263–66, 347–49
  Bush's views on, 419–20

CIA relations with, 29, 72–73,
    111–12
congressional briefings and, 190, 193,
    194, 368–70
Crawford briefing and, 53–64
Dora Farm strike and, 386–92
in election of 2000, 27–28, 87
on foreign policy struggle, 128–29
Iraqi dissidents' meeting with,
    258–60
Iraq War and, 381, 402, 409–12,
    428–29
Iraq war planning and, 25, 53–64,
    72–73, 103–4, 111–13, 122,
    155–57, 163–69, 172, 174–76, 193,
    194, 206, 207, 228–31, 262–67,
    292–95, 342, 416
Middle East trip of, 111–13
in NSC meetings, 164, 176, 234–35
in post-9/11 planning, 25, 30
post-Saddam planning and, 4, 28,
    284, 429
Powell's relationship with, 164,
    175–76, 226, 292, 296, 415
as president of Senate, 28–29, 167
in principals committee meetings,
    13–14, 155–57, 167–68, 174–76,
    182–83, 415
pro-war speeches of, 163–67
on risk in inaction, 103–4, 206, 262,
    429
Saddam as viewed by, 4, 25, 164, 165,
    175, 179, 182, 199
as secretary of defense, 9, 27, 29, 49,
    78, 105, 176, 231, 263, 370
tax cuts and, 28–29
U.N. process doubted by, 153, 157,
    163, 174–75, 180–81, 294, 297
U.N. resolutions and, 174–75,
    180–81, 182, 220–22, 296, 319,
    430
as vice president-elect, 9–12, 18–19
vice presidential duties of, 28–30
weapons inspections and, 164, 165,
    176, 180, 220–21, 223–24, 234–35,
    293–94, 430
weapons of mass destruction and, 29,
    30, 87, 104, 112, 132, 164, 165,
    182, 194, 195, 199, 247–50, 295,
    298, 428, 433, 442
worst-case scenarios and, 29–30, 122,
    237–39
Cheney, Lynne, 112, 129, 409, 410
Chile, 341, 343–45, 364–65
China, 12, 159, 168, 221, 222, 259, 297,
    372, 441
Chirac, Jacques, 129, 222, 225, 241,
    312–15, 346, 357–58
Churchill, Sir Winston, 337, 338

CIA (Central Intelligence Agency), 12,
    18, 26, 53–74, 155, 216, 261, 266,
    272, 289, 350, 435–41
Afghan paramilitary attack by, 5, 6,
    46, 59–60, 67, 71, 109
Cheney's relations with, 29, 72–73,
    111–12
Cincinnati speech and, 201–2,
    294–95
congressional oversight of, 192,
    194–95, 350
covert operations of, 3, 5, 64, 67–74,
    81, 107–8, 115, 116–17, 139–44,
    192, 195, 199, 229, 241–43,
    349–54
in deception of Saddam, 108, 325,
    352–53
Directorate of Intelligence (DI) of,
    70–71
Directorate of Operations (DO) of,
    68, 69, 107–9, 209, 212
French polls and, 186–87
funding of, 109, 139, 306
Iraqi Operations Group of, 68–74,
    107–9, 141–42, 143, 349–54
Iraqi opposition and, 13, 20, 21, 55,
    64, 70, 108, 109, 209
Iraqi paramilitary operations of,
    109, 139–44, 208–12, 241–42,
    264–65, 300, 302–6, 335–37, 350,
    352
Iraqi recruitment efforts of, 73, 108,
    140–42, 209–12, 241–42, 246–47,
    302–5, 336, 352, 374
Jordan's work with, 72–73, 108, 111,
    112, 257, 354
nuclear weapon threat and, 46,
    47
pay offs by, 108, 117, 141, 143,
    209–10, 212, 302–3, 305
presidential findings and, 70, 108–9,
    139, 354
sabotage efforts of, 108, 349–51
Saudi operations with, 72–73, 108,
    229
weapons inspections and, 239–40,
    245–46
weapons of mass destruction and, 12,
    164, 190, 194–99, 201–2, 209,
    244–50, 288, 289, 294–95,
    299–300, 354, 418, 422, 428, 430,
    433, 436–42
on Zarqawi, 300–301
see also National Intelligence
    Estimate; ROCKSTARS
    intelligence; Tenet, George
Ciccone, Christine M., 171
Clark, Adm. Vern, 207
Clement, Bob, 189

Cleveland, Robin, 276–77
Clinton, Bill, 9–12, 19, 26, 30, 67, 139, 434
    Iraq policy of, 10–12, 23, 70, 187, 229, 422
CNN, 14, 179, 202, 382, 389
coalition partners, 238, 379
    in Iraq War, 401, 403, 405, 432
    Iraq war planning and, 83, 102, 151, 155, 156, 285, 328, 329, 330, 357–63, 366, 369
    see also specific countries
Coalition Provisional Authority, 412
coercive diplomacy, 73, 184, 188, 243, 360
Cohen, Stu, 196–97
Cohen, William S., 9–12, 37
Cold War, 69–70, 89, 131, 187, 196, 291
Cole, USS, bombing of, 30
Collins, Susan, 203
commander's estimate, 5, 8, 31, 38
    fifth iteration of, 96–98
    fourth iteration of, 80–83
    second iteration of, 42–43, 54
    third iteration of, 43, 54
Congress, U.S., 17, 19, 79, 276, 287
    Bush's meetings with members of, 169–70, 171, 186–91, 257, 307, 368–69
    Bush's speeches to, 87, 92–93
    CIA relations with, 70, 109, 192, 350
    Gang of Eight in, 193, 194
    Gulf War resolution and, 168, 169, 170
    Hayden's testimony to, 215, 217
    intelligence briefings and, 185–87
    Iraqi opposition funded by, 10, 70
    Iraq war planning and, 99, 137, 329, 368–70
    Iraq war resolution and, 167–72, 187–88, 200–204, 245, 378, 431
    Powell's U.N. presentation and, 307–9
    regime change and, 10, 169, 189
    taxes and, 28–29, 90
    war funding and, 373
    WMD and intelligence failure investigated by, 433, 434, 439
    see also House of Representatives, U.S.; Senate, U.S.
Conrad, Kent, 172
Conservative Political Action Conference (CPAC), 94–95
containment, 132
    of Iraq, 27, 71, 72–73, 137, 154, 170, 272
"Coup Scenario" paper, 315–16
Craddock, Lt. Gen. John, 325–26

Crawford briefing, 53–66, 75, 79–80, 99, 114
Crawford Community Center, 161
Crawford ranch, 162, 253–56
    Bush at, 44, 52–66, 119, 153, 154, 161, 162, 165–66
    foreign rulers' visits to, 119, 319–20
    Franks's visit to, 44, 53–66, 75
CRITIC flash messages, 215–16
cruise missiles, 26, 187
    in Iraq war planning, 55, 62, 64–65, 98, 148
    see also Tomahawk cruise missiles
Cuba, 168, 202, 291, 297
Cuban missile crisis, 202, 291
Curry, Dayna, 36

Dailey, Maj. Gen. Del, 113
Daniels, Mitch, 373
Daschle, Tom, 169–70, 188, 200, 204, 368
Dean, Howard, 430–31
Dean, John, 311
deception, 55, 98, 101, 202, 325
    calculated (spikes), 83–84, 100, 102, 236
    CIA activities and, 108, 352–53
    Saddam's use of, 251, 253, 289
Defense Department, U.S., 15, 29–38, 61, 83, 111, 176, 231, 263, 332
    Bush-elect team briefed in, 10–12
    disorganization in, 14, 321–22
    Iraqi opposition and, 13, 20
    money reprogramming and, 137
    Office of Special Plans in, 288–89
    post-Saddam planning and, 281–84
    September 11 attack on, 24
    as unmanageable, 16–18
    war plan concerns in, 1–2, 31–37
    see also Joint Chiefs of Staff; Rumsfeld, Donald H.
Defense Intelligence Agency, 29, 196
Defense Policy Board, 281
democracy, 150, 152
    in Iran, 87–88
    promotion of, 10, 89, 92–93, 131, 132, 155, 156, 258–60, 281, 284, 315, 328, 342, 412, 413, 419, 427, 428
Democrats, Democratic Party, 127, 168, 185, 189, 307–8, 434, 436
    in election of 2004, 430–32
    Iraq war resolution and, 169–72, 187, 200, 203–4
    in Senate, 28, 29, 169–72, 192–95, 203–4, 308, 368–70, 431–32, 434
Denmark, 382–83
deputies committee, 19–20, 21, 280–81

Derbez, Luis Ernesto, 344
Desert Badger, 11, 64–65
Desert Storm, 96, 118, 125, 353
Desert Thunder, 11
deterrence, 33, 46, 71, 132, 170, 187
de Villepin, Dominique, 222–25, 285
DiRita, Larry, 325–26
dirty bombs, 45–47
Diyarbakir, 209
Dole, Bob, 104
dollar plan, 340
Dora Farm, 374–75, 382–99,
    417–18
Downie, Len, 47
Dukakis, Michael, 371

Eagleburger, Lawrence, 411
East Africa, U.S. embassies bombed in,
    26, 30
Eastern Europe, 100, 346, 427
economic sanctions, 13, 15, 21, 71, 80,
    155, 298, 308, 322
economy, U.S., 179, 189, 228, 324
Egypt, 150, 152, 257, 312, 314, 315
Eisenhower, Dwight D., 131
ElBaradei, Mohamed, 223, 293
elections, 228
    of 1988, 104, 371
    of 1996, 79
    of 2000, 18, 23, 27–28, 79, 86, 87,
        254, 255, 410
    of 2002, 168, 172, 185, 227
    of 2004, 150, 254–56, 420, 428,
        430–32, 435, 443
enclave strategy, 22, 103
Energy Department, U.S., 196
Erdogan, Recep Tayyip, 369
evangelical Christians, 86
Evans, Don, 381
"evil empire," use of phrase, 89,
    412
Executive Steering Group (ESG),
    321–22

F-117A Nighthawks, 388–89, 391, 393,
    397–98
Fahd, King of Saudi Arabia, 229, 263,
    267, 268
Fedayeen Saddam, 212, 343, 405
Feinstein, Dianne, 171–72, 204
Feith, Douglas, 281–84, 288–89, 292,
    321–22, 325–26, 416
    postwar planning and, 282–83,
        328–29, 342–43
1st Marine Division, U.S., 403
Fleischer, Ari, 188, 234, 347, 365–66,
    368, 371, 380, 397
Foley, Laurence, 300
Ford, Gerald, 16–18, 27, 29, 255

Fortress Baghdad, 64, 126, 133, 134–35,
    137, 147, 174, 205, 206, 407
4th Infantry Division, U.S., 264,
    324–25, 330, 369
Fox, Vicente, 343–45
France, 62, 129, 151, 266–67, 285, 290,
    297, 312–15, 320, 373
    intelligence of, 312, 313
    Iraqi relations with, 15, 222, 323
    polls in, 186–87
    U.N. resolutions and, 184, 186–87,
        221–27, 235, 240, 314, 341, 349,
        357, 358, 360, 365, 368
    U.S. backlash against, 333, 346,
        372
Francke, Rend, 258
Franks, Gen. Tommy, 1–3, 5–8, 14,
    40–44, 53, 75–84, 96–104, 109–15,
    117–26, 133–37, 184, 324–32, 416,
    425
    Afghanistan war and, 5–6, 8, 31, 53,
        54, 59, 65
    body language of, 66, 403
    Bush briefed by, 53–66, 79–80,
        98–103, 114, 121–22, 126, 130,
        135–36, 145–50, 173–74, 205, 208,
        237, 244, 257–58, 329–32, 407–8
    CIA and, 81, 350, 352
    commander's estimate of, see
        commander's estimate
    Crawford briefing by, 53–66, 75, 99,
        114, 237
    delay in start date and, 319
    deployments requested by, 231–33
    Dora Farm strike and, 383, 385–90,
        392, 401
    Executive Steering Group and,
        321–22
    Fortress Baghdad and, 64, 126, 133,
        134–35, 137, 205, 407
    4th Infantry Division and, 325, 330,
        369
    Generated Start Plan and, see
        Generated Start Plan
    in Germany, 113, 136
    Hybrid Plan and, see Hybrid Plan
    Iraq War and, 365, 378–79, 401–8,
        413
    "iterative planning" process of, 76–77
    JCS and, 117–19, 207
    on lines of operation, 54–58, 77–78,
        101, 114
    MODEPS and, 231–32
    news conferences of, 65, 130, 188
    in NSC briefings, 98–103, 114,
        124–26, 145–50, 173–74, 329–32,
        407–8
    Op Plan 1003 and, 36–37, 40–41, 54,
        80, 130

Franks, Gen. Tommy (*cont.*)
  on point of no return, 258, 260–61
  post-Saddam planning and, 281, 282
  presidential hints and, 122–23
  in Qatar, 123, 236–37, 404
  ROCKSTARS intelligence and, 304, 383, 401–2
  Rumsfeld's relationship with, 6–7, 31, 44, 75–76, 98, 114, 118
  Running Start and, 97, 134, 135, 136, 145–46, 153
  on Saudi Arabia, 262
  spikes and, 83–84, 100, 102
  targeting and, 65, 75–78, 102, 110, 114, 145, 148, 157–59, 173–74, 205, 277, 331, 383, 385
  U.S. casualties and, 101, 327–28
  on weapons of mass destruction, 173–74
freedom, 155, 427
  Bush's views on, 88–89, 93, 152, 258, 276, 405, 424, 428
Freedom of Information Act, 329
Free Iraqi Force, 322
Friendship Treaty, Soviet-Iraqi (1972), 69
Frist, Bill, 368
Frum, David, 86–87
"Future of Iraq" study (State Department), 282, 283–84

Gallipoli, 324
Garner, Lt. Gen. Jay M., 283, 412, 413
Generated Start Plan, 96, 118, 124–25, 133–36, 162
  Hybrid concept and, 145, 146
  "90–45–90" in, 98–99, 114, 125, 133–34, 135, 145
  overview of, 98–99, 145
Gephardt, Dick, 170, 200
Germany, 113, 129, 136, 221, 266–67, 282, 315, 373, 402, 426, 427
  Iraq war planning and, 62, 113, 136, 346
Gerson, Michael, 86, 201, 289, 340–41, 397
  State of the Union speech (2002) and, 85–87, 89, 90, 92
  ultimatum speech and, 342, 347, 359, 361, 367, 368, 371–72, 392
  U.N. speech and, 156, 161, 180
  war announcement speech and, 390–93
  war victory speech and, 412
  West Point speech and, 130–33
Giambastiani, Vice Adm. Edmund, 32, 33, 36

GID (Jordanian intelligence service), 111, 112, 257
Global Positioning System (GPS), 207
Goldwater, Barry, 119, 192
Gore, Al, 28, 200
Graham, Bob, 172, 192–95, 204, 427–28
Graham, Don, 192
Graham, Katharine, 192
Graham, Philip, 192
Great Britain, 10, 89, 162, 190, 324, 341, 367
  in Azores summit, 347, 357–61
  CIA activities and, 69–70, 107
  Dora Farm strike and, 393, 399
  intelligence gathering of, 45, 107, 202
  Iraq bombed by, 14, 23
  Iraq War and, 401, 403, 405, 420
  Iraq war planning and, 58, 82, 156, 161–62, 177–79, 296–97, 319, 329, 337–39, 346–47
  public opinion in, 177–78, 377
  U.N. resolutions and, 177–79, 183, 221, 296–97, 319, 320, 338, 339, 341
  vote for war in, 375, 378
  on weapons of mass destruction, 190, 202
Greece, 131
Greenspan, Alan, 315
"Guidelines When Considering Committing U.S. Forces" (Rumsfeld memo), 19
Gulf War, 9, 40, 70, 78, 99, 115, 149, 173, 175, 265, 267, 283, 286, 331, 340, 344, 387, 409
  congressional resolution and, 168, 169, 170
  Iraqi military strength after, 75, 80–81
  Iraq war plans compared with, 1, 36, 96, 97, 118, 124, 125, 264, 349, 353
  Kurds slaughtered after, 116
  reparations for, 323
  Saudi role in, 230, 231, 262
  U.N. resolution on, 168, 297
  weapons inspections after, 13, 39, 48
  Wolfowitz-Libby recommendations in, 49–50

Haass, Richard N., 79
Hadley, Stephen J., 21, 49, 168–69, 207, 238, 276, 288–91, 297
  Bush's speeches and, 86–88, 90, 201, 295, 347
  Dora Farm strike and, 383, 386, 388, 397–98
  interagency coordination and, 321, 322
  post-Saddam planning and, 280–83
  second U.N. resolution and, 340–41

Hagel, Chuck, 200
Hanson, Victor Davis, 428–29
Hariri, Rafiq, 313
Harlow, Bill, 295
Harman, Jane, 307
Harrell, Brig. Gen. Gary, 113
Harry S. Truman, USS, 236
Hastert, Dennis, 368
Hayden, Lt. Gen. Michael V., 214–19,
  268–69
HET (Heavy Equipment Transporters),
  15
Hezbollah, 427
Hitler, Adolf, 337, 427
Holocaust, 320
homeland defense and security, 29, 114,
  369, 370, 373, 380
Homeland Security bill, 185, 186
House of Representatives, U.S., 168,
  333
  Bush's meetings with members of,
    186–91, 307, 368–69
  election of 2002 and, 227
  intelligence briefings and, 186–87
  Intelligence Committee of, 109, 193,
    307, 435, 439
  International Relations Committee of,
    187, 190
  Iraq war resolution and, 169–70, 200,
    378
Howard, John, 89, 183, 314, 319,
  362–63, 368, 406–7
Hughes, Karen, 252, 289–92, 361, 390,
  392, 393, 415, 435
Hu Jintao, 372
humanitarian issues, 156, 162, 384, 387
  Iraq war planning and, 55, 147, 259,
    275–78, 283, 308, 313, 327,
    358–59, 405
human rights, 162, 220, 291
HUMINT (human intelligence), 63, 67,
  73, 76, 301–5, 439, 440
  CIA recruitment efforts and, 73, 108,
    140–42, 209–12, 241–42, 246–47,
    302–5, 336, 352, 374
  on Dora Farm, 374–75, 380, 382, 384
  paucity of, 81, 107, 174, 196, 211,
    298
  on weapons of mass destruction,
    246–49, 289, 298, 299–300, 310
Hungary, 322
Hussein, Qusay, 56, 211, 336, 358, 367
  at Dora Farm, 382–86, 398
Hussein, Saddam, 2, 3, 10–14, 16,
  20–22, 51, 56–59, 69–74, 101–4,
  119, 134–44, 159–65, 175–79,
  186–90, 244–54, 256–59, 264–67,
  270–73, 296
  Arab displeasure with, 111, 226, 229
  capture of, 425–26
  CIA efforts against, 68–74, 81, 108–9,
    139–44, 208–12, 229, 325, 351,
    352–53
  coups and, 71, 72, 147, 315–16
  deception used against, 83–84, 98,
    108, 325, 352–53
  deception used by, 251, 253, 289
  Dora Farm strike against, 383–99,
    402, 417–18
  economic sanctions and, 13, 71, 298
  executions by, 202
  exile proposals for, 113, 312–14, 320,
    358, 365, 369
  Fortress Baghdad and, 64, 126,
    134–35, 147, 174
  Gulf War and, 99, 265, 286, 349, 370,
    409
  human rights violations of, 162, 220,
    291
  hunt for, 150–51, 259, 304, 373–75,
    382–87, 391
  Iraq War and, 402, 404, 406–8, 414
  Kurds slaughtered by, 70, 116
  location changes of, 304, 373–75
  noncompliance and, 222–23, 226,
    240, 250–54, 256–57, 261, 270,
    275, 285, 289, 320, 333, 341, 346,
    358, 369, 418, 422
  propaganda of, 286–87, 387, 406
  provocation-of-war contingency and,
    124, 125, 134, 257
  "rational man syndrome" and, 298
  sabotage efforts of, 99, 205, 330, 352
  Saudi concerns about, 265–66, 267
  security service of, 70, 71, 109,
    141–42, 189, 210, 241, 264, 336,
    337
  SIGINT on, 217
  strengthening of, 251, 254, 285, 346
  terrorist links of, 25, 26, 38, 42, 70,
    86–87, 119–20, 159, 188, 199, 220,
    241, 289–92, 300–301, 311, 316,
    407, 428
  as threat, 4, 12, 27, 66, 164, 165, 169,
    170, 171, 177, 178, 186, 187, 258,
    420, 423, 428
  ultimatum for, 330, 341, 342, 347,
    358, 359–63, 365–72, 375, 386
  underground facilities of, 244
  U.N. process used by, 181, 251,
    253
  U.N. weapons inspectors expelled by,
    13, 39, 182, 245
  weapons of mass destruction and, *see*
    weapons of mass destruction
  what-ifs planning and, 97, 124, 125,
    134, 136, 147, 244
Hussein, Sajida, 374, 380, 384

Hussein, Uday, 56, 212, 358, 367, 405
  at Dora Farm, 382–86, 398
Hutchison, Kay Bailey, 171–72
Hybrid Plan, 145, 146, 149, 153, 157,
  162, 173, 205, 232, 237, 257, 287,
  401
hydrology, 205, 244, 278

India, 364
intelligence:
  human, see HUMINT
  investigation of failure of, 433–36,
    439, 442
  Office of Special Plans and,
    288–89
  Rumsfeld's skepticism about, 174,
    179, 330, 383
  SIGINT, 213–18, 269, 384
  on weapons inspectors, 239–40,
    245–46, 293–94, 310
  see also CIA; Defense Intelligence
    Agency; National Security Agency;
    ROCKSTARS intelligence; specific
    countries
Internal Look, 237, 244
International Atomic Energy Agency
  (IAEA), 223, 224, 293
Iran, 128–29, 427, 435
  in "axis of evil," 87–88, 90, 92–95,
    177
  CIA activities and, 69–70
  Iraqi Kurds and, 16, 69–70
  Iraq war plans and, 155, 231, 353,
    370
  Khan's sale of nuclear technology to,
    47n, 439
Iran-Iraq War, 27, 293, 299
Iraq:
  in "axis of evil," 87–88, 90, 92–95,
    177
  Baath regime in, 70, 148, 259,
    329, 339, 351, 369, 425,
    426–27
  British bombing of, 14, 23
  Bush-elect team briefed on, 9–12
  Bush's visit to, 424
  Clinton-era policy toward, 10–12, 23,
    70, 187, 229, 422
  containment of, 27, 71, 72–73, 137,
    154, 170, 272
  democracy promoted for, 10, 150,
    152, 155, 156, 258–60, 281, 284,
    328, 342, 412, 419
  economic sanctions against, 13, 15,
    21, 71, 80, 155, 298, 308, 322
  ethnic strife in, 206, 259, 277, 278,
    369, 427
  freezing of assets of, 340, 343,
    354

  intelligence services of, 56, 60, 71,
    206, 212, 241, 289, 342–43, 351,
    354, 370
  Jordan's relations with, 257
  Kurds in, see Kurds
  military in, see military, Iraqi;
    Republican Guard; Special
    Republican Guard
  no-fly zones in, 9, 10–11, 13–16, 21,
    40, 58, 63, 121, 174, 220–21
  post-Saddam regime in, see post-
    Saddam planning
  regime change in, 10, 21, 41–42, 103,
    107–9, 137–38, 141, 142, 155, 163,
    168–69, 180, 189, 193, 209, 220,
    252, 262, 273, 432
  Shiites in, see Shiites
  Soviet relations with, 69–70, 367
  terrorist links of, 25, 26, 40, 42, 70,
    86–87, 119–20, 154, 159, 188, 220,
    241, 289–92, 300–301, 311, 362,
    428
  torture in, 108, 409, 414, 417
  U.S. as perceived by, 81, 108, 259
  U.S. bifurcated policy on, 4, 71,
    72–73, 164, 241–43, 254, 273,
    413–14
  U.S. bombing of, 9, 10–11, 14, 23, 55,
    56–57, 82, 98–99, 102, 110, 142,
    145, 383–99, 401, 402, 406
  weapons inspections in, see weapons
    inspections
  weapons of mass destruction in, see
    weapons of mass destruction
"Iraq: Goals, Objectives and Strategy"
  (NSPD), 154–56, 228
Iraqi Intelligence Service (IIS), 212, 343,
  351
Iraqi National Congress (INC), 19–20,
  432–33
Iraq Survey Group, 418, 434
Iraq War, 401–14, 416–17, 425
  assessment of, 415–16, 420–29,
    434
  Bush presidency dominated by, 150,
    152
  Bush's decisions leading up to, 4,
    257–62, 266–74, 285
  casualties in, 403, 405, 407–8, 420,
    425, 427
  consequences of, 149–52, 175, 179,
    199, 206, 270, 276, 280, 441
  election of 2004 and, 430–32
  length of, 405–6
  opposition to, 253–54, 280, 286, 332,
    431
  start of, 98, 118, 144, 235, 257–58,
    288, 319, 329–30, 348–49, 357,
    363, 365–99

victory in, 402, 405–6, 408–9, 412–13
violent and uncertain aftermath to,
    413, 424, 426, 430, 432
Iraq war plans and planning:
  Afghanistan war as cover for, 62, 63,
      137
  air bridge in, 61, 146, 287
  air operations in, 54, 55, 63, 78,
      81, 82, 96, 98–99, 110, 124, 134,
      135, 146, 158, 207, 257, 264, 329,
      387
  assumptions of, 36, 61–63, 81
  basing and staging options in, 57–58,
      62, 75, 100, 111, 136, 150, 152,
      257, 330
  Blue, Red and White Plans and, 124,
      125, 134, 135, 146
  Bush-Rumsfeld cubbyhole meeting
      and, 1–4, 30
  chain of command and, 122–23
  Cheney's speeches and, 163–67
  Cheney's visit to Middle East and,
      111–13
  CIA recommendation of, 72–74
  civilian issues in, 55, 56, 57, 81, 148,
      158, 208, 327, 331, 332, 405, 425
  coalition of nations in, 83, 102, 151,
      155, 156, 285, 328, 329, 330,
      357–63, 366, 369
  collateral damage and, 148, 158–59,
      205, 206, 331, 405
  commander's estimate and, see
      commander's estimate
  congressional resolution and, 167–72,
      187–88, 200–204, 245
  contamination concerns in, 61, 136,
      208, 214
  cost considerations in, 42–43, 59,
      121, 123, 126, 136, 137, 276–77,
      373
  in Crawford briefing, 53–65, 75,
      79–80, 99
  credibility issues and, 72, 210, 242,
      251, 260, 262
  Desert Badger and, 11, 64–65
  diplomacy in, 55, 58, 146, 155, 199,
      200
  diplomacy vs., 4, 71, 72–73, 151, 153,
      155, 156–57, 163, 241–43, 269–73,
      333, 365
  enclave strategy and, 22, 103
  force size in, 8, 36, 40, 41, 54, 58, 62,
      76, 77, 80, 82, 83, 96–97, 101, 103,
      118, 121, 123, 125–26, 135, 148,
      232
  fuel considerations in, 120, 136
  funding of, 137, 276–77, 373
  goals of, 41–42, 154–56, 228, 328–29
  ground operations in, 54, 55, 63,

      81–82, 99, 119, 124, 130, 134, 135,
      146, 237, 258, 260–61, 287, 329
  Gulf War plans compared with, 1, 36,
      96, 97, 118, 124, 125, 264, 349, 353
  humanitarian issues in, 55, 147, 259,
      275–78, 283, 308, 313, 327,
      358–59, 405
  influence (information) operations in,
      55, 57, 60, 63, 83–84, 110–11, 126
  invisible components in, 42, 83, 97
  kinetic operations (operational fires)
      in, 55, 56–57, 77, 78, 84, 99
  length of war and, 76, 101, 114, 119,
      121–22, 135, 325–27
  lines of operation in, 54–58, 75,
      77–78, 83, 101, 114
  momentum of, 3–4, 81, 149
  news media reports on, 114–15, 130,
      137, 163, 188
  NSA and, 213–19, 268–69
  Phase Four stability operations in, 96,
      102, 133, 146, 148, 281
  Phase Three in, 121, 146
  Phase Two in, 97, 146
  Phase Zero in, 102
  in post-9/11 planning, 24–26
  preemption doctrine and, 54, 134,
      137–38, 360
  for premature provocation, 124, 125,
      134, 257
  Prominent Hammer and, 114–15
  quick strike considered in, 21–22
  regional problems anticipated in,
      121–22, 150
  second front option in, 83, 123, 126,
      257, 306, 324
  secrecy in, 3, 42, 62, 63, 95, 129,
      130
  selling of, 168–72
  "shock and awe" in, 102
  slices of Iraqi capability or
      vulnerability in, 56–57, 58, 75, 82,
      110, 114
  State of the Union speech (2002) and,
      86–87, 93, 95
  supply system in, 61, 102, 136,
      207–8, 324
  targets in, 65, 75–78, 102, 110, 114,
      145, 148, 157–59, 173–74, 205,
      207, 216–18, 244, 264, 277
  timing in, 36–37, 43, 54, 59–60, 66,
      76, 81–82, 83, 96–97, 99–101, 103,
      114, 118, 121–22, 125, 135, 136,
      146, 244, 287–88, 329–30
  unilateralism in, 61, 83, 96–98, 120,
      155, 160, 175, 290
  urban warfare concerns in, 126, 208;
      see also Fortress Baghdad
  U.S. casualties and, 101, 327–28

Iraq war plans and planning (*cont.*)
  weather in, 100, 101, 214
  what-ifs in, 97, 124, 125, 134, 136,
    147, 244
  see also Generated Start Plan; Hybrid
    Plan; Op Plan 1003; Running Start
Islam, Muslims, 206, 276, 408,
    427
  see also Muslim world
Israel, 258, 290
  CIA activities and, 69–70
  Dora Farm strike and, 387, 390, 393,
    394
  Gulf War and, 49, 97, 173
  Iraq war plans and, 42, 55, 62, 97,
    111, 119, 147, 173, 368, 370
  peace process and, 112, 230–31
  Saddam as threat to, 186, 188, 190,
    230
  Scud missile threat and, 21, 55, 97,
    173, 320, 387
Israeli-Palestinian conflict, 112, 230–31,
    260
Italy, 62, 296, 427
Ivanov, Igor, 225, 366–67, 372
Ivanov, Sergei, 366–67

Japan, 24, 282, 419, 426
Jeffords, James, 29
Jews, 320, 380
John C. Stennis, USS, 112
John Paul II, Pope, 332
Johnson, Lyndon B., 265, 331
Joint Chiefs of Staff (JCS), 5, 14, 133
  Bush-elect team briefed by, 10–12
  commander's estimate and, 5, 38
  Iraq war plans and, 114–15, 117–19,
    207–8, 321–22
  in post-9/11 planning, 25–26
  Powell as chairman of, 78, 80, 105,
    175–76, 231, 263
  Prominent Hammer and, 114–15
  in war plans briefing, 32–33
Jones, Gen. James L., 208
Jonestown communications center,
    335–36, 373, 374, 378, 384–85
Jordan, 20, 300, 314, 379
  CIA work with, 72–73, 108, 111, 112,
    257, 354
  effects of Iraq War on, 150, 152
  intelligence service of (GID), 111,
    112, 257
  Iraq war planning and, 58, 72–73, 97,
    108, 111, 112, 126, 147, 257, 261,
    264, 320, 353
Juan Carlos I, King of Spain, 365,
    366
Jumper, Gen. John P., 207
"just war," concept of, 218

Kalachualan, 209–12, 302–5, 335–37,
    380, 384
Kamel, Hussein, 245, 293
Karzai, Hamid, 92, 260
Kay, David, 418, 422, 423, 434–39
Keating, Vice Adm. Timothy J., 378
Kennedy, Edward M., 203
Kennedy, John F., 131, 185, 202, 410
Kerry, John, 203-4, 430–32
Kessler, Glenn, 415
KGB, 290
Khair, Saad, 111
Khamenei, Ayatollah Ali, 128–29
Khan, Abdul Qadeer, 47n, 439
Khatami, Mohammad, 128–29
Khobar Towers, bombing of, 30
Khurmal, 141
Kim Jong Il, 32
Kirkuk, 141, 351, 408
Kissinger, Henry, 70, 163, 375
Koizumi, Junichiro, 419
Korea, 114, 426
  see also North Korea
Kosovo war, 26, 159
Krauthammer, Charles, 95, 334
Kristol, William, 333–34
Kurdistan Democratic Party (KDP), 141,
    209
Kurds, 10, 11, 20, 316, 323, 342, 370,
    427
  CIA relations with, 55, 64, 69–70, 72,
    116–17, 139–44, 209–11, 384
  CIA sabotage efforts and, 350–51
  Iraq war planning and, 55, 56, 57, 77,
    82, 102, 116–17, 130, 139–44, 206,
    209–11, 330
  in PUK, *see* Patriotic Union of
    Kurdistan
  Saddam's slaughter of, 70, 116
  in Turkey, 69, 77, 116
  Turks' views of, 77, 142
Kuwait, 21, 22, 188, 290, 323, 401
  airfield improvement in, 120,
    136
  Iraq's invasion of, 27, 36, 58, 99, 263,
    349
  Iraq war planning and, 55, 56, 58–59,
    60, 83, 102, 120, 125, 126, 135,
    136, 147, 173, 257, 264, 324
  liberation of, 230, 231, 263
  seaport in, 125, 324
  U.S. troops in, 42, 58–59, 130, 135,
    232, 237, 257
Kwasniewski, Aleksander, 275–76,
    382

Labour Party, British, 177, 337, 365, 375
Laghi, Cardinal Pio, 332
Lagos, Ricardo, 343–45, 364–65

laser guidance, 41, 54, 148
League of Nations, 157
Lebanon, 354
Lee, Robert E., 78
Libby, I. Lewis, Jr. (Scooter), 48–51,
    168–69, 288–92, 297, 322, 388
  in deputies committee, 280–81
  Iraq-al Qaeda connection and,
    300–301
  Iraq War and, 402, 409–10
  Iraq war plans and, 50–51, 72, 207
  in NSC meetings, 49, 50
  State of the Union speech (2002) and,
    90
  terrorist presentation of, 289–92
"Liberation of Baghdad" (planning
    order), 133
"Liberation Strategy, A" (deputies
    committee paper), 21
Libya, 47n, 435, 439
Lieberman, Joseph, 200
Lott, Trent, 28, 171

McCain, John, 200
McDonald, Trevor, 119–20
McGrory, Mary, 311
McKiernan, Lt. Gen. David D., 378
McLaughlin, John, 13, 68, 107–9, 186,
    241, 243
  in deputies committee, 280–81
  Dora Farm strike and, 383, 386
  weapons of mass destruction and,
    197, 244–50, 288, 289, 299–300,
    438, 440
McNally, Bob, 381
McNamara, Robert S., 327
Makiya, Kanan, 259
Manning, David, 337, 393
maps:
  NOFORN, 264–65
  U.S. topographic, 246–47
Marine Expeditionary Brigade (MEB),
    61, 135
Marines, U.S., 290
  in Iraq War, 392, 403, 408
  Iraq war plans and, 36, 55, 59, 61,
    113, 118–19, 126, 208, 287, 352
Marshall, George, 35
Medicare, 90
Meet the Press (TV show), 339, 424,
    432
Mercer, Heather, 36
Mexico, 343–45
MI6 (British Secret Intelligence
    Service), 45
Middle East, 42, 58, 93, 414, 427,
    428
  Cheney's trip to, 111–13
  Cold War and, 69–70

effects of Iraq attack on, 149, 270
  peace process in, 112, 210–11, 241,
    260, 347
  see also specific countries
military, Iraqi, 36, 81
  air force, 81, 142, 217
  CIA relations with, 107, 109, 141
  decline in strength of, 42, 75, 80–81
  in Iraq War, 403, 406, 407, 408
  opposition groups in, 55, 57
  post-Saddam, 283, 342–43
  regular army, 56, 57, 70, 81, 111, 126,
    134, 217, 325, 343, 352, 407
  SIGINT on, 217–18
  training cycles of, 99–100
  WMD warning to, 331–32
  see also Republican Guard; Special
    Republican Guard
military, U.S., 6–7, 26, 155, 434
  in Afghanistan war, 5, 6, 7
  chain of command in, 14–15
  Op Plan 1003 and, 8, 36–37, 40, 54
  war plans' use of, 33
  see also specific branches
Miller, Frank, 321–22, 339–40
MODEPS (mobilization deployments of
    U.S. military forces for war),
    231–32
Mohammed Reza Pahlavi, Shah of Iran,
    69–70
More, Sir Thomas, 133
Morris, Edmund, 52
Moseley, Lt. Gen. T. Michael (Buzz),
    378
Mosul-to-Baghdad rail lines, 350–51
Mubarak, Gamal, 314
Mubarak, Hosni, 112, 312, 313, 314
Mueller, Robert, 369
Muhammad, Khalid Sheik, 439
Mukhlis, Hatem, 258
Murray, Patty, 171–72
Musharraf, Gen. Pervez, 46, 47
Muslim world, 267, 332
  democracy promotion in, 89, 92–93
  Saudi Arabia's position in, 262–63
My American Journey (Powell), 78–79,
    176
Myers, Gen. Richard B., 263–67,
    321–22, 325–26, 413
  Dora Farm strike and, 384–89, 392,
    397–98

National Foreign Affairs Training
    Center, 129
National Foreign Intelligence Board,
    197
National Imagery and Mapping Agency,
    196
National Intelligence Council, 195–97

National Intelligence Estimate (NIE),
    194–99, 203, 219, 238, 244–45,
    288, 428, 440, 442
National Prayer Breakfast, 98
National Security Agency (NSA), 29,
    196, 213–19, 268–69, 309
  ROCKSTARS intelligence and, 303,
    304
  September 11 attacks and, 214–15
  SIGINT and, 213–18, 269, 303
National Security Council (NSC), 49,
    105, 111, 181, 221, 277, 320
  CIA briefings of, 69, 71–72
  critiques of, 414–15
  possibility of terrorist attack and,
    47–48
  post-Saddam planning and, 282–83
National Security Council (NSC)
    meetings, 40, 49, 50, 205, 220
  June 1, 2001, 20
  November 21, 2001, 1
  February 7, 2002, 98–103, 114
  August 5, 2002, 145–50
  August 16, 2002, 161
  September 6, 2002, 173–74
  September 7, 2002, 174, 176
  December 7, 2002, 234–35
  December 18, 2002, 242–43
  February 14, 2003, 315–16
  February 24, 2003, 322–23
  March 4, 2003, 328–29
  March 5, 2003, 329–32
  March 10, 2003, 339–40
  March 11, 2003, 341–42
  March 12, 2003, 342–43
  March 17, 2003, 365
  March 19, 2003, 378–79
  March 29, 2003, 405–6
  April 2, 2003, 406
  April 8, 2003, 407–8
  U.N. resolution and, 220, 224
  see also principals committee meetings
National Security Operations Center
    (NSOC), 215–16
National Security Presidential Directive
    #24, 283
National Security Presidential Directive
    (NSPD), 154–56, 228
Navy, U.S., 42, 54, 65, 378, 385, 392
  Iraq war planning and, 61, 118–19,
    124, 207, 232, 329
Netanyahu, Benjamin, 393
Newbold, Gregory S., 7–8
news media, 93, 202, 243–44, 424,
    438
  in Iraq War, 389, 406, 408
  leaks to, 38–39, 42, 50, 138
  talk shows, 149, 160, 179
  see also specific newspapers and TV shows

Newton, David G., 298
New York, N.Y., 380
New York Times, 36, 38–39, 50, 133, 164,
    172, 179, 339, 410
  Iraq war planning and, 114–15, 130,
    137, 163, 188
  on Rove foreign policy role, 127–28
Nickles, Don, 170, 172
Niger, 202
"Night Note for September 4"
    (Ciccone), 171
NILE (Northern Iraq Liaison Elements),
    109, 208–12
Nixon, Richard, 69, 311–12
nongovernmental organizations
    (NGOs), 276–77
Noriega, Manuel, 105
Northern Alliance, 64
North Korea, 31–33, 307, 372, 435
  in "axis of evil," 87–88, 90, 92–95,
    177
  Khan's sale of nuclear technology to,
    47n, 439
nuclear weapons, 30, 187, 364
  al Qaeda linked to, 45–47
  in Bush's speeches, 201–2, 362
  in Cuban missile crisis, 202, 291
  in North Korea, 32, 47n, 439
  in Pakistan, 45, 364, 439
  proliferation of, 45–48, 439
  of Saddam, 13, 48, 165, 171, 179,
    195, 199, 201–2, 204, 220, 249,
    299
  South Africa's elimination of, 180,
    275

Office of Reconstruction and
    Humanitarian Assistance (ORHA),
    283–84, 413
oil, 155
  price of, 150, 152, 228, 324, 381
  of Saudi Arabia, 147, 228, 324, 381
oil, Iraqi, 104, 111, 205, 257, 258, 290,
    322–24, 330, 352
  CIA sabotage accident and, 350–51
  in enclave strategy, 22, 103
  interruption of flow of, 147, 206, 244,
    381, 387
  Iraq War and, 401, 402, 403, 424, 427
  southern fields of, 22, 57, 99, 103,
    146, 258
Oman, 58, 82, 111, 120
Omar, Mullah, 38, 425
Operation Enduring Freedom, see
    Afghanistan war
Operation Iraqi Freedom, see Iraq War
Operation Just Cause, 105–6
Operation Northern Watch, 10, 42, 102,
    124, 174, 217, 221, 304

Operation Southern Watch, 10, 40, 42,
  58, 84, 102, 121, 124, 174, 217,
  221, 304
Op Plan 1003, 8, 36–37, 40–41, 54, 80,
  114–15, 130
  see also Generated Start Plan
Op Plan 1003 V, 365
Op Plan 5027, 32
opposition groups, Iraqi, 13, 19–22, 55,
  81, 155, 205, 316
  CIA work with, 13, 20, 21, 55, 64, 70,
    108, 109, 209
  in Crawford briefing, 55, 57, 62, 63,
    64
  outside Iraq, 13, 19–20, 258–60, 342,
    432–33
  reconstruction role of, 155, 259–60
  U.S. funding of, 10, 70
O'Sullivan, Meghan, 283–84

Pace, Gen. Pete, 38, 325–28
Pakistan, 5, 45–46, 47, 364, 439
Palestinians, 112, 231, 257, 260,
  300–301
Panama, U.S. invasion of, 105–6
Parliament, British, 337, 342, 347, 361,
  365, 373, 375, 378
Patriotic Union of Kurdistan (PUK),
  141–43, 209, 210, 303–5, 336
Patton, George, 104
Pavitt, James L., 12, 108–9, 350–51,
  374, 439–40
Pearl Harbor, Japanese attack on, 24
Pearl order (Sept. 17, 2001), 26
Pelosi, Nancy, 307–8, 368, 369
Pentagon, *see* Defense Department, U.S.
Perle, Richard, 281
Persian Gulf, 65, 84, 352
Persian Gulf War, *see* Gulf War
Pincus, Walter, 354–55
Pistachio base, 335–36, 373, 378
plutonium, 189
poison laboratories, 140–41, 300
Poland, 275–76, 382, 389, 401
post-Saddam planning, 155–56, 280–84,
  328–29, 339–40, 358–59, 406,
  412–13
  Chalabi's role and, 432–33
  CIA and, 212
  currency in, 340, 424
  dissidents' views on, 258–60
  interim authority in, 339, 340, 342,
    343, 360
  long-term outcomes and, 418–19,
    424, 428
  oil industry and, 322–24, 424
  provisional government and, 62, 340,
    430
  reconstruction and, 155–56, 259–60,

  277–78, 283, 313, 328, 343, 408,
    412
  Saudi role in, 230
  U.N. role in, 359, 360, 367, 370, 372
  U.S. occupation and, 96, 147, 148,
    150, 270
Powell, Colin, 20–23, 78, 147–53, 179,
  369, 429
  aftermath of Iraq War and, 413–16,
    432–37, 440–41
  anti-Saddam coalition as goal of, 39,
    151–53, 156
  Armitage's relationship with, 20, 39,
    50, 79, 149, 176, 183, 299, 415
  Bandar's relationship with, 263, 266
  Blix's second report and, 317–18
  Bush advised by, 22, 91, 149–52
  Bush's relationship with, 79, 149,
    167, 226, 251–52, 436–37, 441
  Bush's U.N. speech and, 180, 182–84
  calls for resignation of, 164
  Cheney's pro-war speeches and, 163,
    164, 166
  Cheney's relationship with, 164,
    175–76, 226, 292, 296, 415
  on CIA, 74, 440–41
  congressional war resolution and, 187
  on consequences of war, 149–52, 175,
    270, 441
  Crawford briefing and, 53–64, 79–80
  credibility of, 291, 299, 411
  diplomatic efforts of, 151–53, 155–57,
    161, 167, 220–27, 232, 235,
    269–73, 339, 413–14
  Dora Farm strike and, 386–90, 392
  enclave strategy and, 22, 103
  foreign policy struggles and, 127–29
  House testimony of, 187
  Iraq War and, 406, 411, 413–14,
    436–37, 441
  Iraq war plans and, 21, 22, 25, 50,
    53–64, 74, 78–80, 99, 101, 103,
    125–26, 147–51, 155–57, 161–62,
    175–76, 251–52, 269–74, 324–25,
    362
  isolation of, 79, 149
  at JCS briefing (Jan. 10, 2001),
    10–11
  as JCS chairman, 78, 80, 105, 175–76,
    231, 263
  Kay's statement and, 435–36
  on "maximalist" approach, 221
  maximum military force and, 78, 80,
    125–26
  memoir of, 78–79, 176
  Middle East peace process and,
    112
  in news stories, 79, 128, 149, 339,
    436–37

Powell, Colin (*cont.*)
  in NSC meetings, 99, 101, 103, 161,
    176, 220, 224, 324, 330, 340, 343,
    365
  popularity of, 411
  in post-9/11 planning, 25, 50
  post-Saddam planning and, 282,
    283–84, 340
  preemption doctrine and, 129
  in principals committee meetings,
    13–16, 125–26, 155–57, 175–76,
    415
  as Reluctant Warrior, 78–79, 151,
    187
  Rove's relationship with, 127–28
  Rumsfeld's relationship with, 15, 23,
    129, 156, 182–83, 283–84
  Senate testimony of, 103
  soft-on-Iraq allegations against,
    38–39, 291
  start of war and, 381
  State of the Union speech (2002) and,
    91, 94
  Straw's meeting with, 161–62
  U.N. presentation of, 291–92,
    297–301, 307–12, 316, 317, 411,
    440
  U.N. resolutions and, 167, 175, 178,
    182–84, 200, 220–27, 235, 296–97,
    330, 339, 340
Powell Doctrine, 78
Prague, 289, 292
precision bombing, 5, 41, 54
  in Iraq war plans, 54, 55, 77, 148,
    207
Predator drones, 41, 190
preemption doctrine, 34, 54, 129,
    132–33, 134, 137–38, 203, 360,
    417
President's Daily Brief (PDB), 186–87,
    289
principals committee, 20, 107,
    197
principals committee meetings, 23, 49,
    415
  February 5, 2001, 13–14
  August 1, 2001, 21
  March 1, 2002, 15–16
  May 10, 2002, 124–26
  August 14, 2002, 154–57
  September 1, 2002, 167–68
  September 6, 2002, 174–76
  September 10, 2002, 182–83
  March 11, 2003, 341–42
  March 14, 2003, 347
Project BioShield, 239
Prominent Hammer, 114–15
propaganda, of Saddam, 286–87, 387,
    406

public opinion, 267, 275, 296, 363, 373
  in Great Britain, 177–78, 377
  in United States, 85, 357, 372
Putin, Vladimir, 225, 315, 372, 404–5

Qatar, 388–89
  Franks in, 123, 236–37, 404
  Iraq war planning and, 58–61, 63, 82,
    99, 111, 112, 123, 236–37
Quanrud, Pamela, 322–23

Rasmussen, Anders, 382–83
Reagan, Nancy, 254
Reagan, Ronald, 34, 93, 245, 254,
    416–17
  Bush compared with, 89, 91, 93, 95
  "evil empire" used by, 89, 412
Red Plan, 124, 125, 134, 135, 146
refugees, Iraqi, 276, 277, 407
regime change, in Iraq, 10, 21, 41–42,
    103, 107–9, 137–38, 141, 142, 155,
    163, 168–69, 180, 189, 193, 209,
    220, 252, 262, 273, 432
Renuart, Maj. Gen. Victor E., Jr. (Gene):
  Black Book of Death and, 7, 145, 146
  at Crawford ranch, 53–65
  Iraq war plans and, 7–8, 40, 42, 43,
    53–66, 76–78, 145, 146, 157–59
Republican Guard, 56–57, 80–81, 82,
    107, 126, 134, 147, 217, 264, 325,
    343, 406
  CIA intelligence on, 211, 212,
    248–49, 299–300, 352
Republicans, Republican Party, 17, 86,
    179, 257, 308, 311–12, 434
  in election of 2002, 172, 185, 227
  Iraq war resolution and, 170–72, 200,
    203
  Rove's research on, 254–55
  in Senate, 28–29, 170–72, 227, 434
Republic of Fear (Makiya), 259
Rice, Condoleezza, 4, 10–14, 23, 68, 78,
    247–51, 276, 373, 419, 435
  Armitage's critique of, 414–15
  Bandar and, 228, 266, 313, 315,
    347–49, 376, 394–96
  British issues and, 337–38, 361
  Bush-Powell meetings and, 149, 151,
    153, 167
  Bush's speeches and, 86–88, 90, 93,
    94–95, 131, 161, 181, 183, 359
  coercive diplomacy and, 73, 188, 243
  Congress and, 168, 169, 307–9,
    368–70
  CPAC speech of, 94–95
  Crawford briefing and, 53–64
  Dora Farm strike and, 388, 393–98
  Fortress Baghdad and, 64, 126, 133,
    174

India-sponsored summit rejected by, 364
intelligence suspicions of, 179, 441
interagency coordination and, 321, 322
Iraq War and, 381, 383, 402, 405
Iraq war plans and, 4, 26, 53–64, 73, 87, 111, 125, 126, 133, 168, 174, 207, 208, 235, 251, 253–54, 269, 313, 337–38, 340–42
Kissinger's meeting with, 375
on leaks, 138
in NSC meetings, 243, 330
post-Saddam planning and, 414, 419–20
Powell's relationship with, 414, 415, 436–37
Powell's U.N. presentation and, 291–92, 307–9
in pre-inauguration briefings, 10–12
in principals committee meetings, 13–14, 23, 49, 125, 154–57, 341–42
ROCKSTARS intelligence and, 374–75
Rove vs., 127, 128
Russian issues and, 366–67
Saddam's exile and, 314, 320
Scowcroft's relationship with, 159, 160
on South African disarmament, 180
U.N. resolutions and, 222, 224–25, 307–8, 340–41
U.S. bifurcated Iraq policy and, 73, 243
weapons inspections and, 39, 223, 235, 250, 254, 293–94, 308
weapons of mass destruction and, 244, 247–50, 288–91, 307–9, 441–42
White House Iraq Group and, 168–69
ricin, 246, 289
Ridge, Tom, 369, 380
Roberts, Pat, 370
ROCKSTARS intelligence, 144, 302–5, 335–37, 352, 373–75, 401–2, 417–18
Dora Farm reports of, 374–75, 380, 382–87, 398, 417
rogue nations or states, 89, 90, 162, 177
Rokan (ROCKSTAR subsource), 374, 382–84, 398
Romania, 221
Roosevelt, Franklin D., 48, 320, 412
Roosevelt, Theodore, 48, 52, 131
Rove, Karl, 67–68, 90–91, 179, 200, 289–91, 333–34, 342, 380, 429–32, 443

election of 2004 and, 254–56, 430–32
foreign policy role of, 127–28
Homeland Security bill and, 185
Rumsfeld, Donald H., 1–8, 13–19, 26, 30–38, 40, 78, 159, 179, 290, 411, 433–35
Adelman's work for, 409, 411
Afghanistan war and, 5–6, 26, 37–38, 41, 110
Bandar's meetings with, 263–66, 349
Bush's relationship with, 149, 251–52
Bush's speeches and, 91–92, 93, 96, 180–83, 392
collateral-damage concerns of, 158–59, 206
cost-consciousness of, 42–43, 121, 277
Crawford briefing and, 53–64, 75
defense strategy of, 31, 33–34
Dora Farm strike and, 383, 386–89, 392
dribbling out of force deployments by, 233–34, 236, 287, 319
Franks's relationship with, 6–7, 31, 44, 75–76, 98, 114, 118
intelligence suspicions of, 174, 179, 330, 383
Iraq War and, 402, 406, 407, 414, 416–17
Iraq war planning and, 1–5, 8, 24–25, 26, 30, 31, 35–38, 40–44, 53–64, 75–77, 80–84, 96–103, 109–11, 114, 120–21, 123, 124, 130, 133–38, 148, 157–59, 170–71, 173–74, 184, 205–7, 231–34, 236, 244, 251–52, 260–69, 277, 287–88, 295, 319, 322, 324–27, 329–32, 416, 425
"iterative planning" process of, 76
at JCS briefing, 10–11
length-of-war estimates and, 325–27
memos of, 19, 205–6, 281
in military chain of command, 14–15, 44
military modernization and, 6–7, 80
MODEPS and, 231–32
news media briefed by, 37–38, 236, 341
in NSC meetings, 173–74, 205, 235, 329–32, 406
in post-9/11 planning, 24–27, 34
post-Saddam planning and, 281–84, 413, 414
Powell's relationship with, 15, 23, 129, 156, 182–83, 283–84
preemption and, 34, 54, 129, 133, 138
in principals committee meetings, 13–16, 156, 182, 347
Running Start and, 97, 134, 135

Rumsfeld, Donald H. (*cont.*)
    Saddam's exile and, 314, 320
    Saul's meeting with, 107
    secrecy of, 18–19, 25
    Senate briefed by, 170–71
    September 11 attacks and, 34, 133
    speaking style of, 182–83
    targeting and, 75–77, 110, 157–59
    on "toolbox approach" to problems,
        281
    TPFDD and, 233–34
    ultimatum and, 330, 347
    U.N. resolutions and, 180–81,
        220–21, 349
    war plan concerns of, 1–2, 31–35
Running Start, 97, 134, 135, 136,
    145–46, 153, 162
Russia, 15, 151, 266–67, 315, 323,
    366–67, 372, 373, 404–5, 441
    U.N. resolutions and, 184, 221, 222,
        225, 349, 358, 365, 366

Saddam International Airport, 353
Salih, Ali Abdullah, 111
Sargat, 141, 142
sarin gas, 198, 294
satellite imagery and intercept, 108,
    141, 148, 289, 291, 298, 304, 310,
    331, 380, 383, 386, 401
satellite phones, 304, 335–37, 374, 380
Saudi Arabia, 46–47, 231, 381
    CIA work with, 72–73, 108, 229
    delay in start of war and, 347–49,
        375–76
    Dora Farm strike and, 390, 394–96
    effects of Iraq War on, 150, 152
    in Gulf War, 230, 231, 262, 323
    intelligence service of, 46, 108
    Iraq war planning and, 55, 58, 61,
        72–73, 97, 108, 111, 147, 228–32,
        257, 261–69, 320, 347–49
    Khobar Towers bombing in, 30
    oil of, 147, 228, 324, 381
    Operation Southern Watch and, 40,
        42
    Prince Sultan Air Base in, 42, 61,
        378–79
    Saddam exile proposal and, 313,
        314
    Scud missile threat to, 21, 55, 97, 387
Saul (Chief, CIA Iraqi Operations),
    68–74, 107–9, 301–2, 325–26, 335,
    349–53
    Dora Farm reports for, 374, 380,
        382–85, 391, 418
    paramilitary teams and, 141–42, 143,
        208–9, 212, 242, 306, 374
    sabotage efforts and, 349–51
    U.S. bifurcated policy and, 241–42

Saxe-Coburg Gotha, Simeon, 366
Schroeder, Gerhard, 129, 315
Schwarzkopf, Norman, 49–50
Scowcroft, Brent, 18–19, 149, 159–60,
    163, 409, 410–11
Scud missiles, 21, 55, 57, 97, 126, 173,
    205, 258, 309, 330, 379, 387, 401
Senate, U.S., 103, 168, 176, 185, 308–9,
    368–70
    Armed Services Committee of, 170,
        308, 434, 435
    Cheney as president of, 28–29, 167
    elections and, 227, 434
    Homeland Security bill and, 186
    Intelligence Committee of, 67, 109,
        171, 172, 192–95, 199, 431–32,
        434, 439
    Iraq war resolution and, 169–72, 200,
        203–4, 378
    Rumsfeld's briefing of, 170–71
    tax cuts and, 28–29
September 11 attacks, 3–7, 48, 60,
    71–72, 85–86, 89, 90–91, 162, 177,
    193, 270, 280, 290, 410, 421, 422,
    428
    Afghanistan war in response to, 3,
        425
    al Qaeda and, 438, 439
    attempts to link Saddam to, 25, 159,
        169, 289, 292, 300
    in Bush's speeches, 86, 98, 362, 392,
        412
    intelligence warnings before, 53, 215,
        438
    NSA shortcomings and, 214–15
    planning of response to, 24–27, 30,
        34, 50, 426
Shales, Tom, 372
Sharon, Ariel, 231, 241, 368, 393
Shays, Chris, 189
Shelton, Gen. Henry (Hugh), 11,
    25–26
Shiites, 21, 55, 70, 162, 206, 259, 409
    CIA relations with, 64, 72
Shinseki, Gen. Eric K., 119, 207–8
"shock and awe," 102, 401
Shultz, George P., 129
SIGINT (signals intelligence), 213–18,
    269, 384
SIS (British intelligence service), 107
Skelton, Ike, 308
Slevin, Peter, 415
smallpox, 198, 238–39
Snow, John, 340
Somalia, 26
South Africa, 180, 275
Soviet Union, 89, 187
    Cuban missile crisis and, 202, 291
    Iraq's relations with, 69–70, 367